The Vaal Uprising of 1984 & the Struggle for Freedom in South Africa

Franziska Rueedi

JAMES CURREY

James Currey
is an imprint of
Boydell & Brewer Ltd
PO Box 9, Woodbridge
Suffolk IP12 3DF (GB)
www.jamescurrey.com
and of
Boydell & Brewer Inc.
668 Mt Hope Avenue
Rochester, NY 14620–2731 (US)
www.boydellandbrewer.com

British Library Cataloguing in Publication Data
A catalogue record for this book is available from the British Library

ISBN 978-1-84701-261-6 (James Currey hardback)
ISBN 978-1-84701-262-3 (James Currey Africa-only paperback)
ISB N 978-1-84701-366-8 (James Currey paperback)

Praise for *The Vaal Uprising of 1984 & the Struggle for Freedom in South Africa*

The Vaal Uprising, which commenced on 3 September 1984, is widely acknowledged as a pivotal moment in the anti-apartheid struggle. ... Franziska Rueedi's *The Vaal Uprising of 1984* is therefore the first in-depth reconstruction and analysis of the events leading to and unfolding on the historic day of September 3, and its aftermath. The book contains a remarkable set of interviews with activists whose recollections about life and politics in the townships occupy a central place in this multi-layered account of resistance from below. A rich collection of archives, especially the Delmas Trial records, complement these oral testimonies to produce original insights into the histories of the Vaal region and its constituent parts, as well as into the nature of emancipatory politics and practices of protest, rebellion, and political violence. For anyone wanting to understand protests and political violence, including the most recent events, this book should be compulsory reading. Rueedi's book makes a significant contribution to the scholarship on the history of the liberation struggle in South Africa and, crucially, the Vaal's role in the insurrection that ended apartheid.
Noor Nieftagodien, University of the Witwatersrand, South African Historical Journal

The Vaal Uprising of 1984 & the Struggle for Freedom in South Africa is a well-researched and easy-to-read book. Franziska Rueedi builds on the existing literature on the 1980s and early 1990s township politics and protests in South Africa. This book is a welcome contribution and will undoubtedly enrich our understanding about the insurrectionary politics in South Africa during this period. Although Rueedi's book largely takes up some of the already known aspects of the 1980s township politics, it does so in a very imaginative way. More importantly, in this book, Rueedi clearly demonstrates the influence of the African National Congress (ANC) on local politics and mass mobilization in the Vaal Triangle townships in the 1980s – an aspect that regrettably the majority of the existing literature downplays. ... Rueedi makes a fascinating and compelling argument in her book. She contends that the uprising, which erupted in the Vaal Triangle townships on September 3, 1984, was not only triggered by socio-economic grievances but it was also prodded by the residents' reimagination of a country and its future and the radical demand for full emancipatory citizenship that included material benefits, equality, and a life free from poverty and oppression.
Tshepo Moloi, University of the Free State, *American Historical Review*

A revealing contribution ... Rueedi takes the literature on the South African struggle in new directions by focusing on popular ideas and subjectivities: how people perceived their position and how they understood "freedom" and a decent life in the city.
William Beinart, University of Oxford

The Vaal Uprising was a pivotal moment in South African history, marking the start of the "township revolt" that led, just over five years later, to the release of Mandela and other jailed political leaders, the unbanning of the African National Congress and the negotiations that led to South Africa's transition to democracy. This first detailed study fills an important gap in scholarship on resistance to apartheid in South Africa.
Jeremy Seekings, University of Cape Town

Related James Currey titles on South & Southern Africa

South Africa. The Present as History: From Mrs Ples to Mandela & Marikana
John S. Saul & Patrick Bond

Liberation Movements in Power: Party & State in Southern Africa
Roger Southall

The New Black Middle Class in South Africa
Roger Southall

Mandela's Kinsmen: Nationalist Elites & Apartheid's First Bantustan
Timothy Gibbs

Women, Migration & the Cashew Economy in Southern Mozambique
Jeanne Marie Penvenne

Remaking Mutirikwi: Landscape, Water & Belonging in Southern Zimbabwe
Joost Fontein

Writing Revolt: An Engagement with African Nationalism, 1957–67
Terence Ranger

Colonialism & Violence in Zimbabwe: A History of Suffering
Heike I. Schmidt

The Road to Soweto: Resistance & the Uprising of 16 June 1976
Julian Brown

Markets on the Margins: Mineworkers, Job Creation & Enterprise Development
Kate Philip

The War Within: New Perspectives on the Civil War in Mozambique, 1976–1992
Eric Morier-Genoud, Michel Cahen & Domingos M. do Rosário (eds)

Township Violence & the End of Apartheid: War on the Reef
Gary Kynoch

Limpopo's Legacy: Student Politics & Democracy in South Africa
Anne K. Heffernan

Cyril Ramaphosa: The Road to Presidential Power
Anthony Butler

Archaeology and Oral Tradition in Malawi: Origins and Early History of the Chewa
Yusuf M. Juwayeyi

Manhood, Morality & the Transformation of Angolan Society: MPLA Veterans & Post-war Dynamics
John Spall

Young Women against Apartheid: Gender, Youth and South Africa's Liberation Struggle
Emily Bridger

Marikana: A People's History
Julian Brown

To Jama and Ingwe, who were born free

Contents

Maps

Maps drawn by Kate Kirkwood.

Abbreviations

ANC	African National Congress
APLA	Azanian People's Liberation Army
ASM	African Students' Movement
AZAPO	Azanian People's Organisation
AZASM	Azanian Students' Movement
BCM	Black Consciousness Movement
CCAWUSA	Commercial, Catering and Allied Workers Union of South Africa
COSAS	Congress of South African Students
DESCOM	Detainees' Support Committee
DET	Department of Education
DPSC	Detainees' Parents Support Committee
ERPA	Evaton Ratepayers Association
FEDSAW	Federation of South African Women
FOSATU	Federation of South African Trade Unions
IDAF	International Defence Aid Fund
LPP	Lekoa People's Party
MAWU	Metal and Allied Workers Union
MK	Umkhonto weSizwe
NDR	National Democratic Revolution
OVAB	Orange Vaal Administration Board
OVDB	Orange Vaal Development Board
OVGWU	Orange Vaal General Workers Union
PAC	Pan Africanist Congress
PWV	Pretoria–Witwatersrand–Vereeniging region

RMC	Release Mandela Committee
SAAWU	South African Allied Workers' Union
SACC	South African Council of Churches
SACBC	Southern African Catholic Bishops' Conference
SADF	South African Defence Force
SANFA	South African Football Association
SASM	South African Students' Movement
SASO	South African Students' Organisation
TRASCO	Transvaal Students' Congress
UBC	Urban Bantu Council
VAC	Vaal Action Committee
VALIMO	Vaal Liberation Movement
VAPTU	Vaal Progressive Teachers' Union
VASCO	Vaal Students' Congress
VAYCO	Vaal Youth Congress
VCA	Vaal Civic Association
VIS	Vaal Information Service
VMSG	Vaal Ministers' Solidarity Group
VOW	Vaal Organisation of Women
VTAB	Vaal Triangle Administration Board
VTCC	Vaal Triangle Community Council
VTUCC	Vaal Triangle Trade Union Co-ordinating Committee
WCC	World Council of Churches
WHAM	Winning Hearts and Minds campaign

Acknowledgements

They say it takes a village to raise a child. Perhaps the same can be said about a book. In this case, the village spans across several countries and includes a great number of people, without whom this book would not have seen the light of the day.

First, I must thank the people of the Vaal Triangle, whose support, hospitality, friendship and willingness to share their (often painful) stories provided the most important foundation for this book. The list of people who assisted in one way or another is very long and it is, unfortunately, impossible to mention everyone by name. An abbreviated list will have to suffice. Edward 'Chippa' Motubatsi, perhaps more than anyone else, went out of his way to locate contacts and to assist with closing gaps in my research. ANC underground operative, MK cadre, civic activist and trade unionist: he wore many hats during the struggle for freedom. During seven recorded interviews and countless unrecorded conversations over more than a decade, Chippa Motubatsi helped me understand the complexity of this period and encouraged me to continue with my research. Ke a leboha. Dorcas and Esau Ralitsela not only provided significant insights into the nature of the relationships between the ANC and civic structures, and the unfolding of protest politics in the Vaal Triangle, they also showed great hospitality and warmth. Khulu Malindi opened many doors during the initial phase of the research for this book and helped me find my way around Sebokeng. Sekwati Mokoena became an important guide and friend, and we shared many conversations at the old police station in Sharpeville, where protestors were shot down more than 50 years ago. Mojalefa 'Jaja' Sefatsa's kindness has been humbling and has touched my life and that of my family. Lekgotla 'Ace' Motaung and Dineo 'Mapikoko' Mokoena spent many hours with me retracing their steps during the period of people's war. Peter Mabuye, veteran journalist, reminded me to include different voices to avoid the research becoming one-sided.

The book draws heavily on research conducted for my doctorate at the University of Oxford, between 2008 and 2013, as well as follow-up research conducted between 2015 and 2019, when I was a postdoctoral researcher in the History Workshop at the University of the Witwatersrand in Johannesburg. Friends and colleagues made Oxford a home away from home. I am grateful for the friendship and intellectual engagement with Moritz Mihatsch, Cassandra Mark-Thiesen, Zoe Marks, Oliver Murphy, Jonathan Waterlow, Andrew Tompkins, Tim Gibbs, Nic Cheeseman and Ria Miller. Countless conversations with

Natacha Filippi, even though mostly taking place via email these days, have significantly contributed towards my intellectual growth. I owe a depth of gratitude to William Beinart for his critical reading of my work, his generous feedback and his willingness to tolerate my need for flexible deadlines and my even greater need to escape British winter for South African summer. William often knew what I wanted to say long before I had found the words, yet never imposed his own interpretation of the material.

In 2011 I travelled back to Johannesburg to conduct some follow-up research. Four months turned into almost ten years, during which time Joburg became my home. The list of people who made me feel welcome and grounded is indeed very long. At Wits University, Noor Nieftagodien, Phil Bonner, Arianna Lissoni, Tshepo Moloi, Julian Brown, Luke Spiropoulos and Sarah Godsell provided a warm and intellectually stimulating environment that profoundly shaped my understanding of local political struggles and their relations to broader issues. The History Workshop's warm hospitality is one of a kind. Khumisho Moguerane, Anne Heffernan, Stacey Sommerdyk and Joel Quirk were always available to discuss ideas over a cup of coffee. Their friendship provided much support and sustained me during the writing of this book.

I am indebted to Elaine and Jan Kramers, Lisa and Mike van Olphen, Marianne Anthonissen, Thuli Mlambo-James and Nadira Omarjee for their hospitality and friendship. In Switzerland, Henri Yéré, Sandra Dütschler, Sandra Eichenberger, Anna Vögeli, Fiona Siegenthaler and Nicole Wehrli-Sarmiento have encouraged and supported me throughout the years. Nicholas Rush Smith at the City College of New York has shared my interest in Sebokeng and I have greatly enjoyed our many conversations over the years. My thanks also go to Madeleine Fullard and Pule Zwane for making documents available, and to Matthew Chaskalson who generously shared his notes and the archival records he collected during the 1980s.

Staff at various archives, including the Mayibuye Archive at the University of the Western Cape, the National Archives in Pretoria and the National Heritage and Cultural Studies Centre at the University of Fort Hare assisted in locating relevant archival sources. I am particularly indebted to Michele Pickover, Gabi Mohale and Zofia Sulej at the Historical Papers Research Archive at the University of the Witwatersrand for providing a wonderful space to work. Several grants and scholarships covered the costs of the research: my doctorate was generously funded by a Clarendon Fund and the Merton College Greendale scholarship, the Beit Fund, the Swiss National Science Foundation and the Janggen Pöhn Foundation. I also wish to thank Judy Seidman for making the sketch used for the book cover available. I am grateful to Kate Kirkwood for drawing the maps, Lee Smith for proofreading the manuscript and Elaine Williams for compiling the index.

My family in Switzerland, including my parents Christa and Jürg Rüedi, and my brother Pascal with his wife Lejla and their children Maurice, Julie and Aurélie, always believed in me and supported my adventures across the world. Even though my path may have led me thousands of kilometres away, they were always there to cheer me on. To Nozithembiso Magengelele (mam'zala), Nokuzola Magengelele (mam'khulu), Nomakhwezi, Linus, Sibusiso, Philile, Mihlali, Lerato (Juju), Lekwezi and Ezam: thank you for your warm welcome into your family.

Finally, my heartfelt gratitude goes to Andile Magengelele. Without his support, encouragement and inspiration this book would not have seen the light of day. Having lived through the horrors of the apartheid era, and having cut his teeth as a young freedom fighter during the 1980s and early 1990s, Andile provided input on drafts and significantly sharpened my understanding of this crucial period in South Africa's history. He accepted my frequent physical and mental absence with grace. Raising an infant and a toddler while finishing a book manuscript during a global pandemic can be daunting, and Andile made sure that our children were well taken care of while I spent my days typing and editing the manuscript.

To our children Jama and Ingwe: you are the light and love of our lives. You keep us grounded and full of hope. May you grow up humbled by the sacrifices so many made to liberate your country. This book is dedicated to you.

All royalties this book may generate will go towards children and youth centres in the Vaal Triangle.

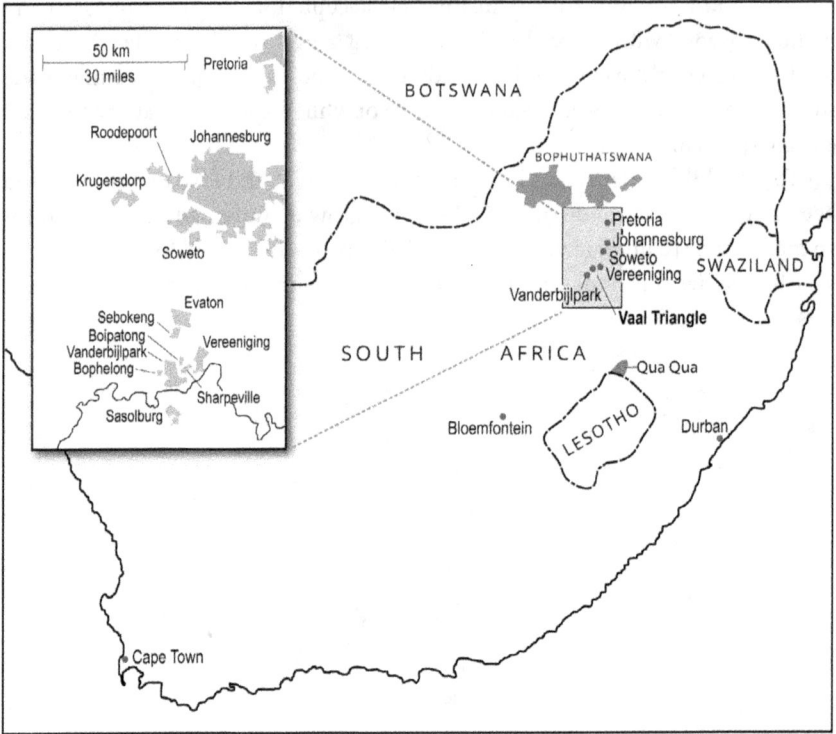

Map 1: South Africa and the Vaal Triangle

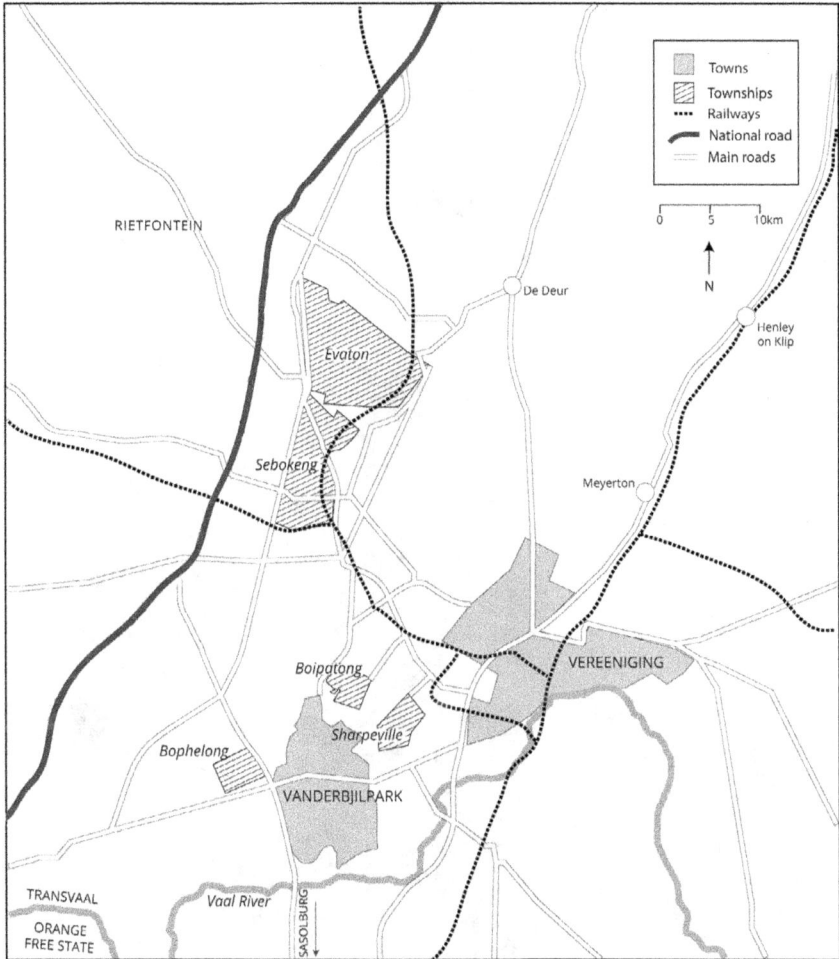

Map 2: The Vaal Triangle

Introduction:
The Struggle for Freedom
and Emancipation

When residents of the African townships of the Vaal Triangle awoke on the morning of 3 September 1984, they found that the unthinkable had become thinkable: a revolt was unfolding that would alter the course of history and catapult the region into the forefront of the struggle for freedom. In some areas, the sound of gunshots punctuated the air, shouts and singing were heard and the air was thick with smoke and teargas. Youth had been confronting police in street battles all night. Rocks and burning tyres had been pushed into the road to ensure no one would go to work or school. A few days prior, a meeting of residents, organised by the Vaal Civic Association (VCA), had resolved that on 3 September all workers would stay away from work and students from school. Businesses belonging to councillors would be boycotted and residents would march to the offices of the Orange Vaal Development Board (OVDB) to demand the resignation of all African councillors and the scrapping of a recent rent increase of R5.90 per month.

The turnout exceeded the expectations of the organisers. Around 8am, thousands of young and old, women and men, started gathering at various meeting points to march to the offices of the OVDB. The mood of the crowd was angry, but participants recalled an excitement that finally something was going to happen: grievances would be made public and dealt with. They were addressed by leaders of the VCA, who reminded them that the march was meant to be peaceful. An hour later, the marchers set off, singing *Siyaya, siyaya ePitoli* (we are going to Pretoria). Fists were clenched and youth were jogging in front of the march. Some of the marchers were holding placards inscribed *asinamali* (we have no money).

State response was as swift as it was brutal. Riot police were out in full force and less than an hour after marchers had left their main gathering point at the Roman Catholic Church in Evaton Small Farms, they were stopped by a contingent of heavily armed riot police in neighbouring Sebokeng township. According to eyewitnesses, police began to shoot without warning. By then, the commander of the riot police, Colonel Viljoen, had already given orders to shoot with live ammunition. All hell broke loose. What was meant to be a peaceful protest march quickly translated into one of South Africa's bloodiest uprisings, known as the Vaal Uprising, which soon found its equivalent in other parts of the country. By the end of the day, young and old lay dead; most of them had been part of the protesting crowds, others were bystanders. Police appeared to be shooting indiscriminately, and angry youth retaliated by stoning police and attacking buildings belonging to government and its African councillors. The townships were plunged into a state of civil war. While the iconic image of Hector Pieterson had demonstrated to the world in 1976 that apartheid's police had no regard for African life, the ruthless shooting of Wiseman Mnisi, a nine-year-old boy who was found with eleven bullets in his back, confirmed that police violence was as gratuitous as it had been during previous public protest.

On the same day, the tricameral parliament was opened in Cape Town, granting the 'Indian' and 'Coloured' populations limited political rights on a national level. But while government had aspired to an august event that would demonstrate to the world the supposed benefits of its recent constitutional reforms, all eyes were on the Vaal Triangle. Images of burning buildings and cars, of toyi-toying (protest-dancing) crowds and police violence were broadcast into the living rooms of domestic and global audiences.

The exclusion of the African majority from political participation at the national level has generally been regarded as the trigger that mobilised people into collective action; yet, as this book aims to show, material concerns and the quest for dignity were equally significant at the grassroots level. Initially, many ordinary people participated not because of overarching ideological concerns, but because of a desire for a decent, dignified life. A lack of secure tenure, quality housing and services, which was a direct consequence of grand apartheid that regarded Africans as 'temporary sojourners' in South Africa proper, shaped the content and direction of the uprising. Popular conceptions of emancipation were therefore informed by people's daily struggles for housing, services and political representation, and the broader visions they held for a dignified life. The violence and rupture of the revolt moulded new political subjectivities and translated these daily concerns into a sustained struggle for political power and social transformation.

Also among the dead were four African councillors, representatives of local government in the townships, who had been attacked by protesting crowds during the course of the uprising. The death of one of them, Kuzwayo Jacob Dlamini, the deputy mayor of the Lekoa Town Council, would later lead to one of South Africa's most infamous murder trials, during which six young people were sentenced to death. Based on the principle of 'common purpose', their presence near the murder scene was disputed and rested on precarious testimonies. The trial of *State v Sefatsa and 7 Others*, popularly known as the Sharpeville Six trial, signified a miscarriage of justice of unprecedented scale and further exposed the regime's illegitimacy.[1] But apartheid's rulers were eager to prove to South Africa and the world that their administrative capacities and coercive power remained intact, and that any attempt to undermine the political order would be harshly punished. This became apparent again when on 23 October 1984, a few weeks after the outset of the Vaal Uprising, 7,000 troops were deployed to Sebokeng and other townships in the Vaal Triangle to cordon off the area, and to conduct a house-to-house search. It was a show of strength, aimed at dissuading other townships from joining the rebellion.

The unfolding of the revolt in this region surprised many. Since the infamous Sharpeville shooting of 21 March 1960, little public protest had occurred and the area was considered to be 'tranquil'. When the student uprisings swept across the country in 1976, schools in the Vaal Triangle remained relatively unaffected; the area was known to be an 'administrator's dream' and a showcase of 'success'. Yet discontent had been brewing for years. Deteriorating living conditions, com-pounded by frequent rent increases and the rejection of a defunct and illegitimate local government, had provided the breeding ground for widespread grievances that would later translate into public protest. Rumours of councillors' rampant corruption, nepotism and malpractice had been circulating since the early 1980s and sporadic confrontations between residents and councillors had rendered visible growing tensions. They were blamed for the misfortune of local residents and were widely regarded as 'collaborators', who were upholding apartheid rule and who were financially benefiting from access to power and resources.

The Vaal Uprising heralded the beginning of the insurrectionary period of 1984–86, which, like no other period in South Africa's recent history, came to signify the search for a new order and demands for full emancipation. The revolt quickly spread to other parts of the country and by 1985, large parts of South Africa's urban townships had become 'ungovernable'. This period inaugurated a new mode of popular democracy known as 'people's power', rooted in grassroots conceptions of representation, transparency and accountability. In response to the insurgency, a blanket of repression was thrown over the embattled townships and by 1986, the police had restablished 'law and order'. But South Africa's political landscape had irrevocably changed and any plans to return to the status quo were shattered.

Violent Revolution or Spontaneous Outburst?

Media coverage of the uprising was extensive. Journalists from across the globe were seeking to establish the chain of events that had triggered the insurgency. Yet despite in-depth media coverage, remarkably little is known about the unfolding of the revolt, the ideas that precipitated mass mobilisation, and the

---

1   The Sharpeville Six trial was named after the six young people who were sentenced to death. Initially, there were eight accused, but two of them, Motsiri Gideon Mokone and Motseki Christian Mokubung, were acquitted of the murder charge.

impact of the revolt on contentious politics and political subjectivities. Many journalists were baffled by what they considered to be an 'eruption' of violence. Most failed to locate the revolt within its historical context and little attention was paid to the longer trajectories that had shaped socio-economic and political struggles. Soon two competing narratives emerged to explain the reasons for the revolt. Government was quick to claim that the revolt had been led by external 'agitators' and 'instigators'. This narrative was undergirded by perceptions that ordinary Africans had little agency and that any large-scale dissent would inevitably have been stirred by larger forces. Conversely, domestic analysts, journalists and scholars emphasised the localised nature of grievances and the spontaneity of the revolt.

These two contending explanatory frameworks were fiercely espoused during the trial *State v Baleka and 21 Others*, popularly known as the Delmas treason trial. Presided over by Judge Kees van Dijkhorst, the Delmas treason trial became one of the longest-running political trials in South African legal history, lasting 437 days in court.[2] The records of the trial provide an unparalled density of fine-grained information on popular mobilisation, everyday life in the townships, as well as state control and repression. Court evidence includes 424 volumes, and thousands of exhibits such as copies of phone books, sketches, letters, pamphlets, magazines, membership lists, handwritten notes, transcripts of speeches, biographical files, poems and songs and other documents that would likely have been lost otherwise.[3] The testimony of 278 witnesses ran to 424 volumes or 27,194 pages while 1,156 exhibits consisted of 14,425 pages.

The 22 accused had been arrested in relation to the revolts that were spreading across the country from September 1984. Their main charge was high treason, with alternative charges of terrorism, subversion, furthering the aims of an unlawful organisation and murder.[4] The great majority of the accused were local civic and student leaders from the Vaal Triangle. Three of the accused, Popo Molefe, Moss Chikane and Mosiuoa 'Terror' Lekota, were high-ranking officials of the United Democratic Front (UDF), and another three were sympathisers

---

2   For an insider's account of the Delmas treason trial, see G. Bizos, *Odyssey to Freedom: A Memoir by the World-Renowned Human Rights Advocate, Friend and Lawyer to Nelson Mandela* (Cape Town, Random House, 2007), pp.442–69.

3   F. Rueedi, 'Narratives on Trial: Ideology, Violence and the Struggle over Political Legitimacy in the Case of the Delmas Treason Trial, 1985–89', *South African Historical Journal*, 67/3 (2015), pp.335–55.

4   The legal definition of treason is vague but implies a hostile intent, which can include incitement or conspiracy to overthrow government by radical and unlawful means. For a discussion, see M. Rayner, 'Law, Politics, and Treason in South Africa', *Human Rights Quarterly*, 471 (1986), pp.471–86.

of the Azanian People's Organisation (AZAPO).[5] Significantly, the make-up of the Delmas treason trial exposed a deeply patriarchal view of emancipatory politics.[6] Even though women were playing a leading role in civic struggles as well as the African National Congress (ANC) underground, all 22 accused were men. Furthermore, the voices of youth activists, many of whom were teenagers when the revolt unfolded, are largely absent from the records. Consequently, court records marginalise the experiences and motivations of significant sections of protestors, whose tactics and visions shaped the uprising to a large extent.

During four years, the state prosecution was at pains to demonstrate that the Vaal Uprising was part of a wider conspiracy, carried out in 31 areas, by the ANC, the South African Communist Party (SACP) and its allies to overthrow the regime by violent revolution. The UDF, formed in August 1983 to oppose the tricameral parliament, was alleged to act as the internal wing of the ANC. By association, its affiliates (including the VCA) were therefore accused of pursuing the ANC's call to render the country ungovernable. As Cathy Albertyn has noted, the state prosecution claimed that separate incidents of protest across the country were part of a 'single grand conspiracy'.[7] For the charge of treason to be upheld, the state prosecution had to prove the connection between the intent of the 22 accused, and the actions of crowds during the uprising. According to the prosecution, the murder of the four councillors during the uprising was a clear indication of the revolutionary intent of the accused; the allegation that the accused had incited violence, later proven to be unfounded, was therefore key to the state prosecution's case.

The defence, on the other hand, carefully divorced localised grievances from the broader strategies and ideology of the banned ANC and its allies. Hundreds of witnesses for the defence testified about the grassroots nature of contentious politics, outlining the grievances that had been plaguing the area. Although a few of the witnesses explained their understanding of liberation and the demand for a representative government, they denied any direct relation to the strategies of the ANC, the Pan Africanist Congress (PAC) or the SACP. This is not surprising. Any association with the ANC in exile would not only have paved the way for government to viciously repress the UDF and its affiliated civic structures, it would also have led to lengthy prison sentences and, if the charge of high treason had been upheld, it would likely have led to the imposition of the death sentence. The naming of an additional 50 organisations and 913 individuals, including

5   They were Thomas Madikwe Manthata, employee of the South African Council of Churches and leading member of the Soweto Civic Association, Reverend Tebogo Geoffrey Moselane, who was at the forefront of protests against rent increases in Sharpeville, and Oupa Hlomuka, leading member of AZAPO in Sebokeng.

6   Rueedi, 'Narratives on Trial'.

7   C. Albertyn, 'A Critical Analysis of Political Trials in South Africa' (PhD thesis, University of Cambridge, 1991).

Bishop Desmond Tutu, Reverend Beyers Naudé and the entire leadership of the UDF, as co-conspirators aimed to hamstring any form of extra-parliamentary opposition to the apartheid regime. But despite concerted efforts by the state prosecution, no evidence of ANC involvement was found and eventually, most of the accused were either acquitted or released with pending sentences. Thomas Madikwe Manthata, Gcina Malindi and the UDF three were sentenced to five years on Robben Island. In 1989, the case went on appeal and judgment was set aside over a technicality.[8]

Inevitably, neither version put forward during the Delmas treason trial is entirely accurate, as this book seeks to demonstrate. Triggered by socio-economic grievances and a lack of representation and political emancipation, what became known as the Vaal Uprising was so much more than a response to immediate bread-and-butter issues. It was the re-imagination of a country and its future, and the radical demand for political power and social transformation that included material benefits, equality and a life free from poverty and oppression; in short, it was the demand for full, emancipatory citizenship and the acknowledgement and realisation of 'human dignity and full personhood'.[9] With the beginning of mass mobilisation localised struggles for housing and services were folded into broader struggles for freedom and emancipation. The ascendancy of the Charterist[10] movement during the early 1980s saw the resurgence of the ideals of the Freedom Charter of 1955, which closely reflected the demands that were being formulated by residents in the Vaal Triangle. Significantly, ANC underground activities had shaped the emergence of mass protests in the Vaal Triangle since 1982, as the book will show. If government's belief that the revolts were orchestrated by the ANC and the SACP was far from the truth, a handful of civic activists with direct links to the ANC in Botswana nevertheless ensured that the strategies and discourse of civic politics in the region would be firmly Charterist. During the 1980s, the Freedom Charter therefore came to symbolise a vision of a post-apartheid order that tallied with popular expectations of African township communities. The mass appeal of the Freedom Charter, and the overlap in political imaginations, is among the reasons why the Charterist movement eclipsed alternative ideologies such as Black Consciousness.

---

8   Judge Kees van Dijkhorst dismissed Professor Willem Joubert, one of his two assessors, over Joubert's signing of the UDF's 'Million Signature' campaign. This led to the court being no longer 'properly constituted', as George Bizos recalls. See Bizos, *Odyssey to Freedom*, p.469.

9   R. Suttner, 'The Freedom Charter @60: Rethinking its Democratic Qualities', *Historia*, 60/2 (2015), p.5.

10   Charterism refers to the political movement that cohered around the principles of the Freedom Charter of 1955.

South Africa's Turbulent 1980s

No other decade in recent South African history has come to represent the urgency with which people sought full emancipation as the 1980s. In what came to be known as the insurrectionary period of 1984–86, the black[11] majority rose in thousands against oppression, discrimination and apartheid violence. While the uprisings of 1976 had been led by students, the revolts of the 1980s saw the participation of all sections of African society. Elderly women marched along-side young people who had not yet reached adolescence, workers downed their tools to join hands with students, and clergy in full religious cloth confronted contingents of riot police. Significantly, and in contrast to earlier decades, the solidarity forged from below constituted a new mode of politics that went beyond narrow interests. By 1985, South Africa was in a state of turmoil. Images of burning townships and toyi-toying youth engaged in battles with police came to signify the crumbling power of the white minority regime.

Yet the two most perplexing questions regarding the revolts of the 1980s are their timing and their geographical pattern and uneven spread. Why was it in the townships of the Vaal Triangle where the 'revolution began in earnest'?[12] Some townships in the Pretoria–Witwatersrand–Vereeniging area (PWV), the complex that encompasses Johannesburg and the Vaal Triangle, remained largely unaffected; in other townships, such as Soweto, where students had scripted an alternative future in 1976, rebellion only occurred at a later stage.[13] Why did popular protests emerge at a time when expectations of police violence were high? Police response to the student uprisings of 1976, the school boycotts of the early 1980s and struggles over rent and bus fares prior to 1984 had demonstrated the state's sheer lack of tolerance for collective action taken by black South Africans. What stirred ordinary people, who had been dissuaded from publicly confronting the regime for more than two decades, into action? What gave them hope that this time change would come? Mass mobilisation was not an inevitable response to oppression and relative deprivation, for had it been, widespread insurrections would have occurred much sooner.[14] In Belinda Bozzoli's words, 'If apartheid was so powerful and oppressive, how

11   I use the term 'black' in its political sense, to refer to the three racial groups who were oppressed under apartheid, namely those classified as 'black' (formerly 'native' or 'bantu'), 'Coloured' and 'Indian'. I use the term 'African' to refer to South Africans who were classified as 'black'.

12   Comment by advocate George Bizos at a thanksgiving function at the Mmabatho stadium in November 1996, quoted in P. Noonan, *They're Burning the Churches: The Final Dramatic Events that Scuttled Apartheid* (Bellevue, Jacana, 2003), p.13.

13   J. Seekings, 'From Quiescence to "People's Power": Township Politics in Kagiso, 1985–1986', *Social Dynamics*, 18/1 (1992), pp.20–41.

14   B. Bozzoli, 'Why Were the 1980s "Millenarian"? Style, Repertoire, Space and Authority in South Africa's Black Cities', *Journal of Historical Sociology*, 13/1 (2000), p.79.

was it that revolts such as these occurred at all? [...] If the African National Congress had been attempting to initiate revolution in South Africa for twenty years, what was it about the 1980s that helped it partly succeed?'[15] This book takes up these questions posed by Bozzoli.

Jeremy Seekings argues that rebellion was often an 'unintended' outcome, resulting from the inability of previous forms of non-confrontational political action to adequately address grievances.[16] He shows that the period of 'apparent quiescence' during the 1970s and early 1980s (with the exception of the student protests in 1976–77) was marked by other, non-confrontational forms of politics.[17] During this period, the benefits of confronting the state were relatively low, while the costs were very high, leading to what he identifies as 'powerlessness' of township populations.[18] Instead, popular grievances were expressed through utilising extra-state structures (such as township courts), 'hidden resistance' (in the form of illegal squatting for example), as well as lobbying and negotiations by 'dissident' councillors, who supported residents in their opposition to rent increases and other council policies.[19] The changing relationship between councillors and residents played a significant role in paving the way for more confrontational political action to emerge.

This is certainly partly true for the Vaal Triangle as well, as this book shows. The devolution of additional responsibilities to African councillors, without giving them meaningful power and sufficient budgets, was key to the emergence of mass protests. Yet what this framework of analysis is missing is the more 'hidden' agenda of radicalised sections of the youth and the ways in which the (albeit modest) strengthening of the ANC underground shaped protest politics during this period.[20] For them, the resolution of material grievances was never sufficient. The VCA's campaigns, even though non-confrontational, always also encompassed a rejection of the political order, which inevitably implied more confrontational political action.[21]

---

15   B. Bozzoli, *Theatres of Struggle and the End of Apartheid* (Johannesburg, Wits University Press, 2004), p.3.

16   J. Seekings, 'Powerlessness and Politics: "Quiescence" and Protest in Pretoria–Witwatersrand–Vaal Townships, c.1973–1985' (Southern Africa in the Nineteenth and Twentieth Centuries seminar paper, Institute of Commonwealth Studies, University of London, 1991), p.84.

17   J. Seekings, 'Quiescence and the Transition to Confrontation: South African Townships, 1978–1984' (DPhil thesis, University of Oxford, 1990); Seekings, 'Powerlessness and Politics'.

18   Ibid.

19   Ibid.

20   This is likely owing to an inability to access this information during the late 1980s.

21   This is particularly apparent in its rejection of the councils and the homeland system that together formed the cornerstones of governance in African areas. See Chapter 3.

If the revolt in the Vaal Triangle was emblematic for a new era of protest politics, it was also unique and rooted in localised social relations, political repertoires and structural conditions. Several factors help explain why the Vaal Triangle took centre stage in protest politics in 1984. The first reason, as Chapter 2 explores, was the intensity of material grievances. Owing to its heavy reliance on manufacturing, the area was particularly hard hit by the faltering of the manufacturing industry during the early 1980s and the onset of economic recession. Real incomes were lower than in other townships of the PWV, with 30 percent of households living below the minimum living level by 1985.[22] The Vaal Triangle Administration Board was reportedly also one of the first administration boards to introduce full economic rental, as stipulated by government policy. Consequently, unsubsidised rents and the costs of developing and upgrading the townships led to a series of rent increases, amounting to 427 percent between 1977 and 1984. By the time the uprising began, the Vaal Triangle was the most expensive area for African people to live.

Secondly, relationships between councillors and their constituents were exceptionally fraught in the Vaal Triangle. In contrast to other townships, where 'dissident councillors' or councillors generally more sympathetic to residents' plight were mitigating the severity of grievances, relations between Vaal councillors and residents were openly hostile.

Thirdly, racial relations in the Vaal Triangle were tense, and as many African residents recall, the towns of Vanderbijlpark and Vereeniging were frequently the scene of violent assaults. Threats of gratuitous violence profoundly shaped the everyday life of many African employees in town. Moulded in this harsh environment, experiences of racial discrimination and oppression in small industrial towns such as Vereeniging and Vanderbijlpark thus differed from other parts of the country. If threats of racial violence may have led to the development of survival strategies (such as avoiding certain parts of town), they also spawned anger and radicalised a younger generation of activists who grew up with a keen sense of injustice.

Fourthly, popular experiences of worsening living conditions need to be seen within the Vaal Triangle's history of forced removals that led to a deep sense of unsettlement and precarity. When Sebokeng township was built during the mid-1960s, the promise of better housing and more urban permanence initially attracted some sections of the upwardly mobile township population. But the dream proved short-lived: from the beginning, the poor quality of housing, overcrowding and a lack of amenities confirmed the failure of 'model townships' to provide improved living conditions. Councillors became the face of this failure and therefore became the embodiment of frustrated aspirations.

---

22   Seekings, 'Quiescence and the Transition to Confrontation', p.51.

Conversely, a lack of shared grievances accounts for the absence of rebellion in other townships. In Kagiso in the West Rand, the weakness of organisational politics and a lack of 'pressing local issues' initially hindered mass mobilisation of the township population in 1984.[23] The mayor of Maokeng township near Kroonstad in the Northern Free State successfully averted public protests by addressing the grievances of his constituents.[24] In Soweto, social differentiation and uneven experiences of material grievances, the subsidisation of rents and the conservatism of the Soweto Civic Association are among the reasons that explain the relative lack of confrontational protest politics in 1984–85.[25]

Yet despite shared grievances and growing hostility towards councillors, political mobilisation remained weak in the Vaal Triangle until 1983, when the VCA was formed. From its inception, the VCA and its sister organisation, the Vaal Organisation of Women (VOW), struggled to attract members into leadership positions, and their campaigns were few. This explains the fifth factor that helped catapult the Vaal Triangle to the forefront of the struggle for freedom: the hesitance of residents to be elected into executive positions of the VCA gave ANC-aligned activists ample space to shape the VCA's discourse and strategies. Remarkably, as the book shows, most of the founding members of the VCA were directly or indirectly linked to the ANC, with several of them being ANC underground operatives. Hence, if civic associations in other townships pursued more moderate politics, the VCA from its inception was shaped by the ANC's ideology and strategic programme.[26] This influence ensured that the VCA was firmly Charterist, and that bread-and-butter issues were always framed within a broader anti-apartheid discourse; bread-and-butter grievances, as underground operatives explained, helped stir mass mobilisation.

In contrast to other townships, where civic associations were actively engaging the administration boards and local government to halt rent increases and address grievances, the VCA barely did this.[27] It pursued few campaigns between

23   Seekings, 'From Quiescence to "People's Power"'.

24   T. Moloi, *Place of Thorns: Black Political Protest in Kroonstad since 1976* (Johannesburg, Wits University Press, 2015).

25   J. Seekings, 'Why Was Soweto Different? Urban Development, Township Politics, and the Political Economy of Soweto, 1977–1984' (African Studies seminar paper, University of the Witwatersrand, 1988). The subsidisation of rent appears to have been unusual.

26   As I have noted elsewhere in this book, the role of ANC underground operatives in shaping civic action remains, with a few exceptions, poorly understood. See pp.13–14.

27   Seekings, 'Quiescence and the Transition to Confrontation', pp.150–52; J. Seekings, 'Broken Promises: Discontent, Protest, and the Transition to Confrontation in Duduza, 1978–1985' (African Studies seminar paper, University of the Witwatersrand, 1990).

October 1983 and August 1984, when the rent increase of R5.90 initiated feverish activities. Partly owing to the intense hostility between residents, the VCA and local councils, and perhaps partly to the radical stance of leading VCA members, a mediated settlement was not on the cards.

Finally, the security branch of the South African Police may have been successful in infiltrating above-ground organisations, but struggled to obtain first-hand evidence of meetings beyond informers' reports. As interviews confirm, police also had no insights into ANC underground activities prior to the uprising; this only changed from 1985, when several underground operatives and Umkhonto weSizwe (MK) cadres were arrested.[28] Even though many ordinary residents may not have had rebellion on their mind when they took to the streets on 3 September 1984, more radicalised (youth) activists and activists aligned to the ANC sought to accelerate the struggle for freedom (see Chapter 4). Their intention was to overturn the system in its entirety. As this book will demonstrate, the uprising was therefore both unintended *and* intended. Some were launching attacks on buildings belonging to councillors and the administration board prior to the protest march.

But if these factors explain conditions that facilitated the mobilisation of residents to join protest action, they do not explain why collective action turned violent. Interviews demonstrate that the scope and the nature of the violence that occurred on that day shocked ordinary residents and politicised activists alike. Key to understanding the escalation into violence are a series of hostile interactions between police, councillors and protesting crowds.[29] Whether the conduct of the riot police would have been more measured under a command other than Colonel Viljoen's is difficult to say. But as eyewitness testimonies suggest, Viljoen's proclivity for excessive violence may well have played its part in inciting the police. Violent retaliation by young protestors was not only in response to direct experiences of police violence but also to widespread rumours of such violence. Rumours of gratuitous violence, and the shooting of children more specifically, turned individualised experiences into collective outrage and the perception of being under attack.[30]

---

28   Former members of the security branch confirm their difficulties in (secretly) recording public meetings in the region. Andries du Toit and Petrus Niemand, interview with author, West Rand, 10 May 2011 (names have been changed). Audio recordings by police informers were also not used as evidence during the Delmas treason trial.

29   For an analysis of how police violence led to the rapid escalation of the conflict in Alexandra, see C. Carter, 'Community and Conflict: The Alexandra Rebellion of 1986', *Journal of Southern African Studies*, 18/1 (1992), pp.115–42; K. Jochelson, 'Reform, Repression and Resistance in South Africa: A Case Study of Alexandra Township, 1979–1989', *Journal of Southern African Studies*, 16/1 (1990), pp.1–32.

30   Belinda Bozzoli explores the role of rumours during the revolt in Alexandra. See Bozzoli, *Theatres of Struggle*, p.76.

The 1980s, with its marches, street battles, strikes and boycotts, have attracted sustained scholarly interest and produced detailed and insightful analyses into the various aspects of popular politics during this period.[31] Surprisingly, and even though the revolt in the Vaal Triangle was one of the great turning points

31   The scholarship on this period is extensive. On the history of the UDF, see J. Seek-ings, *The UDF: A History of the United Democratic Front* (Cape Town, David Philip, 2nd edition, 2015); I. van Kessel, *Beyond Our Wildest Dreams: The United Democratic Front and the Transformation of South Africa* (Charlottesville, University of Virginia Press, 2000); and G. Houston, *The National Liberation Struggle in South Africa: A Case Study of the United Democratic Front, 1983–1987* (London and New York, Rou-tledge, 1999). For a detailed account of a township revolt during this period, see Bozzoli, *Theatres of Struggle*. For accounts explaining the emergence of popular protests, see S. Mufson, *Fighting Years: Black Resistance and the Struggle for a New South Africa* (Boston, Beacon Press, 1990); T. Lodge and B. Nasson, *All, Here, and Now: Black Politics in South Africa in the 1980s* (Cape Town, David Philip, 1991); W. Cobbett and R. Cohen (eds), *Popular Struggles in South Africa* (London, James Currey, 1988); P. Frankel, N. Pines and M. Swilling, *State, Resistance and Change in South Africa* (London, Croom Helm, 1988); M. Chaskalson, K. Jochelson and J. Seekings, 'Rent Boycotts and the Urban Political Economy', in G. Moss and I. Obery (eds), *South African Review 4* (Johannesburg, Ravan Press, 1987), pp.53–74; Seekings, 'Quiescence and the Transition to Confrontation'; M. Mayekiso, *Township Politics: Civic Struggles for a New South Africa* (New York, Monthly Review Press, 1996); A. Marx, *Lessons of Struggle: South African Internal Opposition, 1960–1990* (New York, Oxford University Press, 1992); J. Seekings, 'The Origins of Political Mobilisation in PWV Townships, 1980–84', in Cobbett and Cohen (eds), *Popular Struggles*. Josette Cole explores intra-community conflict in the informal settlement of Crossroads during this period. See J. Cole, *Crossroads: The Politics of Reform and Repression* (Johannesburg, Ravan Press, 1987). For two excellent overviews of the literature, see H. Sapire, 'Township Histories, Insurrection and Liberation in Late Apartheid South Africa', *South African Historical Journal*, 65/2 (2013), pp.167–98 and J. Seekings, 'Whose Voices? Politics and Methodology in the Study of Political Organisation and Protest in the Final Phase of the "Struggle" in South Africa', *South African Historical Journal*, 62/1 (2010), pp.7–28. For an analysis of ANC involvement in the revolts, see T. Simpson, '"Umkhonto we Sizwe, We Are Waiting for You": The ANC and the Township Uprising, September 1984–September 1985', *South African Historical Jour-nal*, 61/1 (2009), pp.158–77 and F. Rueedi, '"Our Bushes Are the Houses": People's War and the Underground during the Insurrectionary Period in the Vaal Triangle, South Africa', *Journal of Southern African Studies*, 46/4 (2020), pp.615–33. Emily Bridger examines the role of young women during the 1980s uprisings in E. Bridger, 'Soweto's Female Comrades: Gender, Youth and Violence in South Africa's Township Uprisings, 1984–1986', *Journal of Southern African Studies*, 44/4 (2018), pp.559–74. For a rare analysis of rural revolt, see I. van Kessel, '"From Confusion to Lusaka": The Youth Revolt in Sekhukhuneland', *Journal of Southern African Studies*, 19/4 (1993), pp.593–614 and P. Delius, *A Lion amongst the Cattle: Reconstruction and Resistance in the Northern Transvaal* (Oxford, James Currey, 1997).

during South Africa's twentieth century, detailed studies of this seismic event are rare. Except for Patrick Noonan's personal account of the uprising,[32] Joyce Mokhesi-Parker and Peter Parker's monograph on the Sharpeville Six trial[33] and Johannes Rantete's eyewitness testimony,[34] the Vaal Uprising is usually referred to in passing, as a watershed to be sure, but with little detail or local nuance.[35] Besides those three works mentioned, Sekibakiba Lekgoathi's analysis is, so far, the most detailed account of the uprising within the broader context of the anti-apartheid struggle.[36] In contrast to a renewed interest in earlier periods, the 1980s township insurrections have attracted limited attention in recent scholarship.[37]

This book aims to address two lacunae that are discernible in the scholarship of the 1980s: firstly, histories produced on grassroots movements have often demoted the role of broader patterns of resistance and the banned liberation movements in analysis. With a few exceptions, there is a lack of understanding of how civic protests during the 1980s related to the ANC's underground machinery.[38] This is partly owing to constraints scholars faced

32 P. Noonan, *They're Burning the Churches: The Final Dramatic Events that Scuttled Apartheid* (Bellevue, Jacana, 2003).

33 P. Parker and J. Mokhesi-Parker, *In the Shadow of Sharpeville: Apartheid and Criminal Justice* (Basingstoke & New York, Macmillan & NYU Press, 1998).

34 J. Rantete, *The Third Day of September: An Eye-Witness Account of the Sebokeng Rebellion of 1984* (Johannesburg, Ravan Press, 1984).

35 Anthea Jeffery's book on people's war dedicates a modest section to the Vaal Uprising. However, her account is biased for it relies exclusively on sources unsympathetic to popular struggles in this region. See A. Jeffery, *People's War: New Light on the Struggle for South Africa* (Johannesburg, Jonathan Ball, 2009).

36 S. Lekgoathi, 'The United Democratic Front, Political Resistance and Local Struggles in the Vaal and West Rand Townships in the 1980s', in South African Democracy Education Trust [SADET] (ed.), *The Road to Democracy in South Africa, Volume 4: 1980–1990* (Pretoria, Unisa Press, 2010), pp.555–610. In contrast to Lekgoathi's chapter, this book draws on oral history interviews with participants in the uprising and therefore provides more of an insider's perspective.

37 A new body of scholarship on the 1970s includes D. Magaziner, *The Law and the Prophets: Black Consciousness in South Africa, 1968–1977* (Athens, Ohio University Press, 2010); J. Brown, *The Road to Soweto: Resistance and the Uprising of 16 June 1976* (Oxford, James Currey, 2016); I. Macqueen, *Black Consciousness and Progressive Movements under Apartheid* (Pietermaritzburg, University of KwaZulu-Natal Press, 2018); L. Hadfield, 'Christian Action and Black Consciousness Community Programmes in South Africa', *Journal for the Study of Religion*, 23/1–2 (2010), pp.105–30 and A. Heffernan, *Limpopo's Legacy: Student Politics and Democracy in South Africa* (Johannesburg, Wits University Press, 2019). Heffernan also writes about the 1980s though focuses on student politics, not the revolts.

38 Exceptions include J. Cherry, 'Hidden Histories of the Eastern Cape Underground', in SADET (ed.), *The Road to Democracy in South Africa, Volume 4: 1980–1990* (Pretoria, Unisa Press, 2010) and T. Moloi, 'The Botswana Connection: The Re-invigoration

when conducting their research; most of the expansive scholarship on this period was produced during the 1980s and 1990s, when research on the ANC was difficult if not outright impossible. Belinda Bozzoli's excellent analysis of the Alexandra revolt, which to date is the most detailed account of a township insurrection, equally does not probe the influence of underground activities on local politics.[39] Conversely, histories written on the ANC barely include the nitty-gritty details of how civic movements overlapped with, responded to and shaped the strategies and ideologies of the banned liberation movements.[40] One of the most expansive and detailed projects that chronicles the struggle for liberation, the South African Democracy Education Trust (SADET), is reflective of the bifurcation between exiled movements and domestic protests, and between above- and underground politics, as Jon Soske, Arianna Lissoni and Natasha Erlank argue.[41] To address this division, Hilary Sapire proposes a 'joined-up history of the liberation struggle' that takes into account its longer trajectories, diverse roots and cross-regional patterns.[42]

Secondly, as Sapire notes, '[m]any analyses of the politics of the 1980s did not locate the dramatic political developments within deeper historical traditions or demonstrate awareness of concurrent historical research into comparable phenomena in earlier periods'.[43] Often, analyses have tended to compartmentalise the different periods with little attention paid to continuities. The insurrectionary period is seen as a logical consequence of the political swell of 1976 and the state reforms and repression that followed in its aftermath. Spectacular moments of resistance are therefore frequently divorced from their broader and longer history of emancipatory thought. Part of the reason for this divorce is the way in which the impact of the Sharpeville shootings of 1960 has been framed. In many analyses, the massacre and the subsequent banning of the liberation

of Confrontational Politics in Thembisa Township, 1979–1990', in A. Lissoni and A. Pezzano (eds), *The ANC between Home and Exile: Reflections on the Anti-Apartheid Struggle in Italy and Southern Africa* (Napoli, Universita degli studi di Napoli L'Orientale, 2015).

39   Bozzoli, *Theatres of Struggle*.
40   Seekings, 'Whose Voices?'
41   J. Soske, A. Lissoni and N. Erlank, 'One Hundred Years of the ANC: Debating Struggle History after Apartheid', in A. Lissoni, J. Soske, N. Erlank et al. (eds), *One Hundred Years of the ANC: Debating Liberation Histories Today* (Johannesburg, Wits University Press, 2012), p.38.
42   Sapire, 'Township Histories', p.170.
43   Ibid., p.169. For exceptions, see, for example, P. Bonner and N. Nieftagodien, *Alexandra: A History* (Johannesburg, Wits University Press, 2008); Delius, *A Lion amongst the Cattle*; C. Bundy, 'Survival and Resistance: Township Organisations and Non-Violent Direct Action in Twentieth-Century South Africa', in G. Adler and J. Steinberg, *From Comrades to Citizens: The South African Civics Movement and the Transition to Democracy* (London, Macmillan, 2000), pp.26–51.

movements ushered in the end of mass protests of the 1950s. What followed was a long hiatus or 'quiescence', which abruptly came to a halt when students rose in thousands during the uprisings of 1976.[44]

The concept of quiescence presumes a sharp distinction between the domestic and the public spheres with politics being located and expressed in the latter, as Julian Brown emphasises.[45] It therefore obscures the diverse forms of politics that existed during the 1960s and early 1970s, as Brown notes.[46] This book concurs with Brown's critique of quiescence. Reducing emancipatory politics to spectacular public protests underplays the significance of diverse forms of dissent that were located in, and related to, the domestic sphere. It also leads to the demotion of the diversity of aspirations and hopes held by Africans, and the 'complex strategies of coping, of seizing niches within changing economies, of multi-sided engagement with forces inside and outside the community'.[47] Moments of intense conflict and resistance cannot be understood without examining their deeper histories and the origins of thought that led people to rebel, and the diverse strategies people adopted to carve out a living and to secure economic opportunities and social transformation.

African Struggles for Citizenship and Power

At a first glance, emancipatory politics during the period of 'quiescence' appear to share few commonalities with the mass protests that shaped the insurrectionary period of the 1980s. Yet a closer look reveals the historical trajectories of emancipatory thought. The denial of full citizenship and secure tenure in the urban townships during the 1960s to mid-1970s shaped aspirations for a better life that informed protest politics later on. Demands for political emancipation therefore became intertwined with demands for a 'good society, a society planned and organised with particular social and economic arrangements to meet the demands of its citizens'.[48] As this book will explore, access to quality housing

44 S. Dubow, 'Closing Remarks: New Approaches to High Apartheid and Anti-Apartheid', *South African Historical Journal*, 69/2, Special Issue: Rethinking 'Apartheid's Golden Age' (2017), p.305.

45 J. Brown, *The Road to Soweto: Resistance and the Uprising of 16 June 1976* (Oxford, James Currey, 2016), pp.8–9.

46 Ibid. For an analysis of ANC underground politics during this period, see R. Suttner, *The ANC Underground in South Africa to 1976: A Social and Historical Study* (Johannesburg, Jacana, 2008).

47 F. Cooper, 'Conflict and Connection: Rethinking Colonial African History', *American Historical Review*, 99/5 (1994), p.1533.

48 R. van Niekerk, 'The African National Congress: Social Democratic Thinking and the Good Society, 1940–1962', in E. Webster and K. Pampallis (eds), *The Unresolved National Question: Left Thought under Apartheid* (Johannesburg, Wits University Press, 2016), p.42.

and secure tenure was key in shaping people's visions of freedom and emancipation. This corresponds with Dickson Eyoh's argument that anticolonial
struggles not only strove for national sovereignty but were inevitably always
'grounded in an understanding of the interconnectedness of socio-economic,
political and cultural subjugation'.[49] Struggles for emancipatory citizenship
therefore not only aimed to achieve inclusion into an existing order, but the
creation of a new social, economic and political order that would ensure
access to material benefits, such as healthcare, education, housing and wages
on a non-racial, equal basis.[50] To be free was closely linked to one's ability to
succeed, progress and establish a dignified, settled life; in short, to realise one's
full human potential in a world free of domination and inequality.

Struggles for freedom and independence had been gaining momentum
since the 1930s and 1940s in different parts of the African continent. In
French West Africa, France attempted to preserve the 'unity of French territory' while assuring Africans of future 'economic, social and political progress'.[51] Using revenues from French taxes, the French colonial authorities
introduced various services and infrastructures. Attempting to legitimise
their rule, the African population under French rule would become 'impe-
rial citizens' with a 'minority voice at the center'.[52] Yet contrary to France's
intention of curbing dissent, 'these policies opened the door to escalating
demands for equality within the French Union'.[53] Similarly, Britain shifted
towards a developmentalist version of colonialism, aimed to stabilise the
African workforce and to increase its efficiency. The Colonial Development and Welfare Act of 1940 made provisions for the use of 'metropolitan'
resources to uplift African communities by expanding access to 'housing,
water, schools, and other social projects', as Frederick Cooper has noted.[54]
In South Africa, similar reforms to upgrade and develop African urban areas
began during the mid-1970s, as this book shows. But significantly, and in

---

49   D. Eyoh, 'Freedom: Overview', in T. Kepe, M. Levin and B. von Lieres (eds), *Domains of Freedom: Justice, Citizenship and Social Change in South Africa* (Cape Town, UCT Press, 2016), p.107.

50   F. Cooper, 'Decolonization and Citizenship in Africa between Empire and a World of Nations', in E. Bogaerts and R. Raben (eds), *The Decolonization of African and Asian Societies* (Leiden, Brill, 2012), pp.42–3. For an excellent analysis of the project of 'worldmaking' that undergirded anticolonial struggles, see A. Getachew, *Worldmaking after Empire: The Rise and Fall of Self-Determination* (Princeton, Princeton University Press, 2019).

51   F. Cooper, *Africa since 1940: The Past of the Present* (Cambridge, Cambridge University Press, 2002), p.53.

52   Ibid., p.56.

53   Ibid., p.53.

54   Ibid., p.41; Cooper, 'Decolonization and Citizenship', p.50.

contrast to French and British colonies, which partly subsidised these developments, the fiscal burden of developing and upgrading the townships was placed on the shoulders of the African population. As was the case elsewhere, these reforms opened up space for new demands to emerge.

In South Africa, the 1940s signified a period of 'political fluidity', during which 'rival notions of citizenship, linked to identity, were developed'.[55] It was a period where 'several "new" South Africa's were imagined' that were 'mutually incompatible', namely Afrikaner nationalism, black African nationalism and a third 'distinct world of possibilities' that was inspired by 'liberal and left-wing internationalist thought'.[56] But by the late 1940s, the containment of influx of Africans undergirded the programme of apartheid, with which the *Herenigde Nasionale Party* won the general elections of 1948. The coming to power of the National Party entrenched and institutionalised segregation that had previously been implemented in a piecemeal fashion.[57] In its aftermath, racial segregation became 'compulsory', with the goal to achieve 'cohesion and comprehensiveness which it had not enjoyed under the United Party'.[58] Race as the organising principle of citizenship became entrenched from 1948, effectively excluding the black majority from the envisaged political community.[59] Two pieces of legislation, the Group Areas Act and the Population Registration Act, both passed in 1950, signified the onset of ruthless classification and separation of different racial groups. With the implementation of the 1951 Bantu Authorities Act, and the 1959 Promotion of Bantu Self Government Act, African 'aspirations to citizenship' were 'pushed into homeland economies', (see Chapter 1).[60] It signalled the 'parting of ways' between South Africa and non-settler colonies, where processes of decolonisation were in full swing.[61] One of the far-reaching

55   S. Dubow, 'Introduction: South Africa's 1940s', in S. Dubow and A. Jeeves, *South Africa's 1940s: Worlds of Possibilities* (Cape Town, Double Storey Books, 2005), pp.11–13.

56   Ibid., pp.2–3.

57   A. Mabin, 'Comprehensive Segregation: The Origins of the Group Areas Act and its Planning Apparatuses', *Journal of Southern African Studies*, 18/2 (1992), pp.405–29.

58   Ibid., p.420.

59   In contrast to African colonies, where those of European descent retained their European citizenship, white South Africans were citizens of South Africa, with only loose ties to Europe. This led the SACP to declare that South Africa was characterised as 'colonialism of a special type' in 1962. See D. Everatt, 'Alliance Politics of a Special Type: The Roots of the ANC/SACP Alliance, 1950–1954', *Journal of Southern African Studies*, 18/1 (1991), pp.19–39.

60   B. Freund, *Twentieth-Century South Africa: A Developmental History* (Cambridge, Cambridge University Press, 2019), p.140.

61   F. Cooper, 'A Parting of the Ways: Colonial Africa and South Africa, 1946–48', *African Studies*, 65/1 (2006), pp.27–44. In settler colonies, processes of decolonisation were far more protracted and violent. See E. Buettner, *Europe after Empire: Decolonisation,*

consequences was a drastic cut in government subsidies for housing and the development of urban African townships.

Model Townships and Housing

African townships have invariably been called 'squalid and drab'[62] and the 'very picture of poverty and oppression'.[63] Sebokeng (meaning 'the meeting place' in Sesotho) and other townships in the Vaal Triangle are certainly no exception. Yet they also once had a reputation for being model townships offering facilities, infrastructure and housing. While Sharpeville was built in the 1940s during a time when government was experimenting with welfare reforms, Sebokeng was established in 1965 during the height of apartheid. They both represented government's plans to stabilise the African workforce, eradicate social ills and ensure political control. Large buffer zones separated African townships from neighbouring 'white' towns and allowed for easy cordoning off in times of upheaval. Houses were built to promote nuclear families with a male head of household. The domestic and intimate sphere was tightly controlled (although this control was subverted in multiple ways). Model townships were deeply patriarchal spaces that reflected apartheid planners' conservative views. African women were particularly vulnerable; their inability to rent a house in their own name forced them into precarious marriages and social relations.[64]

African responses to the establishment of model townships varied. For many, they represented the destruction of their communities and the harshness of life under apartheid. Their uniformity and rigid administrative control served as a reminder that according to apartheid's architects, African life in the city was always seen as temporary. Yet for others, they offered opportunities for improved living conditions; young families and lodgers, for example, who had been renting shacks in Evaton Small Farms, one of the few remaining freehold areas in the country where Africans could own land, benefited from access to private water taps, toilets, privacy, enhanced safety and a larger space.

But irrespective of people's attitudes towards these new townships, the denial of permanent urban rights to the African population, and their resulting treatment as 'temporary sojourners', had two significant consequences

---

Society, and Culture (Cambridge, Cambridge University Press, 2016).

62   Seekings, 'Quiescence and the Transition to Confrontation', p.44.

63   N. Ndebele, *Rediscovery of the Ordinary: Essay on South African Literature and Culture* (Johannesburg, COSAW, 1991), p.37.

64   D. Posel, 'Marriage at the Drop of a Hat: Housing and Partnership in South Africa's Urban African Townships, 1920s–1960s', *History Workshop Journal*, 61 (2006), pp.57–76.

regarding access to housing. Firstly, the precarity of African life in the urban areas went hand in hand with the denial of home ownership and secure tenure. Insecure tenure meant that rent defaulters could be evicted with ease and find themselves in the street. In the words of Leslie Bank, model townships 'offered permanently urbanised Africans a vision of black suburbia by offering them more solid houses to live in, but denied them the right to own these properties or to express their individuality in their new neighbourhoods'.[65] For many, then, the domestic sphere became the space in which they expressed their aspirations and dreams. Dignity was created through the making of 'home'.[66] Secondly, the dwindling of state subsidies led to a severe housing shortage as well as a lack of revenue. In the absence of taxable industries in the townships, rent became the key revenue for administration boards to administer and run the townships. The impact of this lack of revenue became particularly pronounced from the late 1970s, when political and economic reforms were introduced, aimed at creating a new African middle class. De facto property ownership became possible again with the introduction of the 30-year leasehold in 1975, and the 99-year leasehold and home ownership schemes for Africans during the late 1970s.[67] The introduction of these reforms reflected a shift in government's attitude towards urban rights and an acknowledgement of African permanence in the cities. Significantly, the acceptance of African permanence in the cities necessitated the development and upgrading of urban townships; as will be seen, the costs were to be covered through rent increases.

Ideas, Event, Subjectivity

By the late 1970s, the dream of a settled and dignified life in the urban areas was collapsing for many, as living standards were falling. Dissatisfaction over poor living conditions and escalating rent increases was coupled with a growing distrust and rejection of newly elected African councillors. The emergence of contentious politics during this period was not only a clear expression of the widespread rejection of the political order, it also reflected the struggle *for* a different kind of future and a different world. In his book *Thinking Freedom in Africa*, Michael Neocosmos situates emancipatory politics on the continent

65   L. Bank, *Home Spaces, Street Styles: Contesting Power and Identity in a South African City* (Johannesburg, Wits University Press, 2011), p.24.

66   A.-M. Makhulu, *Making Freedom: Apartheid, Squatter Politics, and the Struggle for Home* (Durham, Duke University Press, 2015), p.16. F. Pinto de Almeida, 'Framing Interior: Race, Mobility and the Image of Home in South African Modernity', *Social Dynamics*, 41/3 (2015), pp.461–81.

67   On property ownership in an African context, see B. Freund, *The African City: A History* (Cambridge, Cambridge University Press, 2007).

within a history of thought and contends that at the heart of his analysis is the assertion that 'people think'.[68] While this may seem obvious at first, it is significant; the manner in which people thought about and envisioned liberation and freedom, and the origins of these ideas, warrant greater attention.

The 1980s were shaped by a struggle over what type of life was envisaged as acceptable and desirable. Questions such as 'What is life for? What is an adequate life?' came to be at the centre of political thought.[69] While government reformists advocated for limited political rights on a local level, the African population demanded full emancipation and the transformation of society at the social, political and economic levels. People began to think 'out of place' or 'out of order', as Michael Neocosmos has argued.[70] Without this 'excess', Neocosmos emphasises, the emancipatory project would have failed to develop a vision of an alternative order. The significance of the 1980s, then, does not simply lie in the capacity to challenge the administrative and coercive capacity of the apartheid regime; instead, this period produced new visions of a new order. Grounded in everyday experiences that shaped their political subjectivities, ordinary South Africans imagined and dreamt of a free South Africa. Reforms introduced during this period therefore pushed the issue of rights and representation to the centre of public debate.[71] The politics of petitioning of earlier periods was thus replaced by a politics of demands, which saw ordinary people assert what they thought was theirs.

These ideas were therefore not merely a reflection of material conditions and large structural changes. The political language and visions that were emblematic of the mass-protests of the 1980s were partly rooted in previous repertoires of protest and emancipatory thought, partly shaped by the content, direction and limitations of government's reforms, as well as new experiences of revolt and repression. Significantly, they were also influenced by ideas promulgated in books and magazines and inspired by anticolonial struggles elsewhere. Finally, they overlapped with visions espoused by the banned liberation movements. The Freedom Charter in particular came to represent the aspirations and hopes of ordinary people. Adopted by the Congress of the People as a guiding manifesto in 1955, the Freedom Charter exemplified the search for a different order. It outlined the vision of a free society grounded in principles of equality and justice. Based on inputs collected from thousands of people, the Freedom Charter reflected popular demands.[72] It stipulated that:

68   M. Neocosmos, *Thinking Freedom in Africa: Toward a Theory of Emancipatory Politics* (Johannesburg, Wits University Press, 2016), p.xix.

69   J. Biehl, B. Good and A. Kleinman, 'Introduction: Rethinking Subjectivity', in J. Biehl, B. Good and A. Kleinman (eds), *Subjectivity: Ethnographic Investigations* (Berkeley, University of California Press, 2007), p.5.

70   Neocosmos, *Thinking Freedom in Africa*, p.xxi.

71   Seekings, *The UDF*, p.14.

72   For a discussion, see G. Williams, 'Celebrating the Freedom Charter', *Transformation*, 6

- The people shall govern
- All national groups shall have equal rights
- The people shall share in the country's wealth
- The land shall be shared among those who work it
- All shall be equal before the law
- All shall enjoy equal human rights
- There shall be work and security
- The doors of learning and culture shall be opened
- There shall be houses, security and comfort
- There shall be peace and friendship.[73]

The Freedom Charter combined 'a discourse of rights alongside a discourse of liberation' and thus spoke to both conservative and more radical sections of society, as Jeremy Seekings has argued.[74]

This takes us back to Bozzoli's question regarding the timing of the revolts. The combined effects of growing political and socio-economic grievances, the new language and space provided by the implementation of reforms, the organisational capacity and resources provided by the UDF and its affiliates, and the ideological guidance emanating from the ANC's leadership in exile all forged new political subjectivities that were at the core of emerging mass mobilisation. This new sense of selfhood was also shaped by the '*violences* of everyday life',[75] of which extreme poverty is the most obvious example, and moments of spectacular violence. Defined as 'inner life processes and affective states', subjectivity helps to explain why, how and when people come to envisage new possibilities, and how their particular experiences reconfigure the ways in which they see the world.[76] Political subjectivities that were at the core of mass protests of the 1980s did not emerge in a vacuum but through interpersonal and intersubjective processes.[77] Encounters with African councillors shaped the ways in which township communities came to see their

---

(1988), pp.73–86.

73 'The Freedom Charter', printed in R. Suttner and J. Cronin, *30 Years of the Freedom Charter* (Johannesburg, Ravan Press, 1985), pp.262–66. This is the shortened version of the Freedom Charter, without its subsections.

74 Seekings, *The UDF*, p.7.

75 A. Kleinman, 'The Violences of Everyday Life: The Multiple Forms of and Dynamics of Social Violence', in V. Das, A. Kleinman, M. Ramphele and P. Reynolds (eds), *Violence and Subjectivity* (Berkeley, University of California Press, 2000), pp.228, 238.

76 Biehl, Good and Kleinman, 'Introduction', p.5.

77 A. Kleinman and E. Fitz-Henry, 'The Experiential Basis of Subjectivity: How Individuals Change in the Context of Societal Transformation', in J. Biehl, B. Good and A. Kleinman (eds), *Subjectivity: Ethnographic Investigations* (Berkeley, University of California Press, 2007), p.64.

own oppression. The restructuring of local government, and the devolution of power to the third tier, shifted the blame for socio-economic and political grievances onto the shoulders of newly elected African councillors. Their rampant corruption, misconduct and the violence they meted out not only appeared to confirm their role in impeding meaningful political emancipation and development, they were also seen as violating the moral codes of their communities. The perception of councillors as being the 'enemy of the people' was therefore not only rooted in the political language of the UDF, the ANC and other emancipatory movements, it was also reflective of the collective experience of township communities.

While the decades prior to the uprising had infused emancipatory politics with new ideas, it was the rupture of the uprising and the inversion of the social and political order that refashioned the political imaginary. It was a moment of true struggle that was shaped by 'dimensions of force, uncertainty, domination and disdain, loss and confusion'.[78] The rupture of the uprising laid bare contestations over which strategies and tactics were deemed appropriate, necessary and desirable, and which ones were not. This process of 'subjectivation' – the formation of a 'collective political subject' – was therefore intimately connected to the 'eventfulness' of the uprising and collective experiences of physical violence and threat.[79] Gratuitous police violence and councillors' aggressive behaviour towards their constituencies sparked collective anger that significantly contributed towards the mobilisation of young and old. The aftermath saw the emergence of a more radical form of contentious politics. The uprising itself therefore facilitated the translation of interest-based politics into a broader struggle for political power and social transformation.

The Structure of this Book

This book traces these shifts in emancipatory thought and practice. It locates emerging politics of the 1980s in the social convulsions of the mid-twentieth century and argues that struggles for social transformation and political power were profoundly shaped by aspirations and hopes dating back to earlier periods. The book is divided into seven main chapters. Focusing on social formation and change during the period of industrialisation and urbanisation, Chapter 1 examines the emergence of urban subjectivities and their claim to a decent and

78   G. Pandey, *Remembering Partition: Violence, Nationalism and History in India* (Cambridge, Cambridge University Press, 2001), p.4.

79   On the relation between event and subjectivity, see V. Das, 'On Singularity and the Event', in J. Laidlaw and B. Bodenhorn (eds), *Recovering the Human Subject: Freedom, Creativity and Decision* (Cambridge, Cambridge University Press, 2018), pp.53–73 and Kleinman and Fitz-Henry, 'The Experiential Basis of Subjectivity', pp.53–65.

good life in the cities. Struggles for affordable housing and secure tenure, as this chapter shows, date back to the formation of the African model townships in this region.[80] In Sharpeville, economic rentals were introduced in 1954 and rent increases were key in paving the way for the politicisation of Sharpeville's population during this period. With the consolidation of ethnic state formation, Africans were stripped of their citizenship of South Africa proper; consequently, they were regarded as 'temporary sojourners' whose real future was considered to be in the bantustans.[81] The production of home spaces, as the chapter contends, was therefore deeply political and reflected Africans' claim to citizenship and a stake in the city.

Chapter 2 outlines the failure of these model townships, expressed in falling living conditions and increasing poverty. Significantly, the political crisis of the 1970s ushered in a series of reforms that aimed to create a new African middle class with access to better housing and infrastructure. The (selective) acceptance of African permanence from the 1970s, as this chapter shows, necessitated the development and upgrading of African townships; but a lack of state subsidies and taxable industries led to frequent rent increases that soon provided the matrix for growing dissent. Coupled with a lack of representation, maladministration as well as widespread corruption of newly elected African councillors, the stage was set for the emergence of organised politics. The state's strategy of implementing gradual political and socio-economic reforms, instead of curbing dissent, opened up space for growing demands for equality, rights and emancipation.

Chaper 3 examines the emergence of protest politics. During the early 1970s, the country saw the flourishing of new forms of politics largely rooted in cultural societies, reading clubs, schools and church groups. While these formations remained ephemeral, they groomed a new generation of young political activists who would come to play a leading role during the 1980s. The chapter examines the emergence of these groups and the shift from Black Consciousness to Charterism. With the formation of the Congress of South African Students in 1979 and the UDF in 1983, Charterist ideas gained new momentum. In the Vaal Triangle, the VCA, launched in 1983, and the VOW, established in 1984, came to be at the forefront of mobilisation against rent increases. The ascendancy of the Charterist movement had various

---

80   On model townships, see N. Nieftagodien, 'The Implementation of Urban Apartheid on the East Rand, 1948–1973' (PhD thesis, University of the Witwatersrand, 2001).

81   I follow the suggestion by Shireen Ally and Arianna Lissoni to refer to these entities as bantustans (without inverted commas) or 'homelands' (with inverted commas, to distance myself from the problematic connotations of the concept). See S. Ally and A. Lissoni, 'Preface: "Let's Talk about Bantustans"', *South African Historical Journal*, 64/1 (2012), pp.1–4.

roots: a series of campaigns to popularise the ANC and the Freedom Charter, the (modest) growth of the ANC underground, as well as the identification of ordinary people with the political language, social demands and visions put forward by the Charterists certainly count among the most important factors.[82] For many, the Freedom Charter was the translation of lived experiences into political discourse; growing political activity therefore signified the enactment of the ideals of the Charter. Even though student and civic structures established during the early 1980s operated largely beyond the control of the ANC, they nevertheless drew inspiration and ideological guidance from the ANC.

Chapters 4 and 5 focus on the revolt and its aftermath. Arguing that it constituted a moment of rupture, the Vaal Uprising produced new subjectivities and new political imaginaries. Public protest action reflected ordinary people's claims to full citizenship, and the expectations and aspirations ordinary people held. Chapter 4 traces the unfolding of the revolt in 1984. It focuses on the announcement of a rent increase in early August 1984, and the consequent mobilisation that took place in the townships. As this chapter shows, this increase was the last spark that triggered mass protest on 3 September. The chapter follows the movements and agendas of different actors to highlight the diversity of experiences and agendas, and the variety of tactics employed. It analyses the factors that led a peaceful protest march to turn violent. Here, it is vital to distinguish between the factors that led to the emergence of popular protests, peaking in the protest march on 3 September 1984, and the factors that led to collective violence on the same day. While some of the violence was premeditated and planned, in other instances it was a direct result of councillors and police shooting at advancing crowds. Excessive police brutality and aggression by councillors therefore played a leading role in turning the protest march into a bloody uprising. The contours of conflict and the contours of violence therefore overlapped but also differed. Chapter 5 examines the breakdown of social order and the collapse of organised forms of politics in the aftermath of the uprising. The vacuum of leadership was soon filled by new and often more radical actors, some of whom espoused violence as a tactic. Churches, as this chapter shows, were key in providing guidance and emergency relief, and in publicising the events to a global audience.

---

82   Protest politics in other townships followed the ideology of Black Consciousness. In Zamdela in the Northern Free State, protest politics was spearheaded by youth who largely identified with the Azanian People's Organisation (AZAPO) and its student wing, the Azanian Students' Movement (AZASM). T. Moloi, 'Zamdela Township: The Explosion of Confrontational Politics, Early 1980s to 1990', *Journal of Contemporary History*, 43/1 (2018), pp.111–16.

Chapter 6 examines the way the state responded to the revolt. The use of gratuitous violence and repression signified the crumbling of apartheid power. During this period, as the chapter demonstrates, the state adopted a curious blend of reforms, concessions and repression to curb the swell. The fiscal impact of the rent boycott was severe, and for years local authorities employed diverse strategies to recover rent. In response, local communities made a series of demands, including for reduced rent, home ownership and local democratic structures, that signified contestations over social rights and the political order. Significantly, government claimed that the insurrections that were sweeping across the country had been orchestrated by the ANC, the SACP and their domestic allies.

Chapter 7 analyses the shift towards a more encompassing struggle for social transformation and political power. In what was termed 'people's power', the insurrectionary period of 1984–86 produced a new form of politics that was deeply rooted in demands for people's control over their own lives. To a limited extent, this form of politics was therefore a translation of previous visions and demands into practice. Strategies of withdrawing economic participation through strikes or consumer boycotts were at times linked and at other times in conflict with more clandestine and violent forms of resistance, which corresponded with the ANC's call for a 'people's war' from 1985. During the 1980s, the streets became major sites of conflict, where youth confronted heavily armed riot police. Young comrades'[83] localised tactics of subverting state control were deeply rooted in everyday practices and their knowledge of the topography of the townships. Knowing which streets led to dead-ends, and which houses were safe houses, was key in evading arrest. The home, on the other hand, reflected a system of 'collective care' and communal solidarity where youth activists on the run from the police could seek refuge.[84] Within this context, the home and the domestic sphere became fiercely embattled. By late 1986, as Chapter 7 concludes, the state had successfully re-established 'law and order'. But by then, the dismantling of white minority rule was imminent.

The Conclusion traces the legacy of the 1980s and summarises the main arguments of this book. As the chapter shows, for many ordinary South Africans the dream of a dignified life free from poverty remains out of reach. In response, new social movements have emerged that struggle for socio-economic rights and, in some instances, the transformation of the existing order. Frequent protest action in the urban townships and rural areas reminds us of the revolts of the 1980s; yet their impact and ability to organise across regions remains limited.

83 The term 'comrade' loosely refers to those who were active members of the progressive movement. During the 1980s, it was often equated with Charterist activists.

84 Makhulu, *Making Freedom*, p.24.

This story is of course far from complete. The book does not provide an in-depth analysis of struggles for housing during the apartheid era, but instead shows that housing (as well as social services) was at the core of constructs of citizenship and visions of freedom that informed the revolt of 1984. Evidence shows that Charterist organisations were largely at the centre of the Vaal Uprising. The book therefore focuses on the ascendancy of Charterism and pays less attention to the diversity of politics that shaped the emancipatory project.

1

Urbanisation and the Making of the Home

A Knock on the Door

The knock on the door of the house in Evaton, a freehold area in the industrial complex of the Vaal Triangle, was abrupt – if it was a knock at all. Likely, the sound that disturbed the peace that evening was rather a hammering. In any case, it was unwelcome as it did not announce the friendly visit of a neighbour but the dreaded coming of the infamous municipal police, known as the 'blackjacks'. The year was 1968, eight years after the Sharpeville massacre and the banning of the African National Congress (ANC) and the Pan Africanist Congress (PAC) and three years after the first houses were built in the neighbouring township of Sebokeng. A young boy of eight years had just come back from playing in the street when he witnessed his parents' arrest.[1] Neither his mother nor his father had Section 10 rights under the Native Laws Amendment Act of 1952 and their presence in Evaton was thus considered illegal according to apartheid legislation.[2] To protect her husband, the mother claimed that he was a visitor and not

---

1   WHP AK2117 (*State v Baleka and 21 Others*), Case No.482/85, I2.7, Vol.205, Testimony Malindi, pp.10733–34; Gcina Malindi, interview with author, Johannesburg, 21 July 2010.

2   The 1952 Native Laws Amendment Act (which amended the 1945 Native (Urban Areas) Act) further restricted the movement of South Africa's African population by tightening influx control. It defined three categories of African people who were qualified to live in urban 'white' South Africa. Deborah Posel summarises the sections as follows: 'in terms of section 10(1)(a), Africans who had been born and continuously resident in a particular urban area; in terms of section 10(1)(b), Africans who had served one employer for at least ten years, or several employers within the same area for at least 15 years; in terms of section 10(1)(c), the wives and dependent children of the people who qualified under section 10(1)(a) or (b)'. See D. Posel, 'Influx Control and the Urban Labour Markets in the 1950s', in P. Bonner, P. Delius and D. Posel (eds), *Apartheid's Genesis 1935–1962: Contradiction, Continuity and Popular Struggle* (Johannesburg, Ravan Press, 1993), p.414. Those who did not qualify were regarded as temporary sojourners and were under continuous threat of removal to one of the bantustans.

the head of the household. Asked by one of the policemen whether he knew the man who had just been arrested, the child said no. Despite his young age he understood the gravity of the situation and was aware of his father's precarious legal status. It was neither the first nor the last time his parents would be arrested during a pass raid.

Almost 20 years later, in April 1987, Gcina Malindi, who had by now become a grown man, recalled the incident in court as he was standing trial for his alleged involvement in creating a revolutionary climate to overthrow the South African regime. As one of his lawyers, George Bizos, remembered, Malindi was in clear distress when he recounted the story.[3] It had been a life-changing experience that had influenced his young mind. It was a story symptomatic of life under apartheid, a story that happened countless times all over the country. The constant threat of being removed to one of South Africa's bantustans, and the daily fear of being arrested, shaped the lives of the majority of South Africa's disenfranchised population. These everyday encounters with state oppression, violence and inequality played a leading role in shaping the political consciousness and subjectivity of activists who came to be at the forefront of protest politics during the 1970s and 1980s.

Industrial Expansion and Labour Migration

The Vaal Triangle forms part of the industrial heartland of the Pretoria–Witwatersrand–Vereeniging complex (PWV) of present-day Gauteng, in the former Transvaal. It lies approximately 60 kilometres to the south of Johannesburg and encompasses the area between Vereeniging, Vanderbijlpark and Sasolburg. The climate is harsh with cold, dry winters and hot summers that are punctuated by the frequent thunderstorms the South African Highveld is known for. The heavy pall of smoke, emanating from the local metal giant, Arcelor Mittal, in Vanderbijlpark, formerly known as the South African Iron and Steel Corporation (ISCOR), is a constant reminder of the region's contribution to South Africa's industrialisation. Arcelor Mittal's chimneys stand in stark contrast to the rural face of the Midvaal, approximately 30 kilometres to the northeast of Vanderbijlpark. While the Vaal Triangle signifies industrial expansion, the Midvaal speaks of rural dispossession. These twin economic trajectories of industrial development and agricultural change moulded demographic shifts in the region and significantly contributed towards urbanisation.[4]

3   G. Bizos, *Odyssey to Freedom: A Memoir by the World-Renowned Human Rights Advocate, Friend and Lawyer to Nelson Mandela* (Cape Town, Random House, 2007), p.461.

4   For an earlier history of this region and Vereeniging and Sharpeville in particular, see M. Chaskalson, 'The Road to Sharpeville' (African Studies seminar paper, University of the Witwatersrand, 1986) and S. Trapido, 'Putting a Plough to the Ground: A His-

With the onset of the Second World War, the iron and steel industry experienced enhanced demand to service the armaments industry. By 1944, ISCOR, based in Secunda, chose a new site in Vanderbijlpark to accommodate its growing demand. ISCOR, one of South Africa's largest parastatals, had been established in 1928 to exploit South Africa's rich resources of coal and iron ore. ISCOR's presence entrenched the Vaal Triangle's leading role in the national metal industry, which had emerged during the early twentieth century.[5] South Africa's economy during the Second World War was booming, in contrast to that of its allies. The increased price of gold, an expansion in gold production and a surplus of government revenue allowed South Africa to repay debt and to expand its gold reserves.[6]

Economic prosperity firmly established the region's reputation as one of the most significant industrial hubs in the country. By 1970, the Vaal Triangle was considered to be the most heavily industrialised region in South Africa, with 75 percent of the regional income being produced by industry (as opposed to 25 percent nationally).[7] Nationally, the growth in the manufacturing industry soon resulted in a drastic expansion of African employment. Nicoli Nattrass demonstrates that out of 790,000 workers, 200,000 had volunteered to join the military, thus creating a serious shortage of labour.[8] Consequently, new waves of African migrants, predominantly from Lesotho (then Basotholand) and the Orange Free State, moved to the Vaal Triangle to seek their fortune. These new waves of migration reinforced earlier demographic patterns and

tory of Tenant Production on the Vereeniging Estates, 1896–1920', in W. Beinart, P. Delius and S. Trapido (eds), *Putting a Plough to the Ground: Accumulation and Dispossession in Rural South Africa, 1850–1930* (Johannesburg, Ravan Press, 1986). For a discussion of agrarian change, see T. Keegan, 'The Making of the Rural Economy: From 1850 to the Present', in Z.A. Konczacki, J. Parpart and T.M. Shaw (eds), *Studies in the Economic History of Southern Africa, Volume Two: South Africa, Lesotho and Swaziland* (New York, Routledge, 2013), pp.36–63; T. Keegan, 'The Sharecropping Economy, African Class Formation and the 1913 Natives' Land Act in the Highveld Maize Belt', in S. Marks and R. Rathbone (eds), *Industrialisation and Social Change in South Africa* (London and New York, Longman, 1982), pp.195–211; A. Jeeves and J. Crush, 'Introduction', in A. Jeeves and J. Crush (eds), *White Farms, Black Labor: The State and Agrarian Change in Southern Africa, 1910–1950* (Oxford, James Currey, 1997). On the conquest of African kingdoms and chieftaincies, see P.S. Landau, *Popular Politics in the History of South Africa, 1400–1948* (Cambridge, Cambridge University Press, 2010).

5   See Chaskalson, 'The Road to Sharpeville'.

6   N. Nattrass, 'Economic Growth and Transformation in the 1940s', in S. Dubow and A. Jeeves (eds), *South Africa's 1940s: Worlds of Possibilities* (Cape Town, Double Storey Books, 2005), p.20.

7   M. Chaskalson, unpublished draft manuscript and notes, p.2.

8   Nattrass, 'Economic Growth and Transformation in the 1940s', p.24.

entrenched the region's Sotho-speaking preponderance. A significant number of these migrants joined the *Marashea* gangs (the Russians), established in 1947.[9]

Migration to the towns around the Reef and the Vaal Triangle had begun to pick up pace from the 1920s and further accelerated during the Second World War. Within a decade, between 1936 and 1946, the African population increased by 57.2 percent.[10] The influx of African workers was even greater in Vereeniging, where the African population doubled between 1935 and 1937.[11] For many, employment in the manufacturing industry in the Vaal Triangle provided an attractive alternative to the gold mines of Johannesburg.[12] Factory work paid better than work in the mines and, in contrast to mine workers, factory workers received their salary on a weekly basis.[13] The perceived *oorstrooming* (swamping) of towns by Africans under the banner of *swart gevaar* (black peril) would come to occupy the collective psyche of white South Africa.[14] Poverty and the breakdown of marriages and family life were blamed for rampant crime and juvenile delinquency, which became endemic during the 1920s.[15]

9   J. Guy and M. Thabane, 'The Ma-Rashea', in B. Bozzoli (ed.), *Class, Community, and Conflict: South African Perspectives* (Johannesburg, Ravan Press, 1987), pp.436–55; G. Kynoch, *We Are Fighting the World: A History of the Marashea Gangs in South Africa, 1947–1999* (Scottsville, UKZN Press, 2005); P. Bonner, 'The Russians on the Reef, 1947–1957: Urbanisation, Gang Warfare and Ethnic Mobilisation', in Bonner, Delius and Posel (eds), *Apartheid's Genesis*.

10   D. Posel, 'Curbing African Urbanisation in the 1950s and 1960s', in M. Swilling, R. Humphries and K. Shubane (eds), *Apartheid City in Transition* (Cape Town, Oxford University Press, 1991), pp.20–27.

11   I. Jeffrey, 'Cultural Trends and Community Formation in a South African Township: Sharpeville, 1943–1985' (MA thesis, University of the Witwatersrand, 1991), p.47.

12   On urbanisation during this period, see P. Bonner, P. Delius and D. Posel, 'The Shaping of Apartheid: Contradiction, Continuity and Popular Struggle', in Bonner, Delius and Posel (eds), *Apartheid's Genesis*, pp.1–41; P. Bonner, 'African Urbanisation on the Rand between the 1930s and 1960s: Its Social Character and Political Consequences', *Journal of Southern African Studies*, 21/1 (1995), pp.115–29. On the relationship between the local state and local communities during this period, see H. Sapire, 'Apartheid's "Testing Ground": Urban "Native Policy" and African Politics in Brakpan, South Africa, 1943–1948', *Journal of African History*, 35/1 (1994), pp.99–123.

13   Bonner, 'African Urbanisation on the Rand', p.119.

14   S. Dubow, *Apartheid, 1948–1994* (Oxford, Oxford University Press, 2014), p.5.

15   D. Posel, 'The Case for a Welfare State: Poverty & the Politics of the African Family in the 1930s & 1940s', in Dubow and Jeeves, *South Africa's 1940s*. On the emergence of urban gangs, see P. la Hausse, '"The Cows of Nongoloza": Youth, Crime and Amalaita Gangs in Durban, 1900–1936', *Journal of Southern African Studies*, 16/1 (1990), pp.79–111 and C. Glaser, *Bo-Tsotsi: The Youth Gangs of Soweto, 1935–1976* (Oxford, James Currey, 2000).

Thus, the 1930s saw the rise of social welfarist thinking, which emphasised greater need for intervention into social life (and the family specifically) and the economic sphere.[16] Marriage, parenthood and domestic life became the centre of state intervention. Single women, who arrived in the urban areas often as 'refugees from marriages that had cracked under the strain of rural pauperisation and the migrant labour system', were frequently seen as one of the greatest threats to morality and blamed for social ills.[17] In 1938, the Conference on Urban Native Delinquency emphasised the need for the upliftment of African communities to curb 'moral degradation' and combat 'delinquency'. The conference recommended that central government and municipalities invest in 'better wages, better housing and adequate social services' as well as schools.[18] The development of welfare reforms in South Africa was inspired by international ideas on welfare that emanated from the *Report on Social Insurance and Allied Services* (commonly known as the Beveridge Report), published in Great Britain in 1942.[19] By the mid-1940s, reforms in the social welfare system saw the extension of old age pensions to Africans and Indians, the introduction of a (partial) unemployment insurance, a revision of the education system, moves towards the implementation of universal healthcare and the raising of African wages.[20] Many of these reforms would be undone post-1948, after the electoral victory of the National Party.

The region's prospering economy not only attracted large numbers of African migrants but also firmly cemented Vereeniging's and Vanderbijlpark's status as attractive hubs for the white, mostly Afrikaans-speaking working class and lower middle class. Those segments of white South African society had keenly benefited from social upliftment and were consequently often ardent supporters of policies that entrenched racial segregation and discrimination

16   Posel, 'The Case for a Welfare State', p.65.

17   P. Bonner, 'Desirable or Undesirable Basotho Women? Liquor, Prostitution and the Migration of Basotho Women to the Rand, 1920–1945', in C. Walker (ed.), *Women and Gender in Southern Africa to 1945* (Cape Town, David Philip, 1990), p.227.

18   Posel, 'The Case for a Welfare State', p.72.

19   J. Seekings, 'The Origins of Social Citizenship in Pre-Apartheid South Africa', *South African Journal of Philosophy*, 19/4 (2000), pp.386–404; Seekings, 'Visions, Hopes and Views about the Future: The Radical Moment of South African Welfare Reform', in Dubow and Jeeves, *South Africa's 1940s*.

20   Seekings, 'The Origins of Social Citizenship', p.395; Seekings, 'Visions, Hopes and Views about the Future', p.45. For a differing view, see B. Freund, *Twentieth-Century South Africa: A Developmental History* (Cambridge, Cambridge University Press, 2019). Freund argues that instead of viewing these reforms as 'humanitarian liberal intervention', they were geared towards the promotion of economic development and the modernisation of society. For an analysis of the longer trajectory of welfare reforms, see J. Seekings and N. Nattrass, *Class, Race, and Inequality in South Africa* (New Haven and London, Yale University Press, 2005).

against the African workforce. Vanderbijlpark, a company town built in 1941 on land purchased by ISCOR, was a 'prize project', which, in the words of the director of war supplies, H.J. van der Bijl, would be 'efficient in its layout, sensible in the inter-relationship of the various areas […] but, above all, a town of pleasant surroundings where residents could lead a full and satisfactory life'.[21] Vanderbijlpark's spatial setup reflected modernist urban planning with an 'emphasis on green space and recreation', as Bill Freund notes.[22] The refashioning of white subjectivity and the upliftment of poor whites were underpinned by notions of respectability and orderliness, twin tropes that would also inform the manner in which 'model townships' were engineered.[23]

Sharpeville: The Pride of the Municipality

Social welfare debates impacted on plans to construct a new township near Vereeniging to accommodate the growing African workforce. Sharpeville or Sharpe Native Township, as it was initially known, was named after John Lillie Sharpe, Vereeniging's mayor from 1935 to 1937. Built in 1943, Sharpeville's layout and facilities were in stark contrast to Vereeniging's other municipal township Top Location (Topville), an 'unregulated inner-city township' that had sprung up in 1912.[24] On 19 September 1937, riots broke out in Topville after police raided it to search for 'illegal' visitors and illicit beer brewing, typically one of the most lucrative ways of generating income for migrant Basotho women.[25] For the Vereeniging Town Council, the 1937 riots brought into sharp relief the social volatility of Topville, and the significance of adequate housing in preventing unrest.[26] Subsequently, the Vereeniging Town Council purchased a new site two miles outside the central town.

The removal of Topville's residents began in 1943 and was completed in 1959, when the last residents were forcibly removed to Vukazenzele section in Sharpeville.[27] Rallying around their common experience of forced removals, this last group provided the backbone of support for the PAC in the latter part of 1959 and early 1960. The different nature of removals created animosities and neigh-

---

21   Freund, *Twentieth-Century South Africa*, p.143; H. van der Bijl, quoted in the Vanderbijlpark Town Council, 'Vanderbijlpark – Founded for Progress, Planned for People' (Vanderbijlpark, no date).

22   Freund, *Twentieth-Century South Africa*, p.143.

23   S. Sparks, 'Apartheid Modern: South Africa's Oil from Coal Project and the History of a South African Company Town' (PhD thesis, University of Michigan, 2012).

24   Chaskalson, 'The Road to Sharpeville', p.9.

25   Bonner, 'Desirable or Undesirable Basotho Women?'

26   For a debate on the role of housing in stabilising the African population during this period, see J. Robinson, 'Administrative Strategies and Political Power in South Africa's Black Townships, 1930–1960', *Urban Forum*, 2/2 (1991), pp.63–77.

27   Jeffrey, 'Cultural Trends and Community Formation', pp.65 ff.

bourhood rivalries among Sharpeville's residents, which manifested in local gangs, football clubs and boxing, as Ian Jeffrey has shown.[28]

Sharpeville was a model township and was soon regarded as *'die trots van die munisipale amptenare'* (the pride of the municipal authorities),[29] an 'administrator's dream' and the best-administered African township in South Africa.[30] In contrast to its newer sibling Sebokeng, built later on, Sharpeville was built before the era of grand apartheid and was largely beyond the control of central government; the Vereeniging Town Council therefore had substantial leeway to plan and implement African housing. Owing to its perceived success, Sharpeville was given its status as a blueprint for successful social engineering and was used as a prototype for township planning during the 1950s.[31] Sharpeville's housing and its facilities and infrastructure, which included community halls, a crèche, sporting facilities, a stadium (the George Thabe Stadium where the new constitution was signed in 1996), a beerhall, streetlights, banking facilities and a relatively high number of schools and churches, were considered superior to those in other African townships. Inadequate housing, Vereeniging's officials feared, would foster the 'menace of Communism', or an uprising similar to Mau Mau in Kenya.[32]

Yet discontent with the Vereeniging Town Council was brewing. In 1954, as Matthew Chaskalson highlights, the Native Affairs Department introduced full economic rentals and two years later these new regulations came into effect.[33] The introduction of economic rentals to cover the costs of housing in the townships, and the withdrawal of subsidies, had significant consequences: from the 1950s, rent increases became a key grievance among the African population in Sharpeville. Complaints about overcrowding abounded, as no new housing schemes were built in the entire Vereeniging area.[34] Residents also complained about the lack of tarred roads, sewerage systems, street lights and electricity.[35] By the late 1950s, youth unemployment was spiralling and, consequently, youth

28   Ibid., p.69.
29   Quoted in N.T. Vally, 'The "Model Township" of Sharpeville: The Absence of Political Action and Organisation, 1960–84' (MA thesis, University of the Witwatersrand, 2010), p.44.
30   M. Chaskalson, 'The Road to Sharpeville', pp.1, 11.
31   Ibid., p.9.
32   Ibid., p.12.
33   Ibid., p.16.
34   SMA MS, 'Non-European Affairs Committee, Meeting of August 1956'. On squatter movements in the Vaal during this period, see N. Nieftagodien, 'Vaal Squatters in the 1940s: Occupiers, Speculators and Eye of the City' (unpublished paper, 2012). The passing into legislation of the Prevention of Illegal Squatting Act 52 of 1951 aimed at curbing the proliferation of informal settlements.
35   Jeffrey, 'Cultural Trends and Community Formation', p.181.

gangs proliferated. While the relatively high standard of living partly explains the absence of open political activity during the 1950s, the impact of forced removals, overcrowding, unemployment and increasing police raids soon provided fertile ground for political mobilisation. In 1959, PAC activists from Johannesburg set up a local branch in Sharpeville, and by early 1960 its membership had grown to 150 people, reflecting growing disenchantment in the local population.[36]

What happened next is well documented: on 21 March 1960, police shot 69 women, men and children who had gathered outside the local police station to protest against the pass laws.[37] This heinous act, which came to be known as the Sharpeville massacre, altered the course of history and sent shock waves across the country. While other African countries were preparing for independence, the shooting of protestors in Sharpeville signalled the South African government's unwillingness to tolerate resistance to its discriminatory policies.[38] Ikabot Makiti, a PAC activist who was 17 by the time of the shooting, recalled the comment from an African policeman at the scene of the massacre: 'Now you have got what you wanted. This is your *Izwe Lethu* [our land].'[39]

The Sharpeville massacre heralded the beginning of a period of severe repression. In the aftermath of the massacre, the ANC and the PAC were banned and their leadership went into exile where they would remain for the next 30 years. Both organisations developed underground tactics and adopted the armed struggle. In Sharpeville, open political activity ceased as rapidly as it had begun, and hostility towards PAC members was palpable. 'They are the people that put us in trouble,' Gideon Tsolo remembers hearing from neighbours.[40] The Vaal

36   Chaskalson, 'The Road to Sharpeville', p.29.

37   Under the Natives (Abolition of Passes and Co-ordination of Documents) Act, Act No.67 of 1952 (popularly referred to as the Pass Laws), South Africa's African population was forced to carry an identity book at all times (often referred to as *dompas*). It was one of the cornerstones of apartheid legislation and led to widespread grievances and dissent.

38   The year 1960, while commonly referred to as the 'Year of Africa' that saw the declaration of independence of 17 African nations, also witnessed extraordinary degrees of violence. In Algeria and Kenya, for example, struggles for independence were brutally suppressed, while the Portuguese colonies only achieved independence in 1975, after a protracted armed struggle. See M. Thomas and G. Curless, 'Introduction: Decolonization, Conflict and Counter-Insurgency', in M. Thomas and G. Curless (eds), *Decolonization and Conflict: Colonial Comparisons and Legacies* (London, Bloomsbury Academic, 2017).

39   Ikabot Makiti, interview with author, Sharpeville, 15 July 2010. '*Izwe Lethu*' is a popular slogan among members of the PAC and its formations in South Africa. It refers to the return of the land to African people. On the PAC, see K. Kondlo, *In the Twilight of the Revolution: The Pan Africanist Congress of Azania (South Africa), 1959–1994* (Basel, Basler Afrika Bibliographien, 2009).

40   Gideon Tsolo, quoted in T. Lodge, *Sharpeville: An Apartheid Massacre and its Conse-*

Triangle was singled out for strict police surveillance; activists were harangued and arrested. Evidence of daily life after the massacre remains anecdotal but points towards a culture of fear that seeped into the social fabric and shaped everyday relations in the domestic and the public spheres. Many withdrew into the home. Politics was discussed in whispers, at best, or not spoken about at all: 'They [our parents' generation] were so scared of the regime,' Thami ka Plaatjie recalls.[41] Older residents spoke of an 'almost palpable sense of disaster which seemed to pervade the whole atmosphere, seeping into the most intimate and private social relations'.[42] The impact of the Sharpeville massacre on the collective psyche of the population was significant; expectations of state violence and brutality were high and dissuaded local residents from engaging in public protest action.[43]

While visible forms of resistance fizzled out, cultural life and sports provided temporary relief from the lived reality of oppression and state violence.[44] As elsewhere, boxing and football were popular and Sharpeville produced illustrious champions over the years. Football not only shaped everyday sociality but also laid the groundwork for patronage networks that shaped local politics. One such patron was George Thabe, whose life illustrates the entanglements between politics and entrepreneurship (see Chapter 2).

It was not until the late 1960s when the vacuum that had been left after the banning of the PAC and the ANC was filled by the Black Consciousness Movement (BCM). The BCM's emphasis on the importance of liberating the mind to overcome internalised repression, and its focus on community development, signified an important shift towards envisioning a new world.[45] The Sharpeville Youth Club was launched in 1973 and came to play a leading role in the establishment of a Black People's Convention in Vereeniging.[46] One of the leading

---

quences (Oxford, Oxford University Press, 2011), p.165.

41 Thami ka Plaatjie, interview with author, Vanderbijlpark, 14 June 2010.

42 P. Frankel, *An Ordinary Atrocity: Sharpeville and its Massacre* (Johannesburg, Wits University Press, 2001), p.200; see also Vally, 'The "Model Township" of Sharpeville'.

43 WHP AK2117, S8.10.17, 'Rent Grievances, Sharpeville. Interview with Resident'.

44 Vally, 'The "Model Township" of Sharpeville', p.82.

45 See, for example, D. Magaziner, *The Law and the Prophets: Black Consciousness in South Africa, 1968–1977* (Athens, Ohio University Press, 2010); I. Macqueen, *Black Consciousness and Progressive Movements under Apartheid* (Pietermaritzburg, University of KwaZulu-Natal Press, 2018); X. Mangcu, 'African Modernity and the Struggle for People's Power: From Protest and Mobilization to Community Organizing', *The Good Society*, 21/2 (2012), pp.279–99.

46 See F. Rueedi, '"They Would Remind You of 1960": The Emergence of Radical Student Politics in the Vaal Triangle, 1972–1985', in A. Heffernan and N. Nieftagodien (eds), *Students Must Rise: Youth Struggle in South Africa Before and Beyond Soweto* (Johannesburg, Wits University Press, 2016); Lodge, *Sharpeville*.

figures in the Sharpeville Youth Club was Nkutsoeu Motsau,[47] who was also an executive member of the African Students' Movement (ASM), the predecessor of the South African Students' Movement (SASM) and a member of the Black People's Convention.[48] In 1974, Motsau was banished to the bantustan of Qwa Qwa, after being convicted under the Terrorism Act for 'publishing a poem and a newsletter, both considered by the court to be likely to "engender feelings of hostility between black and white"'.[49] While the BCM's reach remained limited, the intellectual rigour, the networks created and the impact on young people's minds all played a significant part in paving the way for mass resistance later on (see Chapter 3).

Economically, South Africa entered a period of prosperity and growth.[50] Between 1963 and the early 1970s South Africa's economy benefited from investments that 'yielded some of the highest rates of return on capital in the world'.[51] Economic growth and low unemployment rates led to 'unprecedented stability'; for South Africa's white population, an abundance of job opportunities, social advancement and growing affluence were 'major apartheid dividend[s]'.[52] African workers, in spite of earning significantly less income, experienced real wage growth during this period.[53]

From State Welfarism to 'Racial Modernism'

The Sharpeville massacre not only led to a political lull and a climate of fear, it also collapsed Sharpeville's status as a showcase of successful social engineering. Local authorities were eager to remove Sharpeville's residents to Sebokeng, a new township that was envisaged to concentrate the African workforce in the region. Plans to build Sebokeng date back to the early 1950s, when the Mentz Committee was tasked to draw up racial zoning in the entire PWV region. The main task of the Mentz Committee was to address the housing shortage and slum-like conditions of many African settlements, and to 'draw up a set of spatial guidelines for promoting segregated African townships and removing integrated

---

47   Motsau's name is occasionally spelt as Nkutsweu Motsau.

48   N.J. Diseko, 'The Origins and Development of the South African Students' Movement (SASM): 1968–1976', *Journal of Southern African Studies*, 18/1 (1991), pp.40–62.

49   Lodge, *Sharpeville*, p.286.

50   On economic growth, see J. Seekings and N. Nattrass, *Class, Race, and Inequality in South Africa* (New Haven and London, Yale University Press, 2005); W. Beinart, *Twentieth-Century South Africa* (Oxford, Oxford University Press, 2001); Freund, *Twentieth-Century South Africa*.

51   S. Dubow, 'Closing Remarks: New Approaches to High Apartheid and Anti-Apartheid', *South African Historical Journal*, 69/2, Special Issue: Rethinking 'Apartheid's Golden Age' (2017), p.308.

52   Ibid., p.309.

53   Ibid.

living spaces'.[54] Urban planning of the 1950s and 1960s focused on the building of large townships with rigid spatial structures and extensive buffer zones between them and the 'white' towns.[55] This new type of social engineering was reflective of the 'high modernist fantasy' of the apartheid state, with its vision of a 'totalizing order' with 'planning and surveillance' providing the matrices for aspirations of modernity and control.[56] It signified a shift from state welfarism to 'racial modernism', as Belinda Bozzoli points out.[57]

Urban planners projected the area would accommodate around 330,000 Africans by the year 2000.[58] A stretch of land that the authorities called N3-area between the Golden Highway, Houtkop Road and Residensia, a formerly white residential area, was set aside for the new township to be built.[59] But it would take a decade for Sebokeng to be finally developed. This delay points to the difficulties local authorities were experiencing in implementing the Group Areas Act, and the tensions that existed between central and local government. Finally, in 1964, Sebokeng Hostel was built to accommodate migrant workers. A year later Zone 13, Sebokeng's first residential area, was developed. During the same year, the Sebokeng Management Board under the directorship of J.C. Knoetze was established to oversee the administration and management of the area. Knoetze was a 'technocratic administrator' who never joined the National Party.[60] In contrast to most other townships, which were under the

54   P. Hendler, 'Living in Apartheid's Shadow: Residential Planning for Africans in the PWV Region 1970–1990', *Urban Forum*, 3/2 (1992), p.41.

55   On urban apartheid during this period, see N. Nieftagodien, 'The Implementation of Urban Apartheid on the East Rand, 1948–1973' (PhD thesis, University of the Witwatersrand, 2001).

56   D. Posel, 'Race as a Common Sense: Racial Classification in Twentieth Century South Africa', *African Studies Review*, 44/2 (2001), p.100; D. Posel, 'The Apartheid Project, 1948–1970', in R. Ross, A. Mager and B. Nasson (eds), *The Cambridge History of South Africa, vol. 2: 1885–1994* (Cambridge, Cambridge University Press, 2011), p.345.

57   B. Bozzoli, *Theatres of Struggle and the End of Apartheid* (Johannesburg, Wits University Press, 2004), p.43; B. Bozzoli, 'Why Were the 1980s "Millenarian"? Style, Repertoire, Space and Authority in South Africa's Black Cities', *Journal of Historical Sociology*, 13/1 (2000), pp.78–110; see also A. Mabin, 'Varied Legacies of Modernism in Urban Planning', in G. Bridge and S. Watson (eds), *A Companion to the City* (Oxford, Blackwell, 2000), pp.555–66.

58   S. Bekker, 'The Local Government and Community of Sebokeng' (University of Stellenbosch, Occasional Paper No.3, 1978), p.8.

59   NAP BAO, 125, A1/1914, 'Gebiedsbepaling, Residensia, Verklaring van Residensia tot Bantoegebied'; NAP BAO, 1979, A19/1914, 'Bestuursrad van Sebokeng: Residensia: Aankoop van Grond vir Bantoebehuisingsdoeleindes'.

60   M. Chaskalson, 'Apartheid with a Human Face: Punt Janson and the Origins of Reform in Township Administration, 1972–1976', *African Studies*, 42/2 (1989), p.118.

administration of the Non-European Affairs Committees and white municipalities, the Sebokeng Management Board answered directly to the Department of Bantu Affairs and Development. There were two major consequences
of this, as Matthew Chaskalson shows: firstly, the accounts of the Sebokeng
Management Board were divorced from the accounts of white municipalities
and therefore received no indirect subsidies, causing fiscal difficulties.[61] Furthermore, the Sebokeng Management Board served as a pilot scheme for the
administration boards that became responsible for the administration of the
townships a few years later. Consequently, while many white municipalities
under the control of the United Party were reluctant to implement government policy, the Sebokeng Management Board 'followed departmental policy
to the letter'.[62]

Residensia to the north was classified as a white area in 1962, but its residents feared the proximity to the African freehold area of Evaton and urged
local authorities to buy their properties. Two years later, Residensia was
rezoned as an African area and earmarked for further development. Those
houses previously occupied by white residents were in 'tremendous demand'
and accommodated 'mostly well-to-do Africans of the middle class'.[63]

Sebokeng was separated from neighbouring white towns by a vacant strip
of land. Moshoeshoe street, the main road leading in and out of the township, divided Sebokeng into the 'Nguni' and the 'Sotho' side. This 'ethnic'
segregation of the township followed the logic of apartheid ideology that
imagined and constructed bounded ethnic groups, each with their own culture, traditions, language and 'homeland' or bantustan. Strict segregation,
however, was never enforced and most areas remained 'ethnically mixed'.
Like other African townships designed during this period, Sebokeng was
'laid out like a grid', with each zone bordered by a main road and veined
by smaller, mostly untarred streets that 'intersected at 90° angles'.[64] Houses
were numbered with digits while places of worship, administrative buildings and shops and community halls were carefully planned and situated
throughout the township.[65] This physical layout allowed for easy cordoning
off in times of disturbance and unrest, but also produced distinct forms of
'street politics' (see Chapter 7).

Sebokeng's early inhabitants predominantly included former residents of
Meyerton and newcomers from Sharpeville and Evaton. Meyerton, a small
community to the north of Sebokeng in the Midvaal, was declared a 'white area'

61   M. Chaskalson, unpublished draft manuscript and notes, p.9.
62   Ibid.
63   Quoted in Jeffrey, 'Cultural Trends and Community Formation', p.181.
64   J. Dlamini, *Native Nostalgia* (Johannesburg, Jacana, 2009), pp.43–44.
65   NAP BAO, 1798, A19/1914/3/1, 'Stedelike Bantoewoongebiede: Eenhede 8 tot 13, Sebokeng'.

in the early 1960s and by 1970, approximately 200 African families had been forcibly removed to Residensia and Sebokeng.[66] Communal spirit developed very slowly in many areas of Sebokeng as its population's heterogeneous origins reflected the frequent removals during this period, which disrupted 'whatever sense of unity existed'.[67] For sections of the population who had been removed from Meyerton, Evaton or Sharpeville, Sebokeng stood for the destruction of communities and a sanitised urban landscape with little communal spirit and less quality of life: a place that was 'desolate', 'inhospitable', 'unwelcoming' or simply 'pathetic'.[68] Others complained that the yards in Sebokeng were small in comparison to those in Sharpeville.[69]

The social character of each zone in Sebokeng was unique. Class, 'ethnicity' and origins differed and gave areas their distinct reputation. Zone 14 extension, for example, was occasionally referred to as 'Snobville' as it mainly accommodated the more affluent sections of society, including civil servants, nurses, teachers and clerks.[70] Zone 13 was a hub for political activism while Zone 7, popularly referred to as *slag pan* (slaughter pan), was notorious for its gangs and high levels of crime. It brought together the most impoverished residents; its close proximity to Evaton Small Farms, also known for its gangs, added to the distinct social character of Zone 7.[71] In spite of its dreary reputation, Zone 7 also produced a crop of political activists and became home to some of the politically most militant youth groups during the 1980s (see Chapter 7).

While urban planners and administrators envisaged that all other townships in the Vaal Triangle would eventually be demolished and their residents removed to Sebokeng, these plans never came to fruition. Bophelong, Boipatong and Sharpeville were considered to be too close to white areas, and the land upon which they were built was needed for industrial development. Yet even though Sharpeville, Bophelong and Boipatong continued their existence, their development and upgrading were frozen. In Sharpeville, for example, the construction

66   WHP AK2117, S8.10.5, 'Memorandum on Vaal Triangle Background'; Dikeledi Tsotetsi, interview with author, Vanderbijlpark, 14 June 2010.

67   WHP AK2117, S8.10.5, 'Memorandum on Vaal Triangle Background'.

68   Gift Moerane, interview with author, Vereeniging, 29 March 2010; Thami ka Plaatjie, interview with author, Vanderbijlpark, 14 June 2010.

69   M. Chaskalson, unpublished draft manuscript and notes.

70   For an analysis of the politics, cultural life and social markers of the African elite during this period, see M. Brandel-Syrier, *Reeftown Elite: Social Mobility in a Black African Community on the Johannesburg Reef* (New York, Africana Publishing Corporation, 1971).

71   For young men, criminality was often a quick and relatively easy path to success, money and status. See C. Glaser, 'Swines, Hazels and the Dirty Dozen: Masculinity, Territory and the Youth Gangs of Soweto, 1960–1976', *Journal of Southern African Studies*, 24/4 (1998), pp.719–36.

of a social centre, a crèche and the introduction of waterborne sewerage were all cancelled.[72] The freezing of their development and upgrading together with their uncertain fate produced 'a sickening feeling of insecurity' among residents in these three townships, resulting in a lack of interest in home improvements.[73] Many houses in these three townships remained incomplete because residents were 'expecting the axe to fall any day'.[74] The planned removal of these three townships was not only based on government policy, but fiscal interests: the Sebokeng Management Board had taken out several loans, including a loan to purchase land on which Sebokeng's Zones 11, 12 and 13 were built. To be able to repay these loans, it depended on rent payments of an extra 6,000 tenants.[75] These loans, as Chapter 2 will show, contributed towards the financial strain experienced by the board. Sharpeville's status was accepted only in the late 1970s. Its size remained stagnant as government declared that no new houses were to be built outside of Sebokeng.

'We are sick and tired of "baaskaap"'

In contrast to the careful planning of Sharpeville and Sebokeng, Evaton's layout had developed organically. Many of the houses were substantially larger than the 'matchbox houses' in the model townships, with impressive stoeps and surrounded by sizeable tracts of land. Evaton was built on Weldebeestfontein Farm 536IQ, owned by Thomas Adams and Charles John Easton.[76] The farm was subdivided for freehold in 1904 and plots were sold to landless Africans. In contrast to the tightly controlled model townships that emerged several decades later, Evaton offered economic opportunities and access to land for the socially aspirant and upwardly mobile. Its unique status as a freehold area therefore gave rise to a class of land owners and entrepreneurs who fiercely defended their gains. The famous Wilberforce Institute, a mission school established in 1908, was key in producing the local African elite.[77] More than any other township in the region, Evaton was a hub for political activities as early as the 1950s. It was at the centre of the *azikhwelwa* (we will not ride) bus boycott of 1956 and played a key role in political organising that led to the Sharpeville massacre of 1960.[78]

---

72   Jeffrey, 'Cultural Trends and Community Formation', p.180.

73   NAP MSK 335/3/8/2, 'Memorandum by the Vaal Triangle Council, Presented to Dr. P. Koornhof, 28 November 1979'; NAP MSK 335/3/8/2, 'Memorandum: Voortbestaan van Sharpeville-Woongebied'.

74   Ibid.

75   SMA MS 5/4/6, Document 78, 'Notule van 'n Vergadering van die Informele Komitee Aangestele deur die Minister van Bantoe-Administrasie en-Ontwikkeling gehou op Vrydag Augustus 11, 1967'.

76   V.R. Kumalo, 'The African Struggle for Independent Education: A History of Wilberforce Institute, Evaton, 1905 to 1950s' (PhD thesis, University of the Witwatersrand, 2018), p.108.

77   Ibid.

78   T. Lodge, '"We Are Being Punished because We Are Poor": The Bus Boycotts of Evaton

The degree of administration in Evaton in these early days was very light, as Tom Lodge points out: 'A health committee, which was the most rudimentary form of local government, did not exist.'[79] As a result, there was almost no provision of services and most residents were free from influx control and other restrictions. Owing to its social geography and its role in political mobilisation, Evaton was a thorn in the flesh of local authorities. The director of the Sebokeng Management Board, J.C. Knoetze, admonished in a letter to the Bantu Affairs Commissioner in 1971 that '[i]t is common knowledge that Evaton always has been and still is the hiding place for many Bantu who are illegally in the Vaal Triangle.'[80]

With the establishment of Sebokeng, fears of being removed increased.[81] The building of new houses, and the expansion and improvement of existing ones, were prohibited. Under the Land and Trust Act of 1936, the land Evaton was built on was scheduled to be purchased by the Vaal Triangle Administration Board, the successor of the Sebokeng Management Board, and J.C. Knoetze, director of the board, noted its 'powers of expropriation' but emphasised that only proper-ties coming onto the market would be purchased.[82] Property owners wishing to sell their house received no financial reimbursement but were leased a house in Sebokeng instead and granted a few months' free rent.[83] Knoetze cited concerns about what he regarded to be squalid living conditions, resulting in poor public health and ill order, as reasons for Evaton's scheduled replanning. According to Knoetze, Evaton's population was

> living in the most appalling conditions. There was no proper water supply [...], no proper sanitation or rubbish removal, there was an inadequate health ser-vice, there was an inadequate overall administration. To rectify the position, the management board of Evaton, of Sebokeng was created by the Department of Bantu Administration to try and bring order to the community, to provide essential services and to resettle the families who were living there under the most unsatisfactory conditions.[84]

---

and Alexandra, 1955–57', in T. Lodge, *Black Politics in South Africa since 1945* (London and New York, Longman, 1983); E. Mphahlele, 'The Evaton Riots', *Africa South*, 1/1 (1957).

79   Lodge, '"We Are Being Punished because We Are Poor"', p.174.

80   NAP BAO, 9210, A14/1914/1, 'Ministerial Inquiry, Residential Problems: Resi-dents of Evaton'.

81   NAP BAO, 125, A1/1914, 'Letter by Jacob Tshabalala'.

82   Excerpt from Commission of Inquiry into the Riots at Soweto and Other Places in South Africa held on 1 March 1977 (Cillié Commission), Vol.122, Statement by J.C. Knoetze, p.5853. https://www.aluka.org/stable/10.5555/al.sff.document.tra19770 301.026.019?searchUri=s0%3Dps_collection_name_str%2Basc%26Query%3D-Knoetze, retrieved 2 May 2020.

83   M. Horrell and D. Horner (eds), *A Survey of Race Relations, 1973* (Johannesburg, South African Institute of Race Relations, 1974), p.132.

84   Excerpt from Commission of Inquiry into the Riots at Soweto and Other

Knoetze juxtaposed this glum picture with the sanitised and modern facilities Sebokeng provided: '[T]hose are now living in four-roomed houses mainly with waterborne sewage, water laid on, tarred bus routes, a proper health service, a proper administration, and all the other modern facilities which are required in a properly settled community.' His complaints about poor living conditions were matched by the insistence of Evaton's residents that local authorities were doing little to upgrade and develop the township.[85] Yet despite this lack of development, Evaton offered property ownership and economic opportunities. Struggles against the control of the Sebokeng Management Board and its successors and threats to lose freehold rights shaped much of Evaton's history in the second half of the twentieth century.

The Denial of Urban Rights

While many struggled against the removal to Sebokeng, for others it signified aspirations for improved living conditions and urban permanence. These aspirations stood in stark contrast with apartheid social engineering, which regarded Africans as temporary sojourners in the urban areas. Within apartheid logic, modernity was considered to be a hallmark of the refashioned white subjectivity, while African 'ethnic' identities were imagined as bounded.[86] High apartheid, starting in the 1960s, was therefore defined by a distinction between 'white modernity' and 'African tradition'.[87] In contrast to the first decade of apartheid rule, apartheid's social engineers challenged the distinction of urbanised Africans with section 10(1) rights and those whose permanent base was considered to be in the rural areas.[88] This attempt to invert urbanisation of the African population found its apogee in the Promotion of Bantu Self-Government Act of 1959, effectively aiming to 'push Africans back to the reserves'.[89] It prepared the ground for transforming 'native

---

Places in South Africa held on 1 March 1977 (Cillié Commission), Vol.122, Statement by J.C. Knoetze, pp.5852–3. https://www.aluka.org/stable/10.5555/al.sff. document.tra19770301.026.019?searchUri=so%3Dps_collection_name_str%2Basc%26Query%3DKnoetze, retrieved 2 May 2020.

85   NAP BAO 2021/20/1914/2, 'Re: your Letter. A20/1914'. *Isolomuzi* ('eye of the home'), a local community organisation, fought against the replanning of the township.

86   For a discussion of the construction of these 'ethnic' identities, see, for example, L. Vail (ed.), *The Creation of Tribalism in Southern Africa* (Berkeley, University of California Press, 1989) and Landau, *Popular Politics*.

87   This was in contrast to French and British colonial authorities, whose 'ruling fiction of power' was guided by the belief that the African populations would be turned into '"modern" men and women', as Frederick Cooper notes. See F. Cooper, *Africa since 1940: The Past of the Present* (Cambridge, Cambridge University Press, 2002), p.76.

88   Posel, 'The Apartheid Project', p.342.

89   N. Nieftagodien, 'High Apartheid and the Erosion of "Official" Local Politics in Daveyton in the 1960s', *New Contree*, 67 (Special edition, 2013), p.36.

reserves' into self-governing entities, effectively stripping their 'citizens' of South African citizenship.[90] According to apartheid's architects, the creation of these ethnic national states was supposed to mirror processes of decolonisation that were under way elsewhere on the continent, as Laura Evans has argued.[91] 'Ethnic groups' were considered to be 'supra-tribal groupings, destined to realise the hidden ambitions of "nationhood" in the newly created homeland states'.[92] For the next two decades Africans were denied permanency and secure tenure in South Africa proper.[93] The settled urbanised population was redefined as labour supply and the right to reside in the city was linked to employment.

In the case of the majority of the Vaal Triangle's African population, the designated 'homeland' was Qwa Qwa, an area of approximately 480km² at the border between Lesotho, the Orange Free State and Natal. Previously known as the Witzieshoek Reserve,[94] the area was officially declared an 'ethnic home-land' for the Sotho-speaking population in 1969.[95] Qwa Qwa housed only a tiny fraction of South Africa's Sotho speakers; yet according to the Bantu Homelands Citizenship Act of 1970, anyone identified as 'South Sotho' was considered to be a de jure citizen of Qwa Qwa.[96] Between 1970 and 1982, the population of this tiny homeland increased from an estimated 23,860 to about 500,000. Even though these figures need to be interrogated as they stem from different sources, the increase was 'suggestive of mass population relocations of a scale almost unprecedented in South African history', as Isak Niehaus argues.[97] Qwa Qwa was earmarked for industrial development and advertised as a 'land of golden opportunities', allegedly offering economic prospects and

90   Seekings and Nattrass, *Class, Race, and Inequality in South Africa*, p.21. L. Evans, 'South Africa's Bantustans and the Dynamics of "Decolonisation": Reflections on Writing Histories of the Homelands', *South African Historical Journal*, 64/1, Special Issue: Let's Talk about the Bantustans (2012), pp.117–37.

91   Evans, 'South Africa's Bantustans', p.123.

92   L. Bank, 'The Failure of Ethnic Nationalism: Land, Power and the Politics of Clan-ship on the South African Highveld 1860–1990', *Africa*, 65/4 (1995), p.566.

93   Nieftagodien, 'High Apartheid'.

94   The Witzieshoek Reserve was created in 1869 to accommodate two groups of Baso-tho: a group of Bakwena under the leadership of Paulus Mopeli, and a group of Bat-lokwa under the leadership of Koos Mota. For an account of the Mopeli dynasty, see Landau, *Popular Politics*.

95   J. Martiny and J. Sharp, 'Second Carnegie Inquiry into Poverty and Development in Southern Africa: An Overview of Qwa Qwa: Town and Country in a South African Bantustan', Carnegie Conference Paper No.286 (Cape Town, 13–19 April 1984).

96   The ethnic category 'South Sotho' was a colonial construct. The term 'Sotho' will therefore be used throughout.

97   I. Niehaus, 'Relocation into Tseki and Phuthaditjhaba: A Comparative Ethnography of Planned and Unplanned Removals in Qwa Qwa' (University of the Witwaters-rand, African Studies seminar paper No.260, 1989), p.1.

social advancement. To attract the disparate Sotho-speaking population, a concerted propaganda campaign was broadcast via Radio Sesotho.[98] In reality, Qwa Qwa resembled a 'sea of hunger and misery' with high unemployment rates, overcrowding and severe poverty.[99] The promotion of self-governing (and from the 1970s independent) bantustans, and the forced removals to the bantustans of those who were considered to be 'surplus', saw the relocation of large numbers of Africans. By the late 1960s, the state had forcibly removed 3.5 million Africans to the bantustans.

In 1967, government passed legislation to prohibit any further purchasing of houses in urban areas by Africans. '[H]ouses of a higher standard' should be built in one of the designated bantustans, where Africans could 'obtain title for the land', as a circular issued by the Department of Bantu Administration and Development stated in 1967.[100] Township houses had to be rented from municipalities, and later the administration boards. Those who already owned a house could no longer bequeath it to their descendants.[101] State funds earmarked for Africans were therefore largely used for the development of these bantustans, while investment in urban areas drastically slowed down.

In contrast to central government's commitment to reverse urbanisation, local administrators often had a more realistic view. The Sebokeng Management Board acknowledged as early as 1969 that a large-scale removal of the Vaal Triangle's population to Qwa Qwa was unrealistic, and that the African population therefore had to be accommodated in the townships.[102] Administrators on the ground therefore accepted African urban permanence years before central government did. To avert social ills and political instability commonly associated with a lack of housing, administrators therefore sought a pragmatic approach to the urban question.[103] This acceptance, as Chapter 2 will show, placed the Sebokeng Management Board, and later its successor, the Vaal Triangle Administration Board, at the forefront of housing reforms.

Urban Subjectivity and Aspirations for Permanence

The making of home therefore became a significant expression of urban Africans' claim to the cities and their resistance to apartheid's attempt at 'retribalisation'.[104] Consumerism, home improvement and participation in a

98   Ibid.
99   Bank, 'The Failure of Ethnic Nationalism', p.577.
100   Quoted in Nieftagodien, 'High Apartheid', pp.49–50.
101   P. Morris, *A History of Black Housing in South Africa* (Johannesburg, South Africa Foundation, 1981), p.77.
102   See M. Chaskalson, unpublished draft manuscript and notes, p.29.
103   Chaskalson, 'Apartheid with a Human Face'.
104   F. Pinto de Almeida, 'Framing Interior: Race, Mobility and the Image of Home in South African Modernity', *Social Dynamics*, 41/3 (2015), pp.461–81.

cosmopolitan cultural expression through music, dance, poetry, fashion and literature were expressive of the ways the African population appropriated and reinterpreted the monotony of model townships.[105] International rock 'n' roll reached Sharpeville's youth via Radio Lourenco Marques (LM Radio), which broadcast from neighbouring Mocambique. Radio LM was a counter voice to South Africa's conservative Radio Bantu, introduced by the South African government in 1960 and geared towards ethnically homogeneous audiences.[106]

The majority of houses in these new model townships, popularly referred to as matchbox houses, consisted of a four-room unit known as type NE 51/6, with an asbestos roof, two bedrooms, a kitchen and a lounge or sitting room. Toilets, particularly in older zones such as Zone 13 in Sebokeng, were outside. Houses were rented out without plastering, ceilings or internal doors, and it was the responsibility of the tenants to improve these basic structures at their own expense.[107] Any additions had to be approved by local authorities and no compensation was paid for improvements to these houses, once the tenant moved out.[108] For many tenants, these additional costs placed a severe burden on their budgets and caused much grief. Rebecca Ginsburg shows that owing to a lack of funds, it often took tenants many years to complete the renovations.[109] Many prioritised home improvements over buying furniture; to live in a decent and respectable home was key to one's sense of belonging in the urban areas, and it was a way of asserting dignity in the face of the daily indignities and inhumanity of racial discrimination and oppression.[110] Home improvements signified people's claim to the city; it was a form of 'quietly setting down roots', as Ginsburg argues.[111] For those who could not afford home improvements, the stylisation of interiors came to represent a rejection of the 'denial of domesticity'.[112] Closely linked to the enforcement of racial segregation and the denial of full citizenship, the home, and by extension the interior, became one of the most embattled spheres and a significant site of everyday resistance to the state's grand apartheid.

105   Jeffrey, 'Cultural Trends and Community Formation', p.227.

106   S. Lekgoathi, "'You Are Listening to Radio Lebowa of the South African Broadcasting Corporation"': Vernacular Radio, Bantustan Identity and Listenership, 1960–1994', *Journal of Southern African Studies*, 35/3 (2009), pp.575–94.

107   Bekker, 'The Local Government and the Community of Sebokeng', p.29.

108   Morris, *A History of Black Housing*, p.77.

109   R. Ginsburg, "'Now I Stay in a House": Renovating the Matchbox in Apartheid-Era Soweto', *African Studies*, 55/2 (1996), p.132.

110   Ibid., p.138; the most common home improvements were plastering walls and floors, painting, and installating doors and ceilings.

111   Ginsburg, "'Now I Stay in a House"', p.127.

112   Pinto de Almeida, 'Framing Interior', pp.471–72.

The design of Sebokeng and other townships during this period was typical for this period of '*middling modernism*', which, as Leslie Bank emphasises, 'focused principally on reconfiguring the home and domestic life'.[113] Houses were built to accommodate nuclear families, headed by a male head of the household, while women were barred from accessing housing of their own from 1967.[114] While men typically acted as head of the household, the domestic sphere of the home was structured and run by women. In contrast to the feminine space of the home, the street was dominated by men and young boys.[115] Boys were socialised to a large extent through their participation in everyday street life, where forms of sociality were played out from a young age.

This deeply conservative engineering of society not only aimed to stabilise the male African workforce, but to bind the large numbers of independent African women who continued to arrive in towns and who were regarded as a threat to social order and public health. The instability of marriage and family life resulting from 'detribalisation' was considered to be a principal cause for social ills in urban areas. This conservative conception of the African family was not only an attempt to eradicate social ills but also reflective of the discourse among apartheid officials. Underpinned by strong Christian beliefs and a deep-seated patriarchal view of the world, apartheid officialdom 'authored a regime of moral authoritarianism' in response to the perceived 'moral laxity of the "liberal" ways proliferating elsewhere in the West'.[116] The hetero-patriarchal conception of home left little possibility for unmarried men, women or homosexual couples to access housing. It comes as no surprise that the gendered nature of social engineering, and the discrimination against African women in general, shaped relations between the sexes and often forced women 'into marriages of convenience'[117] or 'house marriages', which women entered to qualify for housing.[118] The precarious status of African women in urban areas also shaped the emergence of emancipatory politics later on. Widows had a particularly precarious status, as they relied on male relatives to take over the lease or faced eviction, which often went hand in hand with being sent to one of the bantustans (see Chapters 2 and 3).

113   L. Bank, *Home Spaces, Street Styles: Contesting Power and Identity in a South African City* (Johannesburg, Wits University Press, 2011), p.23, emphasis in the original. 'Middling modernism' refers to a similar set of ideas as Bozzoli's concept of 'racial modernism'.

114   R. Lee, *African Women and Apartheid: Migration and Settlement in Urban South Africa* (London, Tauris Academic Studies, 2009), p.86.

115   Bank, *Home Spaces, Street Styles*.

116   Posel, 'The Apartheid Project', p.335.

117   Bozzoli, *Theatres of Struggle*, p.58.

118   D. Posel, 'Marriage at the Drop of a Hat: Housing and Partnership in South Africa's Urban African Townships, 1920s–1960s', *History Workshop Journal*, 61 (2006), pp.57–76.

Yet for all these problematic assumptions and underpinnings, the new houses offered a 'vision of black suburbia' for those who aspired to climb the social ladder.[119] Corner houses in particular were popular because they had the biggest yards. For those who rented a shack from one of Evaton's stand owners, the move into a house in Sebokeng was a major step towards improved living conditions. Access to one's own toilet and tap, more space, a backyard as well as dignity, privacy and legality were among the reasons that made Sebokeng attractive.[120] Having one's own house signified that 'one had "arrived" socially and culturally […] one had arrived among human beings'.[121] Oupa Mareletse, born in 1961 in Sharpeville, explains the overcrowding and lack of privacy he experienced as a child, and the significance of the family's relocation to Sebokeng:[122]

> It [the house we rented in Sharpeville] was shared by two families. My father was renting the kitchen and one bedroom and the other family was renting another room and sitting or dining room. And I think they shared [the toilet] and then the toilet was outside. […] I remember a guy wearing a black uniform arriving at our house and my father and my mother signing some papers. And I remember my father, my mother jubilating after that. She was jumping in the house. And then when my father came […] she kissed my father and she said 'we've got a house'.

For government, Sebokeng replaced Sharpeville as *the* model township in the region, and perhaps in South Africa at large. It was shown to foreign visitors to demonstrate the alleged 'success' of apartheid racial engineering. The administration board was said to be 'enlightened' and J.C. Knoetze praised his board's ability to consult with the local population and believed that the higher living standards in the area explained its relative quiescence during the student revolts in 1976.[123]

The uprisings of 1976 are well documented: on 16 June 1976, schools in Soweto, Alexandra and elsewhere erupted in protests over the poor quality of education and the announcement that Afrikaans would become a medium of instruction.[124]

---

119   Bank, *Home Spaces, Street Styles*, p.24.
120   Gcina Malindi, interview with author, Johannesburg, 25 March 2010; Richard 'Bricks' Mokolo, interview with author, Orange Farm, 20 March 2010.
121   Brandel-Syrier, *Reeftown Elite*, p.86.
122   Oupa Mareletse, interview with author, Johannesburg, 30 June 2010.
123   *Bantu*, January 1978, p.17. Knoetze's perceived success as the chief director of the VTAB led to his appointment as chairman of the West Rand Administration Board (WRAB), which included Soweto, in 1979. See J. Seekings, 'Why Was Soweto Different? Urban Development, Township Politics, and the Political Economy of Soweto, 1977–1984' (African Studies seminar paper, University of the Witwatersrand, 1988).
124   The literature on the 1976 uprisings is expansive. See, for example, J. Brown, *The Road to Soweto: Resistance and the Uprising of 16 June 1976* (Oxford, James Currey, 2016); S.M. Ndlovu, *The Soweto Uprisings: Counter Memories of June 1976* (Johannesburg, Picador Africa, 2017); H. Pohlandt-McCormick, 'I Saw a Nightmare… ': The Soweto

In the Vaal Triangle, young students were warned by their parents not to join the protests.[125] For sections of the population that had experienced the horror of the Sharpeville shootings of 1960, openly discussing politics or engaging in any form of public protest action was regarded as bearing potentially deadly consequences. Gcina Malindi explains the impact of the shootings: 'It [the Sharpeville shooting] did play a role because often if you tried to speak to the older generation about what you were doing as a student, or trying to encourage them to be involved in the politics of the Vaal Triangle, they would remind you of 1960.'[126] A history of forced removals and the migration of politicised students to Soweto further stifled the emergence of confrontational student politics in the Vaal Triangle in 1976. In contrast to parts of the Eastern Cape or Limpopo (then the Northern Transvaal), for example, the Vaal Triangle lacked centres of higher education that provided a platform for Black Consciousness.[127] Yet despite the relative lack of student mobilisation in the Vaal Triangle townships, local students identified with the grievances of students in Soweto and elsewhere.[128] Significantly, this period produced a new crop of young activists that was catapulted to the forefront of student politics during the early 1980s (see Chapter 3).

Across the country, many of these young students benefited from a drastic expansion of primary schooling from the mid-1950s, and secondary schooling from the mid-1970s, which resulted from an increased demand for skilled labour. If 4 percent of African children attended secondary schooling in 1960, this number had risen to 35 percent by 1980.[129] By then, the Vaal Triangle's African population had become largely urbanised; a survey conducted in 1978 found that 70 percent of Sebokeng's residents were born in, and 77 percent

Uprising, June 16, 1976 (New York, Columbia University Press, 2005); S. Mkhabela, *Open Earth and Black Roses: Remembering 16 June 1976* (Johannesburg, Skotaville Publishers, 2001).

125 Tsietsi 'Speech' Mokatsanyane, interview with author, Pretoria, 13 July 2010; see also P. Parker and J. Mokhesi-Parker, *In the Shadow of Sharpeville: Apartheid and Criminal Justice* (Basingstoke and New York, Macmillan and NYU Press, 1998), p.25.

126 Gcina Malindi, interview with author, Johannesburg, 25 March 2010.

127 Natasha Vally argues that the lack of a political base from which student politics could be reconfigured, the limited reach of Black Consciousness and repression explain the relative absence of student protests in 1976. See Vally, 'The "Model Township" of Sharpeville', p.84.

128 Oupa Mareletse, interview with author, Johannesburg, 30 June 2010; Gcina Malindi, interview with author, Johannesburg, 25 March 2010; Dikeledi Tsotetsi, interview with author, Vanderbijlpark, 14 June 2010; WHP AK2117, S7.6, Statement GP Malindi.

129 P. Pillay, 'The Development and Underdevelopment of Education in South Africa', in W. Nassan and J. Samuels (eds), *Education: From Poverty to Liberty* (Cape Town, David Philip, 1990), p.34; J. Hyslop, *The Classroom Struggle: Policy and Resistance in South Africa* (Pietermaritzburg, University of Natal Press, 1999).

brought up in, an urban environment.[130] The significant change in levels of education gave rise to expectations for a better future, yet economic recession, a lack of resources at schools, the ubiquity of corporal punishment and a series of related grievances, as Chapter 3 will show, led to the emergence of radical student politics. Schools soon became 'sites of expansion, of expectation, of deprivation, and of explosive political potential'.[131] For the broader population, falling living conditions, widespread retrenchments, increasing poverty and overcrowding soon gave the lie to aspirations for social upliftment and a dignified, settled life.

130   Bekker, 'The Local Government and the Community of Sebokeng', p.25.
131   Beinart, *Twentieth-Century South Africa*, p.236.

2

'When it rains, the roof leaks':
Reforms and the Housing Crisis

Economic Decline and the Housing Crisis

To reverse the process of urbanisation, the government drastically reduced funding for housing for the African population outside the bantustans. Between 1968 and 1976, the budget 'was cut by 80 percent from R14.5 million to R2.7 million'.[1] Government loans began to dry up and by 1976, a circular informed the Vaal Triangle Administration Board (VTAB), the successor of the Sebokeng Management Board, that loans for lower-income housing were no longer available. This withdrawal of central government subsidies and loans had dire consequences for administration boards' ability to build new houses for the rapidly expanding population, leading to a severe shortage in housing that made itself felt from the early 1970s. As we have seen, officials of the VTAB had recognised the unfeasibility of relocations to Qwa Qwa, and the building of more housing in the urban townships therefore became a pressing concern.[2]

By that time, the average number of persons in a household was 6.5, half of the houses were overcrowded and one out of six households accommodated ten people or more.[3] Dire financial circumstances, and in some instances pressure from local authorities, forced many to take in lodgers.[4] Overcrowding and the smallness of the houses left almost no room for privacy. Township spaces were a 'private world without privacy' where 'living took place in the street, in the yard's open space or within earshot of either', as Belinda Bozzoli notes.[5] While

1   O. Crankshaw, 'Squatting, Apartheid and Urbanisation on the Southern Witwatersrand', *African Affairs*, 92 (1993), p.43; M. Chaskalson, unpublished draft manuscript and notes.

2   M. Chaskalson, 'Apartheid with a Human Face: Punt Janson and the Origins of Reform in Township Administration, 1972–1976', *African Studies*, 42/2 (1989), p.118.

3   S. Bekker, 'The Local Government and Community of Sebokeng' (University of Stellenbosch, Occasional Paper No.3, 1978), p.30.

4   M. Chaskalson, unpublished draft manuscript and notes, p.13.

5   B. Bozzoli, *Theatres of Struggle and the End of Apartheid* (Johannesburg, Wits University Press, 2004), p.22. Alexandra's social geography as a freehold area was distinct. In contrast to townships such as Sebokeng, yards played a more significant role in

this certainly forged strong social relations within families, it also impacted on the way in which politics was discussed and opposition voiced. And it nurtured the seeds of resistance against inferior living conditions in a new generation of young activists. Roy Matube, who joined the Congress of South African Students during the 1980s, recalls the effect of deteriorating living conditions on his political consciousness: '[I wanted] to fight for what is right. So that people live in decent houses. Bigger and decent houses.'[6]

The economic boom of the 1960s began to stagnate during the early 1970s, when the growth rate dropped from 7 to 5 percent during the financial year 1971/72.[7] The steel industry, with the South African Iron and Steel Corporation (ISCOR) in Vanderbijlpark being a major production site, suffered from decreased demand and retrenchment, owing to a drop in the steel price and growing interest rates. Being part of the industrial heartland of South Africa, the Vaal Triangle was particularly hard hit by the recession that set in in the early 1980s and the faltering manufacturing industry.[8] In 1980, 46 percent of the workforce was employed in the manufacturing industry; five years later, this had fallen to 32.3 percent.[9] In South Africa, the global economic crisis was compounded by a deterioration in the price of gold during the early 1980s.

By the late 1970s, at least a quarter of the residents in Sebokeng were living below the household subsistence level of R152.60 per month.[10] By 1985, 30 percent of households in the Vaal Triangle were reported to be below the minimum living level compared to 26 percent in Pretoria, 22 percent in the East and West Rand and 25 percent in Soweto.[11] Although the average monthly real wages increased by 70 percent in manufacturing between 1970 and 1985, a quarter of the population in the Vaal Triangle experienced falling real incomes.[12] A decline

---

structuring social life. Nevertheless, the small yards of 'matchbox houses' still functioned as a place for social interaction.

6   Roy Matube, interview with author, Vanderbijlpark, 17 June 2010.

7   Chaskalson, 'Apartheid with a Human Face', p.103.

8   M. Sutcliffe, 'The Crisis in South Africa: Material Conditions and the Reformist Response', *Geoforum*, 17/2 (1986), p.148; J. Seekings, 'The Origins of Political Mobilisation in PWV Townships, 1980–84', in W. Cobbett and R. Cohen (eds), *Popular Struggles in South Africa* (London, James Currey, 1988), p.69.

9   Bureau of Market Research, 'Income and Expenditure Patterns of Urban Black Multiple Households in the Vaal Triangle, 1985' (Pretoria, University of South Africa, 1986), p.11.

10 Bekker, 'The Local Government and the Community of Sebokeng', p.29.

11 J. Seekings, 'Quiescence and the Transition to Confrontation: South African Townships, 1978–1984' (DPhil thesis, University of Oxford, 1990), p.51.

12 M. Chaskalson, M. Jochelson and J. Seekings, 'Rent Boycotts and the Urban Political Economy', in G. Moss and I. Obery, *South African Review 4* (Johannesburg, Ravan Press, 1987), pp.53–74; Seekings, 'The Origins of Political Mobilisation in PWV Townships', p.56.

in subsidies on consumer items such as maize and bread and the introduction of a general sales tax (GST) in 1981 shifted the burden of the fiscal crisis onto the shoulders of consumers.[13] Within three years, GST increased from 5 to 10 percent, crippling the consumer capacities of the impoverished population, exacerbated by a surge in inflation from 9 percent in 1977 to 17 percent in 1981.[14]

Households earning more than R12,000 per month increased from 10 percent to 15 percent, while households earning less than R4,000 rose from 22 percent to 26 percent.[15] This growing income gap promoted social stratification that separated the great majority of the population with a low to modest income from a small percentage of high earners. To add insult to injury, rent, including levies, service tariffs and house rental, kept increasing on an unprecedented scale between the late 1970s and 1984.

'Controlled Urbanisation' and Social Stratification

The Durban strikes of 1973 and the student uprisings of 1976 had exposed the structural crisis South Africa was facing, posing a direct threat to its economic and political stability. To counter rising discontent among South Africa's disenfranchised majority, the South African government under P.W. Botha introduced a series of reforms from the mid-1970s onwards. What became known as Total Strategy (in response to the perceived threat of a communist total onslaught) rested on a curious blend of heightened repression and the reformation of certain aspects of apartheid.[16] The key reforms introduced concerned the reformation of urban policy, the formation of a regional as well as a national constitutional framework, a shift in policies pertaining to the bantustans, a change in industrial relations as well as the strengthening of the security forces, particularly intelligence and the military.[17]

A key objective of this reform package was to accommodate political and economic aspirations of conservative sections of the African population. It was thought that allowing limited access to power at the local level, opening up business opportunities and providing better living standards through improved housing and development would foster an African middle class to serve as a

13 W. Beinart, *Twentieth-Century South Africa* (Oxford, Oxford University Press, 2001), p.237.

14 C. Cooper, S. Motala, P. Randall et al. (eds), *A Survey of Race Relations: 1982* (Johannesburg, South African Institute of Race Relations, 1983), pp.59, 207.

15 Bureau of Market Research, 'Income and Expenditure Patterns', p.16.

16 D. O'Meara, *Forty Lost Years: The Apartheid State and the Politics of the National Party, 1948–1994* (Johannesburg, Ravan Press, 1996), p.323.

17 W. Cobbett, D. Glaser, D. Hindson et al., 'A Critical Analysis of the South African State's Reform Strategies in the 1980s', in P. Frankel, N. Pines and M. Swilling (eds), *State, Resistance and Change in South Africa* (London, Croom Helm, 1988), pp.19–51.

buffer between the increasingly militant youth and working class and the white minority. The recommendations of the Wiehahn and the Riekert commissions, both reporting in 1979, played a leading role in defining the direction and content of reforms. The Wiehahn report advocated for 'limited recognition of African trade unions, as long as they registered and subjected themselves to regulation'.[18] While its intention was to depoliticise and separate workers' grievances and organisations from broader political struggles, it achieved the opposite: it opened the path for organised labour to emerge as a key player in collective action during the 1980s. In its aftermath, the Federation of South African Trade Unions (FOSATU) decided to register to secure greater rights but other unions, such as the South African Allied Workers' Union (SAAWU), followed a different path.[19]

While the Wiehahn Commission's findings delineated the contours of labour action, the recommendations made by the Riekert Commission on Manpower Utilisation were of key significance for the direction and content of changing urban policy. It was tasked to make recommendations that would initiate the 'improvement, modernisation and reform of the existing official institutional and statutory framework of the labour market in South Africa, with a view to the better utilisation especially of Black manpower'.[20] At the centre of the Riekert report was a sharp distinction between those with 'permanent' section 10 rights and those without. It was a partial acknowledgement of African urbanisation and Africans' rights to live in South Africa proper.[21] Industry had been pressuring government to relax influx control throughout the 1970s. 'Their concern,' Douglas Hindson argues, 'was to raise labour productivity by encouraging settlement and improved housing, education and training for the urban workforce.'[22] Based on Riekert's recommendations, Africans with section 10 rights were now permitted to move between different urban areas, subject to 'availability and standard of employment and housing in the urban areas'.[23] Significantly, the Riekert report recommended decentralising power and privatising township housing; the combined effects of these two reforms prepared the ground for growing popular protests.

18   Beinart, *Twentieth Century South Africa*, p.246.

19   Ibid., p.249.

20   Manpower Utilisation Commission, quoted in D. Hindson, *Pass Controls and the Urban African Proletariat* (Johannesburg, Ravan Press, 1987), p.83.

21   Ibid., p.83; K. Jochelson, 'Reform, Repression and Resistance in South Africa: A Case Study of Alexandra Township, 1979–1989', *Journal of Southern African Studies*, 16/1 (1990), p.3.

22   Hindson, *Pass Controls*, p.82.

23   D. Hindson, 'Orderly Urbanisation and Influx Control: From Territorial Apartheid to Regional Spacial Ordering in South Africa', *Cahiers d'Etudes Africaines*, 25/99 (1985), p.406.

Even though the implementation of a more relaxed policy with regard to housing and urban rights was mostly carried out after 1976, the origins of these reforms date back to the early 1970s. As Matthew Chaskalson shows, Punt Janson, the Deputy Minister of Bantu Administration and Education from November 1972 to January 1976, played a leading role in spearheading reforms aimed at improving the living conditions of the urban African population.[24] Janson publicly recognised that grand apartheid was untenable, and that the treatment of urbanised Africans was inhumane.[25] Janson was also at the forefront of lobbying for the development of urban townships, citing the stabilisation of the African population as key: 'It is essential for the good relations of whites and non-whites that we create facilities for Bantu in white areas where they can lead a dignified existence,' Janson stated in 1973.[26] While many of Janson's reformist plans were curtailed or altogether abandoned by conservative elements within the National Party, his proposed plans for township development and a change in home ownership had a direct impact on the lives of urban African communities. Janson lobbied for the development of facilities, infrastructure and improved housing, linking a lack of quality housing to delinquency and social instability.[27]

As Chaskalson shows, Janson's reformist approach impacted on J.C. Knoetze's plans to develop the African townships in the Vaal Triangle.[28] During the financial year of 1976/77, the VTAB set aside R13,5 million for township development.[29] Sewerage was upgraded, running water, electricity and street lighting installed and roads tarred; the funds were also meant to cover the costs of building sports centres, libraries, hostels and cinemas. Fulfilling the 'socio-economic aspirations' of the upwardly mobile while granting limited trade union rights to the working class was expected to undermine potential alliances that could pose a threat to the political order.[30] By 1982, 30 percent of Sebokeng's households had been electrified, and all townships except Evaton had waterborne sewerage.[31]

Significantly, the fiscal burden for developing and upgrading the townships was placed on the shoulders of township residents. Owing to a lack of state subsidies, frequent rent increases were therefore not only aimed to cover the maintenance but also the upgrading of township facilities, as well as

24 Chaskalson, 'Apartheid with a Human Face'.
25 Ibid., p.108.
26 Ibid., p.112.
27 Ibid., p.111.
28 Ibid.
29 M. Chaskalson, unpublished draft manuscript and notes, p.33.
30 M. Morris and V. Padayachee, 'State Reform Policy in South Africa', *Transformation*, 7 (1988), p.4.
31 M. Chaskalson, unpublished draft manuscript and notes, p.33.

administrative costs.[32] As Chaskalson, Jochelson and Seekings note, the lack of revenues to pay for township development was at the core of the political crisis that shook local government in 1984.[33] In 1985, for example, a breakdown of total rent of R65 highlighted that house rental was only an average of R13, while R39.30 went towards service charges (including electricity), R10 towards payment for the 'infrastructure of electricity' and R3 towards internal electrification of houses.[34] House rental was calculated to cover the repayment of building loans, while service charges would pay for the upgrading and development of the townships.[35]

Besides providing improved infrastructure, government recognised that quality housing was among the aspirations of the emerging middle class. While the 'model townships' of the 1960s had suppressed class distinction by providing everyone with the same matchbox house, the new policy encouraged new differential housing to be built. Adequate housing was also linked to a decrease in social ills such as delinquency:

> *Wanneer mense opgroei in 'n omgewing war hulle tevrede en waarop hulle trots is, sal die kinders minder geneig wees tot misdaad*

> [When people grow up in an environment in which they are satisfied and that makes them proud, the children will be less likely to commit crime]

an article in the administration board's newsletter remarked in 1983. Owners and tenants were encouraged to express aspiration and class through beautifying and modifying their homes. Regular 'house and garden' competitions were intended to promote residents' pride in their homes.

New houses in Sebokeng's Zone 14 extension were bigger, with painted and tiled walls.[36] In 1975, 20 percent of all new stands were earmarked for the construction of 'better houses' for the professional elite, and the *World* newspaper ran a weekly series on these housing developments.[37] Janson was also spearheading the introduction of the 30-year leasehold during the same year, and he met with building societies and employers to lobby for their support in expanding home ownership schemes.[38] Home ownership, Janson surmised, would not only stabilise urbanised Africans, it would also provide much-needed rev-

---

32   'Rent' included charges for house rental and service charges. Electricity and water were paid for separately.
33   Chaskalson, Jochelson and Seekings, 'Rent Boycotts and the Urban Political Economy'.
34   UWC MA, MCH31 15024, L3F23CA, 'Minutes of a Meeting Held on 2.12.85 to Discuss the Rental Problem in the Vaal'.
35   Ibid.
36   Edward 'Chippa' Motubatsi, interview with author, Vereeniging, 15 April 2010.
37   M. Chaskalson, unpublished draft manuscript and notes, p.11.
38   Chaskalson, 'Apartheid with a Human Face', p.112.

enues to cover the costs of township administration.[39] To own a home would give the African population a stake in the political stability of the country. Yet, Janson's reformist plans were curtailed by *verkrampte* (ultra-conservative) officials within the department.[40] The 30-year leasehold scheme is a case in point. The leasehold could be renewed for up to another 30 years, but was contingent on the possession of a 'homeland citizenship certificate', effectively linking home ownership in the urban areas to citizenship in one of South Africa's bantustans.[41]

Even though the 30-year leasehold scheme was only legalised in 1976, the VTAB had already begun to 'sell' houses the year before. J.C. Knoetze was at the forefront of implementing proto-reforms in housing that would lead to secure tenure and better houses, before it became official policy.[42] As Knoetze emphasised, 'it was important for the people to get security of tenure. It was important to help them extend their houses'.[43] The extension of the 30-year leasehold schemes to 99 years as stipulated in the Urban Areas Amendment Act of 1978 further cemented the promotion of home ownership by an emerging middle class.

In 1983, government declared its intention to sell 500,000 houses country-wide.[44] Tenants who purchased their houses by 30 June 1984 were eligible for discounts of up to 40 percent.[45] This 'sale of the century' was widely advertised in newspapers, television and radio.[46] Tenants who would not opt to purchase their homes were warned of 'drastic rent increases'.[47] To further encourage home ownership, plans were discussed to adjust rent to reflect a return on the capital value instead of the original building costs. Once the rental structure was adjusted, officials surmised, 'it will become clear to all inhabitants that it is more advantageous to buy a house than to rent it'.[48] According to government,

39 Ibid., p.112.

40 Ibid., p.116.

41 P. Morris, *A History of Black Housing in South Africa* (Johannesburg, South Africa Foundation, 1981), p.93; Chaskalson, 'Apartheid with a Human Face', p.116.

42 J.C. Knoetze, interview with Matthew Chaskalson, Sebokeng, 1 February 1988. Private collection of Matthew Chaskalson.

43 Ibid.

44 Mabin and Parnell, 'The Question of Working Class Home Ownership', p.2.

45 P. Wilkinson, 'The Sale of the Century? A Critical Review of Recent Developments in African Housing Policy in South Africa', Second Carnegie Inquiry into Poverty and Development in Southern Africa, Carnegie Conference Paper No.160 (Cape Town, 13–19 April 1984), p.1.

46 A. Mabin and S. Parnell, 'The Question of Working Class Home Ownership', Second Carnegie Inquiry into Poverty and Development in Southern Africa, Carnegie Conference Paper No.159 (Cape Town, 13–19 April 1984), p.10.

47 Wilkinson, 'The Sale of the Century?', p.1.

48 'Gemeenskapsontwikkeling – Funksie Draai Darom', *Bula Ditaba tsa Lekoa*, December 1983, p.1.

out of a housing stock of 21,582 units in Sebokeng, 16,315 (equalling 75 percent) were rented, and 5,267 houses had been bought under the 99-year leasehold scheme and the 30-year leasehold scheme, respectively, by 1987.[49] Figures provided by the Orange Vaal Development Board (OVDB) for the entire region suggest that of a total of 39,232 houses, 22,237 were rented, 9,104 were bonded with the financial assistance of the OVDB, 7,095 were part of self-help housing schemes and 797 had been purchased with the assistance of employers.[50]

In contrast to previous periods, government made provisions for the private sector to invest. First calls to 'allow private investment' in township housing and development date back to the early 1970s, when building societies and members of the United Party called for a relaxation of the law.[51] Between 1975 and 1977, the VTAB raised approximately R10 million in the form of loans from the Allied Building Society and other corporations to finance the building of more houses.[52] These loans were, however, given under the condition that houses built would be of superior quality compared to the 'matchbox houses'. During a meeting in February 1975 local employers emphasised that housing should be planned at a cost of at least R6,000 per house. A standard matchbox house only cost R1,000 and these new houses therefore remained unaffordable for the impoverished majority.[53] The 99-year leasehold scheme allowed African home owners to borrow money from private capital, but an investigation conducted in 1984 reported that only 20 percent of the Vaal Triangle's African population could afford a house purchased under the 99-year leasehold scheme.[54] Furthermore, as Paul Hendler shows, 93 percent of the population in the Pretoria-Witwatersrand-Vereeniging (PWV) were ineligible for building society loans.[55] The privatisation or 'recommodification' of township housing, as Alan Mabin has labelled this process, therefore allowed a small minority to access and own superior houses, while the great majority could not afford them.[56] Government's responsibility would

49   H. Mashabela, *Townships of the PWV* (Johannesburg, South African Institute of Race Relations, 1988), p.131.

50   UWC MA, MCH31 15024, L3F23CA, 'Minutes of a Meeting Held on 2.12.85 to Discuss the Rental Problem in the Vaal'.

51   Chaskalson, 'Apartheid with a Human Face', pp.105–6.

52   Ibid., p.119.

53   M. Chaskalson, unpublished draft manuscript and notes, p.12.

54   Ibid., p.17. For a calculation of costs involved in purchasing a house in Soweto, see Mabin and Parnell, 'The Question of Working Class Home Ownership', p.7. As Mabin and Parnell show, prospective home owners would have had to raise between R500 and R1,000 to finance the initial costs. Living costs for a family of six in Soweto were calculated at R277 per month, and more than 50 percent of Soweto's population earned less than that.

55   P. Hendler, *Urban Policy and Housing: Case Studies in Negotiations in PWV Townships* (Johannesburg, South African Institute of Race Relations, 1988).

56   Mabin and Parnell, 'The Question of Working Class Home Ownership', p.2.

be limited to 'the provision of infrastructure, self-help schemes, controlled corehousing and shell houses'.[57] 'The implication is therefore clear,' officials of the administration board noted, 'the individual will have to take responsibility for the provision of this [sic] own housing.'[58] Fiscal and political aims of central government therefore posed a contradiction: government's financial withdrawal from township development and housing undermined its aims to stabilise the urban population. Furthermore, home ownership schemes also predominantly benefited men. Women's wages were typically lower and therefore women struggled even more to access subsidies and loans to finance home ownership.[59]

Prior to the late 1970s, elite formation followed different trajectories. It was either linked to occupation, with teachers, clerks, doctors and nurses having a higher social status, or it was community elders (popularly referred to as *sakhamuzi*) who had earned respect through their involvement as soccer patrons and community leaders. From the late 1970s, economic opportunities in the urban areas and the bantustans gave rise to a new class of entrepreneurs and businessmen that came to form the backbone of a new emerging middle class. Growing social stratification introduced tensions in the population, particularly if newly acquired wealth was considered to be ill-gotten. Significantly, worsening socio-economic conditions for the majority coincided with the reformation of the local state and the emergence of a new political elite of African councillors, many of whom formed part of the growing new class of businessmen and entrepreneurs.

'The smoothest-running council in the country'

The restructuring of local administration had begun in 1971 when the administration boards, which were directly linked to the Department of Bantu Administration and Development, took over control of the townships from the municipalities. Two years later, the Sebokeng Management Board became the VTAB and took over the administration of all African townships in the Vaal Triangle. This shift reflected government's policy of separate development that sought to bring the townships under stringent influx control aimed at containing African urbanisation.[60] While townships built prior to the introduction of the administration boards had seen uneven implementation of policies, and

57   'Allied Lends a Helping Hand', *Bula Ditaba tsa Lekoa*, April 1983.
58   Ibid.
59   R. Lee, *African Women and Apartheid: Migration and Settlement in Urban South Africa* (London, Tauris Academic Studies, 2009), p.87.
60   The department's name was altered in 1976 to Department of Plural Relations and Development and then to Department of Co-operation and Development. On the role of administration boards, see S. Bekker and R. Humphries, *From Control to Confusion: The Changing Role of Administration Boards in South Africa, 1971–1983* (Pietermaritzburg, Shuter and Shooter, 1985).

municipalities had enjoyed a degree of freedom in the manner in which they ran the townships, the introduction of administration boards aimed to streamline the administration of African townships. In reality, administration boards retained a degree of independence. Key responsibilities included the running of labour bureaux, the development and maintenance of townships and influx control. Administration boards therefore came to play a leading role in implementing forced removals to the bantustans and, for many Africans, they came to represent the precarity of life in urban areas. In 1979, the 22 existing administration boards were reduced to 14; the VTAB became part of the Orange Vaal Administration Board (OVAB), which covered parts of the Northern Free State.

Since the promulgation of the Urban Bantu Council Act in 1961, African representation had been channelled through Urban Bantu Councils (UBCs). They replaced the old system of advisory boards that had served as a platform for Africans to advocate vis-à-vis white municipalities, under whose control the African townships fell prior to 1971. Yet neither of these bodies possessed any meaningful power. Advisory boards were solely dependent on the 'willingness of municipalities to consult them'.[61] UBCs were nicknamed 'useless boys' clubs' as they were generally deemed ineffective and powerless by the urban African population. A few councillors nevertheless enjoyed a certain degree of authority and respect among sections of the township population as 'arbiters of justice' and distributors of patronage, as Jeremy Seekings has noted.[62]

This system of local African representation was once more revised in the aftermath of the student uprisings of 1976, when the inadequacy of the UBCs became glaringly clear. As a direct response to the failure of the administration boards to contain the crisis in the townships, and as part of a gradual move to reform apartheid, the Community Council Act, Proclamation 125 of 1977 was passed. Locally, J.C. Knoetze was at the forefront of supporting the introduction of the councils:

> *Indien woongebied ontwikkeling in Swart woongebiede weklik lewensvatbaar gemaak wil word, dan moet die beplanning daarvan uit die geledere van die Swart gemeenskap self kom.*

> [If residential development in Black residential areas is to be made viable, then its planning must come from the ranks of the Black community itself.][63]

61   N. Nieftagodien, 'High Apartheid and the Erosion of "Official" Local Politics in Daveyton in the 1960s', *New Contree*, 67 (Special edition, 2013), p.38.

62   Seekings, 'The Origins of Political Mobilisation', p.62; Seekings, 'Quiescence and the Transition to Confrontation'.

63   J.C. Knoetze, quoted in M. Chaskalson, unpublished draft manuscript and notes, p.18.

The Vaal Triangle Community Council (VTCC) was the first countrywide to be voted into power in November 1977.[64] It consisted of 36 members, elected in a 20 percent poll. Dissatisfaction with this new system was apparent from the beginning. In Boipatong, one of the councillors had asked people who opposed the new council system to leave the meeting, only to see the entire crowd of 1,000 attendees march out in defiance.[65] Evaton, with its long history of struggling for its status as a freehold area and against the influence of the Sebokeng Management Board, the predecessor of the VTAB, was given the possibility to establish its own community council, although it would normally have fallen under the jurisdiction of Sebokeng.[66] Elections in Evaton were held months later with only 10 percent of eligible voters casting their vote.[67]

Unlike Sharpeville, Boipatong and Bophelong, Sebokeng never had a UBC and councillors standing for election in Sebokeng had no history or experience of community politics. It is thus perhaps not surprising that 11 out of 17 seats were uncontested and councillors presented themselves as individuals without party affiliation. Evaton, in contrast, had a longstanding tradition of making demands and expressing grievances through petitioning and writing letters to relevant authorities. Evaton therefore had a history of organised community politics and the implementation of local government structures was met with widespread suspicion.

The powers given to the newly formed VTCC included the allocation of housing, the right to make recommendations with regard to influx control, the allocation of church, school and trading sites (the latter were allocated by a committee consisting of three members of the community council and three members of the administration board), the 'determination of moral and social welfare', the promotion of community development, a say in the 'beautification and neatness of the different townships', the awarding of bursaries and a say in the destruction of abandoned buildings.[68] All decisions taken by the community councils had to be implemented by the executive committee of the administration board.

64 Bekker and Humphries, *From Control to Confusion*, p.102.

65 WHP AK2117, S8.10.2, 'Vaal Triangle Background: Demonstration of Dissatisfaction among Residents'.

66 NAP BAO, 3/356, A2/14/2/S16, 'Vaaldriehoek: Instelling van Gemeenskaprade'; NAP BAO A2114/2/S16, 'Meeting on 9 August 1977, re: Establishment of Community Councils'.

67 These are the figures given by the South African Institute of Race Relations: see S. Blignaut, C. Cooper, L. Gordon et al. (eds), *Survey of Race Relations in South Africa, 1978* (Johannesburg, South African Institute of Race Relations, 1979), p.345. Figures provided by the defence for the Delmas treason trial quote a voting poll of 15 percent for Sebokeng and 4 percent for the Evaton Council: see WHP AK2117, S8.10.6, 'Memorandum on Vaal Triangle Background, Part II. Community Councils: Introduction and Reaction'.

68 NAP BAO, 3/356, A2/14/2/S16, Gemeenskapraade.

Thabeng Samuel Richard Rabotapi, locally known as Sam Rabotapi, a trained teacher who had taught at the famous Wilberforce Institute for 13 years, was elected first chairman of the Evaton Community Council. Like other local leaders, Rabotapi had been involved in community affairs since the 1950s and had been a founding member of the Evaton Residents' Association. As the 'father of boxing' and founder of the Evaton Football Association, Rabotapi was a well-known *sakhamuzi* who enjoyed his community's respect. George Thabe, local resident and soccer patron of Sharpeville, became the VTCC's first chairman. Locally known as the 'Pele of South African football', Thabe was born in Top Location in Vereeniging and grew up in Sharpeville.[68] He rose to fame through his leading role in forming the South African National Football Association (SANFA), whose first president he became. Significantly, his position as a soccer patron had gained him the support and respect of Sharpeville's community. In 1979, Thabe became the first African director of the United Building Society in Vereeniging.[69]

A year after the VTCC's inception, Thabe addressed the members of the white-controlled administration board and ensured them of his conservative political views:

> We seek for change through consultation and this will continue to be the policy of my council. [...] If we have to raise protest, it will not be in the newspapers; it will be round the conference table where we as a Community Council will say we feel this or that is unjust, can't something be done about it? [...] We will have a most difficult task in trying to convince the residents that we are the authority. You will realise, ladies and gentlemen, that after 300 years of saying the government will do it [...] it is now an almost impossible task to make these people realise that in future we will have to provide the roads, build the schools and that we will have to run our townships.[70]

While Thabe's speech was cautious at best, it nevertheless outlined his understanding of the role he envisaged for councillors as promoters of welfare, change and betterment. Thabe's speech was in line with what the government and the administration board were advocating limited access to political power on a local level. Only a few months later, however, in October 1978, Thabe was ousted as chairman

68   The subsequent biographical information on George Thabe is drawn from I. Jeffrey, 'Street Rivalry and Patron Managers: Football in Sharpeville, 1943–1985', *African Studies*, 51/1 (1992), pp.69–94.

69   Chaskalson, unpublished draft manuscript and notes, p.37.

70   NAP BAO, 3/356, A2/14/3/S16, 'Verbal Comment by Mr George Thabe during the Delivery of his Budget Speech and Address to the administration board on the Powers and Duties of the Community Council (Vaal Triangle) at the Fifty-Fourth Meeting of the administration board held at Sebokeng, on 22 February 1978 to Consider and Approve the Estimates of Income and Expenditure for the Vaal Triangle Black Townships for 1978/79'.

of the VTCC and replaced by another soccer patron: Josiah 'Knox' Matjila, former head of the Transvaal African Football Association.[71] Matjila had initially been Thabe's protégé but was expelled from SANFA in the mid-1970s, after rumours had circulated that he was attempting to replace Thabe as president.[72]

It was clear from the beginning that the two community councils did not aim to push for any meaningful political and social change at the national level. Their goal was to receive full municipal status and to improve local living conditions. The toothlessness of these structures, and the paternalistic attitude government and the administration boards had towards them, was perhaps best expressed in a public statement by the Minister of the Department of Co-operation and Development, the successor of the Department of Bantu Affairs and Development, Dr G. de V. Morrison, who stated in 1980, 'People have to crawl before they can walk. We don't want to give you powers you can't handle. We are not afraid – but you don't have the experience or the know-how.'[73] By 1978, the VTCC was described in the press as the 'smoothest running council in the country', and according to Thabe it was 'well-respected.'[74] Sebokeng was praised as a model township with a local government, which, in the words of sociologist Simon Bekker, was 'reputed to be one of the best in nonhomeland South Africa.'[75] But fiscal pressure, a lack of meaningful power, and corruption, nepotism and maladministration soon brought into sharp relief the council's incapacity to provide welfare and effect social transformation.

'The council is under enormous pressure'

The proposed budget for the financial year 1978/79 by the VTAB was R48 million, of which R27 million should be generated in the townships.[76] Financially, the VTCC was in dire straits from the outset, as a later section will explain. An anticipated deficit of R1.8 million for the financial year 1978/79 was drastically reduced to R301,711 by increasing levies, taxes and rent twice within a year.[77] The shelving of plans to remove Sharpeville's residents and the subsequent need to upgrade the township exacerbated this fiscal crisis. The electrification of Sharpeville and the introduction of waterborne sewerage, costing R8.5 million in total, necessitated further increases in tariffs and levies to balance the budget during the financial year 1980/81.[78]

---

71   *Sunday Post,* 15 October 1978; *Sunday Times Extra,* 15 October 1978.
72   Jeffrey, 'Street Rivalry and Patron-Managers'.
73   *Sunday Post,* 30 July 1979; WHP AK2117, S7.20.34, 'Nusas: Ruling the Townships'.
74   *Sunday Post,* 15 October 1978; *Sunday Times Extra,* 15 October 1978.
75   Bekker, 'The Local Government and the Community of Sebokeng', p.1.
76   Ibid., p.19.
77   NAP BAO 3/4561/A/3/4/2/S16, 'Budget Report 1979/80: Community Council Vaal Triangle'.
78   NAP BAO, 3/3546, A11/4/3/S16, 'Budget Report for the Financial Year 81/82,

Aware of the financial burden it was placing on local residents, the VTCC sought assistance from the Department of Co-operation and Development on several occasions. In a memorandum presented to Dr Koornhof, Minister of Co-operation and Development, in late November 1979, the VTCC emphasised that in order to achieve the 'desired change in the *modern* black township [emphasis added]', certain hurdles had to be removed.[79] While councillors had informed their constituencies that the fiscal needs of the townships could only be met by increasing levies and service tariffs, the awarding of an alleged R11 million to the Soweto Community Council undermined their credibility. 'It does now appear clear [...] that we have been telling untruths because the government is alleged to have given the Soweto Council R11m so that they can meet their deficits and/ or increased service tariffs', councillors bemoaned. The memorandum further pleaded with Koornhof that 'if there is some type of free money to give [...] we wish to make an urgent and earnest appeal to the Government to come to our rescue so that our credibility should remain undented'. Endorsing the VTCC's request, the OVAB urged the Department of Co-operation and Development's Deputy Minister, Dr G. de V. Morrison, that 'the council is under enormous pressure from its residents not again to increase tariffs and rentals [...] unless all community councils are given the same dispensation in regard to financial assistance from the government'.[80] In response, the VTCC was informed that the R11 million the Soweto Community Council was allegedly given was not a subsidy but the permission to use accumulated funds to write off the West Rand Administration Board's deficit.[81]

The administration board's suggestions to increase revenues by being allowed to keep 100 percent of profits from liquor sales, to supplement community councils through income tax and to increase levies paid by employers were all rejected by the department, except for the latter.[82] Instead, the department emphasised that township development and maintenance had to be covered through economic rentals, service charges and levies.

Since their introduction in 1971, the administration boards had been required to be self-financing, partly as a consequence of the policy of separate development and partly because it allowed central government to withdraw from its

Sebokeng and Other Urban Residential Areas'.

79   NAP MSK 335/3/8/2, 'Memorandum by the Vaal Triangle Council, Presented to Dr. P. Koornhof, 28 November 1979'.

80   NAP BAO, 3/4561/A/3/4/2/S16, 'Increased Tariffs: Vaal Triangle Community Council'.

81   Jeremy Seekings shows that the development of Soweto as a 'showpiece to the world' was of key significance. See J. Seekings, 'Why Was Soweto Different? Urban Development, Township Politics, and the Political Economy of Soweto, 1977–1984' (African Studies seminar paper, University of the Witwatersrand, 1988), p.14.

82   Chaskalson, unpublished draft manuscript and notes, p.35.

financial involvement. By the early 1980s, most administration boards in the PWV area were accumulating deficits.[83] The fiscal crisis of the boards had a number of causes including increasing costs for administering the townships, a lack of taxable industries in the townships and an increase in costs for building houses. The privatisation of liquor and beer licences in 1983 further exacerbated the crisis, depriving the administration boards of one of its most important revenues. In contrast to administration boards that were subsidising services, the VTAB had achieved the introduction of full economic rentals by 1977.[84] As Matthew Chaskalson notes, Knoetze played a leading role in ensuring the introduction of economic rentals.[85] During a meeting in 1974, he stated that

> *Ons moet die Bantoe help om op sy eie voete te staan en om self the leer om sy begroting te laat klop... Ons benadering is om die Bantoe geleidelik te leer om te betaal vir wat hy kry*

> [We must help the Bantu to stand on his own feet and to learn how to budget himself... our approach is to gradually teach the Bantu to pay for what he gets].[86]

In the absence of subsidies, rents therefore continued to increase to cover the deficit and anticipated costs of upgrading and development. Between 1977 and 1984, average rental payments were increased by 427 percent.[87] By 1984, the Vaal Triangle had become the most expensive area for African people to live in South Africa.

The Development of Qwa Qwa

While the development and upgrading of townships was slow and often wanting, the injection of funds into the development of infrastructure in the bantustan of Qwa Qwa, as noted in Chapter 1, caused anger and exacerbated anxieties with regard to urban rights. Funds that were set aside to develop Zone 14 were channelled to the building of 4,000 houses in the bantustan of Qwa Qwa, as well as a hostel in Sebokeng.[88] As a memorandum noted, there was a 'widespread belief amongst residents in Sebokeng that their real future and welfare was located in

---

83   Seekings, 'The Origins of Political Mobilisation in PWV Townships', p.60.
84   For a comparison, see Bekker and Humphries, *From Control to Confusion*, p.151.
85   Chaskalson, unpublished draft manuscript and notes, p.35.
86   Quoted in Ibid., p.35. My translation.
87   WHP AK2117, S8.10.17, 'Comparison of Vaal Rents and Other Urban Areas in South Africa'.
88   Chaskalson, unpublished draft manuscript and notes, p.14; J.C. Knoetze, interview with Matthew Chaskalson, Sebokeng, 1 February 1988. Private collection of Matthew Chaskalson.

Qwa Qwa and not in Sebokeng'.[89] Since its inception, the administration board had played a leading role in Qwa Qwa's development. In the early 1970s, for example, it financed the building of 300 semi-detached, four-roomed houses in Qwa Qwa's capital.[90] The VTAB's director, J.C. Knoetze, testified at the Cillie Commission in 1977 that R30,000 had been budgeted for the financial year 1977/78 for the development of Qwa Qwa.[91] He stated that, according to government policy, it was the duty of administration boards to develop the bantustans and as the majority of the population in the Vaal Triangle was of Sotho origin, the administration board's area of responsibility was Qwa Qwa. The amalgamation of administration boards in 1979, and the subsequent creation of the OVAB, cemented these relations. The jurisdiction of the OVAB now shared a border with Qwa Qwa, which was 'intended to facilitate "homeland orientated administration"'.[92]

Besides financial assistance, this close relationship between Qwa Qwa and the administration board manifested itself in exchange of personnel, incentives to invest in the bantustan and visits of officials. Administration board staff sat in various structures of the Qwa Qwa government, while bantustan representatives served as intermediaries in the urban townships. Some of the councillors in the Vaal Triangle belonged to the Dikwankwetla (strong men) party of T.K. Mopeli, the Chief Minister of Qwa Qwa, and stood for election as representatives in Qwa Qwa's government. Prominent local residents were actively recruited to serve in official functions and to establish business ventures there.[93] Elite formation in the townships was therefore closely linked to the development of the bantustans, which offered opportunities for investment and growth.

In 1981, a delegation from Qwa Qwa visited the Vaal Triangle and was shown around by officials from the OVAB. 'Mopeli used to come here to address people. Almost all the bantustan leaders they will come to the urban area. And they will always believe that we are their people,' Reverend Gift Moerane remembers.[94]

89   WHP AK2117, S8.10.5, 'Memorandum on Vaal Triangle Background'; Edward 'Chippa' Motubatsi, interview with author, Vereeniging, 15 April 2010.
90   I. Niehaus, 'Relocation in Tseki and Phuthaditjhaba: A Comparative Ethnography of Planned and Unplanned Removals in Qwa Qwa' (University of the Witwatersrand, African Studies seminar paper No.260, 1989), p.8.
91   Excerpt from the Commission of Inquiry into the Riots at Soweto and Other Places in South Africa held on 1 March 1977 (Cillié Commission), Vol.122, Statement by J.C.Knoetze,pp.5864ff.,http://www.aluka.org/action/showAllText?doi=10.5555/AL. SFF.DOCUMENT.tra19770301.026.019, retrieved 1 April 2020.
92   Bekker and Humphries, *From Control to Confusion*, p.31.
93   Sekwati Mokoena, interview with author, Sharpeville, 30 March 2010.
94   Gift Moerane, interview with author, Vereeniging, 29 March 2010; other bantustan leaders who used to visit the Vaal Triangle were Mangosuthu Buthelezi, leader of KwaZulu and presiding over Inkatha, and Charles Sebe, leader of the Ciskei.

Whenever bantustan leaders were visiting, Matime Moshele Papane recalls, school children were 'lined up on the road, alongside the road with a little flag of the bantustan'.[95] Perhaps one of the most significant links between the Qwa Qwa government and the OVAB was J.M. van Rooyen, chairman of the VTAB from 1974. Van Rooyen was a member of the advisory committee of Mopeli's government, as well as various committees tasked with the promotion of tourism, development and administration. In 1983, van Rooyen left his position at the OVAB to resume the post of Commissioner General of Qwa Qwa.

Even though Mopeli had repeatedly renounced plans for Qwa Qwa's independence, the naming of Qwa Qwa's stadium as 'independence stadium' led to the circulation of rumours that Qwa Qwa would soon follow the Transkei, Ciskei, Venda and Bophuthatswana in declaring independence. The recent incorporation of Ga-Rankuwa, a township outside Pretoria, into the bantustan of Bophuthatswana cemented fears that the Vaal Triangle might face a similar threat. 'It was a general belief that the Koornhof Bills will bring such a situation whereby Qwa Qwa would opt for independence and it would be easy for people in the Vaal Triangle area to be incorporated into this homeland and ultimately lose their citizenship as South African citizens.'[96] The declaration of independence effectively removed South African citizenship of urban Africans who were *de jure* citizens of these bantustans.

In 1983, a landmark decision was passed by the Supreme Court in the case of *Rikhoto v East Rand Administration Board*, confirming that migrant workers with annually renewable contracts would qualify for Section 10 rights after ten years of employment in urban areas. This victory had a significant impact on tens of thousands of migrant workers in the country, including those that were living in the Vaal Triangle. But threats of independence continued to loom large.

Black Local Authorities

The passing of the Black Local Authorities Act 102 of 1982, part of a set of bills that were popularly known as the 'Koornhof bills', further decentralised power by giving town councils increased authority.[97] Under the jurisdiction of the OVAB, four councils were identified to become Black Local Authorities, namely the Vaal Triangle, Evaton as well as Kroonstad and Bethlehem in the Free State. Another 84 townships were identified across the country to follow suit in 1984.[98]

95   Matime Moshele Papane, interview with author, Johannesburg, 6 November 2018.
96   WHP AK 2117, I2.1, Vol.159, Testimony Vilakazi, p.7756.
97   J. Grest, 'The Crisis of Local Government in South Africa', in P. Frankel, N. Pines and M. Swilling (eds), *State, Resistance and Change in South Africa* (London, Croom Helm, 1988), p.93; Seekings, 'Quiescence and the Transition to Confrontation', p.58.
98   'Gemeenskapsontwikkeling – funksie draai darom', *Bula Ditaba tsa Lekoa*, December 1983, p.2.

The replacement of community councils with town councils was an attempt to improve their reputation and to gloss over the fact that the new tricameral parliament, inaugurated in 1983 and consisting of three different houses of parliament for different racial categories, once more excluded the African majority from meaningful political participation. Africans' right to vote in national elections was confined to their respective bantustans, while councils were to represent African interests in urban areas. The Vaal Triangle was the first area to hold elections on 27 November 1983, with 14 percent of registered voters (or 9 percent of the adult population) voting the Lekoa Town Council into power.[99] Elections for the Evaton Town Council were held separately. The Lekoa Town Council included 39 seats and represented six townships: Sebokeng, Boipatong, Bophelong, Sharpeville, Zamdela and Referengkgotso.[100] Both town councils came into being on 1 January 1984.[101] The low turnout was a clear indication of dissatisfaction with the new political framework and testimony to councillors' lack of legitimacy.

Newly elected councillors were vested with augmented powers that had previously been exercised by administration boards. Under the Black Communities Development Act 4 of 1984, administration boards became development boards; in line with new government policy, the function of these boards shifted from overseeing and implementing administrative matters to playing their part in developing the townships. In popular perception, however, they were regarded as the same and many believed that the town councils were under the direct control of the development board. During the inaugural speech, the former chairman of the OVAB reminded newly elected councillors that 'the success of your Council will largely be determined by your leadership and vision to approve and implement only what will be of advantage to your community as a whole'.[102] But the newly elected mayor, Esau Mahlatsi, leader of the Lekoa People's Party (LPP), soon demonstrated his aloofness and his authoritarian leadership style, which left little room for engagement. Councillors of the opposition parties, the Bafutsana Party ('party of the poor'), the Mbumba Party of Josiah 'Knox' Matjila and the Mahlasedi Party, were discriminated against and allegations abounded that they were prevented from using the community halls during the election campaign.[103] After being voted into power, councillors of all parties were told by Mahlatsi that they should forget about party politics and serve in unity.

99   WHP AK2117, S8.5.6, 'Black Local Authorities Elections 1983'.
100   Zamdela and Referengkgotso outside Sasolburg and Deneysville in the Free State fell under the jurisdiction of the OVAB. Owing to their geographic location, civic structures in these two townships were separate from those in the Vaal Triangle.
101   WHP A2243 (*State v Sefatsa and 7 Others*), Case No.698/85, A, Vol.1, Testimony Louw, p.28.
102   'The First Four Town Councils', *Bula Ditaba tsa Lekoa*, February 1984, p.1.
103   WHP AK2117, I1.7, Vol.50, Testimony Mofokeng, p.2530.

For a sizeable section of the Vaal Triangle's impoverished communities, the Bafutsana Party appeared to best represent their interests. Councillors aligned to the Bafutsana Party had been running their election campaign under the banner of 'no rental increases without explanation'.[104] Seekings has argued that some councillors, most of whom were 'dissident' councillors outside the ruling party, retained a degree of support as 'popular conservatives' who were 'inclined towards non-confrontational politics over limited goals'.[105] Members of the Bafutsana Party perhaps most closely fit this description. Yet in contrast to councillors who kept the interests of their constituents at heart, councillors of the Bafutsana Party who voiced their opposition were soon either marginalised or co-opted. During council meetings, none of the eight councillors belonging to the Bafutsana Party voted against the increases that would trigger the uprising in 1984. Subsequently, several members of the Bafutsana Party, who were not serving on the council, resigned in protest. The lack of consultation from their elected councillors, and their support for rent increases, was seen as a violation of party principles. To add insult to injury, other members of the Bafutsana Party soon joined Mahlatsi's LPP. The co-opting of opposition councillors had dire consequences, for it eliminated more critical voices from the council and created resentment among those who had supported them.

News about councillors' floor-crossing was also shared in the media, when *The Star* newspaper published a report shortly after the inauguration of the Lekoa Town Council.[106] According to this report, a group of councillors – including Kuzwayo Jacob Dlamini who had been elected deputy mayor – joined the LPP; for those voters who had elected members of the Bafutsana Party hoping that their socio-economic situation would be addressed, it came as a heavy blow and further undermined the councillors' reputation. Joining the LPP had clear benefits. Only councillors of the LPP were members of the trade committee, one of the most lucrative posts in the council as it was in charge of distributing business and liquor licences.[107]

Mahlatsi's Empire

Most councillors had an occupational background as traders or businessmen, with a few teachers and unskilled labourers.[108] Some had gained respect in their communities through involvement in advisory committees, residents' associations, school committees, church groups and sports clubs. Soccer played a particularly significant role in the rise of these *sakhamuzis*, patrons who were

---

104 Ibid., p.2493.
105 Seekings, 'Quiescence and the Transition to Confrontation', p.109.
106 *The Star*, 28 February 1984.
107 WHP AK2117, S8.5.6, 'Handwritten Notes'.
108 Bekker and Humphries, *From Control to Confusion*, pp.105–6.

well-known and respected figures in their communities. Thabe and Rabotapi are two examples of this. As speeches and minutes of the VTCC and later the Lekoa Town Council demonstrate, councillors' political vision was conservative; many believed in reforming the system from within, by lobbying for limited change.[109]

As such, councillors regarded themselves as elders who did not tolerate dissent and challenge; their relations to their constituencies were hierarchical, authoritarian and paternalistic.[110] Councillors' reliance on patronage politics ran contrary to popular expectations of being treated fairly and equally. Rumours also abounded that elderly residents were too afraid not to support councillors, for fear of being evicted or losing their pension grants. The vote of others was won by providing them with blankets the councillors had received from the administration board for distribution.[111] While their political power was never considered adequate, the blatant disregard for the welfare of their constituencies soon made them the target of popular anger.

Augmented powers in allocating housing and distributing business and trading sites, business licences (and from 1984 onwards liquor licences) soon led to widespread corruption.[112] Two of the councillors at the centre of allegations of corruption were the two most influential men within the council during the 1980s: Josiah 'Knox' Matjila, chairman of the VTCC between 1978 and 1982, and Esau Mahlatsi, mayor of the Lekoa Town Council from 1984. Matjila went on trial at the Vereeniging Magistrate's Court in 1985 for alleged corruption and bribery, together with his former deputy, Ananias Ramogonako Sekobane, as well as councillor and member of the trade committee, Johannes Mabane Monnakgotla.[113] During his hearing, Matjila claimed that his abuse of power was nothing unusual as corruption within the community council was endemic during the period of his chairmanship. He was known for exercising politics through nepotism; he allegedly formed a small and closed group of alliances within the council, excluding those councillors outside his group from receiving bribes and acquiring trading and business licences.[114]

Statistics demonstrate that members of the trade committee distributed business and trading licences and sites first and foremost to themselves, their families and their friends. By 1984, Mayor Esau Mahlatsi, who had been a member of the trade committee since 1978, together with his two brothers Paul and Meshack Mahlatsi, had built a business empire that included bottle stores and super-

109   See the 14 volumes of testimony given by councillors during the Delmas treason trial. WHP AK2117, I1.6.40–I1.8.54, Vols.40–54.

110   C. Charney, 'Vigilantes, Clientelism, and the South African State', *Transformation*, 16 (1991), pp.1–28.

111   Edward 'Chippa' Motubatsi, interview with author, Vereeniging, 15 April 2010.

112   WHP AK2117, S8.5.2, 'Incidents of Corruption by Councillors'.

113   *Sowetan*, 20 November 1985; *The Star*, 12 March 1985.

114   WHP AK2117, S8.10.6, 'Memorandum on the Vaal Triangle Background'.

markets: 12 out of 25 bottle stores belonged to his family and he had interests in another eight.[115] If councillors' corruption and nepotism were topics of discussion among residents, and rumours abounded of excessive spending and inappropriate behaviour towards their constituencies, newspaper reports cemented these beliefs. Reports in widely read newspapers like the *Sowetan* and the *Rand Daily Mail* featured councillors' extravagant spending and lifestyle: money was spent to bring an overseas choir to the Vaal Triangle, cars were repaired at council's expense and councillors were planning a trip to Europe, funded by council money.[116] In May 1984, Evaton's Mayor Sam Rabotapi's dismay with the purchase of a mayoral car was reported.[117] The cause of Rabotapi's anger, the newspaper report alleged, was the cutting of the budget from R28,000 to R25,000 for buying 'a silver grey' car, which Rabotapi claimed he needed for a public function. These newspaper reports had a significant impact as they confirmed popular perception that councillors were wasting money while their constituencies suffered hardship.

Evictions from houses were widespread, and with their augmented powers councillors became the face of these practices. At times tenants were evicted by councillors who wanted to allocate the house to someone else; corner houses were particularly attractive and their tenants were at permanent risk of being removed. Councillors took advantage of the housing crisis when they received bribes from residents who were on the waiting list for a house. As Reverend Peter Lenkoe remarked, 'it was generally accepted that to get what you wanted, you had to grease a councillor's palm'.[118] More widespread than evictions for personal gains were evictions of rent defaulters. By then, a sizeable percentage of the local population was in arrears, and those who failed to settle their bills often found themselves locked out of their homes, with furniture or house doors removed. By far the most vulnerable target for evictions were widows, who lost their right to remain in the house once the male head of household passed away (unless a male relative took over the lease).[119] The eviction of widows signified the merciless manner in which officials and councillors dealt with these personal tragedies.

In addition to corruption and evictions, councillors had a reputation for ignoring grievances voiced by their constituents. Local resident Elizabeth Lefoke, for example, stated in 1985 that 'I have complained to councillors at meetings. They don't listen. I didn't believe the councillors because they never consulted the people'.[120] Rent increases were frequent and often implemented without prior

115   P. Noonan, *They're Burning the Churches: The Final Dramatic Events that Scuttled Apartheid* (Bellevue, Jacana, 2003), p.109.
116   WHP AK2117, S8.10.6, 'Memorandum on Vaal Triangle Background'; *Sowetan*, 5 February 1982.
117   *Rand Daily Mail*, 3 May 1984.
118   WHP AK2117, S8.11.1., 'Affidavit P. Lenkoe'.
119   On African women's struggles for housing, see Lee, *African Women and Apartheid*.
120   WHP AK2117, S8.11, 'Statement by Elizabeth Lefoke'.

consultation; councillors also failed to discuss socio-economic grievances of their constituencies with the relevant administration board officials.[121] And so while election promises included the provision of better services, the upgrading of townships as well as a reduction of rents, they stood in sharp contrast to the realities on the ground. For many, who had been led to believe that rent increases were implemented to cover the costs of upgrading and development, the lack of infrastructure and facilities together with councillors' spending patterns confirmed suspicions that councillors were enriching themselves at the expense of the poor.

'I am a Tsotsi councillor'

Conflict between councillors and their constituencies had been ongoing since their election in 1977. In 1978, a meeting held to announce a rent increase ended with a heated exchange when residents complained about the increases and ongoing evictions. Councillors allegedly told residents not to meddle in the affairs of the council; in response, the audience angrily told them that they were 'selling out'.[122] One of the councillors at the centre of violent confrontations was Knox Matjila, chairman of the VTCC. On 27 July 1980 he addressed a meeting at Khutlo-Tharo Junior Secondary School to announce a rent increase of R2.40.[123] During Matjila's speech residents called on him to scrap the increase, to end the evictions of widows and to upgrade and improve facilities and infrastructure. Matjila, who had a reputation for being aggressive and belligerent, was threatened with assault by members of the audience. Policemen who appeared on the scene were stoned, and Matjila subsequently had to be escorted out in a police van. As a newspaper report stated, 'Tempers ran high when the police came to Mr Matjila's rescue. The crowd shouted at him and demanded that the police should go away.'[124] A year later, the conflict began to escalate in the Vaal Triangle as well as Thembisa in the East Rand when shops were looted, buses burnt and buildings set alight in the aftermath of another meeting convened to announce a rent increase. In the vicinity of Sam Rabotapi's house shots were heard and a crowd of approximately 300 people was seen on the premises.[125] Matjila threatened that he would 'fix' residents who confronted him regarding the increase and the evictions; he was allegedly in the company of an 'old witch doctor [...] who also began threatening assault'.[126]

---

121   WHP AK2117, I1.7, Vol.45, Testimony Mokoena, p.2239; WHP AK2117, I.1.8, Vol.55, Testimony Matthysen, pp.2835–37.

122   WHP AK2117, S8.10.2, 'Vaal Triangle Background. Demonstration of Dissatisfaction among Residents'.

123   *Post,* 28 July 1980.

124   Ibid.

125   *Sowetan,* 7 April 1981; *The Star,* 6 April 1981.

126   WHP AK2117, S8.10.2, 'Vaal Triangle Background. Demonstration of Dissatisfaction among Residents'. The term 'witch doctor' is problematic. The correct term would be *sangoma*.

The steepest increase was announced in 1982, when rent went up by R16 per month, from R30 to R46. The meeting hosted by councillors led to a heated confrontation between them and the audience. Angry residents challenged the councillors, saying that they were no longer going to pay rent increases as they could not see any improvements. Councillor Mofokeng, one of the councillors who addressed the meeting, threatened residents, saying, 'I am not afraid of anybody here. I am a Tsotsi councillor. I can fight anybody anywhere.'[127] Other councillors narrowly escaped being beaten up after the meeting had concluded. During that year, a number of councillors resigned, including George Thabe and Sam Kolisang of Sharpeville. Thabe publicly criticised the council system and stated that it was a powerless body.[128] Kolisang followed suit and emphasised that the rent increases were 'ridiculous and exorbitant'.[129] Matjila's leadership was described as 'inconsiderate and dictatorial' and some of the councillors promised to call for public meetings where they would challenge the decision of the council to increase rents.[130]

Mofokeng's behaviour was symptomatic of the deep-seated disregard many councillors had for their constituencies, and their unwillingness to tolerate dissent. Caesar Motjeane, one of the councillors who died during the uprising of 1984, was said to have 'broken a man's jaw' when evicting him from his house.[131] Motjeane allegedly also praised himself for being able to fight with a knobkierrie, a fist and a gun. Besides his aggressiveness, Motjeane was rumoured to be a womaniser who would 'take away' other men's girlfriends and make inappropriate advances on women.[132] Other councillors' reputation was no better. Jacob Kuzwayo Dlamini, who like Motjeane died on 3 September 1984, was accused of being responsible for the dismissal of workers employed by African Cables.

Conflict between councillors and their constituencies over rent increases, alleged corruption and mismanagement became more and more violent, placing councillors outside the imagined boundaries of community.[133] An increasing

---

127 *Sowetan*, 2 February 1982; WHP AK2117, I2.3, Vol.179, Testimony Nkopane, p.9187.
128 *Sowetan*, 15 July 1981.
129 *Sowetan*, 8 February 1982.
130 Ibid.
131 WHP AK2117, S8.5.4, 'Memorandum on Councillor Caesar Motjeane'.
132 Ibid.
133 F. Rueedi, 'The Politics of Difference and the Forging of a Political "Community": Discourses and Practices of the Charterist Civic Movement in the Vaal Triangle, South Africa, 1980–1984', *Journal of Southern African Studies*, 41/6 (2015), pp.1181–98. Tshepo Moloi's case study of Maokeng township shows a different outcome. Moloi argues that the council in Maokeng township outside Kroonstaad in the Northern Free State averted popular protest action by addressing the needs and grievances of their constituencies. T. Moloi, *Place of Thorns: Black Political Protest in Kroonstad since 1976* (Johannesburg, Wits University Press, 2015).

resort to violence and an abuse of power also became apparent in the work-ings of *makgotla*,[134] courts held by councillors to resolve disputes. One widow approached a *lekgotla* run by a councillor in Sharpeville to report a conflict with her nephew as well as her sub-tenant. She did so 'in good faith because I wanted to discipline the young man but instead it turned out that the councillor was a crook'.[135] The sentence in these courts was often lashing with a sjambok and other forms of corporal punishment. If these *makgotla* initially enjoyed some support, their legitimacy was soon undermined.[136] They were often 'paramilitary rather than judicial institutions' and they relied on using sheer force.[137]

The combination of a lack of transparency and consultation with visible and extravagant spending exacerbated residents' beliefs that councillors were neither representing their constituencies nor taking care of their interests and welfare. In the absence of open communication and information, rumours of misconduct extended beyond personalised experience and reached broader audiences. These rumours therefore played a significant role in the bounding of group identities.[138] The use of language was key in turning the councillors into 'the other': they were seen as a collective group of 'enemies' who were regarded as hindering the attainment of freedom.[139] Councillors were regarded as 'puppets', 'stooges', 'sell-outs' or 'dogs', and this discourse gained promi-nence after the formation of the United Democratic Front in 1983. By 1984, as Matime Moshele Papane, a political activist from Sharpeville, pointed out, 'layers and layers of anger' existed towards councillors, 'around the ways they conducted themselves'.[140] Councillors were blamed for a lack of development and emancipation. The announcement of yet another increase of R5.90, as the next chapter will show, was the final straw that broke the camel's back. The stage was set for rebellion.

---

134   *Makgotla* is the plural of *lekgotla*.

135   WHP AK2117, S8.11.1, Statement by Celistyna Letseka.

136   J. Hund and M. Kotu-Rammopo, 'Justice in a South African Township: The Sociol-ogy of *Makgotla*', *Comparative and International Law Journal of Southern Africa*, 16/2 (1983), pp.179–208.

137   J. Seekings, 'People's Court and Popular Politics', in G. Moss and I. Obery (eds), *South African Review 5* (Johannesburg, Ravan Press, 1989), p.122.

138   Veena Das has examined the role of rumour in shaping collective identities in India. See V. Das, 'Specificities: Official Narratives, Rumour, and the Social Production of Hate', *Social Identities*, 4/1 (1998), pp.109–30. For an analysis of the role of rumour in triggering violence in South Africa, see F. Rueedi, 'The Hostel Wars in Apartheid South Africa: Rumour, Violence and the Discourse of Victimhood', *Social Identities*, 26/6 (2020), pp.756–73.

139   Esau Ralitsela, interview with author, Vereeniging, 5 April 2010.

140   Matime Moshele Papane, interview with author, Johannesburg, 28 April 2010.

3

'Quite a fertile soil':
Civic Protest and the Ascendancy
of Charterism

Ramakgula's Door

It all began with a door. Tebello Ephraim Ramakgula had purchased the house door made of Meranti wood for R78 to provide his rented house in Zone 7, Sebokeng, with safety and privacy. Sebokeng and Zone 7 in particular were notorious for their high levels of crime and the prevalence of gangs. Ramakgula had bought the door in 1977 to replace the old, rotten front door the house had come with when he moved in. Months of discussions with the Orange Vaal Administration Board (OVAB) and the ward councillor in his area had convinced him that he had to take matters into his own hands as the authorities appeared unwilling to provide a new door. Adding to his problems, Ramakgula was told to pay the previous tenant's rental arrears of four months.[1]

In 1983 the door went missing. Ramakgula, an assistant electrician in his thirties with little formal education, enquired at the offices of the OVAB and was informed that the door had been removed owing to his failure to pay rent: a widespread strategy aimed at enforcing the payment of rent arrears.[2] With high crime rates, a missing door was no minor matter but exposed him to insecurity and danger, and it constituted the (temporary) loss of a valuable item. Ramakgula's experiences, typical for township communities in the Vaal Triangle, prompted him to attend the launch of the Vaal Civic Association (VCA) on 9 October 1983 and subsequently to join the area committee in Zone 7. Less than four years later, on 23 February 1987, he appeared in court as one of the accused in the Delmas treason trial for his alleged involvement in fomenting a revolutionary climate in South Africa.

---

1   WHP AK2117, I2.3, Vol.179, Testimony Ramagula [sic], pp.9199–200.
2   Ibid., p.9202.

Cross-examined by George Bizos, he explained his reasons for joining the VCA in 1983. The incident that caused him particular stress, he explained in court, was the removal of his house door. Rampant corruption, unaccountability and aloof behaviour of councillors, the harsh practices of the administration board and his dire economic situation had shaped the context in which the removal of the door came to symbolise everything that was wrong with the system. In his words, the VCA provided a platform 'to come together and discuss with my fellow Blacks, my fellow people, to discuss the problems we have.'[3] Ramakgula's testimony bears witness to the subjective factors that moulded ordinary people's political consciousness. The daily assault on people's dignity and sense of self, and the subjective experiences of poverty, oppression and violence shaped the political ferment of the 1980s.

While bread-and-butter issues played a key role in politicising and con-scientising large sections of African society, the resurgence of Charterism under the banner of the United Democratic Front (UDF) as well as the ideological direction provided by the African National Congress (ANC) nurtured everyday grievances into a sustained struggle for social transformation and political power. Many of the emerging activists who took centre stage during the 1980s had been schooled in the fold of the Black Consciousness Movement (BCM) but shifted towards Charterism during the early 1980s.[4] The BCM, with its focus on com-munity building, upliftment and the liberation of the mind, had inaugurated a new era of black radical thought and activism; yet during the early 1980s, the BCM was eclipsed by the ascendancy of Charterism among township activists. The reasons for this were manifold, as this chapter will explore.

The Death of Johannes Matsobane and the Formation of Networks

As Julian Brown has argued, the notion that South Africa underwent a period of 'quiescence' blots out the many forms of open and clandestine engagement with, and resistance to, the state.[5] This is certainly true for the Vaal Triangle; even though open political resistance was virtually absent, and student protests paled in comparison to Soweto and Alexandra, dissent to white minority rule was expressed through less overtly political groups: cultural clubs, church groups and student societies came to play a leading role as incubators of political ideas and as training grounds where future activists honed their oratorial and organi-

---

3   Ibid., p.9217.

4   Anne Heffernan argues that the two competing ideologies were neither as discrete, nor as contentious, as they are often made out to be. A. Heffernan, 'Blurred Lines and Ideological Divisions in South African Youth Politics', *African Affairs*, 115/461 (2016), pp.664–87.

5   J. Brown, *The Road to Soweto: Resistance and the Uprising of 16 June 1976* (Oxford, James Currey, 2016).

sational skills.[6] Often initiated to keep young people off the streets, these groupings were vital in connecting them.[7] Two organisations played a particularly important role in producing the new crop of leadership: the Vaal Youth Crusade and the Young Christian Workers. The Vaal Youth Crusade was a cultural club located at the African Methodist Episcopal Church in Evaton. It hosted poetry readings, theatre plays and exhibitions, and even though it had no political programme, many of its members used it as a platform to discuss politics. The Young Christian Workers gained nationwide prominence during the 1970s.[8] Gcina Malindi, Edith Letlhake and Simon Nkoli, who emerged as student and civic leaders during the 1980s, all cut their teeth in these two organisations.

Bhekizizwe Peterson argues that the 1970s saw a 'renaissance of cultural work'.[9] It was a period of cultural eclecticism and excitement that witnessed the interrogation and assertion of what it meant to be black in apartheid South Africa. Poetry readings, drama, theatre, art, literature and music were thriving in Soweto and attracted local youth from the Vaal Triangle. The poetry of Mafika Gwala and Ingoapele Madingoane and the theatre of the Mihloti Black Theatre group, the latter two based in Soweto, were heavily influenced by Black Consciousness (BC) and reflected the political awareness of young black South Africans. Madingoane performed his famous poems 'Black Trial' and 'Africa My Beginning, Africa My Ending', published in 1979 and immediately banned by the apartheid regime, widely all over Soweto. Literature on anticolonial struggles such as *Facing Mount Kenya* by Jomo Kenyatta or *Things Fall Apart* by Chinua Achebe were read alongside Karl Marx's *The Communist Manifesto* and *Pedagogy of the Oppressed* by Paulo Freire. The literature by African American intellectuals such as W.E.B. du Bois equally served as an inspiration, as did the struggles of the Black Power Movement, Kwame Nkrumah's Pan Africanism and Frantz Fanon's explorations of the psychology of oppression. The coup in Lisbon in 1974, and the subsequent installation of independent governments in Mozambique and Angola a year later, caused excitement among politicised youth, who drew inspiration from the *Frente de Libertação de Moçambique* (Frelimo) and its successful struggle against Portuguese colonialism.[10]

6   See C. Glaser, '"We Must Infiltrate the Tsotsis": School Politics and Youth Gangs in Soweto, 1968–1976', *Journal of Southern African Studies*, 24/2 (1998), pp.301–23; C. Glaser, *Bo-Tsotsi: The Youth Gangs of Soweto, 1935–1976* (Oxford, James Currey, 2000).

7   T. Lodge, *Sharpeville: An Apartheid Massacre and Its Consequences* (Oxford, Oxford University Press, 2011), p.286.

8   I. van Kessel, *Beyond Our Wildest Dreams: The United Democratic Front and the Transformation of South Africa* (Charlottesville, University Press of Virginia, 1995).

9   B. Peterson, 'Culture, Resistance and Representation', in South African Democracy Education Trust [SADET] (ed.), *The Road to Democracy in South Africa*, Volume 2, *1970–1980* (Pretoria, Unisa Press, 2006), p.161.

10   Sekwati Mokoena, interview with author, Sharpeville, 30 March 2010; on the Frelimo rallies, see Brown, *The Road to Soweto*.

Even though secondary schools in the Vaal Triangle were not in the forefront of protests in 1976, they were nevertheless important sites where new ideas were debated and networks created. Tshepo Themba Secondary School in Residensia, Jordan High School in Evaton, affiliated to the famous Wilberforce Institute, and Lekoa Shandu in Sharpeville were known to be schools with a politically conscious student body. Later on, during the 1980s, a handful of schools in Sebokeng such as Moqhaka Secondary School in Zone 11, Fundulwazi in Zone 12 and Sizanani in Zone 13, the three zones that formed the spatial node of resistance and political mobilisation in that period, would come to produce some of the most radical student leaders in the region.

Others attended secondary schooling outside the Vaal Triangle, and even though their numbers were small, these outside influences brought new ideas to the townships and created political and cultural networks that formed the basis of subsequent student mobilisation. One of them was David Moisi. Born in 1956 in Kroonstad, Moisi joined the famous Orlando High School in 1975 to study mathematics and science at matric level; such courses were lacking at many high schools in the Vaal Triangle.[11] Moisi's first-hand experience of the Soweto uprising strengthened his growing political conscientisation. In 1977, Moisi was part of a handful of students who staged a march against a rent increase of 35 percent; it attracted a few hundred residents and students.[12] Shortly afterwards, following the funeral of BC leader Steve Biko, Moisi left South Africa to join Umkhonto weSizwe (MK), returning three years later for the successful bombing of SASOL II in Secunda on 31 May 1980, for which he was subsequently arrested.[13] After the death of BC's most prominent leader, Steve Biko, on 12 September 1977, South African Students' Organisation (SASO) and other organisations aligned to the BCM were banned. BC would re-emerge through the formation of the Azanian People's Organisation (AZAPO) in 1979, which, for a few years, played an important role in Sharpeville.

The death of another local student activist proved to be a turning point. Johannes Matsobane was arrested for his alleged involvement in the burning of a school in 1977 in Sebokeng. Charged with sabotage and sentenced to imprisonment on Robben Island, Matsobane died a few months later. The circumstances of his death as well as his role as a student leader attracted a large crowd of mourners to attend his funeral.[14] The funeral was disrupted by brutish violence when police teargassed the crowd of mourners, chasing those

---

11   David Moisi, interview with author, Pretoria, 13 July 2010.

12   Ibid.; Oupa Mareletse, interview with author, Johannesburg, 30 June 2010.

13   David Moisi, interview with author, Pretoria, 13 July 2010. Together with his two co-accused Anthony Tsotsobe and Johannes Shabangu, Moisi was sentenced to death for high treason. The sentence was later commuted.

14   *Work in Progress*, 6 June 1978; Richard 'Bricks' Mokolo, interview with author, Orange Farm, 20 March 2010.

who tried to flee the mayhem. In the aftermath, five young men were arrested and charged with attending an 'illegal gathering'.[15] Wanton police violence would become an all too common experience of mourners during funerals from the late 1970s onwards and significantly contributed towards a growing anger against the apartheid government and its security forces, as subsequent chapters will highlight. Matsobane's funeral was one of the first public events in the Vaal Triangle since 1960 and impacted on the emergence of new protest politics, as it 'gave people who had several grievances, the sense that they were not alone in such grievances'.[16]

A Life of Struggle: The Ralitselas

While their lives may be unique in many ways, and their sacrifice and courage exemplary, the processes that shaped the political consciousness of Dorcas and Esau Ralitsela are reflective of the diverse blend of influences that underpinned the struggle for freedom. This married couple were key in framing bread-and-butter issues within a broader political context. Dorcas Ralitsela was born in 1947 in Evaton into a family of nine children.[17] Her family, using the unique economic opportunities Evaton offered during this period, belonged to an aspirant entrepreneurial class; her father owned a general store in which everyday goods were sold. Being raised as a staunch Anglican, Ralitsela was exposed to the political and social teachings of Christianity from a young age. Attending boarding school in Botshabelo in the then Northern Transvaal, Ralitsela completed her secondary schooling at the Morris Isaacson High School in Soweto. During this period, it was known to be one of Soweto's most prestigious schools, which attracted the socially aspirant.[18]

In 1968, Ralitsela enrolled at the University of the North, popularly known as Turfloop, to study social work and psychology. Built in 1959 to cater for students of Sotho, Venda, Tsonga and Tswana ethnic origins, Turfloop came to be at the centre of the BCM.[19] Dorcas Ralitsela's politicisation was therefore heavily influenced by the teachings of Biko and his contemporaries. Perhaps even more so, Turfloop's charismatic BC leader, Onkgopotse Tiro, made a lasting impression on her. 'Politically the message became clear', she recalls, 'that there

15   *Post*, 27 January 1979.
16   WHP AK2117, S8.4.1, 'Memorandum on the Emergence of the VCA'.
17   Dorcas Ralitsela, interview with author, Vereeniging, 1 April 2010.
18   C. Glaser, 'Soweto's Islands of Learning: Morris Isaacson and Orlando High Schools under Bantu Education, 1958–1975', *Journal of Southern African Studies*, 41/1 (2015), p.164.
19   A. Heffernan, 'Black Consciousness's Lost Leader: Abraham Tiro, the University of the North, and the Seeds of South Africa's Student Movement in the 1970s', *Journal of Southern African Studies*, 41/1 (2015), p.174; A. Heffernan, *Limpopo's Legacy: Student Politics and Democracy in South Africa* (Johannesburg, Wits University Press, 2019).

is something that is not right.'[20] Literature by Chinua Achebe and Jomo Kenyatta, among others, framed her own experiences as an African woman within a larger context of anticolonial struggles. While at Turfloop, Ralitsela attended conferences hosted by the Anglican Students' Federation as well as the Anglican Women's Federation, which is when, in her words, she 'began to have a brush with the law' and the security branch of the South African Police warned her to abstain from politics.[21]

Owing to financial strictures, Ralitsela could not complete her postgraduate degree. After stints in Kimberley and later Randfontein, where she began her career as a social worker, Ralitsela was eventually transferred to the OVAB. While her exposure to BC and her upbringing in Evaton undoubtedly had a conscientising and politicising effect, the daily frustrations and tribulations she faced as a social worker and the harrowing stories she witnessed instantiated the gamut of injustice of apartheid. The harshness of influx control, poverty and inequality, as well as the limitations placed on her ability to effect meaningful social upliftment soon found her at loggerheads with administration board officials. It was through her work as a social worker that she got to know Esau Ralitsela, whom she married in 1981.

Born on a farm near the Vaal Dam, Esau Ralitsela had spent his childhood in Evaton Small Farms, where water was shared through communal taps and the living conditions were difficult.[22] In 1968, the family moved into a house in Zone 7 in Sebokeng. Esau Ralitsela was politicised through his discussions with Ntsizi Moremi, an old school friend and priest. An adherent of the BCM, Moremi believed in self-help and community care, as espoused by the Black Community Programmes.[23] His church was a key rallying point where adult literacy, based on the concepts developed by Paulo Freire, was taught, and advice on political and legal matters provided. In 1978, after receiving his banning order, Moremi went into exile, first crossing into Lesotho and later living in Nairobi, Kenya.[24]

In 1978, Ralitsela attended training workshops at the Industrial Aid Society, run by students at the University of the Witwatersrand. Together

20   Dorcas Ralitsela, interview with author, Vereeniging, 1 April 2010.

21   On the Anglican Students' Federation, see I. MacQueen, 'Students, Apartheid and the Ecumenical Movement in South Africa', *Journal of Southern African Studies*, 39/3 (2013), pp.447–63.

22   Esau Ralitsela, interview with author, Vereeniging, 1 April 2010.

23   Ibid.; on the relation between Christian organisations and the Black Community Programmes, see L. Hadfield, 'Christian Action and Black Consciousness Community Programmes in South Africa', *Journal for the Study of Religion*, 23/1–2 (2010), pp.105–30.

24   Ntsizi Elijah Moremi, interview with Gail Gerhart, 1979–80, http://www.disa.ukzn.ac.za/ora19790731000009000, retrieved 20 April 2020.

with Fana Mkhwanazi, he subsequently opened a local branch called the Industrial Aid Centre in Vereeniging, which was funded by the International Confederation of Free Trade Unions (ICFTU). From its inception, the Industrial Aid Centre became an important hub of activities, providing advice and assistance to individuals, but also aiding in the organisation of workers through unions such as the Commercial, Catering and Allied Workers' Union of South Africa (CCAWUSA) and the Metal and Allied Workers' Union (MAWU).[25]

Ralitsela's role at the Industrial Aid Centre placed him in an advantageous position; through his interaction with workers, he was intimately aware of their everyday grievances and he enjoyed their respect. 'The influence [of working closely with workers was] in a socialist way,' Ralitsela recalls.[26] 'That the workers are the ones who must run the country and they must also get all the interests and aspirations realised.' And it facilitated the use of resources such as photocopiers and telephones, which would later come to be of great use when the couple became involved in civic struggles. It was through the Industrial Aid Centre that Esau Ralitsela first met Matseliso Elisabeth Letanta, popularly known as MaLetanta, whom he would recruit into an ANC underground unit a few years later. His contacts with students such as Thabiso Ratsomo as well as his contact with workers laid the basis of a network of people who were at the forefront of the formation of the VCA in 1983.[27]

By the early 1980s, the Ralitselas were in search of a broader political framework for their social activism, and in 1982, the couple travelled to Botswana to meet with Dorcas Ralitsela's sister, who had joined the ANC there in the late 1970s. Upon arrival in Gaborone, the Ralitselas were introduced to ANC members and underwent training.[28] One of their first encounters was with Jackie Seemela (Mogase) and later Billy Masetlha, Florence Mophosho and Ray Alexander, who all came to play a key role in the Ralitselas' political training. They were instructed to act as couriers, distribute ANC material, work towards the formation of above-ground structures and identify potential new recruits. Unusual for their time, the Ralitselas owned a car, which allowed them to visit Botswana and to smuggle in ANC material.

The ANC and the Growth of Charterism

The Ralitselas' task to form above-ground structures in the Vaal Triangle was in line with the ANC's strategic shift towards mass mobilisation. Much has

25   Esau Ralitsela, interview with author, Vereeniging, 5 April 2010.
26   Ibid.
27   Ibid.
28   Dorcas Ralitsela, interview with author, Vereeniging, 1 April 2010; Dorcas Ralitsela, unrecorded interview with author, Vereeniging, 4 November 2011.

been written about the emergence of mass mobilisation, and the ANC's influence on the formation of the UDF in 1983; less is known about the role of ANC underground units during the township revolts of the mid-1980s.[29] The key developments regarding the ANC's strategic shift are worth summarising here, for they contextualise the growth of the domestic underground in the Vaal Triangle, which, as will be seen, linked grassroots struggles to the broader struggle for freedom and emancipation.

The ANC's inability to lead the student revolts in 1976 led it to reassess its strategies, as Howard Barrell and others have argued.[30] After the visit to Vietnam in October 1978 of the ANC's National Executive Committee (NEC) delegation, the Politico-Military Strategy Commission redefined its priorities.[31] Summarised in the Green Book (named after the Green Book by Muammar Gaddafi), the four pillars of the revolution were defined as being the underground, mass mobilisation, the armed struggle and international solidarity.[32] The strategy outlined in the Green Book emphasised that the military aspect of the struggle was secondary to the political one and that the masses needed to be mobilised in order to create a situation in which the broader population would become engaged in a people's war.[33] Mass mobilisation would be guided by trained underground units, and inspired by a concerted propaganda campaign that would include the distribution of printed material, a series of campaigns to popularise the ANC and its leaders, the strengthening of the ANC's presence through songs and other symbols and armed propaganda to mark the domestic presence of MK. In the aftermath of the visit to Vietnam, efforts to strengthen the domestic underground accelerated but experienced uneven success; overall, the ANC underground machinery never had the strength and capacity to provide direct leadership to the domestic struggle, but its symbolic presence and ideological guidance instilled hope in the disenfranchised majority.[34]

29   See, for example, H. Barrell, 'Conscripts to Their Age: African National Congress Operational Strategy, 1976–1986' (DPhil thesis, University of Oxford, 1993); J. Seekings, *The UDF: A History of the United Democratic Front in South Africa, 1983–1991* (Cape Town, David Philip, 2nd edition, 2015).

30   See Barrell, 'Conscripts to Their Age', pp.178ff.

31   Ibid.; S.R. Davis, *The ANC's War against Apartheid: Umkhonto we Sizwe and the Liberation of South Africa* (Bloomington, Indiana University Press, 2018).

32   The Green Book: Report of the Politico-Military Strategy Commission to the ANC National Executive Committee, August 1979, https://www.marxists.org/subject/africa/anc/1979/green-book.htm, retrieved 20 April 2020.

33   Barrell, 'Conscripts to Their Age', pp.184ff.

34   See G. Houston, 'The ANC's Internal Underground Political Work in the 1980s', in SADET (ed.), *The Road to Democracy, Volume 4* (Pretoria, Unisa Press, 2010), pp.133–222.

ANC journals such as *Sechaba, Mayibuye* and the *African Communist*, pamphlets and other written documentation were circulating from the late 1970s, but were read by few. More important than written material was Radio Freedom, which introduced many of the songs sung by MK in the neighbouring countries to listeners in South Africa, kept activists abreast of the latest strategies and tactics espoused by the ANC and also provided practical advice.[35] The annual speeches by the ANC's president, O.R. Tambo, on 8 January became one of the most significant ways in which the ANC communicated with its domestic listeners. While it is difficult to gauge to what extent Radio Freedom influenced the political consciousness of the broader population in the townships, activists recall that they used to meet at particular houses, including the Ralitselas' house, to listen to Radio Freedom.[36] Tapes of these recorded speeches were distributed to a select audience, to publicise the ANC and to spread its messages.[37]

To popularise the Freedom Charter of 1955, the ANC proclaimed 1980 to be 'The Year of the Charter' and copies of the Freedom Charter were distributed widely. During the same year, the Release Mandela Committee (RMC) was launched to take up its campaign to free Nelson Mandela from prison. The RMC's lobbying had a crucial impact on international solidarity, as it gave the struggle a clearly identifiable face and name.[38] While the reach of this campaign remains unknown and it is unclear how many ordinary people were exposed to it, the ANC's symbolic presence provided ideological guidance. If the infiltration of printed material and campaigns to popularise the ANC aimed to provide ideological leadership, armed propaganda had the goal of lifting the morale of the oppressed majority. According to Tom Lodge, there were 533 recorded MK attacks between 1977 and June 1986, with the vast majority occurring in 1985/86.[39] Sabotage acts such as

35   P. Lekgoathi, 'The African National Congress's Radio Freedom and Its Audiences in Apartheid South Africa, 1963–1991', *Journal of African Media Studies*, 2/2 (2010), pp.139–54.

36   Themba Goba, interview with author, Vereeniging, 18 June 2010; Dorcas Ralitsela, interview with author, Vereeniging, 1 April 2010.

37   Dorcas Ralitsela, interview with author, Vereeniging, 1 April 2010.

38   G.L. Klein, 'Publicising the African National Congress: The Anti-Apartheid News', *South African Historical Journal*, 63/3 (2011), pp.394–413; C. Saunders, 'Britain, the Commonwealth, and the Question of the Release of Nelson Mandela in the 1980s', *The Round Table: The Commonwealth Journal of International Affairs*, 106/6 (2017), pp.659–69. For an analysis of African American networks of solidarity in the United States, see, for example, F.N. Nesbitt, *Race for Sanctions: African Americans against Apartheid, 1946–1994* (Bloomington and Indianapolis, Indiana University Press, 2004).

39   T. Lodge, 'State of Exile: The African National Congress of South Africa, 1976–86', in P. Frankel, N. Pines and M. Swilling (eds), *State, Resistance and Change in South*

the bombing of SASOL II in May 1980 or the attack on Voortrekkerhoogte military base in August 1981 were reported in the press, on Radio Freedom and along township networks, and instilled hope that the apartheid regime would be defeated.[40]

In the Vaal Triangle, the Ralitselas formed an underground unit after their return from Botswana and recruited MaLetanta into their unit. MaLetanta was described as an ordinary, semi-illiterate and elderly woman, known for her sharp memory and her quiet demeanour. Born in 1922, MaLetanta was already 60 years old when she joined the unit. One of the many unsung heroes of the struggle for freedom, she not only played an active role in the underground but also came to be a leading figure in the Vaal Organisation of Women (VOW), and she also mediated between students and parents during the education crisis of the mid-1980s (see Chapter 7). She was an ideal candidate for underground work: her age, gender and inconspicuous appearance kept her off the radar of the security branch and her secretiveness ensured that the unit was protected. 'The way she carried herself', Dorcas Ralitsela remembers, 'made her trustworthy.'[41] The patriarchal gaze of the security branch rendered MaLetanta 'invisible', an advantage the unit used to its benefit. By August 1984, MaLetanta had successfully brought ANC material back from Botswana. Having wrapped the material around her body, hidden under layers of clothes, MaLetanta exploited the inherent hesitation of male police and border officials to strip-search an older woman. The Ralitselas placed these pamphlets and written ANC documents at strategic places, where frequent passers-by would take notice, or near police stations to indicate the strength and presence of the ANC.[42] The key mandate for underground units, certainly from 1984 onwards, was to work towards making the country ungovernable and apartheid unworkable, as the Ralitselas recall.[43] Calls for ungovernability had been circulating as early as 1981, but became one of the cornerstones of the ANC's strategic programme during the period leading up to the insurrectionary period of 1984–86. To achieve ungovernability, the ANC's president Oliver Tambo stated, people should 'attack and demolish' the administrative system: 'Having rejected the community councils by boycotting the elections, we should not allow them to be imposed on us. [...] We must ensure that they cease to exist. Where administration boards take over their functions, then these must be destroyed too.'[44] By connecting local debates on rent increases and the councils to the broader political visions of the

---

Africa (London, Croom Helm, 1988), pp.229–58.

40   David Moisi, interview with author, Pretoria, 13 July 2010.

41   Dorcas Ralitsela, unrecorded interview with author, Vereeniging, 4 November 2011.

42   Esau Ralitsela, interview with author, Vereeniging, 5 April 2010; Dorcas Ralitsela, unrecorded interview with author, Vereeniging, 4 November 2011.

43   Esau Ralitsela, interview with author, Vereeniging, 5 April 2010; Dorcas Ralitsela, interview with author, Vereeniging, 1 April 2010.

44   *Sechaba*, March 1984, p.6.

ANC, and by framing popular grievances in the language of the Freedom Charter, the Ralitselas promoted the growth of Charterism in the region.

'Before we are students we are members of the community'

The first legal organisation to formally adopt the Freedom Charter was the Congress of South African Students (COSAS), formed in 1979. In contrast to SASO, which was banned in 1977, COSAS accommodated secondary school students and its ideology was Charterist. During the early 1970s, secondary schooling had expanded drastically, swelling the classrooms. By 1980, approximately 46 percent of the African population was estimated to be under the age of 15; it provided the demographic for an increasingly politicised student body. Economic decline and rising unemployment, however, barred young people from climbing the social ladder. Frustration over a lack of prospects, enmeshed with exposure to inequality, oppression and poverty, planted the seeds of a political consciousness that was deeply rooted in everyday lived experiences of young people. The sharp economic decline in the Vaal Triangle not only led to growing retrenchment of the established labour force, but a decrease in employment prospects for young people. Consequently, youth unemployment rose and school students faced an uncertain future, providing fertile ground for a new generation of radicalised youth with little to lose and much to gain. The first generation of COSAS leaders had been at the forefront of the uprisings of 1976, and through the likes of Joe Gqabi in Soweto, were in contact with the ANC underground. While COSAS initially accommodated both BC adherents and Charterists, its name and direction signalled a clear shift towards Charterism and away from the BC-led movement of the 1970s.[45]

During the following months, local branches of COSAS sprang up across the country. On 21 March 1980, a meeting to commemorate the twentieth anniversary of the Sharpeville massacre, held at Mphatlalatsane Hall in Zone 14, Sebokeng, and organised by AZAPO, led to the establishment of a COSAS branch in the Vaal Triangle. AZAPO, which by then was the only political organisation in the region, had organised the commemoration service and invited AZAPO's Curtis Nkondo and Khehla Mthembu as speakers.[46] While AZAPO and Charterist organisations would soon descend into a bloody feud costing dozens of lives in the Eastern Cape and elsewhere, during the early 1980s these animosities had not yet come to the fore. Gcina Malindi was elected chairman in October 1980 and Simon Tseko Nkoli became secretary.

45   See Heffernan, 'Blurred Lines and Ideological Divisions', p.671.
46   WHP AK2117, S7.6, Statement GP Malindi, 7; WHP AK2117, I2.12, Vol.243, Testimony Nkoli, pp.12957–58.

Reasons for joining COSAS were manifold. First and foremost, COSAS provided a platform for student grievances. The abolition of corporal punishment, the distribution of free textbooks, an end to sexual harassment of female students, the provision of better resources and the introduction of democratically elected Student Representative Councils (SRCs) were all issues on the agenda of students.[47] Some were also concerned about the imposition of age restrictions at schools that disallowed students above a certain age from attending classes. COSAS also afforded its members a degree of protection from harassment and beatings: 'They cannot beat us as much as they used to do. So we can do our things as much as we like now because we are now COSAS!'[48] For other students, it was curiosity that led them to join COSAS, as Oupa Masankane recalls: 'We are kids and we are inquisitive and so on. We attended. And we hear these elder brothers talking about politics.'[49] Most students who joined COSAS regarded their struggle as being part of a broader struggle for freedom. It was the structure of society, and political oppression and socio-economic injustice more broadly, that shaped the daily experiences of young people in the townships.[50]

During its formative years, the Vaal Triangle branch of COSAS had a limited membership and its main activities were restricted to the organisation of commemoration services and addressing student grievances. Significantly, COSAS was the first organisation to take up the rent issue. The socio-economic difficulties, especially rent increases, affected students profoundly as their families experienced being locked out of their houses and as less and less money was available for school fees, textbooks or uniforms.[51] Electricity cut-offs prevented students from studying at night and hence impacted their progress at school.[52] COSAS was therefore acutely aware of the embeddedness of student grievances. Student leader Khulu Malindi noted that 'we maintained the stand of COSAS that if our parents can't afford to pay this, if they pay higher rents it means it's going to affect us and the welfare of us as students'.[53] This sentiment was reflected in official statements issued by COSAS, which called on workers and students to support each other's demands.[54] In 1982, after the announcement by the Vaal Triangle Community Council that

47   Heffernan, *Limpopo's Legacy*.
48   Themba Goba, interview with author, Vereeniging, 18 June 2010.
49   Oupa Masankane, interview with author, Vereeniging, 29 June 2010.
50   WHP A2675, III (396), 'Speech delivered at the 4th National Council, December 1982'; 'United Action for Democratic Education: Interview with COSAS Activists', *Africa Perspective*, 24 (1984), pp.77–80.
51   Thami ka Plaatjie, interview with author, Vanderbijlpark, 14 June 2010.
52   Sakhiwe Khumalo, interview with author, Vereeniging, 23 June 2010.
53   Khulu Malindi, interview with author, Johannesburg, 22 November 2018.
54   Heffernan, *Limpopo's Legacy*, p.158. Heffernan notes that during the early years of COSAS, these alliances were mostly rhetoric.

rents would be increased by R16 (see Chapter 2), COSAS held a series of meetings at the Roman Catholic Church in Evaton Small Farms and organised a modest protest march.[55]

Besides offering a platform to address grievances, COSAS also provided a space in which young black South Africans found a sense of belonging, purpose and excitement. COSAS became an emotional and ideological home that transcended issues of poverty and repression and allowed young activists to dream of a better future. Regular meetings of the Southern Transvaal region, held in Johannesburg and elsewhere, cemented networks and exposed COSAS members to the struggles and plights of students in other regions. While political networks formed in the 1950s and 1960s were lying dormant and little activity was registered among elderly residents, some key figures served as an inspiration and source of information. Student leader Mandla Mazibuko remembered that Levai Mbatha, an ANC stalwart who maintained his communication with the ANC's leadership, would 'tell us about the struggles of the 50s, the bus boycotts. Those make us very proud.'[56]

Armed propaganda, such as the attack on SASOL in 1980, served as an inspiration for many youth. With the symbolic and physical presence of the ANC and its armed wing, youth increasingly identified with MK's soldiers, whom they regarded as their heroes. Subsequently, throughout the 1980s, the political culture of youth became militarised, with symbols of MK present at meetings, rallies and funerals of activists.[57] Songs were sung praising the exploits of MK and the strength and bravery of detained and exiled leaders. Lyrics were changed to adapt to local circumstances: *uMandela ufuna amajoni/amajoni nkululeko*, for example, was changed to *uMatsobane ufuna amajoni/amajoni nkululeko* (Matsobane wants soldiers/soldiers for freedom).[58] Another popular song reflected the role the youth envisaged for themselves: *Singamasosha ka Mandela, sosha sosha... lapho lapho lapho siyakhona, thina silindela ukufa kwethu* (We are Mandela's soldiers... wherever we go, we are waiting for our death).[59] Street wisdom and bravery were key for young activists. It was a highly masculinist environment in which few women played a leading role.[60]

---

55   *Sowetan*, 26 February 1982.

56   Mandla Mazibuko, interview with author, Vanderbijlpark, 22 June 2010.

57   See, for example, T. Simpson, '"Umkhonto we Sizwe, We Are Waiting for You": The ANC and the Township Uprising, September 1984–September 1985', *South African Historical Journal*, 61/1 (2009), pp.158–77; J. Seekings, *Heroes or Villains: Youth Politics in the 1980s* (Johannesburg, Ravan Press, 1993).

58   Gcina Malindi, interview with author, Johannesburg, 21 July 2010.

59   Thami ka Plaatjie, interview with author, Vanderbijlpark, 14 June 2010.

60   Emily Bridger has explored the role of young women in resistance politics during the 1980s. See E. Bridger, 'Soweto's Female Comrades: Gender, Youth and Violence in South Africa's Township Uprisings, 1984–1986', *Journal of Southern African Studies*, 44/4 (2018), pp.559–74.

In May 1982, the NEC of COSAS took a resolution that non-schoolgoing youth should no longer be allowed to be in leadership positions within COSAS. Hence, in early 1982, a meeting attended by over a hundred youth was held to elect a new committee and Gcina Malindi was replaced by his brother Mkhambi as chairman; a few months later, Jerry Tlhopane assumed the position of acting chairman.[61] Both Tlhopane and the Malindi brothers were arrested in late 1984 and charged with treason during the Delmas treason trial. In 1982, a group of COSAS activists began to look into the formation of a regional youth congress to accommodate unemployed and non-schoolgoing youth. These congresses began to spring up across urban townships.[62] Yet in the Vaal Triangle, progress was slow and by 1984, the youth congress had still not been established; this contrasted with Soweto, for example, where the Soweto Youth Congress (SOYCO) was set up in July 1983. Many working and unemployed youth in the Vaal Triangle were out of the reach of organised politics.[63] One of the young men involved in setting up a youth structure was Edward 'Chippa' Motubatsi. Motubatsi and Malindi had both travelled to Botswana to establish contact with the ANC in exile; Motubatsi had been recruited by Esau Ralitsela in 1982 and after his return from Botswana, where he had joined MK, he was given the mandate to oversee the establishment of youth structures. Motubatsi would play an important role during the state of emergency (see Chapter 7).[64] Malindi, with his high profile in the region, was encouraged by the ANC in exile to continue operating above ground and to aid in the formation of youth structures.[65] Malindi's contacts with the ANC were sporadic. Like others, he received instructions from Esau Ralitsela and from ANC operatives during mass rallies.[66]

Smaller groups existed that dealt with local grievances and bread-and-butter issues. The Bophelong Youth Association, for example, established during the early 1980s, ran seminars educating residents about everyday matters including family planning, and they held classes to teach mathematics and science. Tsietsi 'Stompi' Mokhele, one of the leading activists in Bophelong, was later recruited by Motubatsi to join MK in Botswana. For this generation, political education was key and many young people deep-

61   WHP AK2117, I2.7, Vol.205, Testimony Malindi, p.10740; Pelamotse Jerry Tlhopane, interview with author, Sebokeng, 22 November 2011.

62   In the rural areas, this would take longer. See Heffernan, *Limpopo's Legacy*.

63   J. Seekings, 'Why Was Soweto Different? Urban Development, Township Politics, and the Political Economy of Soweto, 1977–1984' (African Studies seminar paper, University of the Witwatersrand, 1988). Seekings notes that SOYCO held regular meetings but played no significant role in overall politics during this period.

64   Edward 'Chippa' Motubatsi, interview with author, Vereeniging, 22 November 2011.

65   Gcina Malindi, interview with author, Johannesburg, 25 March 2010.

66   Ibid., 21 July 2010.

ened their knowledge about history, anticolonial struggles elsewhere, the law and politics through regular debates.[67]

'*Asinamali!*': The Vaal Civic Association

Partly as a consequence of the Ralitselas' work as an underground unit, partly owing to growing discontent among the population, a small group of people came together in 1982 to form an action committee that was later named the Vaal Action Committee (VAC). The group included Thabiso Ratsomo, who had been imprisoned on Robben Island for his involvement in the student protests of 1976, Edward 'Chippa' Motubatsi, Esau and Dorcas Ralitsela, Edith Letlhake, Sam Matlole, Ernest Sotsu and Gcina Malindi.[68] The VCA was a 'semi-clandestine thing', a 'think-tank' as Esau Ralitsela recalls.[69] The majority of the members, with the exception of Sam Matlole and Ernest Sotsu, were in their mid-twenties to mid-thirties. Importantly, almost all of them had direct or indirect contact with the ANC in exile and subscribed to the ideological content of the Freedom Charter.

During the following months, members of the VAC convened several meetings to plan for the formation of a more permanent civic structure that would be operating above ground. Safe spaces for meetings were scarce and much of the more covert planning and debate occurred in small and private spaces that were difficult to surveil. The blurred boundaries between the domestic and the public, the private and the political, would become one of the defining features of resistance politics during the final decade of the struggle against white minority rule.

On 16 June 1983, during the annual commemoration of the student uprisings of 1976, a watershed meeting took place at the Nyolohelo Roman Catholic Church in Zone 12 in Sebokeng. It was chaired by Jerry Tlhopane, the acting chairman of COSAS, and included speakers representing COSAS, AZAPO, and the Orange Vaal General Workers Union (OVGWU).[70] Addressing a crowd of about 900 people, one speaker after another called for the formation of a civic association that would take up socio-economic struggles of the local communities. One of the speakers was Phillip Masia, the general secretary of OVGWU. Masia, who had been collaborating with Esau Ralitsela through the Industrial Aid Centre, had emerged as one of the key unionists in the region and was a strong supporter of the unions' involvement in community affairs.[71]

67   Tsiesi 'Stompi' Mokhele, interview with author, Bophelong, 18 September 2011.
68   Esau Ralitsela, interview with author, Vereeniging, 5 April 2010.
69   Ibid.
70   Pelamotse Jerry Tlhopane, interview with author, Sebokeng, 22 November 2011.
71   While some unions such as OVGWU supported the close collaboration between civic structures and unions, the policy of others affirmed that union activism should

OVGWU promoted non-racialism and mass mobilisation of workers across different trade unions, while opposing registration and industrial councils.[72] Its key demand was wages that would reflect inflation, as well as protection against retrenchment, victimisation and harassment. OVGWU's condemnation of the constitutional reforms and its critique of the harshness of influx control, however, was a clear indication of its belief that workers' struggles were embedded in the broader struggle for freedom.[73] In the Vaal Triangle, the Industrial Aid Centre had long served as a point of contact between the shop floor and community grievances and, through its contacts, the VCA was able to mobilise workers. A survey conducted in the aftermath of the meeting confirmed the local communities' desire for a civic structure that would take up their plight.[74] Key issues that were identified included high rents, a lack of proper road signs, electricity and recreational facilities, and a lack of trust and confidence in community councils.

Finally, on 9 October 1983, the VCA was launched. Reverend Lord McCamel, a local priest from Evaton who was running his own church, was elected chairman. A well-known community leader in Evaton, McCamel had played a leading role in the struggle against the loss of freehold title.[75] His background as a teacher at Wilberforce Institute, his status as a clergyman and his access to church facilities made him an ideal candidate for the VCA executive. Esau Ralitsela was elected vice-chairman, Thabiso Ratsomo treasurer, Johnny Motete secretary and Mike Kgaka vice secretary.[76] Kgaka, like Dorcas Ralitsela, had studied at the University of the North during the early 1970s and retained strong leanings towards the BCM. While Ralitsela, being an underground activist, would have preferred to abstain from involvement in executive functions of above ground organisations, he found it impossible to reject his nomination. This overlap was unfortunate as it exposed him to renewed attention from the security branch, which ANC underground members were encouraged to avoid. Yet given a lack of candidates, Ralitsela accepted his nomination. The other two members of the unit, Dorcas Ral-

---

remain restricted to the shop floor. *Directory: South Africa's Independent Trade Unions,* https://www.sahistory.org.za/sites/default/files/archive-files/LaJan86.0377. 5429.011.003.Jan1986.16.pdf, retrieved 20 April 2020.

72   'OVGWU Proposals for Labour Unity', *South African Labour Bulletin,* 8/5 (1983), pp.57–63. While OVGWU lobbied for the unification of workers, it was opposed to the formation of a federation that would unite the unions.

73   'OVGWU Proposals for Labour Unity', *South African Labour Bulletin,* 8/5 (1983), pp.57–63.

74   WHP AK2117, S8.4.3, 'Memorandum on the Background of the Formation of the VCA'.

75   Lord McCamel, interview with author, Evaton, 2 May 2006.

76   *Sowetan,* 11 October 1983.

itsela and MaLetanta, similarly struggled to avoid serving in the executive committee of the VOW, established a few months later. Conversely, the hesitance of local residents to be elected into leading positions provided space for the ANC-aligned activists to shape the strategies and the discourse of civic politics. From its inception, the VCA was therefore strongly influenced by the Ralitselas' underground activities and the political beliefs of other ANC-aligned activists.

As noted, the emergence of organised politics had been slow in the region. The VCA struggled to attract members into its executive, partly a result of the impact of forced removals, which left residents unsettled and without a sense of community, and partly as a consequence of repression and collective fear of state brutality. 'It took very brave people or very naïve people to go to these meetings. You see people sometimes find themselves in meetings because they were curious to go and listen,' Dorcas Ralitsela recalls.[77]

Similar to the manner in which the Freedom Charter was drafted, pieces of paper were distributed to encourage the audience to write down the demands they deemed important. After receiving these popular inputs, the VCA resolved to

- demand decent housing and security for all
- demand low rentals that we can afford
- demand that we must not be charged for the maintenance of houses
- demand proper roads with adequate road signs
- condemn the disparity between black and white pension grants and the distressing conditions under which African pensioners receive, meagre (little) as they are, their pension grants
- demand unhindered access into community facilities like halls, schools and demand that they be at our disposal
- demand adequate schools and call on our teachers not to turn away pupils for petty issues such as uniforms
- condemn the high bus fares
- demand adequate recreational facilities
- condemn the concerted efforts by the government to strip the Evaton people of their freehold rights; we demand that our people be left in peace
- condemn the community councils as puppet bodies and to boycott the Black Local Authorities elections since we believe that nothing would be achieved by voting
- condemn and reject the homeland system and in particular the Ciskei government for its atrocities committed against our people
- condemn the banning of SAAWU [South African Allied Workers Union]

77   Dorcas Ralitsela, interview with author, Vereeniging, 1 April 2010.

and to pledge our solidarity with our people in the Ciskei
- elect an interim committee comprising five office-bearers and area-representatives.[78]

Points added in handwriting after the resolutions were printed resolved to

- condemn the government's attempts to phase out minibus taxis
- demand special rent concessions for our pensioners, widows and invalid people
- condemn the present education system which dominates blacks and indoctrinates whites and in its place we demand a democratic [illegible] education system
- to strive for the establishment of an advice and information centre
- to form area committees of the association
- to affiliate through the association to the United Democratic Front (UDF)
- We pledge to strive for unity of our people under the banner of the Vaal Civic Association, to strive for unity and cooperation with our people in other areas of the country, and to cooperate with progressive genuine people's organisations in the country.

The VCA's resolutions are noteworthy for a variety of reasons. The language and content bore striking resemblance to the Freedom Charter of 1955; the very opening, demanding 'decent housing and security for all', was almost taken verbatim from the Freedom Charter.

Significantly, and in contrast to the Freedom Charter, the VCA's formulations were couched in a language different from that of the Charter. While the Freedom Charter stated broad objectives, the VCA's resolutions used the language of demands and rights to frame objectives. It was therefore not merely the broad vision of a free and equal society the Freedom Charter espoused, but a clear assertion of what the population felt was their right. While borrowing from the ideological framework of the Freedom Charter, the demands that underpinned the VCA's political philosophy were concrete, rooted in everyday grievances and based on the principles of a social democratic welfare state. The VCA's demands therefore reflected a rejection of government's plans to privatise township housing and reaffirmed a vision that encompassed a decent and dignified life for all. Enmeshed with demands for social rights was the call for representation and political power, and the rejection of the bantustans. These limited demands were translated into an encompassing call for social transformation and political power in the aftermath of the 1984 uprising.

78   WHP AK2117, J3.13, AN13, 'Resolutions of the Vaal Civic Association'.

The formation of the VCA marked the beginning of a period of organised protest. Its structures were democratically elected and aimed at being representative.
As such, the VCA laid the groundwork for the establishment of street and area
committees from 1985 (see Chapter 7). Calculations by the defence lawyers of the
Delmas treason trial later suggested that between 1,500 and 5,000 people attended
the launch of the VCA – a vague number, and less than some Soweto rallies, but
indicative of the support the new civic structure attracted.[79] The rallying slogan
of the VCA, 'Asinamali [we have no money] – organise or be homeless', was well
chosen for its powerful simplicity and its ability to evoke memories of past slogans
of the 1950s. It had been used during the bus boycotts in Alexandra and Evaton in
1955.[80] Guest speakers included Curtis Nkondo, chairman of the Transvaal branch
of the UDF, Dr Motlana, chairman of the Soweto Civic Association and Elliot
Shabangu, another senior member of the UDF, who had been involved in the
ANC underground in Soweto since the 1970s.[81] The choice of speakers embedded
the newly formed VCA within a broader history of resistance and connected the
organisation to the central structures of the UDF; shortly after its formation, the
VCA affiliated to the UDF. Above-ground structures such as the VCA and COSAS
were allegedly infiltrated by informers early on, and information on planned activities and debates was passed on to the security branch.[82] To protect their ANC
underground cell, as operatives Dorcas and Esau Ralitsela noted, discussions
within the VCA were therefore strictly confined to bread-and-butter issues.[83]

The VCA's first campaign was the boycott of local government elections
in October and November 1983. In Bophelong, the campaign was particularly successful and not a single vote was allegedly cast.[84] Together with Boipatong, Bophelong was the smallest township in the Vaal Triangle and for
decades both townships were off the radar of authorities, activists and journalists.[85] With only 1,400 houses, the smallness of Bophelong had a double
effect on the emergence of political networks: on the one hand, activists
could be easily identified and monitored by the security branch, while on
the other hand the relatively small number of households facilitated door-
to-door campaigns and canvassing.

79   WHP AK2117, S8.4.2, 'Memorandum on the Background to the Formation of the
     VCA'.
80   T. Lodge, '"We Are Being Punished because We Are Poor": The Bus Boycotts of
     Evaton and Alexandra, 1955–1957', in T. Lodge, *Black Politics in South Africa since 1945*
     (London and New York, Longman, 1983), pp.153–87.
81   Houston, 'The ANC's Internal Underground Political Work in the 1980s', p.373.
82   Petrus Niemand and Andries du Toit, interview with author, West Rand, 10 May 2011
     (names have been changed).
83   Dorcas Ralitsela, interview with author, Vereeniging, 1 April 2010.
84   Tsietsi 'Stompi' Mokhele, interview with author, Bophelong, 18 September 2011.
85   Kedibone Mogotsi, interview with author, Vereeniging, 26 July 2010.

Structures of mobilisation were based on familiarity and trust. Inspired by the M-Plan, zonal committees were set up shortly after the launch of the VCA to represent the different areas of the townships, to ensure easy communication and to facilitate the mobilisation of residents.[86] Each zonal committee comprised of one representative from that area, who was well known and respected. In the words of Esau Ralitsela, 'Those people were able to mobilise people in those small areas. And as a result [...] we were able to move people.'[87] Not all areas or zones were equally well covered. Some zonal committees were launched as late as August 1984, while others were established shortly after the inception of the VCA in October 1983. Few major campaigns were conducted between the inception of the VCA and the uprising in September 1984, and it appears that the VCA's main function during this period was to provide assistance and advice to residents regarding housing and other socio-economic matters.

Two of the key areas at the forefront of civic politics were Zone 13 and Zone 7 in Sebokeng. They were among the oldest residential areas in Sebokeng and therefore comprised the most settled communities. Both had sympathetic churches in their vicinities that opened their doors for community meetings and political gatherings. From 1984, Zone 12 and Zone 11 provided a large number of the student leadership of COSAS; Boipatong and Bophelong produced their own small leadership. Evaton, with its special status as a freehold area, had developed separate forms of community organisation. There, the Evaton Ratepayers' Association (ERPA), launched in 1978 after the election of the Evaton Community Council, was key in struggling against Evaton's scheduled redevelopment and subdivision, which would have stripped its residents of their freehold titles. ERPA was collaborating with the VCA and had affiliated to the UDF, but maintained its distinct character as a vessel for Evaton's struggle for freehold rights.

'Women were on their own'

In January 1984, VOW was launched to mobilise women into participating in organised politics by addressing their specific needs and grievances.[88] During its

---

86   The M-Plan dates back to the 1940s and was revised during the early 1960s, when the ANC developed a new strategy to organise the population into streets and zones. For an analysis of the M-Plan's impact on the ANC's efforts to build the underground, see R. Suttner, 'The African National Congress (ANC) Underground: From the M-Plan to Rivonia', *South African Historical Journal*, 49/1 (2003), pp.123–46. For an account of the M-Plan's 'failure', see P. Landau, 'The M-Plan: Mandela's Struggle to Reorient the African National Congress', *Journal of Southern African Studies*, 45/6, Special Issue: Reassessing Mandela (2019), pp.1073–91.

87   Esau Ralitsela, interview with author, Vereeniging, 5 April 2010.

88   WHP AK2117, I2.27, Vol.328, Testimony Oliphant, pp.18764ff.; WHP AK2117, I2.27, Vol.328, Testimony Nyembe, pp.18678ff.

launch, Amanda Kwadi of the Federation of South African Women (FEDSAW) and Aubrey Mokoena of the RMC addressed the gathering. The presence of these two speakers was a clear signal that the newly formed organisation saw itself as part of a broader struggle for freedom. Declaring 1984 to be the 'year of the women', the ANC's leadership had called for the formation of women's structures during its 8 January message. The formation of VOW, initiated by Dorcas Ralitsela, undoubtedly followed this call. The abbreviation VOW was reminiscent of the ANC publication *Voice of Women* and chosen for that reason. VOW resolved to affiliate to the UDF and collaborated with FEDSAW, another Charterist organisation.[89]

Yet VOW, chaired by MaLetanta and including Dorcas Ralitsela and Edith Letlhake as secretary, pursued a conservative programme. It was a far cry from a feminist organisation; its significance lay less in its ability to lobby for gender equality and more in its capacity to address everyday grievances of women. VOW was not exceptional in this regard. Gender equality and patriarchy were hardly ever discussed in such organisations, and neither was sexual violence, which was rife during this period. Many women attending VOW's meetings would have been alienated by fiery feminist speech, while activists themselves often prioritised the broader struggle for freedom. Kwadi, for example, raised her suspicions of feminism when she emphasised that '[t]he idea of feminism goes hand in hand with capitalism and imperialism, something which the Women's Federation in South Africa denounces'.[90] These conceptions reflected the deeply patriarchal nature of South African society, and the strict gender divisions that saw women relegated to the home and men assume leadership positions. The executive committee of the VCA, for example, was predominantly male; this imbalance obscured the key role women like Dorcas Ralitsela and MaLetanta played in politicising and mobilising their communities.

But even though organisations like VOW were hardly feminist, it contributed towards the alleviation of women's grievances when it launched a programme of childcare and adult literacy as well as a grocery co-operative.[91] Mobilisation and recruitment was done through tea parties where women's issues as well as broader political concerns were discussed.[92] Under the banner of 'motherism', women's

89   WHP AK2117, J3.13, AN1, 'Letter by the Vaal Organisation of Women to UDF re Affiliation'. On FEDSAW, see for example M. Healy-Clancy, 'The Family Politics of the Federation of South African Women: A History of Public Motherhood in Women's Antiracist Activism', *Signs: Journal of Women in Culture and Society*, 42/4 (2017), pp.843–66.

90   Amanda Kwadi, quoted in van Kessel, *Beyond Our Wildest Dreams*, p.181.

91   WHP A2675 III (440), 'Report Federation of South African Women: Transvaal Workshop'.

92   Dorcas Ralitsela, interview with author, Vereeniging, 1 April 2010.

demands, as reflected in the Women's Charter of Demands of 1954, impacted on the manner in which social rights were conceptualised and envisaged.[93] On a national scale, 'concrete demands went beyond a general political call for the extension of political citizenship and reflected the importance placed by women on the creation of an inclusive welfare state', as Shireen Hassim notes.[94] The building of crèches, the demand for maternity leave, maternity homes and antenatal clinics, for example, were all part of the demands espoused in the Women's Charter.[95] These demands were incorporated into the Freedom Charter a year later, even though the Freedom Charter's formulations obscured the relevance of gender and instead noted the 'need for a national health service and a welfare state'.[96]

During the civic struggles of the early 1980s, women were often in the forefront of attending meetings and marches.[97] Overcrowding, evictions and an inability to access housing all had a very direct bearing on women's lives. They were the ones who had to make ends meet and, due to the patriarchal nature of society, faced a series of issues.[98] While men typically acted as heads of household, in many instances women informally assumed the role. Struggling to access men's wages to pay for rent, household expenses, school fees, books and school uniforms, women were in a particularly vulnerable position. Their status and their ability to reside in a house were often tied to marriage, as noted in the previous chapter, and many widows were evicted as they could not rent houses in their own name. Housing therefore came to be one of the rallying causes for women, as Dorcas Ralitsela recalls.[99]

The Launch of the UDF

Many of these community structures were brought together under one roof with the launch of the UDF on 20 August 1983.[100] Under the slogan 'UDF unites, apartheid divides', a great diversity of groups including youth and student structures, religious groups, civic associations, trade unions and sports clubs united. Yet the link the between the ANC's call for action and the upsurge of popular protest is not as direct as the readings of ANC material might suggest. While the ANC had been calling to form a broad front as early as 1981, and many of the UDF's leaders such as Popo Molefe were directly or indirectly linked to the

93   S. Hassim, 'Turning Gender Rights into Entitlements: Women and Welfare Provision in Post-Apartheid South Africa', *Social Research*, 72/3 (2005), p.625.

94   Ibid, p.626.

95   Ibid., p.625.

96   Ibid., p.626.

97   See J. Seekings, 'Gender Ideology and Township Politics in the 1980s', *Agenda*, 10 (1991), pp.77–88.

98   Dorcas Ralitsela, interview with author, Vereeniging, 1 April 2010.

99   Ibid.

100 See Seekings, *The UDF*; van Kessel, *Beyond Our Wildest Dreams*.

ANC in exile, either by working as underground operatives or by broadly identifying with the ANC's strategies and ideology, the UDF was always much more than a mere front for the ANC, as Seekings and other scholars have shown.[101]

A number of activists from the Vaal Triangle attended the launch of the UDF. A few weeks after its national launch, during the same period that preparations for the launch of the VCA were under way, the Transvaal leadership of the UDF hosted a meeting at the Roman Catholic Church in Evaton Small Farms to introduce the Front's aims.[102] Amongst the speakers were Popo Molefe, the national secretary of the UDF, and Mmereki Bokala, an executive member of the UDF Transvaal. They explained to the audience why the UDF had been formed and talked about the dire effects the 'Koornhof bills' were going to have on township communities. Molefe allegedly tried to harness support for a UDF committee in the Vaal Triangle but was informed that plans to form a civic association were under way.

The VCA supported the UDF's campaigns, such as the 'Million Signature' campaign, launched to voice opposition to the planned constitutional reforms.[103] But as various records demonstrate, the national executive of the UDF was often not well informed about the dynamics and happenings in the various townships. This became particularly evident in September 1984, when protest action in the townships of the Vaal Triangle ignited a large-scale insurrection (see Chapters 4 and 5).[104] The main reason for the physical absence of the UDF as a steering force for change in the townships can be explained by the initial impetus for its formation. Launched in August 1983 to co-ordinate broad opposition to the introduction of the tricameral parliament, it focused on national rather than local politics and was 'born in a context which distracted it from local issues central to African township politics', as Jeremy Seekings has noted.[105] The UDF's aim was therefore to broaden the struggle, while many township activists sought to intensify it.[106] Affiliates thus often followed their own agenda and only loosely associated themselves with the national programme of the UDF. Furthermore, none of the members of the Regional Executive Committee (REC) of the Transvaal region were based in the urban townships of the East Rand, the Vaal Triangle or the West Rand, with the exception of Soweto.[107] During a meeting held

101   Seekings, *The UDF*.
102   WHP AK2117, S8.4.3, 'Memorandum on the Background of the Formation of the VCA'; WHP AK2117, I2.13, Vol.251, Testimony Molefe, pp.13460–62.
103   Edward 'Chippa' Motubatsi, interview with author, Vereeniging, 5 December 2011.
104   See, for example, AK 2117, J2.23.X9, 'Circular to All Regions, September 1984'.
105   J. Seekings, '"Trailing Behind the Masses": The United Democratic Front and Township Politics in the Pretoria–Witwatersrand–Vaal Region, 1983–84', *Journal of Southern African Studies*, 18/1 (1992), p.94.
106   Ibid.
107   Seekings, *The UDF*, p.74. The UDF had a federal structure. The overall structure was

on 10 December 1983, members of the General Council complained that the UDF was not in a position to guide the struggle for liberation in the townships.[108] To improve access to the different regions, the UDF General Council meeting of the Transvaal region held on 30 June 1984 concluded that area committees should be set up, including the Vaal Triangle region. The committees were called a 'priority and matter of urgency', which highlights how much the individual regions were cut off from the central structures of the UDF.[109]

The UDF therefore mainly provided ideological leadership as well as access to resources including printing facilities, T-shirts and stickers. It further linked various regions by organising workshops. From 27 to 29 April 1984, a handful of activists from the Vaal Triangle participated in a workshop organised by the UDF education committee.[110] Opposition to the Black Local Authorities, the strengthening of civic structures, the role of house-to-house campaigns in mobilising communities, the Million Signature campaign as well as the relationship between the bantustans and the urban areas were discussed.[111]

AZAPO and the Different Route of Sharpeville

While large parts of the Vaal Triangle were under the sway of Charterist groups, Sharpeville was home to Africanist and BC-oriented politics. The township was traditionally claimed by the Pan Africanist Congress (PAC) and AZAPO, a descendant of the BCM of the 1970s. The VCA made few inroads and Sharpeville's leadership remained largely unconnected to activists in Sebokeng and elsewhere.

One of the leading protagonists against rent increases in Sharpeville was Reverend Tebogo Geoffrey Moselane. In his capacity as an Anglican priest, he had been running community projects since the early 1980s. Moselane had spent his student days at the seminary in Alice, known for its engagement with Black Theology and adjacent to the University of Fort Hare, which was a hotbed of BC.[112]

---

comprised of the NEC, with a National General Council. This overall structure was duplicated at the regional level, with RECs and regional general councils. The third layer included affiliated organisations, including the VCA and the VOW, among hundreds of others.

108 WHP AK2117, J2.13, N3, 'Secretarial Report to the General Council Meeting Held on 10th December 1983'.

109 WHP AK2117, J2.16, Q1, 'Letter to Affiliates in the Transvaal Region, 5th of July 1984'; Seekings, '"Trailing Behind the Masses"', p.97.

110 WHP AK2117, J2.20, U4-e, 'U.D.F. Education Committee – Education Programme for Civics. 27–29 April 1984, Daleside'.

111 WHP AK2117, I2.6, Vol.200, Testimony Mphuthi [sic], pp.10464ff.

112 See D. Magaziner, *The Law and the Prophets: Black Consciousness in South Africa, 1968–1977* (Athens, Ohio University Press, 2010) and P. Denis, 'Seminary Networks and Black Consciousness in South Africa in the 1970s', *South African Historical Journal*, 62/1 (2010), pp.162–82.

His opposition to Charterism was well known among VCA activists. Through his involvement with the SASO, Moselane had met prominent leaders of the BCM on several occasions, including Steve Biko.[113] During the student uprisings of 1976, Moselane had been a priest in Soweto, where he engaged with some of the student leaders of the Vaal Triangle including Simon Nkoli.

Black Theology was prominent among many of the local ministers in the Vaal Triangle, and Moselane's support for it was no secret. His sympathies for AZAPO, however, for which organisation he was vice president in Soweto in 1979, were less public because of his position as a clergyman within the community. AZAPO had been established in 1979 as successor of the banned BCM and, like its predecessors, AZAPO was as much an intellectual endeavour as one emphasising community care and upliftment. AZAPO, like other political organisations, rejected the introduction of the tricameral parliament and the 'Koornhof bills' that included the Black Local Authorities Act. Even though AZAPO played a significant role in pockets of the Vaal Triangle, it was eclipsed by the VCA in terms of mobilising the broader population.

In the Vaal Triangle, an interim AZAPO committee was established in March 1980, and a more permanent committee formed a few months later with Kebi Shabangu as its chairperson.[114] Shabangu was later succeeded by Oupa Hlomuka. Hlomuka, born in Evaton in 1954, had first-hand experience of socio-economic grievances and the harshness of influx control in his position as clerk for the administration board.[115] He was later involved in the organisation of workers through the Black Allied Workers Union (BAWU), established to spread BC's teachings to the shop floor. A keen admirer of Gibson Kente's theatre, the poetry of Ingoapele Madingoane, the novels of Mosibudi Mangena and Biko's writing, he first came into contact with BC through reading the *World* and was radicalised by Steve Biko's death on 12 September 1977.

In contrast to the success of civic structures in mobilising and organising the township population, AZAPO's strength was in the conscientisation of communities, the running of welfare projects and the organisation of commemoration services. Hence, while AZAPO rejected government structures and opposed co-operation with local councils, it never developed a systematic approach on how to organise the population.[116] It was not a mass-based movement, but a vanguard organisation of educated activists whose intellectual political language failed to capture the popular sentiments of the people.[117] By early 1984,

113 WHP AK2117, I2.10, Vol.229, Testimony Moselane, pp.12152–54.

114 WHP AK2117, S22.3, 'Notes on the Formation of the Vaal Branch of AZAPO'.

115 Oupa Hlomuka, interview with author, Vanderbijlpark, 9 July 2010.

116 WHP AK2117, S22.3, 'A Brief History of the Azanian People's Organisation, Prepared by the President of Azapo, Ishmael Mkhabela'.

117 For an analysis of AZAPO's strategies, see M.V. Mzamane and B. Maaba, 'The Azanian People's Organisation, 1977–1990', in SADET (ed.), *The Road to Democracy, Volume 4*.

relations between AZAPO and Charterist organisations in the Vaal Triangle were tense as Sharpeville followed different strategies. Yet despite their ideological differences and their mutual political intolerance, AZAPO, and Moselane, Hlomuka and Thomas Manthata from Soweto in particular, would later be accused during the Delmas treason trial of conspiring with the ANC and the South African Communist Party to overthrow the South African government. Rather than reflecting the reality on the ground, these allegations were part of the state prosecution's attempt to delegitimise political organisations by casting their activities as treasonous. But notwithstanding the different nature of politics in Sharpeville, the impact of rent increases, poverty and falling living standards led Sharpeville's population to attend meetings at Moselane's church to discuss their grievances. As elsewhere in the Vaal Triangle, the mood was rapidly changing.

4

'Like people having been enclosed suddenly exploding': 3 September 1984

A Change of Mood

The first day of September is traditionally known as Spring Day in South Africa, marking the end of winter and the reawakening of nature. Winter in the Vaal Triangle is harsh, with greatly varying temperatures that occasionally drop below zero degrees at night and reach up to 20 degrees during the day. Blue skies, uninterrupted by clouds, give a sense of infinity while red and brown dust covers the dry grassland vegetation that characterises the majority of the South African Highveld. The mighty summer thunderstorms are still a few weeks away. However, when September arrived in 1984, more than a new season had started: 3 September, referred to as 'bloody Monday' by some, heralded the beginning of the most sustained period of popular protest against the apartheid regime. As advocate George Bizos later recalled, it was in the townships of the Vaal Triangle where 'the liberation revolution began in earnest.'[1]

The nature and timing of uprisings can never be predicted, for the presence of a committed and organised leadership and an ideological programme are not enough. Without the participation of the population and the formation of crowds, there is no uprising. Participation in public protests, particularly within a context in which state repression is probable, requires a change of mood and frame of mind. By the 1980s, the collective memory of the Sharpeville shootings was fading for a new generation of activists, yet response to protests elsewhere left little doubt that the police were unlikely to show much restraint in the event of organised protest action. As will be seen, the escalation of violence surprised many, including local communities and the civic leadership, who had planned a peaceful march and instead witnessed the unfolding of an uprising.

---

1   Comment by advocate George Bizos at a thanksgiving function at the Mmabatho stadium in November 1996, quoted in P. Noonan, *They're Burning the Churches: The Final Dramatic Events that Scuttled Apartheid* (Bellevue, Jacana, 2003), p.13.

For many outsiders, the Vaal Triangle was an unexpected locus of popular protests. After years of apparent 'quiescence' and the Vaal Triangle's reputation as the country's showcase of 'successful social engineering', what transpired on 3 September 1984 appeared out of the ordinary. A closer look, however, reveals that discontent had been brewing for years and tensions between councillors and residents had reached boiling point. Grievances regarding housing and worsening living conditions, together with deepening dissatisfaction with local authorities, provided fertile ground for mass mobilisation. 'People knew what they were doing,' Dorcas Ralitsela remembers.[2] 'Clearly, that September 3 incident was not a spontaneous reaction. And also, it was not just about rents.'

Different explanations are given for the choice of date. Some claim that the warmth of spring would enable a broader spectrum of residents to participate in collective action outdoors. Others argue that the date was chosen to coincide with the first sitting of the tricameral parliament: public protests were aimed at diverting the attention to the townships of the Vaal Triangle to embarrass the South African government and to emphasise the exclusion of the African majority from the new constitutional framework. But the most significant reason was the announcement of the latest rent and service levy increase of R5.90, due to come into effect on 1 September 1984.

Plans began to take shape in July, around the time when a protest march against a rent increase in Tumahole, a small township outside Parys in the Free State, which fell under the jurisdiction of the Orange Vaal Development Board, escalated into violence.[3] Tumahole was not the first locus of confrontation between aggrieved residents and local authorities; townships across the country had seen the emergence of protests over bread-and-butter issues from the early 1980s.[4] The death in detention of one of the protestors, Johannes Ngalo, received global media coverage and led the Detainees' Parents Support Committee (DPSC), the Detainees' Support Committee (DESCOM) and the United Democratic Front (UDF) to issue a joint statement condemning Ngalo's death and the 'government's violent reaction to a peaceful protest'.[5] Owing to the nature of his death, Ngalo's funeral was highly politicised and was attended by activists from across the region including the Vaal Triangle.[6] Tsietsi 'Speech' Mokatsanyane recalls that word about the planned protests on 3 September was

2   Dorcas Ralitsela, interview with author, Vereeniging, 1 April 2010.
3   Gcina Malindi, interview with author, Johannesburg, 25 March 2010; Shaka Radebe, interview with author, Vereeniging, 23 July 2010; J. Seekings, 'Political Mobilisation in Tumahole, 1984–85', *Africa Perspective*, 1/7,8 (1989), pp.105–44.
4   J. Seekings, *The UDF: A History of the United Democratic Front in South Africa, 1983–1991* (Cape Town, David Philip, 2nd edition, 2015), p.121.
5   WHP AK2117 (*State v Baleka and 21 Others*), Case No.482/85, J3.9, AJ24, 'UDF and DPSC Press Statement'.
6   Dikeledi Tsotetsi, interview with author, Vanderbijlpark, 14 June 2010.

spread during Ngalo's funeral.[7] Tumahole's agitation against rent increases was
quickly curbed by police repression and protests fizzled out within days: the failure of Tumahole's activists to sustain the protests served as a lesson for activists
from the Vaal Triangle, as Mokatsanyane states.[8]

Relationships between Tumahole and the Vaal Triangle were close; less than
a hundred kilometres separated the two areas. One man in particular stands out
for the impact he had on political activists in the Vaal Triangle: Fezile Dabi, a law
student at Fort Hare and staunch member of the Azanian People's Organisation
(AZAPO), had visited the Vaal Triangle on various occasions. Dabi's oratorial
skills were legendary and as majestic as his physical build was slight. In Tumahole, he played a leading role in politicising youth through the Tumahole Student
Organisation (TSO), an organisation identifying with Black Consciousness. A
month prior to the rent protests in Tumahole, Dabi was invited to speak at the
annual commemoration of 16 June at the Nyolohelo Roman Catholic Church
in Sebokeng, where he shared a platform with speakers from the UDF, trade
unions and the Congress of South African Students (COSAS).

Mandla Mazibuko, a 16-year-old COSAS activist at that time, recalls that
between June and September 1984 the mood in the townships was changing
as the population became increasingly fed up with the council system and the
frequent rent increases.[9] The eruption of protest in Tumahole on 15 July was the
first clear indicator that public action relating to socio-economic grievances
and the rejection of the council system was gathering momentum. Elsewhere in
the country, tensions were simmering in response to rent increases announced
in these areas. In Atteridgeville near Pretoria, the mayor's house was petrol
bombed, and in Daveyton in the East Rand, six vehicles belonging to the development board were damaged and two schools were stoned.[10] In response, the
Daveyton and Atteridgeville town councils scrapped their proposed increase,
and in Ratanda in the East Rand, three community councillors resigned.[11]

The spark that eventually lit the flame in the Vaal Triangle was the announcement by the mayor of the Lekoa Town Council, Esau Mahlatsi, and the mayor of
Evaton Town Council, Sam Rabotapi, in early August to increase the rent, service
levies and municipal tariffs by R5.90 from an average of R62 to R67.90 per month.
Rent for privately owned houses was raised by R5.50 and residential permits for
standholders in Evaton by R6. The basic levy for electricity was increased from
R10 to R12 a month while the unit price for electricity went up from 52 cents to

7   Tsietsi 'Speech' Mokatsanyane, interview with author, Pretoria, 13 July 2010; Gcina
     Malindi, interview with author, Johannesburg, 25 March 2010.
8   Tsietsi 'Speech' Mokatsanyane, interview with author, Pretoria, 13 July 2010.
9   Mandla Mazibuko, interview with author, Vanderbijlpark, 22 June 2010.
10   'A Chronicle of Six Months of Township Unrest', *Indicator South Africa*, 2/4 (1985),
     p.6.
11   Ibid.

62 cents.[12] Initially, the increase was to be as high as R11.27, scheduled to cover current and capital cost increases.[13] But according to a memorandum issued by the Lekoa Town Council on 2 August 1984, the increase was reduced to R5.90 and the Lekoa Town Council accepted that the gap between the initial increase and the increment of R5.90 would be covered by accumulated funds.[14]

By then, 35,000 out of 60,000 households in the townships of the Vaal Triangle were in rent arrears and thus the announcement of yet another rent increase exacerbated an already volatile socio-economic situation.[15] The highest accumulation of arrears was in Zone 12 in Sebokeng where 70 percent of rentals were outstanding by August 1984.[16] Gcina Malindi remembers, 'It [the rent increase] made black people very angry, even at a political level. So there was for political mobilisation a very nice combination of the political objection to what apartheid was doing with this tricameral parliament and the hardships of the people in the townships and that combination then led to what the Vaal became.'[17]

Residents were informed through notices in the *Vaderland* and the *Rand Daily Mail* newspapers and a circular that was distributed in early August. The *Sowetan*, the most widely read newspaper, carried no notice. Fiscal strictures had stymied the development and upgrading of the townships and by the time the increase was announced, people were fed up. The imposition of yet another rent increase was baffling for many, given that the living conditions of the majority remained dire and little development was visible in the townships.

A meeting held on 5 August to announce the latest increase led to a heated confrontation when the deputy mayor of the Lekoa Town Council, Jacob Kuz-wayo Dlamini, allegedly pointed his gun at the audience.[18] Other councillors were reported to be ridiculing and laughing at residents when confronted.[19] But most councillors failed to hold report-back meetings to inform residents about the increase. Whether they feared their residents' response or whether they simply did not think it was important to consult with their constituencies remains unclear. But either way, the breaking point had been reached. The sheer

12   C. Cooper, J. Shindler, C. McCaul et al., *Race Relations Survey, 1984* (Johannesburg, South African Institute of Race Relations, 1985), p.389.

13   WHP AK2117, I1.8, Vol.55, Testimony Matthysen, p.2821.

14   WHP AK2117, 'Memorandum. Increased Tariffs and House Rental Applicable in the Area of Jurisdiction of the Town Council of Lekoa, Issued by the Lekoa Town Council'. Reference number unknown.

15   *Sunday Tribune*, 9 September 1984.

16   WHP AK2117, J4.15, AAQ24–5, 'Meeting of the Lekoa Town Council on 18 September 1984, Annexure 21, House Rentals, Monthly Debit and Outstanding'.

17   Gcina Malindi, interview with author, Johannesburg, 25 March 2010.

18   WHP AK2117, I2.28 Vol.331, Testimony Mbatyzwa [sic.], p.18903.

19   WHP AK2117, I2.25, Vol.312, Testimony Myeza, p.17918.

insensitivity with which some of the councillors dismissed their constituencies and the capriciousness they exhibited enraged local communities. Councillors who opposed the increase and who sided with residents had increasingly become sidelined and their voices silenced.

'The air was electric'

If the activities of the Vaal Civic Association (VCA) had remained modest in the past, by the time the increase was announced the VCA was plunged into feverish activity. During the month of August, it convened a series of public meetings in churches in all major townships except Sharpeville, to address local residents and to discuss strategies for mass action. Even those who had been too scared to attend meetings before for fear of police violence found themselves sitting in the audience, voicing their anger and concerns. In the words of Father Patrick Noonan, 'the air was electric'.[20] The Roman Catholic Church in Evaton Small Farms, and the Nyolohelo Catholic Church in Zone 12 in Sebokeng, were known for their sympathetic priests, who had long taken a stand against authorities. Authorities initially remained unperturbed in the face of growing opposition but soon came to realise the gamut of dissent. To hamstring opposition, Esau Mahlatsi and Nicholas Louw, the town clerk of the Lekoa Town Council, attempted in vain to convince the local magistrate to ban public meetings; the magistrate responded that reasons were insufficient to impose bans.[21]

The strategy of how to challenge the increase was contested. During a public meeting held at St Michael's Anglican Church in Zone 13 in Sebokeng on 25 August, the VCA proposed a boycott of the R5.90 increase but was allegedly convinced otherwise by the audience, who demanded a total boycott of rent.[22] Speakers at this meeting represented a broad front of Charterist organisations such as the Release Mandela Committee (RMC), the UDF, the VCA and COSAS.[23] During the following meeting on 1 September at the Roman Catholic Church in Evaton Small Farms, the VCA finally lobbied for a complete boycott of rent and a stay-away from work and school on 3 September. Importantly, it was only during this meeting that the decision to march to the offices of the Orange Vaal Development Board (OVDB) to hand over a memorandum was confirmed. Councillors would be asked to resign and their businesses boycotted. Gcina Malindi recalls that 'the momentum of what happened in the Vaal [was] carried by the people who came to the meetings. The Vaal Civic Association [started] conservatively but [was] pushed by that momentum'.[24] Residents had become

20 WHP AK2117, S8.11.1., 'Notes of meeting with Father Patrick of Sharpeville'.
21 *Sowetan*, 16 April 1986.
22 Gcina Malindi, interview with author, Johannesburg, 25 March 2010.
23 WHP AK2117, L12.3, Judgment, p.786.
24 Gcina Malindi, interview with author, Johannesburg, 25 March 2010.

more radicalised and discontent than the VCA had realised. Similar meetings occurred in Bophelong and Boipatong, and it was in Bophelong where initial skirmishes between residents, councillors and police set in place the cycles of confrontation that eventually triggered the uprising, as we will see.

In Sharpeville, given its different political dynamics, Reverend Moselane took centre stage in the struggle against the rent increase; at his church, residents gathered every Sunday throughout August to discuss the increase and strategies to oppose it. In early August 1984 Moselane met with Peter Hlubi and Nozipho Myeza from the Orange Vaal General Workers Union (OVGWU) to discuss the rent increment, the council system, the destitute situation of old-age pensioners, the costs of school fees, uniforms and books as well as transport fees. OVGWU had taken a strong stance after the announcement of the increase and publicly stated that the rise would cripple most African people financially.

A week after the announcement of the increase, on 12 August, Moselane addressed residents at his church in Sharpeville.[25] In the aftermath of this meeting, he travelled to Johannesburg to seek advice on how to halt the rent increase. At Khotso House, the headquarters of the South African Council of Churches (SACC), he met with Thomas Madikwe Manthata, an SACC fieldworker and personal assistant to Bishop Desmond Tutu. Manthata was a seasoned activist, member of AZAPO and founding member of the Soweto Committee of Ten. He advised Moselane to seek legal assistance.[26] Moselane invited Manthata to the next meeting scheduled for Sunday 19 August at his church. It was his presence on the 19th, and (unfounded) allegations of his inflammatory speech, that subsequently added Manthata to the list of accused in the Delmas treason trial. As was common, the meeting opened with songs. 'Rea Ho Boka Morena' (we thank the Lord), a popular church hymn, and 'Nkosi sikelel' iAfrika' (God bless Africa), one of the most popular hymns, as well as freedom songs, were sung. Manthata in his capacity as a guest speaker compared the rent struggle of the people in the Vaal Triangle to the situation in other townships. During his sermon, Reverend Moselane read from Exodus chapter 3, comparing his parishioners' yoke to the subjugation of Israelites under Egyptian rule. This second meeting resolved to boycott the rent increase and to demand the resignation of all councillors.

The atmosphere and content of speeches of the third meeting on 26 August are well documented as it was filmed by Kevin Harris, a film maker commissioned by the SACC.[27] Emotions ran high, revealing the deep-seated anger held by many. Peter Hlubi, the acting general secretary of the OVGWU, reminded the audience of the decisions taken during the previous meeting:

25   WHP AK2117, I2.10, Vol.229, Testimony Tebogo Geoffrey Moselane, p.12175.
26   Ibid., p.12198.
27   Kevin Harris, interview with author, Johannesburg, 15 May 2006.

P. Hlubi: First Sunday we agreed that the rent we would pay. What we
              don't pay is the R5.90 increase. Are we still there all of us?

Audience: Yes! Yes! Yes!

P. Hlubi: The second thing. We agreed that we no longer want councillors
              all together [sic]. Are we still there all of us?

Audience: We don't want them anymore. Yes! Yes! Yes!

P. Hlubi: The third thing. The question arose as to where the money for
              the bottle stores and the money for other things which could be
              of value to the community was and how it is spent. The fourth:
              it was agreed that their garages and shops must not be used. Is it
              still happening the way it was planned?

Audience: It is not happening. [...] If they are telling the truth [...] it is
              happening.[28]

AZAPO's Oupa Hlomuka spoke about the commonalities between the townships
and informed those present that Sharpeville's residents were not alone in their
struggle against the rent increase. A group of youth had allegedly stoned buses in
Sharpeville a few days prior to the meeting, on 20 August 1984 and members of
the audience reminded them to abstain from stoning buses and cars: 'My children
do not fight', one woman urged, 'the Government is not fighting and the law is not
fighting. Leave the busses alone [...]. My children do not destroy busses.'[29] Others
called on the audience to gather their courage and become active:

> If you have to die, you should die. [...] Are you afraid to fall? We have fallen,
> how can we fall again? We can rather rise and go. [...] It is true, we do not
> need our children. This is a minor fight. This is nothing man. It is a thing
> the parents can do. Those are boys, young boys. [...] Let the children be
> educated at school. They can join us in the struggle, but not now.[30]

One speaker after another bemoaned the financial strictures many were experiencing. 'If you are to extend the house this year, he [your child] must leave
school.'[31] Shouts of 'Amandla! Awethu!' (power is ours) and 'Izwe Lethu!' (our
land) concluded the meeting.[32]

     In contrast to Sebokeng, no plans were made to join the protest march on
the 3rd. Instead, the meeting resolved to take the Lekoa Town Council to court
for failing to fulfil the legal requirements of announcing the rent increase within

28   WHP A2675, III (952), 'Translation of Speeches of Sunday, 26 August 1984', pp.3–4.
      This document is only available in English.

29   Ibid., p.8.

30   Ibid., p.12.

31   Ibid., p.18.

32   'Izwe Lethu', the popular slogan of the PAC that demanded the return of the land,
      was used by AZAPO as well.

an appropriate time and widely enough; should the court interdict fail, Sharpe-ville's group envisaged petitioning the town council. Inspired by the legalistic approach of the Soweto Civic Association (the successor of the Soweto Com-mittee of Ten), the approach adopted in Sharpeville was therefore different and rested on the use of the law in contesting rent increases and evictions.[33] The final meeting in Sharpeville, as elsewhere, took place on 2 September, and it was during this meeting that Sharpeville's leadership was allegedly 'shouted down' by the audience, who argued that they were sick and tired of the situation and that they wanted to join the protest march.[34]

Contestations over the appropriate strategies to oppose the increase, as well as Moselane's absence from Sharpeville on 3 September, led to Sharpe-ville's march being inadequately organised and led. Was it a coincidence that the townships with weak or absent civic structures were the ones to explode into violence first? The answer is likely to be more complex than that. Yet police accounts demonstrate that Sebokeng, the township with the strongest civic presence, was relatively quiet until the morning of the 3rd, while the smaller townships of Sharpeville, Bophelong and Boipatong expe-rienced tensions from late August. Contrary to popular perceptions, it was not in Sebokeng where tensions first escalated but in the small township of Bophelong near Vanderbijlpark. On 29 August, a meeting between residents and councillors escalated, setting the stage for the revolt. Tsietsi 'Stompi' Mokhele recalls:[35]

> It was all the elderly people inside. They started posing questions. [...] These people [the councillors] are just not answering anything. And the whole place was surrounded by the police. Now on the outside we started mobi-lising [...] We need to make sure we beat these people [the councillors] up when they come out of this place. That they never come to our township ever again! Now I don't know whether by design or by default electricity went off in the hall. And they were up there. Man! They were clapped and beaten up I don't know what else.

Police were called in and responded with gratuitous violence, shooting three people.[36] Tensions in Bophelong were mounting, and the leadership of the VCA feared that an uncontrolled escalation would threaten the success of the planned

33   As Seekings shows, the use of courts proved unsuccessful in opposing rent increases in Soweto. See J. Seekings, 'Why Was Soweto Different? Urban Development, Township Politics, and the Political Economy of Soweto, 1977–1984' (African Stud-ies seminar paper, University of the Witwatersrand, 1988).

34   Gcina Malindi, interview with author, Johannesburg, 25 March 2010.

35   Tsietsi 'Stompi' Mokhele, interview with author, Bophelong, 18 September 2011.

36   WHP AK2243 (*State v Sefatsa and 7 Others*), Case No.698/85, A, Vol.1, Testimony Louw, p.18.

action a few days later. In the aftermath of the shooting in Bophelong, the air was redolent with tension and trepidation.

According to the security branch of the South African Police, they were well informed about the planned march on 3 September.[37] The townships had been flooded by pamphlets, calling on young and old to observe the planned action, while a network of informers kept the security branch abreast of debates within the VCA.[38] COSAS activists were doing the rounds, knocking on doors and demanding that residents observe the stay-away. Fake pamphlets calling off the protest march and stay-away received little attention, for their design was wrong. The townships were buzzing with rumours, further exacerbating tensions.[39] Matime Moshele Papane recalled that, 'People were beginning to talk, they had enough of this, they must get rid of this.'[40]

Despite their knowledge of the planned protest action, the security branch claims that their hands were bound and that they were not 'above the law'.[41] Instead of arresting activists, they threatened legal consequences should the protest march go ahead. Significantly, the security branch struggled to access evidence beyond informers' reports; according to their own testimonies, it was almost impossible to secretly tape meetings of the VCA. And while they had successfully infiltrated the VCA and COSAS, they were largely in the dark regarding activities of the African National Congress (ANC) underground.[42] The vice chairman of the VCA, Esau Ralitsela, was threatened with a charge of treason and sabotage if he did not call off the protest march. Ralitsela in turn suggested that if Esau Mahlatsi would appear on TV and publicly resign and scrap the increase, he would do his part in liaising with residents.[43] According to local authorities, this could not be arranged. As we have seen, the Ralitselas' mandate as an ANC underground unit was to organise and mobilise residents into civic structures with the aim of dismantling the councils, which in turn would contribute towards achieving ungovernability. Mahlatsi's resignation would therefore have been insufficient.

37 Andries du Toit and Petrus Niemand, interview with author, West Rand, 19 May 2011 (names have been changed).
38 Ibid.
39 WHP AE862, G37.8, United Democratic Front, Black Sash et al., 'Repression in a time of reform. A look at events in the Transvaal since August 1984' (Johannesburg, 1984), p.10.
40 Matime Moshele Papane, interview with author, Johannesburg, 28 April 2010.
41 Andries du Toit and Petrus Niemand, interview with author, West Rand, 10 May 2011.
42 Remarkably, none of the VCA activists with direct links was arrested for ANC activities prior to the uprising. See also Andries du Toit and Petrus Niemand, interview with author, West Rand, 10 May 2011.
43 Esau Ralitsela, interview with author, Vereeniging, 5 April 2010.

'Our allegiance with God has been tampered with'

Moselane was not the only priest who had become involved in community politics. While many clergy had initially mainly engaged in welfare projects and counselling, their role began to change during the period prior to the uprising. Inspired by the teachings of Black Theology of the 1970s, and the liberation theology emanating from Latin America, many priests began to openly side with the plight of residents. Conscientised and alerted by the desperate situation of their parishioners, they began to 'embrace the memory of an alternative tradition' with an emphasis on liberation from oppression, equality and human rights.[44] The growing radicalism of the clergy and the political content of their sermons widened the reach and scope of grassroots struggles by drawing in more conservative sections of society.

Churches therefore became important sites of protest as they were centrally located, offered space for large crowds to assemble and were generally regarded as safe and respectable. Prayers and sermons played their part in politicising and conscientising parishioners: '[You give] three messages in one sermon. A message for the ordinary people, a message for the impimpi, the spies, and a message for the politically minded. All in one,' as Father Patrick Noonan recalls.[45] Like his colleague Father Edward Lennon, Noonan, an Irish priest who had arrived in South Africa during the early 1970s, was residing in the townships in open defiance of the Group Areas Act. The opening of church doors for community politics did not go down well with officials. A series of threatening letters by the Orange Vaal Administration Board's (OVAB) chief director, D.C. Ganz, exposes the lengths local authorities went to to halt political activities at the churches. They also reflect a deep-seated level of anxiety about growing community mobilisation and the role of churches in facilitating dissent. Prior to the launch of the VCA at Nyolohelo Catholic Church in Sebokeng in 1983, the priest in charge of the church, Father Edward Lennon, had received threatening letters informing him that church premises should be used for 'bona fide' purposes only.[46] To the authorities' great irritation, Father Lennon defied the instructions of the OVAB and continued to open the doors of his church for community meetings. Four months later, in January 1984, he received another letter threatening to cancel the leasehold of his church. Ganz went as far as complaining to the Catholic Diocese in Johannesburg that

---

44   T.A. Borer, *Challenging the State: Churches as Political Actors in South Africa 1980–1994* (Notre Dame, University of Notre Dame Press, 1998), p.7.

45   Ibid.

46   WHP AK2117, J4.15, AAQ30C, 'Letter to Father Edward Lennon, Roman Catholic Church Zone 12, Sebokeng, Issued by the Chief Director of the Orange Vaal Administration Board, D.C. Ganz (13 September 1983)'; Noonan, *They're Burning the Churches*, pp.126–28.

the use of Nyolohelo Church for political purposes 'tend[s] to encourage the deterioration in the relationship between Blacks and the Government instituted organisations'.[47]

By August 1984, clergy and local authorities were in open conflict. To regain control over the situation, representatives of ten different churches were invited by Esau Mahlatsi to attend meetings in Sharpeville and Sebokeng.[48] Discussions produced few tangible solutions to the crisis and clergy alleged that they were threatened by councillors to abstain from politics or else.[49] After the meetings, a joint letter sent by the clergy accused Mahlatsi of heresy and urged him to resign in order to be 'saved'.[50] The letter challenged Mahlatsi and asked, 'Whose word is this that you brought to us? Defunct OVAB's or Town Council's? For us this connivance smacks of hypocrisy and heresy and should be declared anathema.'[51] The clergy insisted that their primary duty was to serve their God:

> In this case particularly, our allegiance with God has been tampered with. The church cannot dichotomize life into material and spiritual or run away from the material. [...] Non-involvement on the part of Church leaders in the affairs that affect people amounts to silence and withdrawal which is not only perilous to our credibility and that of the Gospel of Jesus Christ, but also leads us to support injustices. [...] We appeal to you therefore, your excellency, to repent and desist from this wanton order and system that continuously breeds hatred, injustice and violence and be saved.

This letter not only offers priceless insights into the conflict between local ministers and councillors at that time but also reflects broader debates around heresy, morality and duty to the community. Discourse on the immorality of apartheid had become prominent with the drafting of a *status confessionis* by the World Council of Churches in 1982 that declared apartheid to be a sin and its theological justifications heretical. The SACC adopted the statement in its national conference during the same year.[52] The continuous harassment by the police divided the clergy: it conscientised and radicalised many, while reinforcing the belief of others that any involvement in community politics would have dire consequences.

47 WHP AK2117, J4.15, AAQ30A, 'Letter to the Chancellor of the Catholic Diocese in Johannesburg, Issued by the Director of the OVAB, D.C. Ganz (13 February 1984)'.

48 WHP AK2117, J4.18, AAT14 and 15, 'Letter by N. Louw, Town Clerk re Discussion between Church Leaders in the Vaal Triangle and the Town Council of Lekoa, August 14 1984'.

49 WHP AK2117, S8.10.3, 'Diary of Events – Vaal Triangle, by Father Patrick Noonan'.

50 WHP AK2117, S8.2.5, 'Memorandum by Church Leaders in the Vaal Triangle to the Mayor of Lekoa Town Council'.

51 Ibid.

52 Borer, *Challenging the State*, p.105.

Moselane's harassment was a case in point. He was physically assaulted and his property was damaged twice within two weeks: on 31 August, a group of people led by a local councillor threatened to assassinate him and expel his family from the mission house unless he abstained from his political involvement.[53] In the aftermath of the uprising, his house would be attacked again. Councillors were not the only ones threatening Moselane. Summoned to the offices of the security branch in Vereeniging, Moselane was urged by Captain Steyn to cancel a meeting scheduled for 2 September at his church or be held accountable for any acts of violence that might occur in the aftermath.[54] Father Lenkoe, at whose church in Sebokeng the decisive meeting of 25 August had taken place, allegedly received similar threats from Steyn: '*Ek weet hulle gaan brand. Ek weet mense nie gaan werk nie. Op daardie dag bloed gaan vloei en daardie bloed wat vloei sal op jou hande wees.* [I know that they're going to burn. I know that people will not go to work. On this day, blood will be shed and this blood will be on your hands].'[55]

On Sunday 2 September activists from all townships and representatives of the zonal committees met to prepare for the day to come. The plan was clear: residents from Evaton and Sebokeng were to meet in the morning of the 3rd at the Roman Catholic Church in Evaton Small Farms and the Nyolohelo Catholic Church in Zone 12 in Sebokeng. Residents from other townships would march to the offices of the development board in Houtkop from their respective townships.[56] As police testimonies demonstrate, that day violence erupted in Bophelong after yet another meeting by local residents was disrupted by the police and three young men were shot.[57] Rumours about these deaths spread rapidly, creating a sense of trepidation and foreboding. Expectations of police violence were high. But while the march had been agreed upon, smaller groups were discussing alternative plans. For some of them, a protest march was insufficient to express their anger and opposition. The polyphony of voices and the variety of experiences is difficult to capture; testimonies by participants in the main protest march, smaller groups acting independently, councillors as well as police provide a glimpse of the complexity and messiness of the revolt.[58] Court testimonies of the riot police, given during the Delmas treason trial, are heavily biased and structured to serve the legal purpose of prosecuting the civic leadership. Their advantage is that they provide a bird's-eye view that

53   *Sowetan*, 7 September 1984.
54   WHP AK2117, I2.11, Vol.232, Testimony Moselane, pp.12313ff.
55   WHP AK2117, S8.11, 'Statement Obtained by Rev. Peter Lenkoe'.
56   Esau Ralitsela, interview with author, Vereeniging, 5 April 2010; WHP AK2117, I2.3, Vol.171, Testimony Nkopane, pp.8790ff.
57   WHP AK2117, I1.10, Vol.68, Testimony Coetzee, pp.3571–73.
58   I am grateful to Peter Mabuye for his suggestions on how to capture the diversity of experiences.

helps us analyse the unfolding of the revolt, and the ways in which contingent confrontations in different locations led to the escalation of violence. They also confirm that violence began prior to the protest march. For that reason, they are worth paying close attention to.

'Siyaya Epitoli'

The morning of the 3rd was windy and cool, and light smoke was hanging over the roofs of the houses. At around 8am inside the Roman Catholic Church in Evaton Small Farms, Esau Ralitsela addressed a group of several hundred people. He reminded the audience that this was going to be a peaceful march and explained the purpose of the event.[59] Outside the hall, the group was joined by thousands of people coming from all directions. The elderly and the young, women and men all assembled to express their discontent. 'It was unbelievable. It was unbelievable. But you see, the turnout of people I'm still also amazed. We were not in control of the whole situation.'[60] Exhilaration, defiance and anger textured the mood of the crowd. Rumours of police harassment of some of the participants compounded these emotions. Tsietsi 'Speech' Mokatsanyane, a member of COSAS who went into exile shortly afterwards, recalled his emotions: 'We are happy. We wanted to die for freedom. We are really happy.'[61] Journalist Leonard Khumalo of the *Sowetan* newspaper was capturing the scenes with his camera, but later had the photographs confiscated by the police.[62]

The march finally set off at about 9am, leaving in the direction of Sebokeng along Selbourne Road. At the Masenkeng bus terminal it turned into Vilakazi Street, which borders Zone 7 in Sebokeng. From there the march continued along Wessels Mota Street towards the post office, where Moshoeshoe Street converged with Houtkop Road, which leads towards the offices of the development board. 'Siyaya, siyaya ePitoli' (we are marching to Pretoria) was sung, fists were clenched and groups of youth jogged in front of the march. COSAS members acted as marshalls to guide the marchers and to keep them in line. Many of the marchers shared a feeling that, finally, their grievances were finding an outlet. It was 'like people having been enclosed suddenly exploding', Toy Manqa, a COSAS activist, remembers.[63] Anger over political disenfranchisement was compounded by years of frustration with maladministration, corruption and the daily indignities of life under apartheid.

59   Esau Ralitsela, interview with author, Vereeniging, 5 April 2010.
60   Dorcas Ralitsela, interview with author, Vereeniging, 1 April 2010.
61   Tsietsi 'Speech' Mokatsanyane, interview with author, Pretoria, 13 July 2010.
62   Leonard Khumalo, interview with author, Rust-ter-Vaal, 9 May 2010.
63   Sarhili 'Toy' Manqa, interview with author, Vereeniging, 26 May 2011.

As the marchers passed the house of Caesar Motjeane, one of Sebokeng's unpopular councillors, shots were heard and rumours spread among the marchers that he had been killed. These rumours greatly unsettled the leadership and debates ensued on how to control the march. Eventually, the decision was taken to continue the march to the offices of the development board. Gcina Malindi explains: 'The decision was if we stop here we'll be accused of having led the march to this point. If we're going to be arrested, we'll be arrested at the destination so that it's clear we achieved what we wanted to do and we had nothing to do with the attacks on the councillors.'[64] AZAPO leader Oupa Hlomuka recalls the marchers were 'getting worried. Something happened at the front. As we were discussing, we came near the front of the march. People started guiding the marchers not to go somewhere else.'[65]

Shortly afterwards, at Hunter's garage in Zone 12 in Sebokeng, as the marchers were turning into Houtkop Road, the crowd encountered a contingent of riot policemen who had blocked the road with Casspirs and other police vehicles. What is perhaps surprising is that the marchers had reached the intersection in the first place: Hunter's garage is approximately six kilometres from the Roman Catholic Church in Evaton Small Farms, where the march had originated. Some of the marchers continued to walk towards the police in order to negotiate a continuation of the march.[66] Naphtali Nkopane, one of the members of the VCA, argued, 'The agreement was that we are going to plead with them to let us pass, let the march proceed to its destination and should they refuse us permission to proceed then ours [sic] will be to talk to the marchers, that is the community in the march, to disperse.'[67] He also stated that should this be the case, a small delegation would nevertheless hand over the memorandum to the officials at the development board in Houtkop. But the marchers never reached their destination.

When the first marchers were about 40 metres away, the police began to shoot at the crowd. Witnesses later claimed that there had been no warning.[68] And this was when, as participants of the protest march recalled, 'all hell broke loose': 'It was chaos. It was chaos. We don't know where to go now. What to do now.'[69] Within seconds, the leadership lost control over the march. Panicking, people began to run in all directions, away from the main road and into the side streets. Those unlucky ones within the police's reach were sjambokked and shot at. By then, riot police had dismounted

64   Gcina Malindi, interview with author, Johannesburg, 25 March 2010.

65   Oupa Hlomuka, interview with author, Vanderbijlpark, 9 July 2010.

66   WHP AK2117, I2.7, Vol.206, Testimony Malindi, pp.19858ff.

67   WHP AK2117, I2.3, Vol.171, Testimony Nkopane, p.8801.

68   WHP AK2117, I2.7, Vol.206, Testimony Malindi, pp.10848ff.; WHP AK2117, I2.30, Vol.347, Testimony Vilakazi, pp.19858ff.

69   Tsietsi 'Speech' Mokatsanyane, interview with author, Pretoria, 13 July 2010.

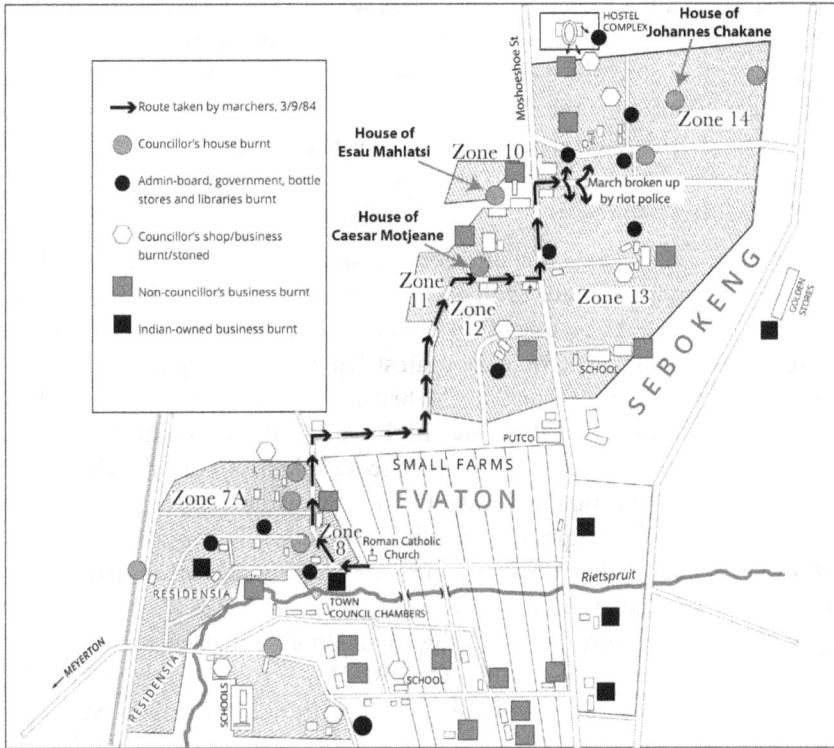

Map 3: Sebokeng on 3 September 1984, with confrontations marked.
This map is based on a sketch found in the archive. It is without scale and
oriented south. See WHP AK2117, S8.12.

their vehicles and were chasing protestors through the streets. Young people were jumping fences, old people were trying to escape the mayhem. They sought refuge in houses and were hiding under beds, in washing baskets and other places. Anger over the shooting was textured by fear of further violence. Some desperately tried to provide leadership by assisting the wounded and deterring angry crowds from burning and looting shops. Youths' response to the police shooting was immediate and fuelled by anger, as one activist recalls: 'We retaliated by throwing stones at police. By burning any government building we may come across.'[70]

As this statement shows, police violence triggered counter-violence by young activists, initiating a cycle of violence that continued for days.[71] The air was thick

70   Peter Nhlapo, interview with author, Vereeniging, 8 July 2010 (name has been changed).
71   This pattern of violence corresponds with research conducted on other uprisings and collective mobilisations. On the role of police violence in triggering crowd violence during the student uprisings in 1976, see for example A.K. Hlongwane, 'The Mapping of the June 16 1976 Soweto Student Uprisings Routes: Past Recollections,

with teargas and the sound of gunshots served as a reminder of past violence. For many township communities, it was a familiar sight that would be repeated time and again across the country, as thousands rose in defiance of apartheid rule. The breaking up of the march had significant consequences. It was the last trigger that turned peaceful public action into an uprising.

'Caesar, our fathers' money, our fathers' houses!'

Rumours about attacks on councillors circulated at least a couple of days before the uprising started. Evidence given in the murder trial of Philemon Leburu 'Dutch' Diphoko, one of the councillors killed in Evaton, claims that there had been threats of violence against Diphoko as early as 1982.[72] From 1 September onwards, Mayor Esau Mahlatsi was warning fellow councillors that they would be attacked on the 3rd. In court, he later recalled, 'We had heard rumours that councillors are going to be killed.'[73] Councillors had been blamed for the misfortune of residents since the early 1980s (see Chapter 2) and allegations of corruption were rife, with councillors widely viewed as 'sell-outs', 'stooges', 'puppets of the regime' or 'dogs', epithets that placed them beyond the boundaries of the community.

To defend themselves, some of the councillors were given guns, two-way radios and fire extinguishers by the OVDB.[74] While guns were mostly distributed to councillors belonging to the mayor's party, only those deemed 'important' and 'well-known' were given two-way radios. The handing out of radios and guns had a significant impact on councillors' reaffirmed perception of being under threat: by the time crowds began to gather in early September, councillors were up in arms, expecting to be attacked.

One of the first councillors to come under attack was the deputy mayor of the Lekoa Town Council, Jacob Kuzwayo Dlamini. His house was stoned in the evening of 2 September, leading to broken windows. A short while later, Dlamini called the OVDB's town clerk, Nicolas Louw, telling him that 'it is bad, send security', but none arrived.[75] Police equally failed to respond and by late that night, his wife tried to convince him to seek safety at a neighbour's house. But

Present Reconstructions', *Journal of African Cultural Studies*, 19/1, Special Issue: Performing (In) Everyday Life (2007), pp.7–36; S. Nlovu, *The Soweto Uprisings: Counter Memories of June 1976* (Johannesburg, Picador Africa, 2017); S. Mkhabela, *Open Earth and Black Roses: Remembering 16 June 1976* (Johannesburg, Skotaville Publishers, 2001). Leslie Bank notes a similar pattern for the East London riots of 1952. See L. Bank, *Home Spaces, Street Styles: Contesting Power and Identity in a South Africa City* (Johannesburg, Wits University Press, 2011), pp.61–65.

72   WHP AK2305 (*State v Nhlapo and 5 Others*), Case No.344/86, Vol.6, Testimony D (in camera hearing), pp.145–46.

73   WHP AK2117, I1.9, Vol.60, Testimony Mahlatsi, p.3124.

74   WHP AK2243, A, Vol.1, Testimony Louw, p.19.

75   Ibid.

Dlamini insisted on staying. Whether he simply misjudged the seriousness of the situation or believed that his gun would protect him, Dlamini's refusal to leave his house would cost him his life.

In the early morning of the 3rd, his house was pelted with stones again and several petrol bombs were hurled. The crowd that had converged outside called on Dlamini to come out. They demanded that he join their march, and they wanted answers regarding the rent increase, the lack of development and his role in upholding an illegitimate political system. What happened next was as predictable as it was tragic: panicking as he saw the large group of people outside his home, Dlamini fired shots into the crowd and wounded a young man, Motsiri Gideon Mokone, who was later charged with Dlamini's murder but acquitted. Subsequently, Dlamini's car was set alight, he was overpowered, drenched in petrol and dragged onto the car where he burnt to death. Dlamini's murder led to the infamous Sharpeville Six trial, where eight young people in their twenties and thirties were tried under the principle of common purpose (see Chapter 6). News of Dlamini's death spread rapidly and caused fear among other councillors. It confirmed what they had been suspecting for months: that they were no longer safe. Councillor Kolisang, who had been serving in various official capacities in Sharpeville since the 1940s, was convinced that he was going to suffer a similar fate. Hiding in his bathroom, Kolisang was terrified when he overheard a group of young people outside his house discussing Dlamini's death.[76] Shortly afterwards, his car was set alight but he remained physically unharmed.

Court records and oral testimonies confirm that violent confrontations between councillors and crowds were contingent. Even though the civic leadership was later accused of having incited violence against councillors, the evidence put forward by police and the state prosecution for the Delmas treason trial is unconvincing and contradicted by countless witnesses who were at the scene.[77] Instead, the councillors' murder was a tragic consequence of an escalating stand-off between panicking councillors and enraged crowds. In most cases, the guns they had been given by the OVDB did little to protect them; on the contrary, guns afforded a false sense of security and fostered a siege mentality that increased the risk of pre-emptive violence. In the case of the councillors who died at the hands of enraged crowds, they accelerated the escalation of the situation: all four councillors who died had shot and wounded members of the crowds outside their houses.

76   Samuel Kolisang, interview with author, Sharpeville, 15 July 2010.
77   See, for example, Kevin Harris's video footage of the meeting in Sharpeville on 26 August 1984, *The Struggle from Within*, directed by Kevin Harris (Johannesburg, Kevin Harris Productions, 1984/85). The documentary is available online at https://kevinharris.co.za/the-struggle-from-within-1984-1985/, retrieved 5 March 2020.

Among these crowds were small groups of politicised youth. Their movements are worth paying attention to, for they highlight the diverse agendas and
tactics individual participants in the uprising pursued. Many youth had spent
the night before the march writing placards and preparing for the day to come.
One such group of COSAS activists, consisting of a handful of young men in
their late teens, serves as a lens through which to read the complexity of violent
encounters during that day. Aiming to enforce the stay-away from work, the
group left their base in Sebokeng at around 2:30am to force the local bakery to
close and to chase its employees away. From there the group moved to the bus
stop in Zone 11 to ensure that nobody would catch an early bus to go to work.
Within 30 minutes they broke up to go to the various train stations, taxi ranks
and bus stations to prevent people from going to work. As they started pushing
rocks into the roads to block them, they were teargassed by approaching police.
According to one in the group, this was when the uprising began in earnest. At
about 4am, 'people were now woken up by teargas, by the shouts, by the singing
and people joined'.[78] Taunting the councillors, the group sang 'Ayasaba amag-
wala' (the cowards are afraid).

What followed was an exercise in hide-and-seek between the police and the
youth, who knew the alleys, dead-ends and byways of the townships in contrast
to the majority of the riot police, who were not familiar with the terrain. This
knowledge allowed the youth to evade arrest for several hours. Jumping over
fences, seeking out hiding spaces in houses and knowing which streets led to
a dead-end, and which ones to safety, provided the youth with an advantage.
Initially, the group had planned to join the main march along the way but since
they were close to Councillor Caesar Motjeane's house, they decided to demand
that he resign and join the march; none in the group seriously considered that
Motjeane would join.[79] Motjeane was known to be an aggressive man; confronting him was therefore likely to end in violence.

Testimonies of what transpired at Motjeane's house are contested but what
is clear is that the small group of youth were not the only ones who had gathered there. Long before the marchers reached the intersection near his house,
smaller crowds had already gathered outside it. One of his neighbours recalls the
crowd chanting, 'Caesar our fathers' money, our fathers' houses!'[80] The content
of the chant confirms that Motjeane was personally held accountable for the dire
poverty and lack of housing that prevailed. When Motjeane's bodyguard shot
a young boy, the enraged crowd retaliated with violence and killed the guard.
COSAS activists recall their futile efforts to prevent the crowd from attacking

78   Shaka Radebe, interview with author, Vereeniging, 23 July 2010.
79   Bongani Mhlobo, interview with author, Vereeniging, 12 July 2010 (name has been
      changed).
80   WHP AK2117, S8.11.1, Statement Alinah Mogkatla.

Motjeane.[81] Fearing for his life after realising that his bodyguard had died, Motjeane barricaded himself in the house and began shooting out of the window. One eyewitness recounts that 'at that time people are counting the bullets. The shots. One [...] and after six people stormed that house'.[82] Motjeane was dragged out of the house, stoned and stabbed to death.

Around the same time, Mayor Esau Mahlatsi, like many other councillors, came under attack. According to Mahlatsi's own estimates, just after 7:30am on 3 September, he was standing in the street when he saw a group of more than 300 people approaching his house. One among the group shouted 'that's him', Mahlatsi recalled.[83] As the crowd approached, Mahlatsi fired shots into the air, further angering the crowd. They were counting the shots and when five bullets had been fired, they told him, 'Now you're left with one bullet.'[84] After Mahlatsi fired his final shot the crowd closed in on him. According to an eyewitness, Mahlatsi shot a child, and as a result, 'If they had caught him, they would have killed him or injured him seriously. [...] We, the older ones had to retreat, the young ones chased Mahlatsi.'[85] Finally, Mahlatsi jumped over the fence surrounding his property and ran away. His house was set alight and, looking back, he saw smoke coming from it.

His colleague Jacob Chakane was less fortunate. The crowd rapidly grew and began moving towards Chakane's house nearby but the marchers were dispersed by a police helicopter shooting live ammunition. 'They started shooting randomly,' one of the youth activists recalls, explaining that 'that's where people were angered. That was between Zone 12 and Zone 13 and Zone 14 [in Sebokeng] and then people they went for shops now. Burnt down shops, burnt down garages and that was the start of the whole thing.'[86] Chakane's body was later found with 'several injuries' and asphyxia in his blood, suggesting suffocation.[87]

Almost all councillors suffered some kind of attack. Their houses were stoned and burnt down and many narrowly escaped with their lives. Even though these attacks were widespread, evidence suggests that they were not centrally co-ordinated but rather organised ad hoc. Unwelcome in their communities, many councillors spent a life under heavy protection. At a meeting on 23 October 1984, the town council of Lekoa presented a list that included the damage to private houses, shops and vehicles of councillors as well as buildings belonging to the development board. According to this list, claims included R166,398 for houses;

81   Bongani Mhlobo, interview with author, Vereeniging, 12 July 2010 (name has been changed).
82   Ibid.
83   *Sowetan*, 11 April 1986; WHP AK2117, I1.9, Vol.60, Testimony Mahlatsi, p.3121.
84   WHP AK2117, I1.9., Vol.60, Testimony Mahlatsi, p.3121.
85   WHP AK2117, S8.11, 'Statement by David Maloka'.
86   Bongani Mhlobo, interview with author, Vereeniging, 12 July 2010 (name has been changed).
87   WHP AK2117, S8.11.1, 'Report on a Medico-Legal Post-Mortem Examination, Death Register No. 594/84, Jacob Chakane'.

R944,924 for contents; R146,918 for vehicles; R133,369 for buildings belonging to the development board; R440,278 for shops of councillors; R1,312,340 for the content of shops; and R64,581 for shops belonging to the development board.[88] The councillors further noted with concern that almost none of them were insured against damage caused by riots and they proposed seeking financial assistance from the Department of Co-operation and Development.

'The most violent unrest': Narratives of the Riot Squad

According to police, complaints that stones and broken windscreen glass were obstructing the Golden Highway (the main road leading out of Vanderbijlpark) began pouring in during the evening of 2 September. In contrast to Sebokeng, Bophelong was only separated by a road from neighbouring Vanderbijlpark and its proximity undoubtedly exacerbated fears of violence spilling over into town. Officer Bruyns alleged that upon arrival in Bophelong, he found the road obstructed and skirmishes between police and small groups of youth ensued. By the end of the evening, the offices of the development board, a bottle store, a beerhall and several houses had been stoned and set alight. Schlebusch, one of the OVDB's inspectors, allegedly fired into the crowd after being attacked with petrol bombs and stones.[89]

Shortly before midnight, Colonel Viljoen arrived with reinforcements from Roodepoort and Krugersdorp, the regional headquarters of the riot police in the West Rand. Viljoen was no newcomer to situations of political protest and public disorder. By the time violence began in the townships of the Vaal Triangle, he had served in the South African Police Force for 25 years. He had also been stationed as a major at Jabulani police station in Soweto during the uprising in 1976 and had become the head of the West Rand riot police in 1980.[90] Little is known about Colonel Viljoen, other than his professional background. But what is clear is that he gained notoriety for his encouragement and use of gratuitous violence against protestors and during funerals. Undoubtedly, his iron-fisted approach exacerbated the already volatile situation and added further fuel to the fire. While Viljoen was called 'a remarkable peace maker' in an article in the *Sunday Times*, extensive evidence demonstrates the opposite.

The contingent of about 200 policemen was divided and dispatched to all townships in the area. Sporadic stoning of the police and their vehicles in Bophelong continued until they left for Sharpeville at 2am in the morning of 3 Sep-

---

88 WHP AK2117, S8.2.6, 'Damage Caused to Private Belongings of Councillors of the Town Council of Lekoa, Supplement Report: Town Council of Lekoa, 23 October 1984'.

89 WHP AK2117, I1.10, Vol.69, Testimony Schlebusch, pp.3698ff.

90 WHP AK2117, I1.10, Vol.67, Testimony Viljoen, p.3526; WHP AK2117, I1.10, Vol.68, Testimony Viljoen, p.3565.

tember. According to Warrant Officer Niemand and Colonel Viljoen, Sebokeng seemed quiet until about 6am, particularly compared to Bophelong, Boipatong and Sharpeville where roadblocks were seen and occasional incidents of stoning occurred throughout the night.[91] In Sharpeville, the house of a member of the security branch was set alight.[92] Police testimonies claim that the frequency of incidents of stone-throwing, as well as the burning of vehicles and houses, began to pick up from 6am on the 3rd.

In Sharpeville, the main road had been blocked and reports indicate that the police were quickly losing control of the situation. Major Crons, a pilot who flew over Sharpeville at 7.30am, noted that 'the unrest was much heavier than in other black areas'.[93] At around the same time, news reached the police that Councillor Dlamini's house was being stoned anew. Upon arrival, Viljoen claims that he found Dlamini with a 9mm pistol and tried to convince him to leave his house. Dlamini refused and by the time Viljoen returned, Dlamini was dead.[94] In Sebokeng and Evaton, according to the police, incidents of stoning of buses and vehicles ensued from 6am and crowds began to form shortly afterwards. The groups in Evaton and Sebokeng were reported to be much larger than in other areas. By 7.20am aerial observation over the two townships recorded three houses burning: one in Zone 7, one in Zone 13 and one in Evaton.[95] Just before 10am, the offices of the development board were set alight.[96]

Viljoen later claimed that the violence had been organised and that it was not spontaneous, as specific targets and people were attacked, including councillors, policemen, their houses, beerhalls and buildings belonging to the development board.[97] Viljoen and other riot policemen alleged that crowds were urged on by political and student leaders, who they claimed to be identifiable by the T-shirts they were wearing. Riot police testimonies therefore all followed a similar pattern when describing crowd action: an 'unruly mob' (*oproerige skare*) was led and incited by small groups of leaders to attack councillors and police.[98] To substantiate his claims that the attacks in the Vaal Triangle had been planned,

91   WHP AK2117, I1.10, Vol.70, Testimony Niemand, p.3726; WHP AK2117, I1.9, Vol.63, Testimony Viljoen, p.3359; WHP AK2117, I1.10, Vol.69, Testimony Schlebusch, pp.3700ff.
92   WHP AK2117, I1.10, Vol.68, Testimony Coetzee, p.3575; WHP AK2117, I1.10, Vol.68, Testimony Bruyns, pp.3619–21.
93   WHP AK2117, I1.10, Vol.71, Testimony Crons, p.3796.
94   WHP AK2243, A, Vol.18, Testimony Viljoen, p.893.
95   WHP AK2117, I1.10, Vol.71, Testimony Crons, pp.3803–04.
96   WHP AK2117, I1.10, Vol.69, Testimony Keyter, p.3662.
97   WHP AK2117, I1.9, Vol.64, Testimony Viljoen, p.3397.
98   F. Rueedi, 'Narratives on Trial: Ideology, Violence and the Struggle over Political Legitimacy in the Case of the Delmas Treason Trial, 1985–89', *South African Historical Journal*, 67/3 (2015), pp.335–55.

Viljoen compared the situation to the uprisings of 1976, where he had been stationed previously: 'This was the most violent unrest I have witnessed in my entire career,' he alleged.[99]

At 9.46am Colonel Viljoen gave orders to shoot with live ammunition, as 'the situation could not be brought under control with the use of less dangerous weapons'.[100] His claims that the use of live ammunition was necessary to avoid the loss of 'life and property' were part of a widespread discourse among the police during this time. In 1982, the amended Internal Security Act had empowered police above the rank of warrant officer to use force to disperse gatherings. However, section 49 specifically stated that lethal weapons should only be used if the gathering could not be dispersed otherwise, or if lives and property were being threatened.[101] In court, police later claimed that their conduct had been 'orderly, purposeful and controlled', in stark contrast to the 'unruly' and 'senseless violence' by youth.[102] This discourse, as Deborah Posel shows, was key to government's propaganda war during this period, which aimed to delegitimise black protest action by casting it as violent and a threat to public order and the state.

The countless deaths during the uprising, however, give the lie to the police's claim. Court testimonies, oral history interviews and affidavits collected by the Southern African Catholic Bishops' Conference all confirm that police were shooting indiscriminately.[103] The violence meted out, as these sources highlight, was as gratuitous as it had been during the student uprising of 1976. The shooting of young children paints a particularly harrowing picture. Wiseman Mnisi, aged nine, had been on his way home from his grandfather's house when the police opened fire on him, shooting him 11 times in the back.[104] His mother testified that by the time a neighbour brought him home, he was sobbing and could no longer speak.[105] Any attempt to call an ambulance was in vain and Mnisi died on the back of a relative who was carrying him to the hospital.[106]

99   WHP AK2243, A, Vol.18, Testimony Viljoen, p.894; Rueedi, 'Narratives on Trial'.
100 WHP AK2117, I1.9, Vol.64, Testimony Viljoen, pp.3372ff.
101 N. Haysom, 'Licence to Kill, Part 1: The South African Police and the Use of Deadly Force', *South African Journal of Human Rights*, 3/1 (1987), pp.3–27.
102 D. Posel, 'A "Battlefield of Perceptions": State Discourse on Political Violence, 1985–1988', in J. Cock and L. Nathan (eds), *War and Society: The Militarisation of South Africa* (Cape Town, David Philip, 1989), 269–71.
103 The evidence is extensive. For an overview, see WHP A2675, III (344), 'Report on Police Conduct during Township Protests, August–November 1984, Compiled and Published by the Southern African Catholic Bishops' Conference (SACBC)'.
104 WHP AK2117, I1.9, Vol.65, Testimony Viljoen, p.3442; *Los Angeles Times*, 3 September 1986, http://articles.latimes.com/1986-09-03/news/mn-13186_1, retrieved 5 March 2020.
105 WHP AK2117, S8.11.2, 'Sebokeng G.O. 231/84, Betty Mnisi Verklaar'.
106 WHP AK2117, S8.11.2, 'Sebokeng G.O. 231/84, Emily Kunene Verklaar'.

Rumours of the death of Mnisi and another young child, Alinah Mnyanda, spread rapidly and inflamed an already volatile situation. The gratuitous violence dispensed by police and the shooting of children created the impression that a war was being waged against communities. The attire and attitude of policemen, their use of weapons, vehicles and camouflage uniforms further entrenched this perception. Rumours also circulated that some of the young policemen were laughing as they shot at young people to frighten them.[107] Within the tense context of the uprising, the shootings by councillors and police triggered popular anger that had been simmering for years. As Karen Jochelson has argued for Alexandra, '[i]n popular opinion the police had crossed the moral boundaries of law and order'.[108] The brutal assault on mourners attending funerals to bury the victims of the uprising, as will be seen in the next chapter, further confirmed beliefs that the police were assaulting African communities with impunity. Incidents continued throughout the day. While Sharpeville, Boipatong and Bophelong seemed to become quieter, violent clashes were picking up in Sebokeng.[109] During the late afternoon reinforcements of 360 policemen arrived from Pretoria, swelling the number of police on patrol. By then, the townships had come to resemble a war zone.

The Spatiality of Protest and the Formation of Crowds

The degree to which crowd behaviour was controlled during the uprising came to be at the heart of the Delmas treason trial (see Chapter 6). The police claim that crowds were controlled by individual leaders was refuted by experts called by the defence for the accused civic leaders. Drawing on French social psychologist Gustave le Bon, sociologist Brunhilde Helm emphasised the irrationality and emotionality of the crowds, whose accountability was therefore reduced. In her words, 'people are capable of excesses [...] of which they would be incapable when acting on their own'.[110] The reference to Le Bon, whose theory had been widely refuted by then, was used for strategic purposes. The legal strategy of the defence rested on a two-pronged argument, namely that legitimate grievances had led to the mobilisation of ordinary residents, culminating in a peaceful protest march on 3 September.[111] The leadership rapidly lost control, the defence argued, when police and councillors began shooting at the crowds.

107 WHP AK2117, I1.9, Vol.65, Testimony Viljoen, p.3449.
108 K. Jochelson, 'Reform, Repression and Resistance in South Africa: A Case Study of Alexandra Township, 1979–1989', *Journal of Southern African Studies*, 16/1 (1990), p.9.
109 WHP AK2117, I1.9, Vol.65, Testimony Viljoen, p.3373.
110 WHP AK2117, M3.2, 'Report Professor Brunhilde Helm', p.28868.
111 Sociologist Mark Swilling outlined the different theories on crowd behaviour and advised the defence on which theories to use. See WHP AK 2117, S8.10.1, M. Swilling, 'Interpretations of Crowd Behaviour, Protests and "Riots": Some Thoughts on the Vaal Uprising', no date.

Recent research has refuted the strict separation between emotions and rationality, and emphasised that they are often mutually constitutive. Anger, joy, exhilaration and fear have all been shown to shape the ways in which crowds behave.[112] Participation in crowds can therefore lead to a sense of empowerment that is at the heart of social change.[113] Collective action is often socially meaningful, instead of predominantly negative, as Le Bon and others had argued.[114] Recent literature suggests that participants in crowds 'shift from behaving as disparate individuals to behaving in terms of a context-specific social identity'.[115] As Drury and Reicher argue, collective action therefore produces and reconfigures new social identities.[116] As this chapter has discussed, emotions prevalent during the protest march ranged from exhilaration that finally action was being taken, to anger over the injustices suffered. The most significant turning point was the brutal manner in which the police quelled the protests and halted the march, and the shooting of participants in the crowds. Rumours of violence, perpetrated by both the crowds and the police and councillors, therefore inflamed an already volatile situation and facilitated collective action.[117]

112 J. Drury and S. Reicher, 'Collective Psychological Empowerment as Model for Social Change: Researching Crowds and Power', *Journal of Social Issues*, 65/4 (2009), pp.707–25; S. Stürmer and B. Simon, 'Pathways to Collective Protest: Calculation, Identification, or Emotion? A Critical Analysis of the Role of Group-Based Anger in Social Movement Participation', *Journal of Social Issues*, 65/4 (2009), pp.681–705; D.B. Gould, *Moving Politics: Emotion and ACT UP's Fight against AIDS* (Chicago, University of Chicago Press, 2009). Charles Carter argues that anger shaped political action in Alexandra township during the mid-1980s. See C. Carter, 'Community and Conflict: The Alexandra Rebellion of 1986', *Journal of Southern African Studies*, 18/1 (1992), pp.115–42.

113 Drury and Reicher, 'Collective Psychological Empowerment'.

114 J. Drury and S. Reicher, 'Collective Action and Psychological Change: The Emergence of New Social Identities', *British Journal of Social Psychology*, 39 (2000), pp.579–604. The literature on collective action and crowd behaviour is vast. For an overview, see G. Martin, 'Collective Behaviour', in B.S. Turner (ed.), *Wiley Blackwell Encyclopedia of Social Theory* (Oxford, Wiley Blackwell, 2017); E. DeMarrais and T. Earle, 'Collective Action Theory and the Dynamics of Complex Societies', *Annual Review of Anthropology*, 46 (2017), pp.183–201.

115 Martin, 'Collective Behaviour'.

116 Drury and Reicher, 'Collective Action and Psychological Change'.

117 The role of rumour in collective action has been analysed in different contexts. See, for example, G. Rudé, *The Crowd in the French Revolution* (Oxford, Clarendon Press, 1959); G. Lefebre, *The Great Fear of 1789: Rural Panic in Revolutionary France*, trans. Joan White (New York, Pantheon Books, 1973); V. Das, 'Specificities: Official Narratives, Rumour, and the Social Production of Hate', *Social Identities*, 4/1 (1998), pp.109–30; S. Kakar, 'Rumors and Religious Riots', in G. Fine, V. Campion-Vincent and C. Heath (eds), *Rumor Mills: The Social Impact of Rumor and Legends* (New Brunswick, Aldine Transaction, 2005); J. Glassman, *War of Words, War of Stones:*

Anger as a framework to explain the escalation of violence was drawn upon by journalists and local residents alike. Edward 'Chippa' Motubatsi recalls that 'people were angry. That frustration, you see, years of frustration. They would then avenge it. Anybody who's associated with the security forces or the government, any structure of the government [people would attack]. People were absolutely angry'.[118] Articles in the alternative press and letters to the editor also situated attacks on buildings and councillors within a context of heightened emotions; violence was narrated as a form of punishment. This view was reflected in Johannes Rantete's eyewitness account *The Third Day of September*. His poem titled 'Sebokeng You Are Great' stated that 'The wrath you showed was more than/ That of a tempted black mamba/When you demolished everything to ashes'.[119] But violence was neither random nor erratic and uncontrolled. Most deaths resulted from police shootings, and there is no evidence that local residents were killed indiscriminately by the crowds. The majority of buildings that were burnt down were either regarded as symbols of apartheid, such as administrative buildings, police stations or beerhalls, or they belonged to councillors and members of the development board. The only exception was the widespread burning and looting of Indian shops, houses and a mosque in Evaton.[120] Dorcas Ralitsela suggests that owing to prejudice, some community members believed that Indian traders were exploiting African communities.[121] Whether the burning of Indian shops and the mosque points towards the limitations of a non-racialist solidarity is difficult to assess; in all likelihood, these incidents were reflective of the divergence between the ideology of non-racialism and beliefs and grudges held by some people on the ground. Others suggest the role of an agent provocateur in instigating violence against Indian traders: '[It] seems he [an alleged police agent] was promoting divisions between the blacks and the Indians of Evaton. So it's many cases that the system played some tricks on the people [...] to put an idea that the people are confused of what they wanted at that time'.[122]

Racial Thought and Violence in Colonial Zanzibar (Bloomington, Indiana University Press, 2011); F. Rueedi, 'The Hostel Wars in Apartheid South Africa: Rumour, Violence, and the Discourse of Victimhood', *Social Identities*, 26/6 (2020), pp.756–73.

118   Edward 'Chippa' Motubatsi, interview with author, Vereeniging, 15 April 2010.

119   J. Rantete, *The Third Day of September: An Eye-Witness Account of the Sebokeng Rebellion of 1984* (Johannesburg, Ravan Press, 1984), p.43.

120   *The Star*, 3 September 1985; *Financial Mail*, 7 September 1984. It is unclear why the mosque was burnt down.

121   Dorcas Ralitsela, interview with author, 1 April 2010; see also Edward 'Chippa' Motubatsi, interview with author, Vereeniging, 15 April 2010.

122   WHP AK2117, S8.11.1. Patrick Noonan writes about some of the 'dirty tricks' used by government to divide people and discredit activists. See Noonan, *They're Burning the Churches*. For an overall account of dirty tricks, see D. Potgieter, *Total Onslaught: Apartheid's Dirty Tricks Exposed* (Cape Town, Zebra Press, 2012).

The agenda of participants in the crowds was diverse: some were converging spontaneously and independently outside the houses of councillors to demand their resignation and to call on them to join the protest march, as we have seen. Others held personal grudges against a councillor and joined the crowds to settle scores, to seek revenge or personal benefits. Eyewitnesses confirm that the crowds included young and old, both ordinary residents and politicised activists.[123] This corresponds with Stathis Kalyvas' argument that conflict is usually shaped by a master cleavage, with several more contingent cleavages motivating actors on the ground.[124] Matime Moshele Papane recalls, 'Some people had their own discontent with [councillors]. I had a friend who was working with us […]. And he [the councillor] beat him up into a pulp because he wanted to evict him. […] Now there was that thing in the factory, people were saying "ey, we want to avenge what happened to this guy".'[125] Yet others were bystanders who were led by curiosity and who found themselves pulled into a rapidly escalating situation.

Looting ensued within the general upheaval. Evidence suggests that a great variety of age and social groups participated either out of opportunism or as a form of punishment of shop owners. 'There was now generally also a criminal element playing itself out. Because there were money safes in these offices and these bottle stores so criminals were taking over now,' Mandla Mazibuko, a COSAS activist, recalled.[126] Archival evidence further suggests that policemen on duty also participated in several incidents of looting.[127] By the afternoon of 3 September, shop owners were therefore up in arms. In one particularly tragic incident, a shopkeeper in Zone 11 reportedly fired indiscriminately at a crowd that had gathered outside his shop.[128] A young boy of 14, who had tripped as he attempted to flee, was shot in the head in a way that resembled an execution.

For some, violent tactics therefore emerged as the most efficient means to express their anger, to mete out punishment and, finally, to achieve ungovernability. One youth activist explained his involvement in the burning of houses and shops during that day: 'The plan was that we're going to march. But some

123   Shaka Radebe, interview with author, Vereeniging, 23 July 2010.

124   S. Kalyvas, 'The Ontology of "Political Violence": Action and Identity in Civil Wars', *Perspectives on Politics*, 1/3 (2003), pp.475–94; S. Kalyvas, *The Logic of Violence in Civil War* (Cambridge, Cambridge University Press, 2006). For an analysis of Kalyas' framework in a South African context, see G. Kynoch, *Township Violence and the End of Apartheid: War on the Reef* (Woodbridge, James Currey, 2018); Rueedi, '"Siyayinyova"!'

125   Matime Moshele Papane, interview with author, Johannesburg, 28 April 2010.

126   Mandla Mazibuko, interview with author, Vanderbijlpark, 22 June 2010.

127   WHP A2675, III (344), 'Report on Police Conduct during Township Protests', pp.18–20.

128   WHP AK2117, S8.11.2, 'Statement re Death of Lawrence Pekeer; WHP AK2117, S8.11.2, Gerektelike Doodsondersoek, No.163/85'.

of us had already said "no, let's develop another agenda. We can't just go there and leave the sell-outs here." So we went to the houses, burnt them down. We torched few shops. Went to the Indian shops.'[129] As Chabani Manganyi argues, crowd behaviour reflects social and political antagonisms and struggles.[130] Crowd behaviour thus brought to the fore underlying social and political conflicts within local communities. It highlighted changing social relations that had been fraught with tension for years and it exposed the fault lines of what was deemed acceptable and desirable.

In spite of Evaton's long history of resistance, and Sharpeville's role in politics in 1960, most political networks in the area were in their infancy by the time the uprising began. The VCA had only been established the year before, and the number of activists willing to serve in leadership positions remained low. Sebokeng's local population, marked by a long history of forced removals and relocations that deeply unsettled the social cohesion, could not build upon a memory of resistance. Repertoires of protest were therefore invented on 3 September and new political and social identities were forged on that day. This lack of sustained networks as well as the context of the uprising provided a testing ground for new tactics to emerge; arson, for example, became embedded in protest politics from September 1984. The success of such tactics, reflected by the departure of councillors from the townships, convinced many young people that increasing force would accelerate the crumbling of apartheid control and power.

The heightening of the conflict between councillors and local communities from the early 1980s had seen the emergence of small crowds that appeared ad hoc in situations of conflict. It was during the uprising of 1984 that crowds as a political force for change became significant on a larger scale, signalling the end of a period of internalised repression that had shaped the collective psyche since 1960. While crowds had played a significant role at various times and places in South Africa's history, they became particularly prominent during the mid-1980s as mass mobilisation and popular protests gained momentum. It was a period that saw the increasing use of public space in expressing and staging protest.[131] Funerals became important sites of protest, where some of the most significant political mobilisation took place (see Chapter 5). Contrary to 1960, police brutality no longer deterred local communities from engaging in public protest; instead, it radicalised and conscientised the broader population and entrenched

---

129 Sipho Johnson, interview with author, Vanderbijlpark, 7 June 2010 (name has been changed).

130 C. Manganyi, 'Crowds and Their Vicissitudes: Psychology and Law in the South African Court-Room', in C. Manganyi and A. du Toit (eds), *Political Violence and the Struggle in South Africa* (London, Macmillan, 1990), pp.287–303.

131 B. Bozzoli, *Theatres of Struggle and the End of Apartheid* (Johannesburg, Wits University Press, 2004), p.67.

the perception that apartheid had to be overthrown for peace to prevail and freedom to be gained. The street resumed greater importance and profoundly shaped politics during this period. Crowds symbolised mass dissent and acted as human barriers, hindering police, the military and other government representatives from entering the townships.

Crowds need space for their formation. It was hence the main roads and open spaces that enabled large gatherings that proved impossible to control. The smaller, untarred side roads on the other hand became the scenes of tactics that resembled urban guerrilla warfare; they allowed for more clandestine forms of resistance politics to take shape. This became particularly prevalent from 1985, as clandestine youth units began targeting houses of police and anyone else deemed to be a collaborator (see Chapter 7). Many of those side scenes became difficult for police to control, as they lacked knowledge of the local terrain. The uniformity of townships such as Sebokeng and Sharpeville therefore impeded effective policing: to the outsider, houses all looked the same, landmarks were almost completely absent and streets often ended in dead-ends.[132] For police, these smaller roads were also more unsafe, for they were scenes of frequent roadblocks set up by youths to hinder vehicles from entering.

The period starting with the Vaal Uprising therefore combined repertoires of protest, including strikes, boycotts and marches, with tactics that were developed in the course of the uprising. Large crowds and small, clandestine groups that espoused political violence both came to shape protest politics during the insurrectionary period (see Chapter 7). Besides political pressure through protest and mobilisation, the economic implications of the rent boycott were severe. It was this eclectic mix of dissent and protest that proved difficult to crush and necessitated new strategies by government to re-establish 'law and order'. Not long after, the revolt spread to other townships across the country. By late September, protests over rent increases and the council system were escalating in the Eastern Cape and large parts of the Pretoria–Witwatersrand–Vereeniging region (PWV), including the East Rand, the West Rand and Pretoria.[133] This situation, as will be seen in Chapter 6, led to the imposition of a partial state of emergency in 1985, followed by a nationwide state of emergency in 1986. What had begun as a protest march against rent increases and the two local town councils in the Vaal Triangle therefore heralded the insurrectionary period of 1984–86, which profoundly altered protest politics and shifted the balance of power, at least for some time.

---

132   Petrus Niemand, interview with author, West Rand, 29 September 2011 (name has been changed).

133   'A Chronicle of Six Months of Township Unrest', *Indicator South Africa*, 2/4 (1985).

5

Turning the Tide:
The Uprising and its Aftermath

Event

When night fell on 3 September, the sky was illuminated by fire. Overturned cars had been turned into smouldering wrecks while houses, beerhalls, shops and buildings belonging to the Orange Vaal Development Board, councillors and other businessmen presented their hollow shells, emptied of goods and reduced to rubble. In some areas, the air was thick with smoke: the smoke of burning buildings merged with the smoke emanating from coal stoves and the vapour of the industrial plants in Vanderbijlpark. Added to the fumes and smoke, the stench of teargas made those in the streets cover their faces and reach for the buckets of water and wet cloths placed next to houses. Gunshots added to the eerie atmosphere; the presence of death was almost palpable. The air was filled with the 'repugnant stench of death that gusted like a gale force through the Vaal', one journalist noted.[1] It was an apocalyptic scene that witnesses would later remember with great distress. Death had visited the townships of the Vaal Triangle once more and, for some, the actions of the police conjured up memories of the Sharpeville massacre of 1960.

Elderly women were lying on the ground, overcome by teargas. Children as young as six were standing outside the burnt shops of the mayor of the Lekoa Town Council, Esau Mahlatsi, giving the Black Power salute. One woman was seen wearing the mayoral gown of Sam Rabotapi, the mayor of the Evaton Town Council.[2] Calling herself the first mayor, she was dancing in the street. And people were heard saying that Jacob Kuzwayo Dlamini, the councillor who had been burnt in Sharpeville, had been turned into a 'Kentucky fried chicken'.[3] Anecdotal as they may be, these scenes were symbolic of a breakdown of

---

1   *The Star*, 8 September 1984.
2   J. Rantete, *The Third Day of September: An Eye-Witness Account of the Sebokeng Rebellion of 1984* (Johannesburg, Ravan Press, 1984), p.8.
3   P. Tom, *My Life Struggle: The Story of Petrus Tom* (Johannesburg, Ravan Press, 1985), p.64.

social order; hierarchies of power were turned on their head while accepted forms of sociality were suspended. The revolt signified an interregnum, where everything seemed possible and nothing was certain. Administrative structures had collapsed, the Vaal Civic Association (VCA) was struggling to maintain a sense of control, and government in Pretoria wanted to know what was happening. It was a moment of struggle in its truest sense that came with great levels of uncertainty, disdain, loss and confusion. While the messiness of the uprising curtailed effective political mobilisation and severely challenged communities' capacities to go about their everyday lives, it also provided opportunities to renegotiate what was feasible, thinkable and doable. The occurrence of violence necessitated new narratives to explain what had transpired and social relations had to be refashioned. The killing of the four councillors constituted a transgression of social norms and a break from past confrontations. While many residents were eager to return to a more stable and peaceful form of life, the routines and rhythms of everyday life changed in the aftermath of the uprising.

New subjectivities were moulded within a context of social convulsion and political upheaval. While collective action prior to the uprising had largely been guided by immediate interests, the uprising reconfigured the possibilities. People began to 'think out of place', as Michael Neocosmos argues.[4] If demands to scrap the rent increase of R5.90 and that councillors should resign had initially motivated residents to join the protest march, many were radicalised by the experiences of violence during the revolt. 'The 1984 uprising in this area […] mobilised our people. […] It started to change the mentality of our people', as Congress of South African Students' (COSAS) activist Sakhiwe Khumalo recalls.[5] This 'displacement', Neocosmos emphasises, therefore equalled the transcending of narrow interests and the development of a more radical vision of what constituted a dignified, equal and free life. New futures were imagined and emancipatory politics moved from focusing on bread-and-butter issues to more encompassing demands for a new social, economic and political order.

Aftermath

The extent of violence and the scale of protests surprised many. Neither the civic and political leadership nor the police or other authorities had anticipated an uprising that would change the social and political landscape of the area. Word spread rapidly across the region that something momentous had occurred in the Vaal Triangle; that an uprising had begun. Journalists flocked in from Johan-

---

4   See M. Neocosmos, *Thinking Freedom in Africa: Toward a Theory of Emancipatory Politics* (Johannesburg, Wits University Press, 2016), pp.12–14.

5   Sakhiwe Khumalo, interview with author, Vereeniging, 23 June 2010.

nesburg, London and New York, and photographers transfixed the world with pictures of the revolt. Footage of burning townships was broadcast into the homes of domestic and global audiences. For those white South Africans eager to protect their status and racial privilege, the uprising confirmed their deepest anxieties about the threat of the *swart gevaar.*

In the Vaal Triangle townships, some houses were filled with debates and explanations of what had transpired while others experienced a deafening silence. For days, street battles with police, looting and arson continued. Renamed 'Beirut', the area around the post office in Zone 12 in Sebokeng, opposite the politically active Nyolohelo Roman Catholic Church, became a battlefield and remained so for years.[6] Roy Matube, a COSAS member remembers that, 'I felt that now it's bad. Police are going to kill us as well.'[7] 'People were bowing their head. To say ey ey ey we are going to account for what happened today', Edward 'Chippa' Motubatsi recalls.[8] For some among the civic leadership, a sense of sadness, loss and trepidation prevailed. 'You become sad if you hear stories that so-and-so has been killed, some shops have been burnt down.'[9] But the uprising also instilled hope that the end of white minority rule was near. In the words of Motubatsi, 'At that point I see the unity of the people of the Vaal there's something I had never seen. And it made me more confident that we *are* going to be liberated.'[10]

The Ralitselas' house in Zone 7, popularly nicknamed 'United Nations' for its role in bringing people together, served as a meeting point to discuss the events and to exchange the latest news. But within hours, the Ralitselas moved out of their house. It was the beginning of years of frequent moves between safe houses to avoid arrest and attacks on their lives. Soon after their departure, police arrived at the house and shortly afterwards, it was gutted by a fire. Rumours abounded that the house had been booby-trapped and blown up by police.[11] Esau Ralitsela recalls being informed by his lawyer that 'there's no more warrant of arrest for you. There is an execution order now for you. Shoot on sight.'[12] The Ralitselas were not the only ones whose lives were threatened. Reverend Moselane, who had been assaulted and threatened in late August, was under attack again when tear gas canisters were thrown into his house in Sharpeville and seven rubber bullets were fired through the window on the evening of 3 September.[13] The

6   Sarhili 'Toy' Manqa, interview with author, Vereeniging, 26 May 2011.
7   Roy Matube, interview with author, Vanderbijlpark, 17 June 2010.
8   Edward 'Chippa' Motubatsi, interview with author, Vereeniging, 15 April 2010.
9   Esau Ralitsela, interview with author, Vereeniging, 5 April 2010.
10 Edward 'Chippa' Motubatsi, interview with author, Vereeniging, 5 December 2011.
11 Dorcas Ralitsela, interview with author, Vereeniging, 1 April 2010; Esau Ralitsela, interview with author, Vereeniging, 5 April 2010; *Rand Daily Mail*, 25 September 1984.
12 Esau Ralitsela, interview with author, Vereeniging, 5 April 2010.
13 *City Press*, 9 September 1984.

methods of attack, as well as the police vehicle seen near the scene, raised suspicions that the police were actively involved in the assault.[14]

Many progressive organisations were anxious to receive news. Officials from the United Democratic Front (UDF) and the South African Council of Churches (SACC) hosted a series of meetings in Johannesburg to discuss the way forward, and to identify needs for assistance and relief. One figure in connecting the Vaal Triangle to the SACC was Thomas Madikwe Manthata, who had been involved in one of the meetings hosted by Reverend Moselane prior to the uprising (see Chapter 4). In his capacity as a fieldworker for the SACC and assistant to Bishop Desmond Tutu, Manthata visited the Vaal Triangle on several occasions to brief the SACC about the crisis on the ground. Tutu recalls that he 'had the credibility and sensitivity necessary to bring a rational, calming influence to bear on the situation'.[15]

But the reports were harrowing and assistance was desperately needed. The gutting of houses had left people homeless, delivery trucks no longer entered the townships, and the looting of shops was causing a severe food shortage. This dire situation affected every facet of people's lives and they were left vulnerable to exploitation. Organisational capacities and infrastructure were in a state of disarray. Soon stories began to circulate that gangs were roaming the streets, demanding donations for families of the injured or dead; many allegedly used the money to enrich themselves.[16] Pamphlets issued by the UDF blamed the town councils for this situation, called for a continuation of the struggle against high rents and service tariffs and expressed solidarity and sympathy with those who had lost family and friends. Some pamphlets also urged people to abstain from looting and provided phone numbers for those who needed medical or legal assistance.[17] The burning and looting of Indian shops raised concern among the UDF leadership and led to an emergency meeting between Indian shop owners, UDF leaders and members of the VCA. The meeting, held in Roshnee, the township designated to the Indian population in the region, led to heated debates and angry confrontations when shop keepers blamed the civic leadership for the violence.

Even though key leaders of the UDF had been involved in seeking solutions to the crisis in the Vaal Triangle and other areas, the UDF's national and regional structures were remarkably ill-prepared and struggled to provide leadership. Three weeks after the beginning of the Vaal Uprising, the UDF stated in an emergency working document that area committees should be set up, including one in the Vaal Triangle, to strengthen the organisation and

14   WHP AK2117, J7, DA12, 'Letter to SAP, Vanderbijlpark from Rev. T. Moselane re Police Action Against Him, 15 October 1984'.
15   *The New York Times*, 5 December 1988.
16   WHP AK2117, S8.10.4, 'Events in the Vaal Triangle by Lisa Seftel'.
17   WHP AK2117, J3.13, AN15, 'Pamphlet Vaal Civic Association Calls – Asinamali!'.

provide direction.[18] In a meeting of the Regional Executive, the necessity to provide medical and legal assistance as well as 'social work' was affirmed.[19] The lack of leadership was spelt out most clearly during the National Executive Committee meeting in Johannesburg on 10 and 11 November 1984, when the UDF acknowledged its failure to respond to the crisis in the townships and to provide guidance.[20] Reasons for this lack of leadership, as noted in Chapter 3, were rooted in the strategies and modus operandi of the UDF.[21]

In Sebokeng and Sharpeville, branches of the Vaal Information Service (VIS) opened at churches in late 1984.[22] The VIS closely collaborated with the Detainees' Parents Support Committee (DPSC), an anti-apartheid organisation which had been set up in 1981 to provide legal, financial and material assistance to detainees.[23] Dikeledi Tsotetsi, who at some point was the secretary of the local branch of the DPSC, recalls the system of care the DPSC put in place for those whose families were unable to support and visit them. Detainees who were not from the region were 'adopted' by female members of the DPSC 'to have someone who will be your mother'.[24] For many detainees facing torture, hardship and fear, the DPSC was a beacon of light which gave them hope that they had not been forgotten. The DPSC also served as the link between the SACC and detainees and distributed small grants from the SACC to families of those in prison. Another organisation set up to monitor the situation of detainees was the Detainees' Support Committee (DESCOM), run by local activists such as Reverend Gift Moerane, COSAS activist Thomas Maleka and others. Both organisations provided counselling, channelled legal and financial assistance and brought families of detainees together.[25] Through attorney David Dison, the VIS centres were linked to Amnesty International, which enabled information on repression to be publicised internationally.[26]

18   WHP AK2117, J2.3, C118, 'Emergency UDF Working Document, 25 September 1984'.

19   WHP AK2117, J2.18, S11, 'The Meeting of the Regional Executive of UDF, Held on 4 October 1984'.

20   WHP A2675, III (869), 'Minutes of National Executive Committee Meeting, Johannesburg 10 & 11 November 1984'.

21   This analysis is based on J. Seekings, *The UDF: A History of the United Democratic Front in South Africa 1983–1991* (Cape Town, David Philip, 2nd edition, 2015), pp.123–28.

22   *City Press*, 20 April 1986; Gift Moerane, interviews with author, Vereeniging, 29 March 2010 and 17 May 2006; WHP A2675, III (869), 'Secretarial Report from the Transvaal, November 1984'.

23   T. Shakinovsky, S. Court and L. Segal, *The Knock on the Door: The Story of the Detainees' Parents Support Committee* (Johannesburg, Picador Africa, 2018).

24   Dikeledi Tsotetsi, interview with author, Vanderbijlpark, 14 June 2010.

25   Thomas Togo Maleka, interview with author, Vereeniging, 21 June 2010.

26   P. Noonan, *They're Burning the Churches: The Final Dramatic Events that Scuttled Apartheid* (Bellevue, Jacana, 2003), p.145.

Many of those injured sought medical assistance at makeshift clinics based at churches, afraid of being arrested on suspicion of being participants in the uprising. The Azanian People's Organisation in collaboration with the Health Workers Association and the National Medical and Dental Association (NAMDA) set up a mobile clinic, which according to a report in the *Sowetan* treated 144 people.[27]

On 5 September, a delegation of Sharpeville residents, led by Reverend Ben Photolo, went to the offices of the development board in Houtkop.[28] The minutes of the meeting indicate both demands and grievances, including the release of all detainees, the reduction of rents to R30, the replacement of councillors with 'people of their own choice', the withdrawal of the police from Sharpeville, the provision of buses to take people to work, scrapping the increase in service charges, visits to detainees in prison, a call for a commission of enquiry into the allocation of businesses and the burial of victims without police interference.[29] The demand to reduce rent to R30 was based on calculations that had been conducted by local leaders of what would be a fair and appropriate rent. While the VCA supported a total rent boycott, Sharpeville was not in agreement and the campaign to reduce rent to R30 remained confined to Sharpeville. This differing approach, as noted in Chapter 3, was based on Sharpeville's distinct politics and the belief of some of its leaders that a complete boycott was not feasible.

Two report-back meetings to inform residents about the state of negotiations, held at the Anglican Church in Sharpeville and the Nyolohelo Catholic Church in Sebokeng, were banned and ended in violence when the clergy decided to proceed anyway.[30] The brutality with which the police dispersed the meeting bore the imprint of Viljoen's merciless orders: within minutes after their arrival, 'all hell broke loose' as they teargassed and opened fire on the crowd inside the church. Youth retaliated by throwing stones and petrol bombs. The gratuitous violence meted out by police radicalised and conscientised the public at large as well as local priests who experienced and witnessed the teargassing, shooting and sjambokking during such events. Some of the most atrocious assaults occurred during funerals, when police regularly harassed, assaulted and violated mourners.

---

27   *The Star*, 10 September 1984; *Sowetan*, 10 September 1984; WHP AK2117, S5, 'Statement Patrick Noonan'.

28   *Rand Daily Mail*, 6 September 1984; WHP AE862, G37.8, United Democratic Front, Black Sash et al., 'Repression in a Time of Reform: A Look at Events in the Transvaal since August 1984' (Johannesburg, 1984), p.27.

29   WHP AK2117, J4.18, AAT12, 'Meeting Between the Town Clerk and a Delegation +/- 500 Residents from Sharpeville on Wednesday, 5 September 1984 to Discuss the Rent Issue'.

30   WHP AK2117, S8.7.8., 'Handwritten notes by Father Lennon'.

Funerals, Defiance and Police Violence

Official police statistics released on the first day of the uprising alleged that 14 people had died, and eight policemen and 32 civilians had been injured.[30] Unofficial statistics compiled by community leaders estimated that approximately 250 had been injured on the first day of the uprising, and by November, the death toll had risen to 72.[31] The majority of those who died were between the ages of 14 and 35, with the youngest victim, Maud Nzunga, being seven months old, and the oldest one, Martha Ndabambi, being 58 years old.[32] Both had died as a consequence of being teargassed. When the name of baby Nzunga was read during the service, mourners allegedly broke down in tears.

On 15 September, two mass funerals in Sharpeville and Sebokeng, held to bury the victims of police violence, were attended by thousands of mourners. Tebogo Moepadira, a COSAS activist, recalled that the mass funerals were meant to be a platform for people to heal and to accept what had happened. The burial of the dead was, Moepadira argued, not a matter that concerned only affected families but 'it was a matter of saying that as the Vaal community we are affected and we lost the young ones.'[33] Newspaper reports suggest that the two funerals were attended by between 40,000 and 60,000 people.[34] Patrick Noonan estimated the number of mourners to be around 6,000.[35]

The scenes that unfolded at the church and later the cemetery were as horrific as they were familiar. At the centre of the violence that was unleashed was Colonel Viljoen, regional commander of the riot squad, who had overseen the quelling of the uprising. In Sharpeville, police entered the cemetery as the coffins were lowered into the graves. Anger and frustration were mounting as mourners told the police, 'we have come to bury our heroes and we want to do it with respect and dignity. Go away!'[36] Two hundred mourners marching towards the police were said to be chanting, 'Kill us as well. Kill us.' At the mass funeral at Evaton Small Farms, mourners were rounded up and told to sit down in a circle where they were mercilessly sjambokked and later arrested.[37] Other mourners were arrested while riding on a bus which police diverted to the police station,

---

30 WHP AE862, G37.8, United Democratic Front, Black Sash, et al. 'Repression in a Time of Reform', p.25.

31 WHP AK2117, J4.15, AAQ33, 'List of the Dead – Vaal Triangle, 2 September–1 November 1984'; *City Press*, 7 October 1984.

32 Ibid.

33 Interview, Tebogo 'Exec.' Moepadira, Vanderbijlpark, 23 June 2010.

34 *Sowetan*, 19 September 1984; *Vereeniging en Meyerton Ster*, 21 September 1984.

35 Noonan, *They're Burning the Churches*, p.80.

36 *Sowetan*, 4 September 1984; WHP AK2117, S8.10.4, 'Events in the Vaal Triangle by Lisa Seftel'.

37 WHP AE862, G37.8, United Democratic Front, Black Sash, et al., 'Repression in a Time of Reform', p.17.

where its occupants were viciously assaulted.[39] Some of them later laid a charge against police for assault. These case dockets, in addition to mortuary reports, detail the vicious violence meted out by police, and the manner in which police violence appeared to be random.[40]

While the brutality with which police had quelled the uprising undoubtedly aggrieved and angered local communities, the assault on mourners exacerbated these sentiments. During the 1980s, as death stalked the townships, political funerals not only signified the violence African communities were subjected to, but they came to serve as one of the key platforms to express anger, defiance and opposition to the regime. Funerals, as Belinda Bozzoli and Charles Carter show in the case of Alexandra, also often led to a further escalation of violence.[41] The same is certainly true for the Vaal Triangle. The police frequently restricted these events and attended in force. Viljoen's conduct did not go unnoticed; unknown to him, footage of these assaults was captured on video and later used during the Delmas treason trial to discredit his claim that the police had acted with restraint.[42]

If anger prevailed over general police conduct, the death of children was an indictment of the police's disregard for African life. It whittled away the last fragments of trust communities had in the police and it imprinted on young people's minds the belief that they had to be expunged from the townships. While some of the children buried during this time were victims of stray bullets, others, like Wiseman Mnisi, were shot in a manner that resembled an execution (see Chapter 4). Similarly, ten-year-old Nicholas Mgudlwa was shot dead by the police while chopping firewood in the backyard of his parents' house.[43] 'The family heard a shot being fired from the street. Mr Mgudlwa closed the front door and called his son, Nicholas to come inside. From the kitchen door he could see Nicholas lying on the ground. He rushed to him and heard the kombi speed off.'[44] Mr Mgudlwa identified the kombi driving past their house at the time of his son's death as a police kombi, and the bullet found outside their house was a rubber bullet. In the aftermath of Nicholas Mgudlwa's funeral, youth pelted the car of a white woman with stones, leading

39 Noonan, *They're Burning the Churches*, p.92; file in the possession of the Missing Persons' Task Team, National Prosecuting Authority. MPTT NPA, Case Docket, M.R. No.480.01.85, 'Julia Mokhefe Tunza Verklaar [sic]'.

40 See, for example, MPTT NPA, Case Docket, M.R. No.482/01/85, Jacob Rooi.

41 B. Bozzoli, *Theatres of Struggle and the End of Apartheid* (Johannesburg, Wits University Press, 2004); C. Carter, 'Community and Conflict: The Alexandra Rebellion of 1986', *Journal of Southern African Studies*, 18/1 (1992), pp.115–42.

42 George Bizos, interview with author, Oxford, 23 February 2011.

43 WHP A2674, III (344), 'Report on Police Conduct During Township Protests', pp.7–8.

44 Ibid.

to the death of her infant son.[44] The tragic death of the infant received wide-spread media coverage and brought the insurrection into the homes of white South Africans. Based on evidence that rested on precarious testimonies, two young men from Sebokeng were convicted of culpable homicide, assault with the intention to do grievous bodily harm and contravention of the Internal Security Act 29, section 54.[45] Police who shot African children in the townships, on the other hand, acted with impunity.

The funerals of the four councillors were held separately. Jacob Kuzwayo Dlamini, the councillor who had died in Sharpeville on 3 September, was buried secretly and under heavy police guard. Details of the funerals of other councillors were not released and local clergy conducting the funerals received threats.[46] Councillors who emerged from their hiding places to attend the funerals admonished the political leadership, arguing that change would only come through peaceful negotiations.[47]

A funeral etched in popular memory for its political significance is that of Joseph Sithole on 23 September 1984. Sithole, a student activist with a reputation for militancy, had died in mid-September: he was allegedly beaten and killed by a crowd, said to be close to local shop owners, for his involvement in the burning of shops on 3 September.[48] By then, most activists were in hiding to evade arrest, but many felt that they needed to show support to their communities and respect to Sithole's family. Due to his status as a political activist, the local branch of COSAS wanted to bury him separately from the other victims. Newspaper reports initially announced that the funeral was to be held at the Roman Catholic Church.[49] Subsequently, Vanderbijlpark's magistrate issued an order restricting the number of people who were allowed to attend the funeral and defining the route and proceedings of the service.[50] According to witnesses, mourners knew nothing about the orders as the venue had changed to the Baptist Church in Zone 13. As thousands of people assembled outside the church, the riot squad arrived. Colonel Viljoen demanded that no freedom songs should be sung, that the coffin was not to be carried in the street, that no banners should be carried and that mourners were not allowed

44   *City Press,* 14 October 1984; *Rand Daily Mail,* 13 October 1984.

45   UWC MA, MCH31 (Records of the International Defence and Aid Fund), 5032/ L3F23C4, Supreme Court of South Africa, Appelate Division, Petition in the Matter between Themba Alfred Lata and Piet Mntambo and the State.

46   *Vereeniging en Meyerton Ster,* 21 September 1984.

47   *The Star,* 13 September 1984.

48   Tsietsi 'Speech' Mokatsanyane, interview with author, Pretoria, 13 July 2010; Shaka Radebe, interview with author, Vereeniging, 26 July 2010.

49   Noonan, *They're Burning the Churches,* p.82.

50   VT CPN, 'Prohibition of Gathering in Terms of Section 46 of the Internal Security Act (Act 74/1982)', no reference number.

to walk or march to the graveyard.[51] Only those already participating in the church service would be allowed to attend the burial at the graveyard.

Speakers in the church included members of COSAS, the Azanian Student Movement (AZASM) and the Evaton Ratepayers Association.[52] After the church service, the coffin was placed in a hearse and mourners got into buses to drive to the Evaton cemetery. The flanking of the procession by police raised tempers and caused great anger. The last prayers had barely been said at the graveside when police surrounded the cemetery and started shooting and sjam-bokking those present. Colonel Viljoen was heard inciting the police, shouting racist abuse: '*slaan* [beat] *die kaffir! Donder* [lay into] *die kaffir!*'[53] The scenes at the cemetery were nightmarish for their cruelty. One woman testified seeing policemen cutting people's hair, presumably to humiliate them.[54] A policeman with a bloodied butcher's knife was allegedly overheard telling his colleague that he had just stabbed someone.[55] Gcina Malindi recalled that no one was spared: even priests, who were usually protected by their status, were 'beaten to a pulp'.[56] At the house of Sithole's family, pots containing food and drink were wasted because of teargas while others were spilt.[57] A stampede and panic broke out as thousands of people attempted to escape the pandemonium, some of them falling into, and others trying to hide in, open graves.

After the funeral, 598 people were arrested for attending an 'illegal gather-ing'; some of the youngest arrested had barely reached adolescence.[58] Including arrests in other townships, the numbers were estimated to be as high as 900. Among them were Gcina Malindi, former chairman of COSAS, who was shot during his arrest; Patrick Baleka, an Azanian Youth League activist from Soweto; and Simon Nkoli, all of whom later stood accused in the Delmas treason trial. Baleka recounted being kicked in the chest by Viljoen as he was handcuffed and kneeling on the ground.[59] Malindi had made plans to go into exile the next

51   WHP AK2117, I1.5, Vol.36, Testimony MacCamel [sic], pp.1643–44; Lord McCamel, interview with author, Evaton, 2 May 2006; WHP AK2117, S8.7.8, 'Handwritten Notes by Accused No.13 Regarding the Funeral on 23 September 1984'.

52   WHP AK2117, S8.7.8, 'Handwritten Statement by Accused Nos 1, 5, 6, 12 & 13 Con-cerning Funeral of 23 September'.

53   Noonan, *They're Burning the Churches*, p.84; Gcina Malindi, interview with author, Johannesburg, 25 March 2010; WHP AK2117, I2.7, Vol.206, Testimony Malindi, p.10838.

54   WHP A2674, III (344), 'Report on Police Conduct During Township Protests', p.23.

55   WHP AK2117, S7.7, 'Statement Morake Petrus Mokoena'.

56   Gcina Malindi, interview with author, Johannesburg, 25 March 2010.

57   Shaka Radebe, interview with author, Vereeniging, 26 July 2010.

58   *Sowetan*, 24 September 1984; *Rand Daily Mail*, 27 September 1984.

59   WHP AK2117, S8.7.8, 'Handwritten Notes by Accused No.1 Regarding the Funeral on 23 September'.

day with student activist and close friend Tsietsi 'Speech' Mokatsanyane. But their ways parted when Mokatsanyane narrowly escaped being caught by police and Malindi was arrested. Mokatsanyane would spend the next few years in exile where he joined Umkhonto weSizwe. Malindi, on the other hand, soon stood accused in the Delmas treason trial for his role in the insurrections that were spreading across the country.[60] After being arrested, the ordeal was not over. Dozens of people had to run a gauntlet between two rows of policemen who were lashing out at them.[61] Malindi recalls:[62]

> Hundreds of people crammed into one space, and police just beating them. Getting exhausted, sit down, take a break and then lay into people again, it was horrific. […] There was such incredible defiance by the people. […] People were kicking back, fighting back and it was not a scream of pain 'let me be', it was screams of agitation against what was happening.

A group of arrested youth were threatened by a policeman who demanded to know where his jacket was. After being told that none of the youth knew the whereabouts of the jacket, the policeman shot one of them, Jacob Moleleki, at point-blank range. Subsequently, the youth were ordered to wash Moleleki's blood from the van in which they had been kept.[63] In response to this brutish violence, youth stoned and set vehicles alight.[64] As was the case again, police conduct triggered cycles of violence that would last for days. In Sharpeville the houses belonging to a businessman, an employee of the Orange Vaal Development Board (OVDB) and a police constable went up in flames.

Exile

Within days after the beginning of the uprising, civic structures were collapsing, while the police were looking to arrest the leadership.[65] The uprising severely undermined the administrative and coercive capacities of the state and endangered government's reform process, therefore exposing its lack of legitimacy. Captain P.E.J. Kruger from the security branch in Krugersdorp was tasked with heading the investigations; the case would turn out to be one of the most significant investigations of his career. Among the most sought people were Dorcas and Esau Ralitsela, whom the police suspected of having orchestrated the revolt. Aware that their arrest was imminent, the couple left their house within days

60 Tsietsi 'Speech' Mokatsanyane, interview with author, Pretoria, 13 July 2010; Gcina Malindi, interview with author, Johannesburg, 25 March 2010.
61 WHP A2674, III (344), 'Report on Police Conduct during Township Protests', pp.26–27.
62 Gcina Malindi, interview with author, Johannesburg, 25 March 2010.
63 WHP A2674, III (344), 'Report on Police Conduct during Township Protests', p.8.
64 *Sowetan*, 25 September 1984.
65 Petrus Niemand and Andries du Toit, interview with author, West Rand, 10 May 2011 (names have been changed).

of the beginning of the uprising. To protect the identities of those they had been working with, and to report back to the African National Congress (ANC) in exile, they decided to leave the country. The journey was, however, anything but straightforward and it would take them several months before they finally reached their ANC contacts in Gaborone in Botswana.

Their first destination was Johannesburg, where, with the assistance of Beulah Rollnick, an advice worker at the Black Sash offices, they relocated to a safe house. Under constant threat of being detected, they changed from one safe house to the next and travelled to Winterveld and Mafikeng, close to the Botswana border, where they stayed with relatives. In a twist of fate, the mayor of the Evaton Town Council, Sam Rabotapi, had also sought refuge in Mafikeng. For the Ralitselas, Rabotapi's presence threatened their anonymity, and after the police had visited the town they knew that they were no longer safe.

> Now we're waiting for people to help us to cross the border. We didn't have pass-
> ports, we didn't have anything. And days were going, days were going, trying to
> find a way. Now we have lost the telephone numbers of people in Botswana [and
> so we could not contact them].[66]

If their journey into exile reflects the deep anxieties and uncertainties the couple faced, it also highlights the breakdown of communication with the ANC in exile, and the hasty nature of their departure. Once the Ralitselas reached Gaborone, they were finally able to brief their contacts within the ANC about the unfolding of the revolt in the Vaal Triangle. For the next six years, they would play a crucial role in linking the ANC in exile to the Vaal Triangle, recruiting and training new operatives and providing logistical and practical support for those who wanted to leave the country. Through their connection with MaLetanta and 'Chippa' Motubatsi, the Ralitselas smuggled ANC literature into the country and recruited new members into underground work. During the infamous raid on Gaborone on 14 June 1985, which led to the killing of a dozen people (including women and children) at the hands of the South African Defence Force (SADF) and the security branch, the Ralitselas narrowly escaped with their lives.[67]

Life in exile was harsh, lonely and full of fear. Apartheid South Africa was dangerously close; cross-border raids by the SADF alternated with incursions by the security branch, who were looking for ANC exiles. 'Every day you're not sure whether tomorrow morning you would be alive. You wouldn't want to sleep in the same house for more than a month', Dorcas Ralitsela remembers.[68] While it may be tempting to imagine the South African exile community in Botswana as a supportive environment in which political discussions abounded, the truth was more complicated. Due to the high levels of infiltration, trust was hard-won

66   Dorcas Ralitsela, interview with author, Vereeniging, 1 April 2010.
67   Ibid.
68   Ibid.

and even within ANC circles, activists kept a low profile and barely disclosed the nature and degree of their political work. In Botswana, Dorcas Ralitsela worked for the Department of Local Government and Lands and lectured at the University of Botswana. In 1986, she underwent military training in Angola and received additional political training in the Soviet Union.

While the Ralitselas' life was profoundly altered by their departure for exile, the disruption of normal life for activists who remained in South Africa was no less severe and the price they paid for their activism was high. Many left their homes and families and spent years in hiding from the police, frequently moving between different safe houses. Tsietsi 'Stompi' Mokhele recalls, 'I knew from that night on [3 September] it's the last night sleeping like that. The last night of spending time with my family.'[69] The threat of being arrested loomed large; fear was a constant companion, as being arrested almost inevitably meant assault, torture or worse. For their families, constant worry and anxiety about the fate of their activist daughters, sons, grandchildren, siblings and spouses was compounded by police harassment.

Edward 'Chippa' Motubatsi was detained for two weeks under section 30 of the Internal Security Act (ISA) of 1982.[70] Two days after his release, he was rearrested and accused of having been involved in the killing of Councillor Caesar Motjeane. Charges were later dropped but due to serious assault and torture, the ANC in exile advised Motubatsi to leave the country, which he declined for private reasons.[71] Others departed for different parts of the country, where they had family or friends providing shelter and safety. Lord McCamel, the VCA's chairman, was arrested on 8 November 1984 under section 29 of the ISA and later held under section 31 for 16 months.[72] McCamel eventually turned state witness for the Delmas treason trial.[73]

The Vaal Ministers' Solidarity Group

With key civic leaders gone and others in hiding or detention, the structures of the VCA virtually collapsed after the uprising. Fledgling civic structures, and the dire need for leadership and material, legal and spiritual assistance thrust another player into the forefront. Under the umbrella of the SACC and the Southern African Catholic Bishops' Conference (SACBC), churches began to

69   Tsietsi 'Stompi' Mokhele, interview with author, Bophelong, 18 September 2011.

70   Edward 'Chippa' Motubatsi, interview with author, Vereeniging, 15 April 2010; WHP AK2117, S5, 'Statement Edward Motobatse [sic]'.

71   Edward 'Chippa' Motubatsi, interviews with author, Vereeniging, 15 April 2010 and 22 November 2011.

72   WHP AK2117, S8.10.20, 'The Vaal Triangle During the Unrest, 1984–1985 (September to January) by Rev. Patrick Noonan'; *City Press*, 11 November 1984.

73   *Sowetan*, 4 March 1986.

play a key role in filling the lacunae the harassment and persecution of the local leadership had left. On 6 September, three days after the beginning of the uprising, the SACC and its affiliates held a meeting to discuss the situation in the Vaal Triangle and the East Rand, the second area where popular protests had translated into an uprising.[74] The list of attendees was impressive: chaired by Bishop Desmond Tutu, also present to discuss possible strategies to provide assistance were other prominent figures of the UDF and the SACC: general secretary of the SACC, Frank Chikane, Allan Boesak and Smangaliso Mkhatshwa.[75] Briefed by local clergy and community leaders, the SACC harshly condemned police conduct and the insensitivity of local authorities in responding to popular grievances, as the press statement released in the aftermath of the meeting highlights. The SACC stated that it:

1.   Records its shock and anger at the irresponsible and uncontrolled action of some members of the South African police, and the manner in which some unruly elements in the areas concerned hijacked a legitimate protest.

2.   Expresses its distress and concern regarding the manner in which the Government refuses to admit publicly the root causes of the unrest, which can only increase unless genuine grievances are heard and dealt with in a manner, which recognises the human dignity and rights of all South Africans.

3.   Calls on all members elected to the House of Representatives and the House of Delegates to resign forthwith, and on those involved in the Government agencies, which are responsible for the unrest to withdraw their participation forthwith.

4.   Calls on its member Churches, and all ministers and congregations, to offer the support and the facilities of the Churches to those affected by the unrest.

5.   Expresses its solidarity with the tenants, workers, students and parents in their struggle for justice and participatory society.

6.   Calls on the Government a) to consult with the acknowledged leaders of the communities and the students concerned; b) to release all people arrested or detained during the recent elections for the House of Representatives and the House of Delegates.

7.   Pledges itself to pray and strive for society in which the rights and responsibilities of all South Africans are recognised, which this Council believes to be the only permanent answer to the recurring unrest which has become endemic in South Africa ever since June 16th, 1976.[76]

---

74   WHP AE862, G37.8, 'Handwritten Notes re Emergency Meeting'.
75   WHP AK2117, S8.10.3, Diary of Events.
76   WHP AE862, G37.8, 'Handwritten Notes re Emergency Meeting'.

A telex sent to Kairos, the Dutch anti-apartheid organisation, by the Transvaal branch of the UDF highlighted the situation of the population under siege in the Vaal Triangle and stressed the 'need for transport and assistance to help hungry people in the areas'.[78] Food prices had become 'exorbitant' and medical care was non-existent for many. Concerned about the escalation of violence in the townships of the Vaal Triangle, the SACC sent telexes to P.W. Botha and cabinet ministers, pleading with them to adopt a sensitive approach towards protest action in the region.[79]

Besides playing a significant role in publicising the atrocities, the SACC provided material, financial and spiritual assistance. International funding through the International Defence Aid Fund (IDAF) was channelled through the SACC and distributed to activists who had to go into hiding, to students in need of bursaries and to pay for legal costs that arose in relation to political trials. Many youth who had been expelled from township schools due to their activism continued their education with the assistance of the SACC. In the case of the trial of the Sharpeville Six and the Delmas treason trial, the SACC and its member churches were vital in assisting in organising transport to visit the trials, in counselling the defendants and in aiding their families.[80] Furthermore, they lobbied for their release and maintained relations to international media, pressure groups and governments. On an informal level, churches offered sanctuary and hiding places for those evading the police. Within a context of increasing state repression, the support of churches therefore protected, at least to some degree, activists who were on the run from the police.

The other religious body that resumed a crucial role in monitoring the situation in the townships was the SACBC. When the SACC issued its press statement on 6 September, the SACBC followed suit on the same day, condemning the violence and calling for restraint on all sides.[81] It urged the government to establish a commission of inquiry that would look into the causes of the uprising and warned that, should grievances not be addressed, similar uprisings were bound to occur.

While progressive clergy across South Africa had long played a role in voicing their dissent, it was during the course of the uprising that they resumed a more active role. Guided by their belief that as clergy they needed to be in solidarity with the oppressed, they took a more open political stand (see Chapter 4). In mid-September, a group of 17 clergy formed the Vaal Ministers' Solidarity Group (VMSG).[82] It was the largest inter-denomina-

78 WHP AK2117, J3.12, AM62, 'Message to Kairos Holland by UDF Tvl'.
79 WHP AK2117, S8.10.4, 'Events in the Vaal Triangle by Lisa Seftel'.
80 Noonan, *They're Burning the Churches*.
81 VT CPN, 'Press Release, SACBC Administrative Board, 6 September 1984', no reference number.
82 WHP AG2613, F11, 'A Report from the Vaal Triangle'; Noonan, *They're Burning the Churches*, pp.71–72.

tional formation of clergy that the region had seen. Lord McCamel, the former chairman of the VCA, was elected chairman; Edward Lennon, a Roman Catholic priest known for his support of political activists, became treasurer; while Reverend Peter Lenkoe of the Anglican Church, an ardent supporter of Black Consciousness and outspoken critic of local authorities, acted as secretary. The VMSG played a diverse role that included negotiating with local authorities, organising funerals, establishing food relief centres in collaboration with the Red Cross, organising legal aid, monitoring the death toll, supporting those who were appearing in court, co-ordinating medical aid centres, establishing a relief fund for those who had lost family members during the uprising, monitoring police conduct as well as providing information to the media.[82] But their growing outspokenness was a thorn in the flesh of local authorities; on more than one occasion, churches were firebombed and attacked at night, to leave the impression that parishioners were rejecting the activities of the priests.[83]

Although most of them were not radical, their leadership and presence was vital in providing assistance and sanctuary and keeping communication with the outside world going. At a time when government was clamping down on political dissent, the clergy's relations with the SACC and the World Council of Churches (WCC) proved vital in ensuring that information would reach the media, international pressure groups and foreign governments. On 17 October 1984, British Labour Party MP Donald Anderson visited the Vaal Triangle on his tour through South Africa.[84] He held discussions with local clergy, community leaders, lawyers as well as officials of the UDF at the Emmanuel Roman Catholic Church in Zone 14, Sebokeng. Anderson, describing the South African government as 'evil', appeared to be shocked by the occurrences in the Vaal Triangle and the high degree of violence that was ravaging the townships. Such negative publicity was a thorn in the flesh of the South African government, which by then had launched a propaganda war to steer international opinion in its favour (see Chapter 6).

Even more than the visit of Anderson and other international observers, the publication of a booklet on police conduct challenged the government's attempt to portray police action as reasonable and measured. The investigation launched by the SACBC into police brutality in the Vaal Triangle and the East Rand caused an uproar and exposed the gratuity with which police meted out violence against protestors, bystanders and township communities at large. Allegations of wanton violence by police had emerged during

---

82   WHP AG2613, F11, 'A Report from the Vaal Triangle'.
83   Noonan, *They're Burning the Churches*.
84   Patrick Noonan, interview with author, Sebokeng, 24 March 2010; WHP AK2117, S8.10.20, 'The Vaal Triangle During the Unrest, 1984–1985 (September to January) by Rev. Patrick Noonan', p.4; *City Press*, 21 October 1984.

the course of the uprising, when the Health Workers Association reported cases of people's backs, buttocks and legs being 'riddled' by buckshot – demonstrating that they had not been facing the police when shot.[85] One of the doctors treating victims of police violence aired his concerns when he said, 'I do not believe that the behaviour of the police is preventative at all. It is punitive in the extreme.'[86] The SACBC's public relations officer, Sarah Crowe, with the assistance of local clergymen Patrick Noonan and Edward Lennon and advocate Nicholas Haysom, identified victims and eventually collected dozens of affidavits detailing police conduct. Random sjambokkings and beatings, humiliating behaviour, reckless and punitive use of teargas, indiscriminate shootings, participation in looting as well as rape all formed part of a long list of atrocities police were accused of. While the security forces justified their conduct as necessary to re-establish public order, allegations of rape undermined such claims.[87] Other evidence suggests that policemen laughed, drank liquor and hurled racist abuse while assaulting people.[88]

By December 1984, enough evidence had been collected to publish the report. It sharply criticised police conduct and concluded that 'the police appeared to believe they were at war'.[89] Patrick Noonan recalls that the booklet was in fact 'a not-so-veiled condemnation of the policing of Brigadier Gerrit Viljoen', in charge of the riot squad, who had been promoted to the rank of brigadier shortly after the uprising.[90] The booklet was launched at a press conference at Khanya House, the headquarters of the SACBC in Pretoria, on 6 December 1984. Not surprisingly, the police denied the allegations. Complaining that they had not been consulted, they accused the bishops of conducting the investigation for 'ulterior purposes'.[91] A few weeks after its publication, a lengthy statement by Viljoen, in which he responded to the different allegations made in the booklet, aimed to refute the allegations.[92] It was the second time the SACBC published a report criticising the government and its security forces; the first report, published in 1982, had challenged the conduct of SADF in Namibia.[93]

85 *Sunday Mirror*, 16 September 1984.
86 WHP A2674, III (344), 'Report on Police Conduct during Township Protests', p.29.
87 Sarah Crowe, interview with author, Johannesburg, 11 May 2006.
88 WHP A2674, III (344), 'Report on Police Conduct during Township Protests', p.23.
89 Ibid., p.28.
90 Noonan, *They're Burning the Churches*, p.114.
91 *Rand Daily Mail*, 7 and 8 December 1984.
92 MPTT NPA, Case Docket, M.R. No.480.01.85., 'Gerrit Johannes Viljoen Verklaar'.
93 Archbishop Dennis Hurley, interview with Padraig O'Malley, Durban, 6 July 1985, http://www.nelsonmandela.org/omalley/index.php/site/q/03lv00017/04lv00344/05lv00345/06lv00347.htm, retrieved 14 May 2020.

A few weeks after the launch of the booklet, on 17 January 1985, the SACBC demonstrated its solidarity and support once more when 28 bishops and cardinals visited Sebokeng to attend Mass at Emmanuel Church in Zone 14.[94] In what was dubbed 'the Mass of the rubber bullet' by a reporter from the *Sunday Times*, symbols of the crisis were displayed, including a rent invoice, the booklet on police conduct, school books, a rubber bullet, a teargas canister, a change of clothes (to remember those in detention) and a list of those who had died.[95] Archbishop Denis Hurley in his prayer stated that 'peace had been so severely broken that he stood before God asking for reconciliation'.[96] But the police were not the only ones at the forefront of escalating repression: by late 1984, government had adopted a multi-pronged approach to curb resistance while attempting to win the support of the majority of the population. Doomed to failure, this approach reflected the crumbling of the apartheid regime's power base. Gratuitous violence and the use of the courts and the media to delegitimise black protest, coupled with attempts to appease the larger population, came to be a signifier of the inherent tension of the late apartheid period, as the following chapter will explore.

94   Noonan, *They're Burning the Churches*, p.129.
95   VT CPN, pamphlet outlining the purpose of the Mass, no reference number.
96   *Sowetan*, 29 January 1985.

6

'Instigators and agitators':
The State Responds

'Where peace at all cost was to be'

On 6 September 1984, when the dust had not yet settled and the townships were in a state of chaos, the Minister of Law and Order, Louis le Grange, spoke at a press conference to comment on the recent upheavals in the Vaal Triangle. Le Grange emphasised that, 'I'm not convinced that the rent increase is the real reason for the problems we have here. There are individuals and other forces and organisations that are very clearly behind what is happening in the Vaal Triangle.'[1] Earlier le Grange had visited the townships of the Vaal Triangle in the company of three other ministers: General Magnus Malan, Minister of Defence, F.W. de Klerk, Minister of Internal Affairs and MP for Vereeniging, as well as Dr Gerrit Viljoen, Minister of Co-operation, Development and Training and MP for Vanderbijlpark.[2] In Sebokeng, the group, accompanied by councillors and travelling in an armoured vehicle, had to turn around as they were confronted by several hundred local residents who had blocked the road.[3]

Le Grange was not entirely wrong in thinking that the upsurge of popular protest and mass mobilisation in the Vaal Triangle was not merely a result of the latest rent increase but reflected increasing opposition to the apartheid regime. What le Grange, however, failed to respond to was the severity of socio-economic grievances that had been plaguing the residents of the townships and the pernicious implications an increase in rent of R5.90 had on the already tight funds of the population. A cartoon published in the *Sowetan* a few days after le Grange's statement depicted him searching a garbage bin with a magnifying glass to discover 'the causes of the rioting'.[4]

1   *The Star*, 7 September 1984; *Sowetan*, 7 September 1984.
2   Dr Gerrit Viljoen and Brigadier Gerrit Viljoen are two different people.
3   *Rand Daily Mail*, 7 September 1984.
4   *Sowetan*, 19 September 1984.

Le Grange further alleged that the uprising had been timed to coincide with the introduction of the new constitution – a claim that was confirmed by some activists.[5]

Only months before the rebellion started, State President P.W. Botha toured Europe to win the international community's favourable opinion of his reform programme. Buoyed by the signing of the Nkomati Accord, which had been a major blow for the liberation movements in exile, Botha exuded confidence that domestic resistance had fizzled out and global public opinion had swayed in favour of the government's reforms. Nothing could have been further from the truth. The unfolding of the revolt in the Vaal Triangle and elsewhere caused embarrassment to apartheid's politicians and gave the lie to their myopic dream of averting dissent by implementing partial reforms. Internationally, the revolt confirmed that apartheid could not be reformed, and that only the dismantling of the regime would lead to lasting peace and political stability. In July 1985, Botha's diminishing confidence became apparent when he stated during a meeting of the State Security Council (SSC) that the nationwide insurrections posed a 'spiralling threat' and that the 'brain of the revolution', which he believed to be inside the country, needed to be eradicated.[6] Yet beyond the threat of political and social disorder, government also had to grapple with the failure of the reforms and the growing urban crisis, as well as the 'ideological challenge posed by "people's power"', as Karen Jochelson has noted.[7]

Images of burning tyres, toyi-toying crowds and police violence, broadcast into the homes of domestic and global audiences, affirmed the regime's loss of control. The increasing loss of its coercive capacity was by no means unique to apartheid South Africa but emblematic of late colonialism in other African countries during the 1950s and 1960s. In Kenya, for example, the British colonial regime in its war against the Mau Mau insurgency stripped the revolutionaries of their human rights while attempting to maintain an image of transparency, accountability and justice.[8] The South African state followed a similar logic. The paradoxical marriage between reform and repression came to symbolise the crumbling power of the apartheid regime and an inherent contradiction between the way the state viewed itself, and its use of force. While it increasingly relied on draconian laws, harsh repression and terror,

---

5   *City Press*, 9 September 1984.

6   Quoted in N. Rousseau, 'Counter-Revolutionary Warfare: The Soweto Intelligence Unit and Southern Itineraries', *Journal of Southern African Studies*, 40/6 (2014), p.1346.

7   K. Jochelson, 'Reform, Repression and Resistance in South Africa: A Case Study of Alexandra Township, 1979–1989', *Journal of Southern African Studies*, 16/1 (1990), p.13.

8   D. Anderson, *Histories of the Hanged: Britain's Dirty War in Kenya and the End of Empire* (London, Phoenix, 2006), pp.5–6.

the state imagined itself as transparent, accountable, modern, reasonable and bound by the rule of law.[9] It was anxious to uphold this image in the eyes of its white constituency and the international community.

From the mid-1980s onwards the South African regime therefore waged a propaganda war that aimed to criminalise political protest while portraying itself as the defender of law and order in the face of an alleged communist onslaught. A secret memorandum to all members of the SSC in November 1984 outlined the language to be used by the media when reporting on protests in the townships: protestors were to be depicted as members of faceless crowds, engaging in 'unreasonable' and 'senseless' violence. Protests should be referred to as 'unrest' and any positive connotation was to be avoided.[10] By late 1985, a meeting comprised of the heads of intelligence agreed that 'negotiations with the ANC [African National Congress] were inevitable and that security strategy should direct all its efforts at weakening the ANC (and especially its South African Communist Party [SACP] ally and other radicals) as much as possible before such negotiations took place.'[11]

For government, a popular uprising in the Vaal Triangle not only posed a challenge to its administrative and coercive capacity, but also exposed the severe flaws in its reform programme. The Vaal Triangle was a testing ground for new policies and shown to foreign visitors to demonstrate the 'success' of segregated development. In the words of Father Patrick Noonan, 'This was the model town, where peace at all cost was to be. The last thing that was to happen here was revolt. Everything seemed to be going so well and then it all went wrong in the eyes of the government.'[12] It was the last place where government had expected rebellion. The repression that followed therefore had two aims: to deter other townships from joining the rebellion, and to discredit the genuineness of grievances and demands by claiming the uprising had been orchestrated by outside forces.

Pretoria's politicians were quick to claim that the United Democratic Front (UDF), under the guidance of the ANC and the SACP and in conspiracy with the Azanian People's Organisation (AZAPO) and others, had orchestrated a nationwide uprising to overthrow government by

9   F. Rueedi, 'Narratives on Trial: Ideology, Violence and the Struggle over Political Legitimacy in the Case of the Delmas Treason Trial, 1985–89', *South African Historical Journal*, 67/3 (2015), pp.335–55.

10   D.J. Louis Nel (Adjunk Minister van Buitelandse Sake), 'An Alle Lede van die Staatsveiligheidsraad. Onlussituasies: Vorgestelde Terminologiese Riglyne van Amptelike Segsmanne', 12 November 1984, http://www.disa.ukzn.ac.za/mem19841112040024084, retrieved 15 May 2020.

11   Rousseau, 'Counter-Revolutionary Warfare', p.1346. Rousseau argues that the acknowledgement that negotiations with the ANC were inevitable met with considerable resistance from the security branch.

12   Patrick Noonan, interview with author, Sebokeng, 24 March 2010.

violent means. Le Grange alleged that 90 percent of the UDF's leaders were ANC operatives, and that 'the United Democratic Front is pursuing the same revolutionary goals as the banned ANC and South African Communist Party, in actively promoting a climate of revolution'.[13] This claim was at the heart of two of the most significant political trials of the 1980s: the Delmas treason trial and the Pietermaritzburg treason trial, which both emphasised the UDF's role in violence and protest.[14]

As noted in the Introduction, during the three years the Delmas treason trial lasted, the state prosecution and the defence for the accused called on more than 200 witnesses to impress on Judge van Dijkhorst their version of what had transpired in the Vaal Triangle and elsewhere. The state prosecution's argument that localised rebellions were part of a wider strategy of the UDF and its allies to overthrow government aimed to discredit popular protest by linking it to violent revolution. Such trials, as Cathy Albertyn notes, served to publicly censure individuals and their organisations.[15]

At the core of the trial was the perception that organisations were lacking a broad political constituency and that ordinary people had been incited to participate in protests. This perception informed much of government's counter-insurgency strategy, including the campaign of Winning Hearts and Minds (WHAM) in the aftermath of the uprising. The concept of WHAM had been coined during the war between guerrillas and Commonwealth forces in Malaya from 1948 to 1960 and shaped subsequent counter-insurgency strategies of the British colonial forces.[16] To isolate 'agitators' from society while appeasing the broader population would eventually introduce peace and stability. This belief was endorsed by local authorities. Esau Mahlatsi, the mayor of the Lekoa Town Council, was quoted as saying that 'troubles' had been caused by 'agitators and instigators'.[17] At a press conference, Mahlatsi claimed that only 3 percent of the local population participated in protests; yet how Mahlatsi arrived at this number remains unknown.[18] The town clerk of the Lekoa Town Council, Nicholas Louw, supported this view when he stated that

13   Louis le Grange, quoted in T. Simpson, *Umkhonto we Sizwe: The ANC's Armed Struggle* (Cape Town, Penguin Books, 2016), pp.335–36.

14   On the role of political trials during this period, see C. Albertyn, 'A Critical Analysis of Political Trials in South Africa 1948–1988' (PhD thesis, University of Cambridge, 1991); R. Abel, *Politics by Other Means: Law in the Struggle against Apartheid* (New York, Routledge, 1995).

15   Albertyn, 'A Critical Analysis of Political Trials'.

16   K. Hack, 'Everyone Lived in Fear: Malaya and the British Way of Counter-Insurgency', *Small Wars and Insurgencies*, 23/4–5 (2012), pp.671–99.

17   *SASPU National*, 5/7 (September 1984), p.4.

18   WHP AK2117, S8.10.20, 'The Vaal Triangle During the Unrest in 1984–85 (September to January), by Rev. Patrick Noonan'.

only a small group of people in the Vaal Triangle had actively participated in the protests, which were 'inspired by subversive elements from outside'.[19]

Blame was also put on local priests when a judge stated in court that 'I have reasons to believe that priests are behind the unrest in the Vaal Triangle', referring to Reverend Moselane in particular.[20] Quite unexpectedly, the mayor of the Evaton Town Council, Sam Rabotapi, found another explanation for the recent occurrence. At the funeral of Philemon 'Dutch' Diphoko, Rabotapi allegedly blamed apartheid.[21] Government's attempts to single out individual 'agitators' rapidly found expression in a series of court cases. By the time the Delmas treason trial commenced, another legal and human drama that focused on collective violence was unfolding at the Supreme Court in Pretoria. While the Delmas treason trial aimed to delegitimise the UDF and its affiliates, the murder trial *State v Sefatsa and 7 Others*, popularly known as the Sharpeville Six trial, served another purpose: based on the principle of common purpose, it aimed to effectively criminalise participation in collective action and to reinstall faith in the council system. Yet it had unintended consequences: the blatant miscarriage of justice further exposed the rottenness of the apartheid regime and caused an international outcry.

A Miscarriage of Justice: The Trial of the Sharpeville Six

The trial of the Sharpeville Six began on 23 September 1985.[22] The eight young people were directly charged with the murder of the deputy mayor of the Lekoa Town Council, Kuzwayo Jacob Dlamini, on 3 September 1984 in Sharpeville. It was the most infamous of four murder trials that dealt with the death of the councillors during the Vaal Uprising. Police were anxious to provide suspects in the murder cases of the four councillors; their deaths had proven a major blow for government and it was vital to depoliticise the murders to maintain the claim that the council system held validity among township communities.

19 WHP AK2243 (*State v Sefatsa and 7 Others*), Case No.698/85, A, Vol.1, Testimony Louw, p.39.

20 WHP AK2117, S8.10.20, 'The Vaal Triangle During the Unrest in 1984–1985' by Rev. Patrick Noonan.

21 Ibid.

22 For a first-hand account of this trial, see the monograph published by Prakash Diar, the lawyer for the accused. P. Diar, *The Sharpeville Six: The South African Trial that Shocked the World* (Toronto, McClelland and Stewart, 1990). See also P. Parker and J. Mokhesi-Parker, *In the Shadow of Sharpeville: Apartheid and Criminal Justice* (Basingstoke and New York, Macmillan and NYU Press, 1998) and P. Noonan, *They're Burning the Churches: The Final Dramatic Events that Scuttled Apartheid* (Bellevue, Jacana, 2003).

Based on the judicial doctrine of common purpose, the presence of the accused near the scene of the murder was sufficient to sentence six of them to death, even though evidence that some of them had been near the scene was disputed and no direct involvement in Dlamini's murder could be proven.[23] The doctrine of common purpose was not only particularly notorious but also reflected the perception that crowds formed coherent entities that followed a particular logic. As Chabani Manganyi observes, this approach portrayed the crowd as an ahistorical homogeneous entity that acted outside the realm of social and political struggles.[24]

On 10 December 1985, Judge Human sentenced Reid Mokoena, Theresa Ramashamole, Reginald Mojalefa 'Jaja' Sefatsa, Duma Kumalo, Francis Don Mokhesi and Oupa Moses Diniso to death by hanging.[25] Motsiri Gideon Mokone, who had been shot by Dlamini on the 3rd, and Motseki Christian Mokubung were acquitted on charges of murder but found guilty of alternative charges of public violence and subsequently sentenced to eight years' imprisonment. Judge Human, in a grossly unfair judgment, rejected most of the evidence given by the defendants. He accepted statements made under duress and based his findings largely on the testimony of two state witnesses. Pleading for their lives, their brief speeches after being sentenced are harrowing. While at first some of them asked for clemency, their words speak of increasing resignation and frustration. But their pleas fell on deaf ears; all six were led to the section of the prison reserved for inmates on death row. After being sentenced to death, Duma Kumalo recalls he could not sleep all night: 'It was difficult. I was crying all night long until I fell asleep.'[26] Kumalo had been studying at the Sebokeng Teachers' Training College at the time of his arrest. He recalls that he had no particular interest in politics but 'some inklings'. He joined the march on 3 September without having attended any of the meetings pre-dating it. Like many other local residents he equated town councillors with oppression. When hearing that Dlamini had died, he stated during his hearing at the Truth and Reconciliation Commission, 'I was sort of happy because I felt that the reign of the boers had fallen down.'

23   On the doctrine of common purpose, see N. Matzukis, 'Nature and Scope of Common Purpose', *South African Journal of Criminal Justice*, 1/2 (1988), pp.226–34.

24   C. Manganyi, 'Crowds and Their Vicissitudes: Psychology and Law in the South African Court-Room', in C. Manganyi and A. du Toit (eds), *Political Violence and the Struggle in South Africa* (London, Macmillan, 1990), p.293.

25   WHP AK2243, B, 15, Vonnis (Judgment), pp.1508–11.

26   Truth and Reconciliation Commission, Human Rights Violations. Submission Duma Joshua Kumalo, Case No.861 (5 August 1996), http://www.justice.gov.za/trc/hrvtrans/sebokeng/seb861.htm, retrieved 10 August 2018.

Reginald Mojalefa Sefatsa, a 29-year-old street hawker who had left school after standard six, was arrested on 9 November 1984.[27] The two policemen searching his house punched him, resulting in a broken jaw. His wife, eight months pregnant at that time, was slapped in the face. At the police station, Sefatsa was blindfolded and tortured with electric shocks. The other accused recounted similar stories of assault and torture, leading them to make false statements under duress. Sefatsa was not politically active and had not planned to join the protest march.[28] Instead, he assisted in helping a security branch policeman who was being attacked by a group of youth on that day, but to his distress, the policeman refuted Sefatsa's alibi in court. Like his co-accused, Sefatsa was trying to come to terms with his fate: 'You see, if you are in jail, you start to ask yourself "why me? Why only me?" And then I didn't take any part [in the murder of Dlamini].'[29] Sefatsa recalls his thoughts after hearing that all attempts had failed to overturn the judgment:

> We were supposed to be killed on Friday. You see I accepted that. Because apartheid was too difficult for everybody. […] They will sentence you. Without any proof. […] I was ready to die. I was not scared anymore. […] We were so many who get the death sentence even we didn't do any crime. I said 'no ok. It's how the government runs the country. They kill me, it's ok'.[30]

In his understanding, the reason why he was detained was because the police failed to arrest the perpetrators and hence turned them into scapegoats. Theresa Ramashamole, the only woman among the six, who was 24 years old at the time of her arrest, was accused of having incited the crowd to kill Dlamini.[31] She had made her statement, in which she implicated herself and others, under duress.[32]

On 16 March 1988, the United Nations Security Council adopted Resolution 610, urging the South African government to commute the sentences and to stay the execution of the Sharpeville Six, which was scheduled for 18 March. One day after the adoption of Resolution 610, a one-month stay of execution was granted. After three years on death row and winning two stays of execution, the case was taken to the Court of Appeal to hear new evidence. The defence for the accused argued that two of the key state witnesses had been forced by the police to implicate the six.[33] Appeal was rejected in June 1988, leading the Security Council to adopt Resolution 615 on 17 June 1988. Resolution 615 stated

27 WHP AG2918, 2.3.1.1.1, SATIS, 'Save the Sharpeville Six. No to Apartheid Executions (1986)'.
28 Reginald Mojalefa 'Jaja' Sefatsa, interview with author, Vereeniging, 3 July 2010.
29 Ibid.
30 Ibid.
31 Theresa Ramashamole, interview with author, Vanderbijlpark, 15 June 2010.
32 WHP AK2117, S8.11, 'Theresa Ramashamole Verklaar'.
33 WHP AK2243, G6, 'Interview 18 June 1988 with Mr. Bham'.

that the hanging of the six would 'further inflame an already grave situation in South Africa'.[34] In response to the rejection of the appeal, the House of Representatives in the United States passed HR1530, which called for comprehensive sanctions against South Africa.[35] A day after the adoption of Resolution 615, on 18 June, one of the state witnesses recalled his evidence during a conversation with one of the lawyers. During the same month, Joyce Mokhesi, the sister of one of the accused, toured Europe and the United States to lobby for support from various organisations and governments to reopen the case.[36] Pressure was mounting inside South Africa as well as abroad. In Sharpeville, the local branch of the Detainees' Parents Support Committee in collaboration with the UDF launched the 'Save the Sharpeville Six' campaign.

The trial of the Sharpeville Six captured the imagination of South Africans and global pressure groups. The director of Freedom House in New York sent a telex on 16 March 1988 stating that it was 'imperative that clemency be granted to the Sharpeville Six'.[37] In Britain, TV presenter David Frost confronted the South African ambassador over the fate of the Sharpeville Six.[38] The moral outrage the trial caused in many countries was unprecedented and increased the pressure on the South African government. And it was a major blow to the government's attempt to influence international opinion. Eventually the death sentence was commuted into prison terms ranging from 18 to 25 years. In 1991 the six were finally reprieved but not acquitted.

'A friend does not carry a gun': Operation *Palmiet*

While the Sharpeville Six trialists faced an uncertain future, repression in the townships intensified. One of the most visible signs that the police's coercive capacity had been severely compromised was the deployment of the South African Defence Force (SADF) troops in October 1984. Around 4am on 23 October, 7,000 policemen and military conscripts entered Sebokeng in Buffels, a type of armoured vehicle, and immediately began to cordon it off.[39] Operation *Palmiet* (bulrush) had begun, launched to effectively 'rid the area of criminal and revolutionary elements' and to 'restore law and order',

34   *Washington Post*, 18 June 1988; WHP AG2918, 2.3.1.1.2, 'Resolution 615 (1988), Adopted by the Security Council at Its 2817th Meeting on 17 June 1988'.

35   *Washington Notes on Africa*, Summer 1988, p.5; American Committee on Africa, *Action News*, Fall 1988, p.25.

36   *Washington Notes on Africa*, Summer 1988, p.7; Parker and Mokhesi-Parker, *In the Shadow of Sharpeville*.

37   WHP AK2084, Af9, 'Telex from Freedom House, New York, to Helen Suzman re Clemency for Sharpeville Six, 16/03/1988'.

38   WHP AK2243, G7, 'Transcript of Interview between David Frost and Rae Killen, South African Ambassador to Britain'.

39   *City Press*, 26 October 1984; *Ecunews*, December 1984, pp.23–24; *Sowetan*, 24 October 1984.

as le Grange stated.⁴⁰ For many of the young conscripts it was their first experience of an African township, and the first time they were confronted by protesting crowds.

Police assisted by the soldiers embarked on a house-to-house search. Every ten metres, a soldier was placed to reinforce and support police roadblocks. Residents were only allowed to pass through once they had received red ink on their thumb, signalling that they had passed the check-up. An army helicopter was flying over the townships announcing that the army had come to protect the local population. A pamphlet was distributed, declaring 'We are here to promote normal social life, continued education, safe travel, stability, a healthy community, the delivery of food. Trust us'.⁴¹ The pamphlet was also published in the newsletter of the Orange Vaal Development Board (OVDB), *Bula Ditaba tsa Lekoa*, in October 1984 in Sesotho and English.⁴² But these attempts by the SADF to portray itself as anything but an occupying force fell on deaf ears. 'A friend does not carry a gun in your house and later detain your son,' one resident remarked.⁴³ For Sebokeng's residents, the presence of troops signified a declaration of war. A letter to le Grange, written by a resident of Evaton, highlights the anger experienced by many. The author demanded that the SADF and the police leave the townships, described several incidents of excessive and wanton violence by policemen and warned le Grange that 'the frustration caused to blacks is irreparable. I would not like the Minister to be here when blacks obtain their freedom.'⁴⁴

Rumours soon began to spread that special forces had been brought in from Namibia and Angola to deal with the unrest. Among the conscripts in Sebokeng, stories were told that members of *Koevoet*, the notorious counter-insurgency unit that had been set up in northern Namibia in 1978, were driving around in Nyalas, the distinct yellow police armoured vehicles, with 'bad boys' written on the side.⁴⁵ The deployment of specialised counter-insurgency units indicated the degree of threat government believed itself to be under. For the local population, it increased their sense of being at war.

By 8.30am, 348 people had been arrested for the possession of drugs, banned literature, unlicensed arms and ammunition and for pass law offences.⁴⁶ No evidence of guns and ammunition could be found.⁴⁷ For the local

40   C. Cooper, J. Shindler, C. McCaul et al., *Race Relations Survey: 1984* (Johannesburg, South African Institute of Race Relations, 1985), pp.751–52.
41   *Bula Ditaba tsa Lekoa*, October 1984, pp.6–7.
42   Ibid.
43   *SASPU National*, 5/7 (December 1984), p.3.
44   *Rand Daily Mail*, 29 November 1984.
45   Nick Miller, interview with author, Alberton, 9 May 2006 (name has changed).
46   *The Star*, 23 October 1984; *Sowetan*, 24 October 1984.
47   *The Guardian*, 24 October 1984.

population, Operation Palmiet would come to symbolise the day 'the army came to catch a thief'.[48] Shortly afterwards, the operation was repeated in the townships of Boipatong and Sharpeville. In the afternoon, several senior police officers, including the commissioner of police, General Johan Coetzee, flew into Sebokeng to evaluate the situation and members of parliament were briefed on the use of troops. A few weeks later, on 13 November, Thembisa was sealed off, followed by Thokoza in the East Rand on 22 November; the revolt had been picking up pace in these two areas.

Two days after Operation Palmiet, the Regional Executive of the UDF held an emergency meeting to discuss the situation in the Vaal Triangle townships.[49] Churches were asked to ring their bells in solidarity with Sebokeng's population, a protest meeting was scheduled and a pamphlet drawn up to counter the one distributed by the SADF. During a UDF rally in Cape Town on 26 November, Frank Chikane called the deployment of troops 'armed to the teeth against our defenceless people in the Vaal' a reaction to the state's inability to curb protest and stressed the necessity of armed units in the townships to protect the population.[50]

The presence of troops in the townships became a widespread phenomenon from the mid-1980s onwards and reflected the reality that the SADF was involved in warfare on two fronts: abroad and inside the country. It was a clear indication that the police had no capacity to curb the revolts. And it was a show of strength by the state to discourage other areas from joining in the protests. Operation Palmiet received widespread condemnation in international media. *The Guardian* called it both 'sinister' and 'silly', stating that the government was 'short on using the airforce against pickpockets' and blaming the 'brutal system of race discrimination' by the South African government for the upheavals in the townships.[51] The US government, increasingly more critical towards the apartheid regime, proclaimed that the military occupation put into question the government's willingness to engage with internal problems through reforms and consensus.[52]

---

48   Noonan, *They're Burning the Churches*, p.92.
49   WHP A2675, III (868), 'Emergency Regional Executive Meeting of the United Democratic Front held 25/10/1984'.
50   WHP A2675, III (870), 'Police Recording of UDF Meeting, Claremont, Cape Town, 26 November 1984'.
51   *The Guardian*, 24 October 1984.
52   *The Star*, 24 October 1984.

'Mahlatsi's village': The Lekoa Town Council

Local government was in a state of disarray in the aftermath of the uprising. With most of their houses burnt down and their safety at risk, councillors were relocated to a complex in Zone 10 in Sebokeng and placed under 24-hour guard. Many of them remained for years in what some residents called 'Mahlatsi's village'.[53] The Lekoa Town Council and the Evaton Town Council were not the only ones facing heavy opposition; across the country, councillors went into hiding. Eight days after the onset of mass protest in the townships of the Vaal Triangle, the UDF issued a press statement reaffirming its position that all councillors should resign.[54] During the same month, on 11 October 1984, the town clerk of the Lekoa Town Council, Nicholas Louw, addressed a meeting attended by employers and the press to comment on the crisis of local government. Stating that councillors had no intention of resigning, he confirmed that the conflict had indeed reached a deadlock.[55]

Despite statements by Esau Mahlatsi and officials of the OVDB that councillors would not resign, by 23 October there were five vacant seats out of 39 in the Lekoa Town Council, owing to three deaths (Diphoko had been a member of the Evaton Town Council) and two resignations.[56] A year later, in September 1985, the number had increased to 11 vacant seats.[57] By-elections held in November 1985 produced only one candidate from Sharpeville, and although the Lekoa Town Council never entirely collapsed, elections remained on hold for years to come as candidates feared for their lives. Countrywide 240 councillors had resigned by July 1985 and eight town councils had resigned en masse.[58] Local authorities across the country were in a state of disarray, demonstrating the failure of local government reforms and the growing demand for political representation.

Mahlatsi refused to step down, arguing that only his constituency could ask him to resign.[59] At the first anniversary of the Vaal Uprising, his intransigence was apparent when it was reported that he still failed to understand the causes of the uprising and that he was unwilling to 'move one iota from his position of a year ago'.[60] In contrast, his two relatives (Paul and Meshack Mahlatsi, who were also councillors) submitted letters of resignation on 10 January 1985. In their

---

53   *Sowetan*, 4 September 1986.
54   WHP A2675, III (867), 'Press Statement, 1984/11/09, Resignation of the Councillors'.
55   *Sowetan*, 12 October 1984.
56   WHP AK2117, J4.15, AAQ25, 'Minutes of the 9th Ordinary Meeting of the Town Council of Lekoa, 23 October 1984' (this document is listed as missing in the inventory).
57   WHP AK2243, A, Vol.1, Testimony Louw, p.23.
58   *The Star*, 17 June 1985.
59   *Sowetan*, 20 September 1984 and 19 June 1985.
60   *The Star*, 3 September 1984.

letters they cited 'the failure of the Lekoa Town Council to meet the people's grievances' as well as 'lack of decisive powers of the Lekoa Town Council over a.) house rental and b.) land'.[61] No mention was made of the corrupt practices that members of the council had been accused of by local residents. According to the *Sowetan*, they argued that they were 'disgusted with the whole set-up. We are not helping the very people we purport to be representing'.[62] Their resignation was announced during a meeting with representatives at the headquarters of AZAPO in Johannesburg, where Meshack Mahlatsi asked members of the organisation to plead with local communities to accept them back into their fold.[63] The position of councillors who had resigned was not clear-cut to everyone. Whether councillors should be welcomed back into the community led to major disagreements and divisions within the Congress of South African Students (COSAS) and the Vaal Civic Association (VCA) as well as between different townships in 1985, as some of the comrades 'wanted them dead'.[64]

Despite widespread calls for the scrapping of the Black Local Authorities, the apartheid government continued to endorse the devolution of power to the third tier, as the Minister of Cooperation, Development and Training, Dr Viljoen, who succeeded Dr Piet Koornhof, emphasised in his speech at a function of the OVDB in Sebokeng on 27 October 1984.[65] To improve their reputation and combat malpractice, councillors signed a code of conduct and made an oath of allegiance a few months later.[66] In 1985, major reforms were announced in the Regional Services Councils Act, which introduced multi-racial councils that aimed to integrate the white municipalities and the black town councils.[67] It was part of a new series of reforms that had been pursued since late 1984.[68]

The Rent Boycott

A special meeting of the Lekoa Town Council on 18 September 1984 decided that no increase in service charges, electricity and water tariffs or any other tariffs would be implemented until the end of the financial year on 1 July 1985.[69] The budget report of 1984/85 stated that 'it is bad financial policy not to implement the increase of R5.90', but the volatility of the situation left little choice.[70] Major

---

61   WHP AK2117, S8.2, 'Re: Resignation from Lekoa Town Council'.

62   *Sowetan*, 11 January 1985.

63   *The Star*, 10 January 1985; *Sowetan*, 11 January 1985.

64   Shaka Radebe, interview with author, Vereeniging, 23 July 2010.

65   *Bula Ditaba tsa Lekoa*, November/December 1984, p.1.

66   *Bula Ditaba tsa Lekoa*, June 1985, p.1.

67   *Bula Ditaba tsa Lekoa*, May 1986, pp.6–7.

68   The other key pillars included a restructuring of labour control and influx regulations, and a change in regional development strategies through industrial decentralisation.

69   SAHA AL2457, 6.2, 'Town Council of Lekoa, Revision of the 1984/85 Budget'.

70   SAHA AL2457, 6.2, 'Budget [of the Lekoa Town Council] 84/85'.

cutbacks in development and infrastructure were scheduled to compensate for the fiscal loss the scrapping of the rent increase would cause.[71] A letter by the OVDB's town clerk, Nicholas Louw, to announce the shelving of increases threatened that the 'refusal to pay their monthly dues will result in the losing of their houses through legal proceedings, the disconnection of electricity, the ceasing of refuse removal, sewage disposal and the maintenance of houses, roads and water reticulation.'[72]

While scrapping the R5.90 may have averted the revolt, in its aftermath it was no longer regarded as sufficient. For many, rent was unaffordable even without the implementation of the increase, and by late 1984, a great majority of residents were participating in a complete boycott of rental payments. Figures suggest that the boycott was supported by around 60 to 70 percent of the local population.[73] Although the scrapping of the rent increase followed the initial demands of local residents, cutbacks on capital projects in areas that were already suffering from poor infrastructure and service delivery did little to enhance the quality of urban life or attitudes towards local government. Widespread debates about the nature of local government, the provision of services and the affordability of rent produced localised understandings of what was considered fair, reasonable and affordable. High service charges were considered unfair; a visible lack of development and upgrading of living conditions confirmed widespread beliefs that service charges should be reduced. As discussed in Chapter 2, a large percentage of what was labelled 'rent' was, in fact, service charges. In contrast to government's stance that only those below the poverty line would qualify for subsidised housing, popular demands envisaged a subsidy of urban services for all communities by the central state. Quality housing, services such as electricity and water, as well as education should be accessible to everyone, irrespective of their income.[74] Local government should be representative and have the welfare and emancipation of their constituencies at heart.

The total boycott of payment for rents and service levies and tariffs proved to be an enormous fiscal blow for local government, which had already been suffering from a lack of revenue prior to the boycott. The town treasurer of the Lekoa Town Council calculated that while the council had been short of R341,932 per month between January and August 1984, by November 1986 the deficit was almost R2 million per month.[75] Eight months into the boycott, 16,000

71 Ibid.
72 VT CPN, 'Letter by the Town Clerk of the Lekoa Town Council, N.P. Louw, 23 October 1984', no reference number.
73 WHP AK2243, A, Vol.1, Testimony Louw, p.23.
74 For a statistical analysis of popular perceptions and demands, see P. Frankel, 'Socio-Economic Conditions, Rent Boycotts and the Local Government Crisis: A Vaal Triangle Field Study' (unpublished report, June 1987).
75 WHP AK2117, G2.1.16, 'Verklaaring EHK Matthysen'.

households were in arrears, owing a total of R13 million and by May 1987, the Lekoa Town Council was short of just under R58 million.[76] By 1986, around 500,000 households in 54 townships across South Africa were participating in the rent boycott, leading to a loss of revenue of R40 million a month, which was required to finance administration and the costs for upgrading and developing the townships.[77]

To prevent a complete fiscal collapse of local government, the Lekoa Town Council introduced a stop order system in November 1984 under Proclamation 186 of 1967, which would allow them to deduct rent directly from people's salaries without their consent.[78] By late November, out of 30,500 households under the jurisdiction of the Lekoa Town Council, 18,000 had received notices that money for rent and tariffs would be deducted from their wages.[79] Local employers were hesitant to implement the order for fear of shop floor mobilisation and because the legality of such action was questionable. On 16 January 1985, employers in the commercial and industrial sector met with representatives of the OVDB and the Department of Co-operation and Development to discuss alternative ways to recover rental arrears. The use of Proclamation 186 remained short-lived, however. Widespread anxieties among officials about mass resistance and strikes led to its revoking in March 1985.[80]

Failing to break the boycott, local authorities sent out letters in October 1985 warning residents of pending legal action should they continue to boycott the payment of rent and service tariffs.[81] To make an example of them, selected residents in stable employment were served with summonses to appear in court. The Vaal Triangle Trade Union Co-ordinating Committee (VTUCC) warned that legal action against rent defaulters could lead to renewed violence and shop floor unrest.[82] Residents were encouraged to ignore the summons and refuse to go to court. VTUCC, established in May 1985 and representing 30,000 workers from six different unions, including the Federation of South African Trade Unions (FOSATU), the Council of Unions of South Africa (CUSA), the Orange Vaal General Workers Union (OVGWU) and other unions, as well as the Industrial Aid Centre, had been involved in negotiations with the Vaal Chamber of Commerce and major industries since June to find

76   *Hansard*, 30 April 1985, Col.1340–41.
77   M. Swilling, 'The United Democratic Front and Township Revolt', in W. Cobbett and R. Cohen, *Popular Struggles in South Africa* (London, James Currey, 1988), p.107.
78   WHP AK2243, A, Vol.1, Testimony Louw, p.44.
79   *Rand Daily Mail*, 30 November 1984.
80   WHP AK2243, A, Vol.1, Testimony Louw, pp.44–45; Letter by S.J. de Beer, published in *Sowetan*, 10 July 1985.
81   *Sowetan*, 24 October and 1 November 1985.
82   *Sowetan*, 25 October 1985.

a solution to the stalemate.[83] One of VTUCC's key demands was a reduction of rent to R30, a demand that had originated in Sharpeville (see Chapter 4). It signified what residents believed to be a fair rent, based on the quality of housing and the services received. While government argued that those earning R450 or more per month were obliged to pay full economic rentals, and that subsidies would only apply to 'welfare cases', VTUCC demanded greater government subsidy in rent, infrastructure and development.[84] Talks eventually broke down owing to mutual distrust between government officials and VTUCC's leaders and a year after its formation, VTUCC dissolved when ideological differences pulled the organisation apart.[85]

A few weeks later, in November 1985 the chief director of the OVDB, D.C. Ganz, stated that the fiscal crisis had crippled the council to the extent that it could no longer meet its payment to the Rand Water Board and Eskom, creating severe health hazards.[86] Funds earmarked for development and maintenance had been used to provide basic services. The failure to collect night soil on a regular basis in those areas that relied on the bucket system not only caused disgruntlement but proved to be a hygiene disaster. As a result, government adopted a multi-pronged approach to collect outstanding rents, tariffs and levies.[87] In December 1985 it presented a document entitled 'Strategy for the collection of arrear rental and service charges' to the media. The document, in line with government policy reflected in the growing importance of Joint Management Centres to bring economic, security, administrative and political bodies together, suggested a combined use of the courts, police and community guards to enforce payments.[88]

By August 1986, Louw announced that 1,800 eviction orders had been authorised by the Magistrate's Courts in Vereeniging and Vanderbijlpark and residents would be evicted in groups of 13 on a weekly basis by the newly established municipal police force, which had become a key player in breaking the rent boycott.[89] Those on the list to be evicted had their furniture either locked inside the house, removed to the yard or in some instances taken away to defray costs, only to be given back if rent arrears were paid off. Houses were placed under the guard of municipal police to prevent families from moving back in. Insult was added to injury when by March 1986,

83 *Sowetan*, 21 August 1985.
84 H. Mashabela, *Townships of the PWV* (Johannesburg, South African Institute of Race Relations, 1988), p.128.
85 Richard 'Bricks' Mokolo, interview with author, Orange Farm, 11 May 2006.
86 *The Star*, 21 November 1985.
87 WHP AK2117, J4.15, AAQ23, 'Town Council of Lekoa, Executive Committee, Fifteenth Special Meeting' (this document is listed as missing in the inventory).
88 *The Star*, 20 December 1985.
89 *The Star*, 12 August 1986; *Sowetan*, 11 August 1986.

42 heads of household were imprisoned for 30 days for not paying rent.[90] In October 1986, the VCA's application to have the evictions stopped was heard in the Rand Supreme Court. A few days later, in late November 1986, eight out of 35 families that had been evicted were allowed to move back into their homes after litigation at the Rand Supreme Court.[91] Louw's unpopularity was confirmed when his house was petrol bombed, causing damage of around R2,500.[92]

A survey conducted by Philip Frankel in 1987 suggests that 84 percent of the respondents indicated that they had had problems paying rent and rates in the past, with an overwhelming 42 percent explaining it as a result of insufficient funds.[93] A further 84 percent felt that the rent and services charges were 'unfair' while a staggering 97 percent said they were not paying rent at the time of the survey.[94] Better housing was cited as the leading demand by residents, followed by the creation of more employment. By that stage, 90 percent felt that the Lekoa Town Council did not represent the interests of local residents, with a vast majority associating the council with corruption and misuse of funds; respondents overwhelmingly felt that the fiscal crisis was not the reason why the council failed to provide adequate services.[95] Half of the respondents argued that the rent boycott should only be ended if houses were made available for purchase and previous rent used as a deposit. This view was widely held. Residents recalled that 20 years prior they had been promised that they could own their houses once the total amount paid in rental had covered the purchase price.[96] While the rent boycott had initially been triggered by the increase and opposition to the council, three years later demands reflected broader demands for social upliftment and political transformation.

As Hilary Sapire shows, the lack of housing and high rents produced another outcome: from the mid-1980s, informal settlements began to mushroom across the Pretoria–Witwatersrand–Vereeniging (PWV) area.[97] They housed the poorest sections of society: those who could not afford a house or did not qualify for formal housing, for one reason or another. Widows and women whose marriage

90   *The Star*, 18 March 1986.

91   *Sowetan*, 25 November 1986.

92   *The Star*, 29 September 1986.

93   P. Frankel, 'Socio-economic Conditions, Rent Boycotts and the Local Government Crisis: A Vaal Triangle Field Study' (unpublished report, June 1987), pp.1, 18–19.

94   Ibid., pp.21–24.

95   Ibid., pp.51–55.

96   WHP AK2117, S8.10.19, 'Notes of Discussion with Phillip Masia, General Secretary of the Orange Vaal General Workers' Union'.

97   H. Sapire, 'Politics and Protest in Shack Settlements of the Pretoria–Witwatersrand–Vereeniging Region, South Africa, 1980–1990', *Journal of Southern African Studies*, 18/3, Special Issue: Political Violence in Southern Africa (1992), pp.670–97.

had broken down, for example, could no longer access formal housing and were therefore crowded out of formal townships. Informal settlements remained largely outside of the orbit of civic structures and pursued their own politics.[98]

Winning Hearts and Minds

While repression became the order of the day, in late 1984 the government tasked Prof. Tjaart van der Walt, rector of the University of Potchefstroom, to head an investigation into the roots of local grievances, and the school boycott that had been ongoing since 3 September.[99] Van der Walt submitted his original report in December, and an edited version in January 1985.[100] It was based on interviews with 137 people and organisations as well as submissions made by various political, educational, religious, community and social organisations. While dismissing the increases in rent, tariffs and levies as the sole cause leading to the uprising, he acknowledged that the over-hasty, unwise, clumsy and insensitive handling of the issue by local authorities had caused grievances that eventually ignited the spark.[101]

Van der Walt's report produced six main recommendations, which were mostly geared towards improving the functioning of local government: the need for better communication and training between the public, town councils and the OVDB; a recommendation to launch an official investigation into the composition of municipal rates and levies in comparison with other areas; the need for additional sources of revenue in black townships; the suggestion to allow residents to spread their arrear payments over several months; a recommendation to establish an official enquiry into allegations of corruption and nepotism of local councillors; and a call to allow greater political participation of black constituencies in national political-decision processes that affected 'their own interests'.[102] In the aftermath of the report on 2 January 1985, Deputy Minister of Education and Development Aid, Sam de Beer, issued a statement concluding that van der Walt's recommendations were being implemented.[103] The findings of the report were widely rejected by AZAPO and the UDF, who argued that 'it was no more than an attempt to justify the failure

98   Josette Cole's powerful analysis of the rise of violent vigilantism in Crossroads remains one of the most detailed studies of politics in an informal settlement during the mid-1980s. See J. Cole, *Crossroads: The Politics of Reform and Repression* (Johannesburg, Ravan Press, 1987).

99   WHP AK2117, J4.15, AAQ34, T. van der Walt, *'Report on the Investigation into Education for Blacks in the Vaal Triangle Following Upon the Occurrences in September 1984 and Thereafter'* (Pretoria, Government Printer, 1985).

100   Ibid., pp.iii, xiii–xiv.

101   Ibid., p.29.

102   Ibid., p.ix.

103   Ibid., p.vi.

of the National Party policies'.[104] For township communities, these measures barely scratched the surface and did not address popular demands for representation, equality and social and political rights.

Government launched campaigns to address the lack of housing and to develop and upgrade the townships. Besides these plans to improve infrastructure and housing, the OVDB also acknowledged the dire need to extend welfare and to provide better social services. The hiring of more social workers and hospital staff, better medical services at hospitals, provision of recreational and educational facilities and bridging programmes for school leavers were all seen to be part and parcel of community development.[105]

In line with the findings of the van der Walt report, local government embarked on a propaganda campaign to enhance the reputation of the councils and to discredit political organisations. The propaganda campaign included the 're-education' of youth in special youth camps as well as the use of media to improve the image of local authorities.[106] In 1985 the OVDB launched the Eagle's Clubs, formed to organise youth activities and to keep the youth away from politics. Similar attempts to break the rent boycott by 're-educating' the youth were done in other parts of the country.[107] Declaring the 'Year of the Youth', the OVDB had been given R37,000 by the Department of Co-operation and Development to organise activities for the youth in 1985.[108] In September 1986, two camps were organised for the Sebokeng Hostel Club and the Sharpeville Club in Qwa Qwa and Bultfontein near Rustenburg.[109] In the early 1990s, reports leaked that the Eagle's Clubs had been funded under Strategy 44 of Military Intelligence and channelled through the local Joint Management Centre (JMC).[110]

To improve the reputation of local authorities, monthly features were published in the newsletter of the OVDB on how to promote leadership and administrative skills.[111] Other articles explained the history, structures and working of the Lekoa Town Council. Besides propaganda in the newsletter

104   *Rand Daily Mail*, 3 January 1985; *The Star*, 4 January 1985.

105   'Community Development in Evaton and Lekoa', *Bula Ditaba tsa Lekoa*, February 1987, p.1.

106   *The Star*, 19 December 1985.

107   WHP AK2117, S8.2.1, 'Sukses met Betrekking tot Huurinvordering van die Wes-Transvaalse Ontwikkelingsraad deur Middel van Jeugdiges'; also see P.S. Kunene, 'From Apartheid to Democracy: A Historical Analysis of Local Struggles in Phomolong Township, Free State, 1985–2005' (MA thesis, University of the Witwatersrand, 2013).

108   *Bula Ditaba tsa Lekoa*, May 1985, p.9.

109   *Bula Ditaba tsa Lekoa*, September 1986, p.10.

110   Noonan, *They're Burning the Churches*, pp.131–32.

111   *Bula Ditaba tsa Lekoa*, February 1986, p.5.

Bula Ditaba tsa Lekoa, the OVDB used Radio Sesotho to broadcast information on local government.[112] From 1985 onwards, the newsletter reflected the
broader propaganda war of the government by quoting the Bible, denouncing
communism and condemning political violence.[113]

'Disappeared from the face of the earth': State of Emergency

By 1985, insurrections in the townships had become so widespread that a partial
state of emergency was declared on 21 July 1985 in 44 magisterial districts, cover-
ing the Witwatersrand, the Eastern Cape and the Western Cape. It was followed
by a nationwide state of emergency, declared on 12 June 1986. These states of
emergency threw a blanket of repression over townships, effectively allowing the
security forces to act with impunity. The key features were de facto military rule,
widespread detentions and tight censorship. During the second state of emergency in 1986 an estimated 10,000 people were detained.[114] In the words of Tsietsi
Mokhele, they often 'disappeared from the face of the earth'.[115] Activists from the
Vaal Triangle were taken to either Leeuhof or Groenpunt, the two prisons near
Vereeniging, or other institutions such as John Vorster Square, Diepkloof prison
(ironically dubbed Sun City) or Potchefstroom. If the detainees had links to other
regions, investigations were conducted across regional borders, resulting in activists from the Vaal Triangle being detained elsewhere.

Political policing was fraught with contradictions between the use of excessive force and the need to co-opt at least part of the population. For the security branch, mass detentions were therefore a double-edged sword; while they
curbed 'unrest', they also enhanced the status of activists, attracted international
and domestic attention and forged new networks, as General Johan van der
Merwe, second in command of the security branch during this period, recalled.[116]

The conditions in prison were ghastly; besides the frequent harassment,
beatings and various forms of torture, the food was often of very poor quality,
nights were spent without blankets and information was inaccessible. Detention
disrupted the routines and rhythms of the everyday; time became suspended.
Despair and fear were coupled with defiance and anger; but while some were
released from prison with a firmly held belief that resistance was the only way
forward, others broke. Solitary confinement was the most traumatic form of
detention, where detainees were often kept naked and in darkness, without any
sense of whether it was day or night. The stories of these experiences, recounted
during the hearings of the Truth and Reconciliation Commission, are expressive

---

112   WHP AK2117, S8.2.1, 'Letter to Mnr Spangenberg, from AJ Watson, Radio Sesotho'.
113   *Bula Ditaba tsa Lekoa*, January 1985 and March 1985, p.9.
114   WHP A2084, Ad6.1.2.1, 'DPSC Report for June/July 1986'.
115   Tsietsi 'Stompi' Mokhele, interview with author, Bophelong, 18 September 2011.
116   Johan Velde van der Merwe, interview with author, Pretoria, 18 May 2011.

of the total onslaught the prison system imposed on people's psyche and body.[117] As Natacha Filippi shows, the sensory deprivation and hardship experienced in solitary confinement put the detainee at risk of becoming 'totally disoriented' and showing symptoms of 'a person with psychosis – disturbance of the mind – such as high levels of anxiety, panic, delusions'.[118]

The majority of political detainees were detained under section 29 of the Internal Security Act (ISA), followed by section 50 of ISA, the Act allowing for preventive detention.[119] Both sections were notorious. Despite the new regulations introduced following the recommendations of the Rabie Commission into security legislation in 1982, detention often provided little safety and few control mechanisms.[120] A study conducted by Diane Sandler and Don Foster in 1985, for example, found that 83 percent of detainees had reported physical torture while 'no cases reported an entire lack of psychological abuse'.[121]

The two organisations that were at the forefront of monitoring detentions, the Detainees' Parents Support Committee (DPSC) and the Detainees' Support Committee (DESCOM), regularly published lists with details of those detained and they compiled reports in which they outlined the rights of detainees, the conditions in prisons and legal action that could be taken. Prior to the implementation of a state of emergency, detentions could be challenged in court and a substantial number of cases were declared invalid.[122] With the declaration of a state of emergency, members of the SADF and the South African Police were exempt from civil and criminal prosecution for acts 'done in good faith'.

While detention had become one of the most far-reaching tools in the regime's attempt to curb the insurrection, a more sinister and covert form of counter-insurgency soon emerged: the 'dirty tricks' of political assassinations, intimidation, smear campaigns and disappearances.[123] In some parts of the coun-

---

117   See, for example, D.H. Foster and D. Davis, *Detention and Torture in South Africa: Psychological, Legal & Historical Studies* (Cape Town, David Philip, 1987); N. Filippi, 'Deviances and the Construction of a "Healthy Nation" in South Africa: A Study of Pollsmoor Prison and Valkenberg Psychiatric Hospital, c.1964–1994' (DPhil thesis, University of Oxford, 2014).

118   Filippi, 'Deviances and the Construction of a "Healthy Nation"', p.70. For an in-depth study on the effects of solitary confinement, see L. Guenther, *Solitary Confinement: Social Death and Its Afterlives* (Minneapolis, University of Minnesota Press, 2013).

119   WHP A2084, Ad6.1.2.1, 'DPSC March 1986 Report'.

120   Foster and Davis, *Detention and Torture in South Africa*.

121   AG2918, 2.2.6.5, D. Foster and D. Sandler, 'A Study of Detention and Torture in South Africa: Preliminary Report' (University of Cape Town, 1985), pp.27–31.

122   WHP A2084, Ad6.1.2.1, 'DPSC March 1986 Report'.

123   K. O'Brien, *The South African Intelligence Services: From Apartheid to Democracy, 1948–2005* (London and New York, Routledge, 2011); D. Potgieter, *Total Onslaught: Apartheid's Dirty Tricks Exposed* (Cape Town, Zebra Press, 2012).

try, such as the Eastern Cape, assassinations by hit squads were particularly rife. At the heart of this campaign of terror and bloodshed were covert units associated with the police and the military. Vlakplaas, a farm north of Pretoria, gained particular notoriety as a base for the counter-insurgency unit C10 (later called C1) of the South African Police, set up to monitor and curb the activities of the ANC and the Pan Africanist Congress.[124] This secluded farm saw dozens of captured guerrillas of Umkhonto weSizwe (MK) and the Azanian People's Liberation Army (APLA) being 'turned' to work for the police as spies or *askaris*.[125] The security forces went to great lengths to cover up the killing of activists; coded language such as 'to neutralise', 'to take out' or to 'eliminate' created a vocabulary that allowed insiders to understand commands without being too explicit while corpses were carefully disposed of and traces covered up.[126] Torture and assassinations were kept secret, for public knowledge of the regime's onslaught on the population would have further undermined its credibility and legitimacy in the eyes of global and domestic audiences. For political activists, however, it was common knowledge that being arrested would lead to torture or worse. This harsh political climate shaped new tactics to undermine the coercive and administrative capacities of the apartheid regime, as the following chapter explores.

124 E. de Kock and J. Gordin, *A Long Night's Damage: Working for the Apartheid State* (Johannesburg, Contra Press, 1998); J. Pauw, *Into the Heart of Darkness: Confessions of Apartheid's Assassins* (Johannesburg, Jonathan Ball, 1997).

125 J. Dlamini, *Askari: A Story of Collaboration and Betrayal in the Anti-Apartheid Struggle* (Johannesburg, Jacana, 2014).

126 See N. Rousseau, 'The Farm, the River and the Picnic Spot: Topographies of Terror', *African Studies*, 68/3 (2009), pp.351–69.

7

'And then you begin to push harder and harder': People's Power and the Dawn of the New

The Visit

On 4 June 1987, State President P.W. Botha visited the townships of the Vaal Triangle in the company of his wife Elize and a group of cabinet ministers. Local school children were seen waving flags, welcoming the president and his entourage. Botha, his wife and the group of cabinet ministers were taken on a tour through Sharpeville and Sebokeng, where he addressed an audience at the Mphatlalatsane Hall in Zone 14, Sebokeng.[1] It was a carefully orchestrated spectacle, aimed at creating a semblance of normality and endorsement of the government's reforms. The mayor of the Lekoa Town Council, Esau Mahlatsi, provoked local dismay when he presented Botha with the Freedom of Lekoa. In Mahlatsi's words, the Lekoa Town Council had invited Botha to 'see for himself the conditions under which blacks live'.[2] Local residents, however, were quoted as saying they found the visit 'absurd'. They called on Botha to address their grievances, namely to release the Delmas treason and the Sharpeville Six trialists, to halt evictions and reduce rent, and to unban the liberation movements.[3] Botha's failure to visit the graves of the victims of the Sharpeville shooting and the Vaal Uprising confirmed their view that he had little respect for the African population. A spokesperson of the Vaal Civic Association (VCA) sharply condemned the visit, calling it a 'miserable failure'.[4]

For some, Botha's visit not only signified the hubris of government but caused outright fear. One pensioner from Sharpeville, who was paid a surprise visit, was distressed about his association with the state president: 'I curse the

1   *Bula Ditaba tsa Lekoa*, June 1987, p.6.
2   *Weekly Mail*, 12–18 June 1987.
3   *The Star*, 3 June 1987.
4   *Weekly Mail*, 12–18 June 1987; *The Star*, 1 and 3 June 1987.

day Botha set his foot on my doorstep – it has made my life a misery.'[5] Worried that he might be seen as a sell-out, he spent restless nights in fear of having his house burnt down. His fear was not unfounded; by then, arson had become a widespread strategy to rid the townships of informers, police and anyone else suspected of collaborating with the apartheid regime. Rumours of being a 'sell-out' or informer could bring a death sentence.

Violence had begun to escalate since September 1984. While some of this violence was contingent and in response to local grievances, many youthful comrades saw themselves as carrying the banner of Umkhonto weSizwe (MK), the armed wing of the banned African National Congress (ANC), and, to a lesser extent, the Pan Africanist Congress (PAC). Increasingly violent tactics, aimed at forging a new social and political order, were also a direct response to escalating repression and state violence. Police brutality and the use of 'dirty tricks' turned townships into spaces where life was precarious and shaped by fear and uncertainty.

Older repertoires of protest, including strikes, boycotts and marches, were therefore shadowed by newer and more radical forms of contesting the social and political order. These different ways of challenging the regime were at times in open conflict, at other times enmeshed, but often followed the strategies and visions espoused by the ANC. It was therefore during the insurrectionary period that the ANC's symbolic hegemony that it had begun to establish from the late 1970s onwards was cemented. By the mid-1980s, large parts of the urban townships had become ungovernable, and even though the insurrections had not been led by the ANC, its strategies, peaking in the call for a 'people's war' in 1985, tallied with the realities on the ground.[6] Yet while violence shaped the contours of the struggle for freedom during this period, it was by no means the defining feature. Instead, the insurrectionary period saw the dawn of a form of politics that was rooted in popular democratic practices, referred to as 'people's power'.[7] It signalled what Michael Neocosmos terms a shift towards a 'political subjectivity that was centrally located in popular control of conditions of life'.[8]

'We were doing things on our own': Towards People's Power

With the banning of indoor meetings of more than two people from 11 September 1984, and the harassment and arrest of activists, political mobilisation was severely curtailed. As the majority of the leadership had either gone into exile or

5   *Weekly Mail*, 12–18 June 1987.
6   F. Rueedi, '"Our Bushes Are the Houses": People's War and the Underground during the Insurrectionary Period in the Vaal Triangle, South Africa', *Journal of Southern African Studies*, 46/4 (2020), pp.615–33.
7   See M. Neocosmos, *Thinking Freedom in Africa: Toward a Theory of Emancipatory Politics* (Johannesburg, Wits University Press, 2016), pp.134–56.
8   Ibid., pp.136–37.

was in detention, the rebuilding of the VCA was fraught with problems: 'So you had to start almost from scratch,' Matime Moshele Papane recalls.[9] Fake pamphlets were circulating countering information provided by civic bodies, police surveillance increased and smear campaigns were aimed at discrediting the leadership.[10] On 22 December 1984, civic structures organised several meetings at churches to campaign for local support of 'Black Christmas', a campaign by the United Democratic Front (UDF) to commemorate the dead of the uprisings and to express protest against state repression.[11] In Sharpeville, thousands of local residents participated in cleaning the graves of those who had died during the Vaal Uprising. In other areas, including Sebokeng, the meeting of 22 December led to renewed violence and confrontations between police and protestors.

The UDF's efforts to organise regions intensified. In late 1984, Matime Moshele Papane from Sharpeville was employed as a full-time organiser of the Vaal Triangle region.[12] Papane, who had been schooled in the political philosophy of the Black Consciousness Movement (BCM), had recently returned from Soweto, where his stay with a fellow activist of the Soweto Civic Association had hastened his conversion to Charterism. By 1985, the VCA had re-emerged and a new leadership was elected under the chairmanship of Litau Litau. One of the most significant forms of collective action during this period were consumer boycotts, aimed at weakening the economic base of apartheid and asserting workers' demands. In December 1986, the boycott of OK Bazaars was widely supported in the Vaal Triangle; it was the largest consumer boycott and the 'largest national strike during this period'.[13]

Citing fiscal reasons, the Lekoa Town Council stopped providing services from late 1984. Waste removal ceased and electricity and water were temporarily cut off, plunging the townships into darkness and creating sanitary problems. To avoid health hazards and to uphold a semblance of normalcy, streets were cleaned, often by youth who volunteered to become involved. Electricity and water meters were hacked and reconnected, parks were built and childcare facilities established.[14]

This breakdown of the administrative and policing capacities of the state accelerated the emergence of street, block and area committees, which took over the functions of the police and the municipality.[15] They were an 'attempt

---

9   Matime Moshele Papane, interview with author, Johannesburg, 28 April 2010.

10   WHP AE862, G37.8, 'Repression in a Time of Reform'.

11   WHP AG2918, 3.9.1.2.1, 'An Account of the Ongoing Activities in the Vaal and Parys Townships'.

12   Matime Moshele Papane, interview with author, Johannesburg, 28 April 2010.

13   B. Kenny, *Retail Worker Politics, Race and Consumption in South Africa: Shelved in the Service Economy* (Cham, Palgrave Macmillan, 2018), p.84.

14   Tsietsi 'Stompi' Mokhele, interview with author, Bophelong, 21 September 2019.

15   The street committee was the smallest unit; block committees included the different

to grapple with social chaos' by creating a new order, and they reflected the 'radical aspirations of people's power'.[16] Occasionally referred to as the 'G-Plan' or 'Goniwe's Plan', modelled after the M-Plan, street committees emerged in 1984 in the township of Lingelihle in the Eastern Cape under the leadership of Matthew Goniwe, the popular community leader and teacher who was abducted and assassinated in 1985 by the police in collaboration with members of Vlakplaas.[17] In the Vaal Triangle, street, area and block committees built upon the zonal structures the VCA had created prior to the uprising. The frequent detentions of student and civic leaders necessitated the broadening of structures to ensure that the struggle would continue, as Tsietsi 'Stompi' Mokhele, civic activist and MK commander, recalls: 'Every layer we created they went and arrested that whole layer. Until finally we decided you know what, we can't lead this through activists. Let's create street committees and block committees and make sure that the communities run their own lives.'[18] Mokhele alludes to a significant aspect of these committees: aimed at being non-hierarchical and participatory, they came to represent ideals of grassroots democracy.

But their success was uneven; in 1987, a survey concluded that only a third of the 1,155 respondents indicated that their street had been organised into a committee.[19] Organisational capacities were limited, while growing repression undermined the effective functioning of these structures.[20] As Heidi Brooks has argued, the practice and discourse of people's power also differed; on the ground, people's power owed its origins to a diverse set of needs, experiences and ideas that included material needs of local communities (such as waste removal), a 'long tradition [...] of self-help and community organising', and inspiration drawn from international forms of community activism.[21] It also reflected aspirations for participation and equality; taking control over conditions of life would lead to empowerment and social change. For others, peo-

---

leaders of the street committees while area committees were the all-encompassing structure tasked to report to the VCA.

16   K. Jochelson, 'Reform, Repression and Resistance in South Africa: A Case Study of Alexandra Township, 1979–1989', *Journal of Southern African Studies*, 16/1 (1990), p.12.

17   On the building of networks in the Eastern Cape, see J. Cherry, 'Hidden Histories of the Eastern Cape Underground', in SADET (ed.), *The Road to Democracy, Volume 4* (Pretoria, Unisa Press, 2010).

18   Tsietsi 'Stompi' Mokhele, interview with author, Bophelong, 18 September 2011.

19   P. Frankel, 'Socio-Economic Conditions, Rent Boycotts and the Local Government Crisis: A Vaal Triangle Field Study' (unpublished report, June 1987), p.41.

20   See, for example, Jochelson, 'Reform, Repression and Resistance in South Africa', pp.1–32.

21   H. Brooks, 'Popular Power and Vanguardism: The Democratic Deficit of 1980s "People's Power"', *Politikon*, 45/3 (2018), pp.314–15.

ple's power was considered a stepping stone towards the seizure of power and therefore 'primarily a method of struggle'.[22]

For local activists in the Vaal Triangle, who were deeply invested in scripting a new future, the aim of these committees was threefold: they were meant to ensure efficient communication with the VCA, to provide structures that would take over the running of daily affairs in the townships and to create a platform to conscientise and politicise local residents. Soon street committees, and the VCA more broadly, began to handle matters concerning housing, including, for example, the allocation of housing.[23] While such allocation had been steeped in corruption and malpractice, and councillors had frequently abused their powers, the VCA's unofficial involvement in allocating and managing housing was aimed at ensuring fairness and transparency. Based on the concept of popular democracy, the VCA and its street committees came to signify an alternative form of government, one that would be representative, transparent and just, and therefore a significant stepping stone towards 'people's power'. By 1987, half of the respondents in a survey stated that townships should be administered by the VCA, while the other half preferred non-racial municipalities, combining townships and towns, to take over administration.[24]

Policing and the pursuit of justice were also taken over by popular structures known as 'people's courts'.[25] During this period, approximately 400 people's courts sprang up across the country.[26] The policing of townships had long focused on the suppression of political activism and neglected the punishment of common crime. Consequently, incidents of assault, rape and theft, for example, had been plaguing townships for decades and the risk of becoming a victim of violent crime was high. This led to a sense of insecurity, exposure to violence and the necessity to be streetwise, which in turn informed the emergence of a form of street masculinity that was key to the political culture of young comrades during this period, as a later section will explore.[27] Established to take over policing functions, people's courts were therefore set up to deal with a variety of offences including marital disputes, adultery, drunkenness, child beatings, the

22   Ibid., p.316.

23   Edward 'Chippa' Motubatsi, interview with author, Vereeniging, 5 December 2011.

24   P. Frankel, 'Socio-Economic Conditions, Rent Boycotts and the Local Government Crisis' (unpublished report, June 1987), p.73.

25   In contrast to Belinda Bozzoli's detailed case study of Alexandra, no similar records could be located for the Vaal Triangle and hence the information on people's courts in this region remains scant.

26   J. Seekings, 'People's Court and Popular Politics', in G. Moss and I. Obery (eds), *South African Review 5* (Johannesburg, Ravan Press, 1989).

27   C. Glaser, 'Whistles and Sjamboks: Crime and Policing in Soweto, 1960–1976', *South African Historical Journal*, 52/1 (2005), pp.119–39.

breaking of boycotts, theft and sexual assault.[28] The legitimacy of these courts therefore largely rested on their ability to combat crime and disorder.[29]

Popular justice and dispute resolution had a long history in the townships in the form of *makgotla*, courts that were usually run by conservative sections of society such as councillors.[30] Hence, people's courts built on a tradition of community justice that prioritised social coherence and stability, but in contrast to *makgotla*, which rarely aimed to supplant state institutions, people's courts 'sought to transform existing power arrangements by contesting state hegemony over the legal field'.[31] For this reason they played a leading part in the establishment of people's power. Their main goal was to ensure safety in the townships and to turn townships into 'liberated' or self-governed areas by taking over functions of the state.

Belinda Bozzoli argues that in the case of Alexandra they were 'ordered – even ritualised – and at the same time used theatrical methods to appropriate a degree of power'.[32] They therefore differed from ad hoc forms of popular punishments such as spontaneous necklacings by crowds that 'lacked a repeated organizational form'.[33] Popular justice was hence both punitive and redemptive and aimed to deter others from violating perceived social norms. While evidence from Alexandra suggests that specific locations came to serve as people's courts, they appear to have been run in an ad hoc manner from people's private homes in Sebokeng.

In some instances these courts gained notoriety for imposing harsh sentences. Meant to be under the control of street committees, some of them failed to account to the civic structures or street committees.[34] In contrast to the earlier forms of *makgotla*, many of these people's courts were soon run by youth, which inverted generational hierarchies. This inversion created tensions between the older generation and the new crop of youth leaders. 'We could see fear in our

---

28   W. Schärf and B. Ngcokoto, 'Images of Punishment in the People's Courts of Cape Town, 1985–7: From Prefigurative Justice to Populist Violence', in C. Manganyi and A. du Toit (eds), *Political Violence and the Struggle in South Africa* (London, Macmillan, 1990), pp.326–40.

29   Seekings, 'People's Court and Popular Politics', pp.126–28.

30   In African societies, conflict management and resolution has traditionally been the domain of elders. *Lekgotla* are based on this generational hierarchy. People's courts therefore need to be distinguished from the more conservative *makgotla* as well as ad hoc forms of popular punishments such as necklacings by crowds. People's courts were held regularly and were (often loosely) structured. See Seekings, 'People's Court and Popular Politics' and G. Pavlich, 'People's Courts, Postmodern Difference, and Socialist Justice in South Africa', *Social Justice*, 19/3 (1992), pp.29–45.

31   Pavlich, 'People's Courts, Postmodern Difference, and Socialist Justice', p.29.

32   B. Bozzoli, *Theatres of Struggle and the End of Apartheid* (Johannesburg, Wits University Press, 2004), p.151.

33   Pavlich, 'People's Courts, Postmodern Difference, and Socialist Justice', p.31.

34   Edward 'Chippa' Motubatsi, interview with author, Vereeniging, 5 December 2011.

parents' eyes,' youth activist Oupa Modikoane recalls.[35] In a cultural context where respect for elders is paramount, the leadership of the youth violated social norms. 'They take over and they then dictate to their elders as to how they conduct themselves. And it divided communities.'[36] Others used people's courts to settle scores and promote their own interests. One incident that highlights the harsh punishment some of these courts meted out occurred in Sebokeng in July 1986. Two men had poured petrol over a house in which they had locked their girlfriends, killing them as well as a visitor and a baby.[37] Subsequently, a group of comrades bailed the perpetrators out of jail and allegedly stoned them to death in an open field.

By then, struggles over leadership had created rifts; frequent detentions provided an opportunity for new activists to emerge who enjoyed limited legitimacy and whose actions were considered misdirected by the older and more established leadership. Claiming to represent the VCA, some of them began to operate through a politics of coercion. Boundaries between what was considered political and what was deemed criminal became blurred, giving rise to the phenomenon of 'com-tsotsis'.[38] Protection money and harsh punishment of anyone perceived to be a 'sell-out' or in violation of the demands and expectations of these groups became widespread. Edward 'Chippa' Motubatsi recalls, 'People were now living in fear. And we could not tolerate that.'[39] The struggle over who was a legitimate representative of community interests was also structured along ideological delineations, with Charterist groups regularly asserting their presence in meetings of groups adhering to different ideologies. One such group was the Sharpeville Civic Association (SCA), which from 1985 developed its own strategies in countering the state's attempt to break the rent boycott.[40] In the different townships, a 'Committee of Ten', comprised of more conservative sections of society and established during the investigations of the van der Walt commission, soon provoked the ire of politicised activists when they began to negotiate with local authorities to end the rent boycott.[41]

With the declaration of the first nationwide state of emergency on 20 July 1985, open mobilisation was hamstrung. Most meetings had to occur in secret as any public gatherings other than bona fide sports events were prohibited.[42]

---

35 Oupa Modikoane, interview with author, East Rand, 1 July 2010.

36 Edward 'Chippa' Motubatsi, interview with author, Vereeniging, 5 December 2011.

37 *City Press*, 20 July 1986.

38 The term 'com-tsotsi' combines the terms 'comrade' and 'tsotsi', township slang for thug.

39 Edward 'Chippa' Motubatsi, interview with author, Vereeniging, 15 April 2010.

40 *Sowetan*, 28 January 1985.

41 Matime Moshele Papane, interview with author, Johannesburg, 28 April 2010; Richard 'Bricks' Mokolo, interview with author, Orange Farm, 11 May 2006.

42 *Government Gazette*, 27 September 1985.

This effectively outlawed any public engagement with civic issues. With the banning of public meetings, house meetings became a safe and effective option to discuss grievances and tactics. Motubatsi, who by then had taken over the running of the Industrial Aid Centre, and who was involved in both the VCA and the ANC underground, recalls the manner in which some of the clandestine meetings were convened: 'I will tell you as to where we are going to meet. But not at one point. You see. Different points. So I'll go and collect, take you to the venue, [you] don't leave. I go out and bring another group in.'[43] Motubatsi, who was trained in Military Combat Work (MCW) in Botswana, knew the rules of clandestine work.[44] Trust became key. During this period, many activists spent years in hiding, moving from one safe house to the next to avoid arrest. Often not sleeping for longer than three nights in one place, the lives of activists were disrupted; for many, the movement became their surrogate family.

'The Freedom Charter was chanted all over the township'

If politics prior to the uprising had been marked by demands that increasingly overlapped with the broad vision outlined in the Freedom Charter, the insurrectionary period saw a translation of some of these demands into practice. Politics during this phase of the struggle cohered around the concept of 'the people', who included anyone who subscribed to the vision of a new moral, social and political order. Following the first principle of the Freedom Charter, 'The people shall govern', people's power signified a shift towards representation and democracy. It was based on an idea of 'class alliance' and 'national unity' that would lead to the National Democratic Revolution (NDR).[45] Conceptualised as a two-stage revolution, the NDR foresaw the advent of universal democracy during the first stage, followed by the implementation of a socialist order during the second stage.[46] This model was contested and debated among ANC supporters, some of whom advocated for a one-stage revolution through insurrection that would lead to a seizure of power and the installation of a socialist regime. The Freedom Charter's demotion of class as a key tenet of the struggle explains why it was rejected by left groups, who saw the leading role of workers in the struggle for freedom diminished.

43   Edward 'Chippa' Motubatsi, interview with author, Vereeniging, 22 November 2011.

44   Tsietsi 'Stompi' Mokhele and Edward 'Chippa' Motubatsi, interview with author, Bophelong, 21 September 2019. On the concept of MCW, see, for example, S.R. Davis, *The ANC's War against Apartheid: Umkhonto we Sizwe and the Liberation of South Africa* (Bloomington, Indiana University Press, 2018), pp.147–48.

45   S. Thwete, 'Understanding the Charter Clause by Clause', in R. Suttner and J. Cronin (eds), *30 Years of the Freedom Charter* (Johannesburg, Ravan Press, 1985), p.210.

46   E. Webster and J. Mawbey, 'Revisiting the National Question', in E. Webster and K. Pampallis (eds), *The Unresolved National Question: Left Thought under Apartheid* (Johannesburg, Wits University Press, 2016), p.5.

By 1985, the Freedom Charter had gained in popularity and events to cele-brate its thirtieth anniversary abounded. The ANC ran a series of articles on the Charter in its journals such as *Sechaba*, explaining its content and importance. On 26 June, the VCA hosted a meeting at the Roman Catholic Church in Evaton Small Farms, the very same church from which the protest march had taken off in 1984, to celebrate the anniversary. Speakers explained the different sections of the Charter and contextualised its relevance within a context of growing repression and resistance.[47] The meeting was broken up by police, and it was this confrontation between police and the Congress of South African Students (COSAS) activists that sparked a series of petrol bombings of policemen's houses that same night and led to the formation of a clandestine youth unit called the Vaal Liberation Movement (VALIMO).[48]

Besides 'primary citizenship' and power, the Freedom Charter demanded economic and social transformation that would lead to a 'good society' in which people would live in prosperity and peace.[49] Political power was therefore intertwined with the attainment of equal social rights and eco-nomic change. This vision closely responded to grassroots understandings of emancipation and freedom that emerged during the 1980s. Access to decent housing, perhaps more than any other social right, and the implementation of representative political structures, were at the heart of popular struggles in the townships of the Vaal Triangle during this period, as previous chapters have shown. The ability of Charterist groups to address and speak to popular griev-ances therefore played a significant part in their ascendancy during the 1980s. But for all its support, the meaning of the different principles was contested and some of its content was outright rejected by groups aligned to the BCM and the left. In Sharpeville, for example, Reverend Moselane made no secret of his antipathy for the Charter, which he allegedly considered to be watering down the struggle for freedom.[50]

Even though it never formally adopted the Charter, the UDF's campaigns were strongly influenced by its efforts to popularise the Charter and by its ideological content. Many of the UDF's affiliates, including the VCA, were openly Charterist. Among activists aligned to the VCA, COSAS and other Charterist organisations, the Freedom Charter was widely discussed, analysed and taken as a basis for envisioning an alternative future. 'The Freedom Char-

47   Electronic conversation with Edward 'Chippa' Motubatsi, 25 August 2018.
48   See also F. Rueedi, '"Siyayinyova!" Patterns of Violence in the African Townships of the Vaal Triangle, South Africa, 1980–86', *Africa*, 85/3 (2015), pp.395–416.
49   R. van Niekerk, 'The African National Congress: Social Democratic Thinking and the Good Society, 1940–1962', in Webster and Pampallis, *The Unresolved National Question*.
50   Tsietsi 'Stompi' Mokhele, interview with author, Bophelong, 18 September 2011.

ter was chanted all over the township,' Reverend Gift Moerane remembers.[51] Its demands found traction among those who envisaged a complete and radical change of the existing order. It was also an organising tool, as a youth activist explains:

> On the one hand it is a set of ideas, embodying analysis of the social situation, and laying out principles on which a new order should be established. [...] On the other hand, it is an 'organising instrument'. This means that it serves very much as a flag: it enables people to identify themselves, group together, and act unitedly [sic].[52]

Few pamphlets have survived from this period. Those that found their way into the archives highlight the similarity of demands made by the VCA before and after the uprising: the abolishment of the Black Local Authorities system and the lowering of rents remained at the centre of campaigns.[53] In contrast to those produced prior to the uprising, pamphlets from the mid-1980s exhibit an overtly political tone; by then, the release of political prisoners, the creation of a non-racial government and the end of emergency rule had become intertwined with the struggle for housing and affordable rent.[54]

'Freedome in our lifetime': The Banning of COSAS

Another key tenet of the Charter, access to free and quality education, had been at the centre of COSAS campaigns since its inception in 1979. As was the case with civic structures, COSAS demands became more overtly political in the aftermath of the uprising. Besides demands to scrap age limits, which excluded older students, an end to corporal punishment and sexual harassment and the introduction of democratically elected Student Representative Councils (SRCs), COSAS called for a withdrawal of troops, the resignation of councillors, the release of detainees and an end to the harassment of student leaders.[55] Students' demands were channelled into the Education Charter campaign, which laid out an alternative form of education.[56] 'Each one teach one' became a leading concept that saw the promulgation of 'people's education' for all classes.

From late 1984, new members were swelling the ranks of COSAS and sub-branches were set up in the different parts of the townships, co-

---

51   Gift Moerane, interview with author, Vereeniging, 29 March 2010.

52   C. Carter, '"We are the Progressives": Alexandra Youth Congress Activists and the Freedom Charter, 1983–85', *Journal of Southern African Studies*, 17/2 (1991), p.204.

53   WHP AK2117, G3.9.1.3-6 and G3.9.1.17, 'Pamphlets Issued by the Vaal Civic Association'.

54   Ibid.

55   WHP A2675, III (397), 'COSAS NEC Statement on DET's Response to Students' Legitimate Demands'.

56   Roy Matube, interview with author, Vereeniging, 20 April 2010.

ordinated by the Vaal Students Co-ordinating Committee.[57] During the same period, factional fights over political approaches ensued as student leaders struggled to gain control over the future of the local branch.[58] While the first generation of COSAS leaders had been exposed to the political philosophy of the BCM, this new crop of leaders had limited memories of the student uprisings of 1976 and their ideological outlook was less influenced by the BCM. COSAS networks became a significant way in which young activists sharpened their political understandings and honed their skills in leadership and public speaking. Regional conferences became a platform where the COSAS leadership would transmit directives received from the ANC leadership in exile.

The immediate experience of repression as well as a newly found confidence in collective action that emerged out of the 'success' of the Vaal Uprising shaped new understandings of appropriate strategies and tactics. 'Now they [the children] are singing songs based on their own local experiences, singing about the soldiers and le Grange,' one member of the VCA stated.[59] Colin Bundy has argued that the political perspective of this generation of young activists was shaped by an 'impatient anticipation of imminent victory, a hubristic assessment of progress made, and a naïve underestimation of the resources of the state.'[60] Violence, as this chapter will show, was seen as a means to accelerate the attainment of freedom.

For many, the tactics developed during the uprising were adopted and refined to give rise to a new understanding of how to liberate the country. Young people believed that freedom was 'around the corner', and that they would see the end of white minority rule in their lifetime. 'I had a hope that things would change. Remember we had that slogan which said "Freedom in our lifetime",' Khulu Malindi, student activist and former chairperson of the Vaal Students' Congress (VASCO), recalls.[61] 'We committed ourselves and said we are the generation that should bring freedom. And that is why the most militant generation was our generation,' Malindi added.

Relations between organised labour and students became increasingly important. While the UDF's leadership was slow in responding to the crisis in the townships, activists within COSAS and the Release Mandela Committee

---

57 Shaka Radebe, interviews with author, Vereeniging, 23 July 2010 and 23 May 2011; Morris More, interview with author, Sebokeng, 2 December 2011.

58 Sakhiwe Khumalo, interview with author, Vereeniging, 23 June 2010; Shaka Radebe, interview with author, Vereeniging, 26 July 2010.

59 Quote by a member of the VCA in *The Star*, 3 September 1985.

60 C. Bundy, 'Street Sociology and Pavement Politics: Aspects of Youth and Student Resistance in Cape Town, 1985', *Journal of Southern African Studies*, 13/3 (1987), pp.322–23.

61 Khulu Malindi, interview with author, Johannesburg, 22 November 2018.

(RMC) sought to intensify the struggle by calling for a stay-away on 17 September 1984 to express solidarity with communities under siege in the Vaal Triangle. The success of the stay-away was uneven but strengthened the conviction of those within COSAS and the RMC who felt that the time was right to accelerate efforts to bring the economy to its knees. Under the leadership of the Transvaal Area Committee, a regional stay-away from school and work was called for 5 and 6 November 1984.[62] The committee demanded the withdrawal of army and police from the townships, a halt to rent and bus fare increases, the resignation of 'all community councillors', the 'release of all political prisoners and detainees', a 'reinstatement of dismissed workers' and the scrapping of the General Sales Tax (GST) and other 'unfair' taxes.[63] COSAS further demanded that the Department of Education and Training (DET) deal with the education crisis. The November stay-away was one of the most successful of its kind and was supported by approximately 400,000 students from 300 different schools as well as 800,000 workers.[64] According to the Labour Monitoring Group, the participation rate was around 80 percent.[65]

School boycotts that had started on 3 September continued until January 1985, with 93,000 local pupils reportedly boycotting class.[66] This amounted to an almost complete boycott of schooling in the region.[67] Students informed a meeting on 5 October 1984, attended by members of the Orange Vaal Chamber of Commerce, the taxi association, the Vaal Ministers' Solidarity Group and student bodies that they would continue the school boycott until community grievances were addressed and detainees released.[68] A series of meetings were held in local churches during December of the same year to discuss the future of the school boycotts.[69] Meetings were infused by political content; invoking the names of the imprisoned Rivonia trialists, the students expressed their support for the banned ANC and its leadership in prison and exile.

62   WHP A2675, III (869), Pamphlet, 'Stay Away!'
63   WHP AK2117, J3.2, AB7, 'Documents re Regional Stay-Away'.
64   M. Swilling, 'The United Democratic Front and Township Revolt', in W. Cobbett and R. Cohen (eds), *Popular Struggles in South Africa* (London, James Currey, 1988), p.102.
65   M. Swilling, 'Urban Social Movements under Apartheid', *Cahiers d'Etudes Africaines*, 99 (1985), p.369.
66   *City Press*, 30 September 1984.
67   The exact number of pupils at local schools remains unclear; the figures are drawn from the investigation conducted by Tjaart van der Walt; see WHP AK2117, J4.15, AAQ34, T. van der Walt, 'Report on the Investigation into Education for Blacks in the Vaal Triangle Following Upon the Occurrences in September 1984 and Thereafter' (Pretoria, Government Printer, 1985), p.7.
68   *Sowetan Sunday Mirror*, 7 October 1984.
69   WHP AG2918, 3.9.1.2.1, 'An Account of the Ongoing Activities in the Vaal and Parys Townships'.

The question of whether or not to return to school created divisions among the student body: while COSAS was in full support of the school boycott, the Azanian Students' Movement (AZASM) as well as the Sharpeville Students' National Resistance Movement promoted a return to classrooms. A meeting organised by local priests on 3 January 1985 to resolve the issue eventually ended in an uneasy agreement that respected the wishes of those who wanted to return to the classroom.[70] By mid-January 1985, a large percentage of primary and secondary school pupils had returned.[71] Although the regional school boycott was eventually called off, sporadic boycotts continued. The slogan 'liberation before education' became a rallying call for many students who regarded the attainment of freedom as a prerequisite for quality education.

Many parents supported the school boycott because of their sympathy with their children's plight or because they were worried about sending their children back to school where they would encounter police and the military.[72] Progressive parents formed the Education Crisis Committee; MaLetanta, who by then was actively involved in the ANC underground, came to be an important link between students and parents. Her age and status as a parent gave her the ears of more conservative parents, whom she talked to about the grievances of the students and their role in the broader struggle for freedom. Teachers such as Ronjo Hailela, a member of the VCA, played a mediating role. These progressive teachers later formed the Vaal Progressive Teachers' Union (VAPTU). Relationships also varied between different principals and students. While some schools were headed by conservative principals who were passing information to the police, others, such as Moqhaka Secondary School in Zone 11 in Sebokeng, had a sympathetic principal who supported the students.

The lack of schooling provided many with ample time to become politically active and to hold discussion groups and debate political theory, history and poetry.[73] Progressive lecturers and students at the University of the Witwatersrand held informal classes and made banned literature accessible. Political education classes, widely known as *umrabulo*, were conducted regularly. They aimed to deepen knowledge on the history of the struggle for freedom, the paths taken in different countries, theories of revolution and the history of Marxism, and were meant to ensure that everyone was in line with the principles of the Charterist movement. The content of the Freedom Charter and the meaning of the NDR, as espoused by the ANC, were two hotly debated topics. 'You discuss with those close to you. How do you

70   WHP AK2117, S8.10.20, 'The Vaal Triangle During the Unrest, 1984–1985 (September to January) by Rev. Patrick Noonan'.
71   *Rand Daily Mail*, 16 January 1985.
72   *The Star*, 24 October 1984.
73   Shaka Radebe, interview with author, Vereeniging, 26 July 2010.

understand the Freedom Charter, what is entailed? We used to unpack it. [We used to] talk about historical materialism [and] imperialism,' COSAS activist Morris More remembers.[74]

While indoor meetings of small groups were convened to strategise, develop tactics and debate, the streets became the scenes of open confrontation where the newly acquired knowledge was tested. Street battles with police became one of the defining features of youth protest from the mid-1980s.[75] The street had always been an important space for socialisation; yet the 1980s saw the streets emerge as a key locus of protest and violence.[76] Crowds of youth, armed with rocks, petrol bombs and lids of dustbins (which served as shields), fought with police in full riot gear. Crowds of advancing youth were led by call and response: *Niyabasaba na?* (Are you scared of them?) one of the leaders would call. *Hayi asibasabi siyabafuna! Phambili, phambili* (No, we are not scared of them, we want them. We are going forward), the crowd chanted, reminding each other that not even death would halt the political swell.[77] Toyi-toying and songs praising the exploits of Umkhonto weSizwe, lamenting the imprisonment and exile of the political leadership and calling people to action were a daily feature of youth politics during this period.[78] Toyi-toying, a form of dance brought in from Zimbabwe, produced emotionally charged crowds. It aimed to instil courage and bravery and give a sense of unity. Townships became war zones, where youth painted over house numbers to make the townships illegible and ungovernable. Trenches were dug to hinder armoured vehicles from moving around, and slogans on walls proclaiming 'Tambo in – Botha out; ANC in – SADF out; Viva ANC' served as a visible reminder of the illegitimacy of the regime.

For activists it was a harsh life, shaped by fear of arrest, frequent moving and violence. Death stalked the townships and many young people did not expect to live a long life. Weekly burials of comrades not only reminded young people of the precarity of life and the brutality of the regime, but also served as platforms to mobilise and call for action. The slogan 'freedom or death' captured the readiness of many young people to lay down their life for the struggle

---

74   Morris More, interview with author, Sebokeng, 2 December 2011.

75   See Rueedi, '"Siyayinyova!"'

76   See Bundy, 'Street Sociology and Pavement Politics'; Bozzoli, *Theatres of Struggle*; L. Bank, *Home Spaces, Street Styles: Contesting Power and Identity in a South African City* (Johannesburg, Wits University Press, 2011); K. Naidoo, 'The Politics of Youth Resistance in the 1980s: The Dilemmas of a Differentiated Durban', *Journal of Southern African Studies*, 18/1 (1991), pp.143–65.

77   Oupa Masankane, interview with author, Vereeniging, 29 June 2010.

78   See, for example, A. Sitas, 'The Making of the "Comrades" Movement in Natal, 1985–91', *Journal of Southern African Studies*, 18/3, Special Issue: Political Violence in Southern Africa (1992), pp.629–41.

for freedom.[79] But for many, it was also a time of dreaming about a new order, envisaging how life would be in a free South Africa. But while some youth used the opportunity to further their knowledge and to engage in political activities, others became involved in petty crime. Rising unemployment produced generations of young people with high levels of frustration, time on their hands and experiences of violence and repression. Groups of tsotsis were fighting with student leaders over control and access to territory.

At the national conference of COSAS in Durban in January 1985, the need for the establishment of a national youth organisation was therefore stressed to ensure that unemployed and working youth would be politically educated and organised.[80] With the banning of COSAS on 28 August 1985 and the detention of its regional leadership, the establishment of new structures gained even greater importance to channel political activism among the youth and to ensure that new groups would be guided by Charterist principles.[81] The establishment of youth congresses in South Africa dates back to 1982. In the Vaal Triangle, this process was delayed by three years. Eventually, two organisations were launched: VASCO and the Vaal Youth Congress (VAYCO), which suffered from a weak presence in townships other than Sebokeng.[82] VAYCO aimed to organise the unemployed, working and religious youth, to keep them off the streets and to conscientise and politicise them.[83] VASCO, established a year before VAYCO in March 1986, essentially pursued the same aims as COSAS.[84] The idea to form a student congress had emerged during the detention of local COSAS activists, when they discussed possibilities of continuing the struggle after the banning of COSAS.[85] To ensure coherence and unity, student congresses such as VASCO and its Sowetan equivalent, the Soweto Student Congress (SOSCO), were later brought together under the umbrella of the Transvaal Students' Congress (TRASCO).

79　Oupa Modikoane, interview with author, East Rand, 1 July 2010.
80　WHP A2675, III (397), Report of the National Conference Held in Durban on the 12th and 13th Jan.; J. Seekings, *Heroes or Villains? Youth Politics in the 1980s* (Johannesburg, Ravan Press, 1993), p.37.
81　COSAS was banned under section 4(1) of the Internal Security Act (ISA) (Act 74/1982). Section 4(1) of ISA stated that an organisation may be declared 'unlawful' if it endangered national security or the maintenance of law and order (4(1a)), the promotion or furthering of communism (4(1b)), if it was deemed to be controlled by an organisation under section (a) or (b) or if it was furthering the aims of a banned organisation. The vague definition of each section gave the government sweeping powers to declare organisations unlawful. See *Government Gazette*, 9 June 1982.
82　Edward 'Chippa' Motubatsi, interview with author, Vereeniging, 5 December 2011.
83　Tebogo 'Exec.' Moepadira, interview with author, Vanderbijlpark, 23 June 2010.
84　Mandla Mazibuko, interview with author, Vanderbijlpark, 22 June 2010.
85　Lekgotla 'Ace' Motaung, interview with author, Sebokeng, 28 June 2016.

The banning of COSAS led to widespread arrests and most of the COSAS activists in the Vaal Triangle were detained.[86] The average age of those detained ranged between 16 and 20 years – reflecting the nationwide phenomenon that a large number of detainees by that time were in fact under age.[87] Sharing cells with up to 20 people, detention was a time for political discussions often led by senior political detainees. Many youth who had been conscientised through their lived experience of poverty and violence deepened their understandings of politics and history in detention. Significantly, even those who were detained for ad hoc participation in protest action, and who had a poor understanding of the ideological contours, the history and the strategic programme of the banned liberation movements, were exposed to *umrabulo*, in-depth debate, and were thus politicised. One of the senior activists who played a role in conscientising and politicising detained youth was Morakabe 'Raks' Seakhoa, who had been released from Robben Island in late September 1984 and detained again in mid-1985 for possession of explosives.[88] 'We will smuggle a ballpen and Raks will then take a tissue paper. And he will write on the discussion paper. Maybe about the national democratic struggle, the Freedom Charter and then in the afternoon [we will] discuss it.'[89] This exposure allowed many to forge new links with the exiled movements once they were released. Therefore, while Robben Island, nicknamed 'the University', may have been the most famous prison in which these debates were raging, many smaller detention centres that held political activists served a similar purpose, as interviews with youth activists demonstrate.[90]

Strengthening MK in the Townships

The response by the exiled leadership to the insurrection in the Vaal Triangle in 1984 brought into sharp relief its disconnect from what was happening on the ground. Even though the Ralitselas' cell had been stirring civic action in the region, the events in the Vaal Triangle caught the ANC leadership in exile largely by surprise. Howard Barrell points out that the ANC in exile 'failed to seize a moment in which popular militancy, together with weakness and confusion within the apartheid state, was at unprecedented levels'.[91] In the Vaal Triangle, MK was virtually absent in September 1984, and therefore had no capacity to militarily reinforce the uprising. The planned infiltration of MK cadres into the

---

86   Themba Goba, interview with author, Vereeniging, 18 June 2010.

87   WHP A2084, Ad6.1.2.1, 'DPSC Report on Detentions'.

88   Electronic conversation, Morakabe 'Raks' Seakhoa, 1 September 2018.

89   Themba Goba, interview with author, Vereeniging, 18 June 2010.

90   Ibid.; Sarhili 'Toy' Manqa, interview with author, Vereeniging, 26 May 2011.

91   H. Barrell, 'Conscripts to Their Age: African National Congress Operational Strategy, 1976–1986' (DPhil thesis, University of Oxford, 1993), p.8.

country was stalled when the army occupied the townships.[92] To address this lack of military support, Edward 'Chippa' Motubatsi, who had already joined MK in 1982, was tasked by the ANC's leadership in October 1984 to accompany Tsietsi 'Stompi' Mokhele, and one other civic activist, to Botswana to report to the ANC structures in October 1984.[93] In exile, Mokhele and the other activist formally joined MK and the three men underwent two months of military training, instruction in how to conduct clandestine work and political education. Two of the key texts discussed were Joe Slovo's book *No Middle Road* and the Soviet doctrine of MCW.[94] One of their key contacts was Thami Mnyele, co-founder of the Medu Art Ensemble and MK cadre who had been trained in the Soviet Union.[95] Mnyele, as Motubatsi and Mokhele remember, played a leading role in teaching them what it meant to be a disciplined and 'good' cadre.[96]

Mokhele recalls that the unfolding of the large-scale insurrections in the townships accelerated the ANC's commitment to enter a new phase of the struggle. In exile, they were told by the leadership that 'you need to keep the fires burning but more than that, you need to create the infrastructure for the growth of our struggle and the revolution'.[97] Mokhele and Motubatsi were therefore not tasked to engage in military operations, but to create conditions favourable to the infiltration of MK cadres, in line with the concept of people's war. Weak rear bases, fraught lines of communication, cross-border raids, a difficult topography and the challenges of maintaining a supply of weapons and ammunition had all limited the success of MK operations in South Africa. The infiltration of MK cadres and ANC underground operatives therefore aimed to 'facilitate the situation of making sure that the ANC as a political party and MK as an armed wing are placed in the country to provide the political leadership in structures and to lead the armed struggle from within'.[98]

After their return in December 1984, the men went separate ways: Motubatsi was tasked to act as a courier and to continue working towards the formation of youth structures. Mokhele, on the other hand, moved to Parys in the Northern Free State, from where he planned most of his operations. Popularly known

92   Tsietsi 'Stompi' Mokhele and Edward 'Chippa' Motubatsi, interview with author, Bophelong, 21 September 2019.

93   Ibid.

94   Ibid. On MCW, see, for example, Davis, *The ANC's War against Apartheid*, pp.147–48.

95   D. Wylie, *Art and Revolution: The Life and Death of Thami Mnyele, South African Artist* (Johannesburg, Jacana, 2008).

96   Thami Mnyele was among the victims of the Gaborone raid in 1985, when security forces killed 12 people.

97   Tsietsi 'Stompi' Mokhele and Edward 'Chippa' Motubatsi, interview with author, Bophelong, 21 September 2019.

98   Ibid.

as 'the commander', Mokhele soon became a key contact for young people who wanted to join MK in exile. Mokhele also came to play a significant role in locating safe houses for new MK cadres arriving in the area, and like many other MK guerrillas, he facilitated the infiltration of weapons into the country.[99] One of Mokhele's first recruits was Ernest Sotsu, an ANC veteran from the Eastern Cape who had joined the ANC in 1949 and been active in the Boipatong branch of the VCA prior to the uprising. Known for his militancy, Sotsu was active in above- and underground structures for most of his life. After his recruitment, he played a leading role in establishing contact between politically active youth and the ANC leadership in exile.[100] Kedibone Mogotsi was another operative who was in contact with the ANC in exile through Mokhele. Born in 1945, she was already middle aged when she became involved in underground work and, like MaLetanta, her gender and age offered protection and allowed her to operate beyond the radar of the security branch. Mogotsi's house in Bophelong became a safe house for many activists on the run, and she hid weapons she received from her MK contact in dead letter boxes (DLBs).[101]

Some of the youth who wanted to join MK were still in primary school and many of those who were under age were instructed by the ANC to complete their education first.[102] By then, it had become increasingly difficult to leave South Africa via Botswana as border control had tightened in the aftermath of the revolts and the signing of the Nkomati Accord of 1984. New recruits were instead taken to Ficksburg, where they crossed the border into Lesotho. The knowledge of dagga smugglers, Mokhele recalls, was particularly useful in determining safe passage; local people who were known as 'butterflies' assisted the recruits to go unnoticed.[103] Once they had crossed the border, the next destination was the United Nations Centre for Refugees in Maseru, where they were given food and shelter and eventually airlifted to a country of choice of the ANC.[104]

99   Tsietsi 'Stompi' Mokhele and Edward 'Chippa' Motubatsi, interview with author, Bophelong, 18 September 2011.

100   Sarhili 'Toy' Manqa, interview with author, Vereeniging, 26 May 2010. Sotsu was arrested in 1986 and eventually transferred to Mthatha in the Transkei, where he was sentenced to six years' imprisonment. He re-emerged in the late 1980s and came to play a leading role during the violent conflict that ravaged the Vaal Triangle between 1990 and 1994. In 1991, Sotsu's wife, daughter and grandson were murdered at their home in Boipatong township by a criminal gang aligned to the Inkatha Freedom Party (IFP). Truth and Reconciliation Commission Human Rights Violations Hearings, 6 August 1996, Case 211, https://www.justice.gov.za/Trc/hrvtrans/sebokeng/seb211.htm, retrieved 5 November 2020.

101   Kedibone Mogotsi, interview with author, Vereeniging, 26 July 2010.

102   Ibid.

103   Tsietsi 'Stompi' Mokhele and Edward 'Chippa' Motubatsi, interview with author, Bophelong, 18 September 2011.

104   UWC MA MCH31, ISO34/XIRIOAI (*State v Tsietsi Elias Mokhele*), case number unknown.

Despite taking precautions, Mokhele was arrested in August 1985 for his alleged involvement in MK activities and ANC underground work and taken to a small police station close to the Vaal River called Barrage.[105] The police station, which only had a handful of cells, had been emptied of other prisoners and owing to its remote location, it had been turned into an interrogation centre for political detainees. For Mokhele, the remoteness was devastating. 'It was me and God in that place,' he remembered.[106] During the following weeks, Mokhele was brutally and relentlessly tortured and denied any medical care. When Mokhele was finally charged and given access to a lawyer, the prosecution offered to drop six out of seven charges if he admitted to being a member of a banned movement, the ANC. For the police and the prosecution, Mokhele, whom they suspected of being a member of the ANC underground and MK, was a vital witness to prove the link between civic structures and the ANC in exile. The Delmas treason trial was under way, and the state prosecution was anxious to prove that civic structures were operating in collaboration with the ANC. As the Ralitselas had gone into exile, and other underground operatives remained off their radar, the police were under pressure from headquarters in Pretoria to supply evidence; such evidence would have sunk the Delmas trialists and led to the banning of the UDF and its affiliates. Mokhele, however, denied any involvement and was eventually released on bail after the defence discovered that the key state witness, an *askari*, was using various identities to testify at three different trials. Shortly afterwards, Mokhele skipped bail and went into exile, where his journey led him to Mozambique, Angola, Zambia and the Soviet Union, among other places. Years later, in December 2000, he appeared before the Truth and Reconciliation Commission to testify about the disappearance of his spouse Nomasonto Mashiya, an MK cadre codenamed 'Nokuthula Nkomo', and the kidnapping of their then one-year-old son in 1987 in exile.[107]

People's War and the Formation of Armed Units

Mostly in response to the mutiny in MK's camps in Angola, and on recommendation of the Stuart commission, which had been tasked to investigate the crisis within MK in 1984, the ANC called for a National Consultative Conference. The conference eventually took place between 16 June and 23 June 1985

---

105   Tsietsi 'Stompi' Mokhele and Edward 'Chippa' Motubatsi, interview with author, Bophelong, 18 September 2011.

106   Ibid.

107   It remains unclear what happened to Nomasonto Mashiya. Security police admitted to abducting Mashiya and three other MK cadres in Lesotho in 1987, and taking them to a farm in Ladybrand for interrogation. They were never seen again. Truth and Reconciliation Commission Amnesty Hearings, 7 December 2000, AM7715/96, https://www.justice.gov.za/trc/amntrans/2000/2001207.htm, retrieved 25 January 2021.

in Kabwe, Zambia.[108] For several days, the 250 delegates discussed the future of the liberation struggle and the way forward.[109] The delegates acknowledged that while the ANC had been gaining popularity among South Africa's oppressed, its organisational capacities and its ability to provide guidance and direction remained fraught with problems. Although in some areas uprisings were related to the work of ANC underground cells, the impact of the underground was generally considered 'uneven and erratic'.[110] The infiltration of weapons and MK cadres to train internal recruits and the arming of the population to implement 'people's war' were seen as paramount.[111] The tactics of guerrilla warfare should be used to continue rendering South Africa ungovernable by seizing weapons and making local government unworkable.[112] As Hugh Macmillan emphasises, the conference was 'enthusiastic about "people's war", but rejected any suggestion of "terrorism".'[113] But only two and a half hours of the entire conference were dedicated to discussions on the internal situation, and no comprehensive guidelines were developed with regard to strategies and tactics.[114] This lack of clarity severely hampered the ANC's capacity to lead domestic insurrections, and to reinforce them militarily. Furthermore, the ANC failed to implement a 'system of command and control' that would ensure the implementation of a people's war under its guidance.[115]

In Kabwe's aftermath, members of MK and the ANC underground were given the task of identifying youth, giving them basic training in the use of weapons and distributing hand grenades, rifles and other weaponry. A large-scale distribution of weapons was neither feasible nor desirable; instead, politically educated and disciplined activists should be trained under the guidance of MK cadres.[116] The training and arming of these units in the townships was meant to ensure that MK would increase its base in South Africa and that the armed struggle would be rooted inside the country. But by October 1985, a year after the beginning of the uprising

---

108   Hugh Macmillan explains that the mutiny was triggered by MK's involvement in the war against União Nacional para a Independência Total de Angola (UNITA) in Angola, and was exacerbated by grievances among MK cadres such as deteriorating living conditions in the camps, unequal treatment, the use of violence by the ANC's security department Mbokodo, and the return of disgruntled cadres. See H. Macmillan, *The Lusaka Years, 1963–1994: The ANC in Exile in Zambia* (Johannesburg, Jacana, 2013), pp.162–63.

109   For a personal account of the Kabwe conference, see C. Nqakula, *The People's War: Reflections of an ANC Cadre* (Johannesburg, Mutloatse Arts Heritage Trust, 2017).

110   UWC MA MCH01, 47.3, 'Internal Mobilisation', p.2.

111   Ibid.

112   UWC MA MCH01, 15.2, Radio Transcript, *Dawn Breaks* (5 November 1985).

113   Macmillan, *The Lusaka Years*, p.195.

114   Ibid., p.194.

115   S. Ellis, *External Mission: The ANC in Exile, 1960–1990* (Oxford, Oxford University Press, 2013), p.224.

116   UWC MA MCH01, 47.2, 'Kabwe: Pre-Conference Discussion Document: Report of Commission on Military Training Improvement of Skills and Deployment'.

in the Vaal Triangle, the ANC had barely made any inroads in respect of reinforcing the insurrections by sending cadres, training activists and supplying weapons. Thula Simpson quotes Chris Hani, MK's chief political commissar, voicing his frustration that MK's contribution to the uprisings was insufficient: 'If our people had AKs [AK47s], the situation would be radically changed in a few months.'[117]

While the ANC's plans to implement a people's war under its guidance hardly materialised, many youth in the townships embraced the ANC's call for a people's war and formed clandestine, militarised units. One of the earliest such units was the South African Suicide Squad (SASS), formed in the late 1970s in Soweto.[118] Like similar units in different parts of the country, the SASS petrol bombed houses of police, informers and councillors. Despite its ambiguous relationship with units such as SASS, by 1983 the ANC had acknowledged their relevance and recommended providing 'guidance and political training coupled with military upgrading since they form a component of People's War.'[119] Similar units began to spring up in many urbanised townships during the insurrectionary period.[120]

Many of these units regarded themselves as part of the ANC's armed struggle, yet the extent of their training and education, their lack of formal affiliation through taking MK's oath, and their access to weapons, knowledge and support distinguished them from formally trained MK cadres.[121] While some of these units were trained by MK cadres, others had indirect links and no mandate. The ANC's annual speech on 8 January, during which its president Oliver Tambo spoke to the South African population, served as an inspiration to many young activists

---

117 T. Simpson, '"Umkhonto we Sizwe, We Are Waiting for You": The ANC and the Township Uprising, September 1984–September 1985'. *South African Historical Journal*, 61/1 (2009), pp.158–77.

118 Rueedi, '"Our Bushes Are the Houses"'.

119 UWC MA MCH01, 47.2, 'Kabwe: Pre-Conference Discussion Document: The Place of the Armed Struggle', p.8. I explore the formation of these units and their relationship to the ANC in exile more fully in Rueedi, '"Our Bushes Are the Houses"'. See also Simpson, '"Umkhonto we Sizwe, We Are Waiting for You"'.

120 Research on these units remains scant. For case studies outside the Vaal Triangle, see for example T. Moloi, 'The Botswana Connection: The Re-invigoration of Confrontational Politics in Thembisa Township, 1979–1990', in A. Lissoni and A. Pezzano (eds), *The ANC between Home and Exile: Reflections on the Anti-Apartheid Struggle in Italy and Southern Africa* (Napoli, Universita degli studi di Napoli L'Orientale, 2015) and J. Cherry, 'Hidden Histories of the Eastern Cape Underground', in SADET (ed.), *The Road to Democracy, Volume 4* (Pretoria, Unisa Press, 2010). Cherry details the complex interaction between violent and non-violent strategies, and the role of young comrades, the *amabutho*, during people's war in the Eastern Cape.

121 Thula Simpson distinguishes spontaneous rioting from attacks conducted by MK with sophisticated weaponry. See Simpson, '"Umkhonto we Sizwe, We Are Waiting for You"'. My own research shows that these boundaries were often less rigid. See Rueedi, '"Our Bushes Are the Houses"'.

and guided their actions. Their actions were also significantly shaped by their subjective experiences of police violence and oppression, and a desire to protect their communities.[122] During the same period, the Azanian People's Liberation Army (APLA), the armed wing of the PAC, embarked on attacks on policemen. In Sharpeville, ten policemen were allegedly killed by APLA in 1986.[123]

In the Vaal Triangle, the VALIMO was formed on 26 June 1985, after the meeting held to celebrate the thirtieth anniversary of the Freedom Charter was broken up by police.[124] VALIMO consisted of young, mostly male activists who had met each other through COSAS. Their main campaign was to expunge the police, informers and anyone else regarded as an 'agent' of the regime from the townships.[125] Operating at night, VALIMO petrol bombed houses of police and informers. In their view, arson was the most efficient way of heeding the ANC's call to make the townships ungovernable and to ensure that 'organs of people's power' could be successfully established. Ridding the townships of police and informers was also meant to protect activists and the community at large; by then, widespread harassment and police violence had become ingrained in daily life. VALIMO's operations remained ephemeral and by late 1985 most of its members had been detained for public violence, arson and intimidation. In detention, they linked up to MK networks and after their release, VALIMO's members began to access weapons and military training.[126]

VALIMO's members had first attempted to access weapons in 1985, when they were approached by Joe Mamasela, the infamous Vlakplaas *askari*, who was posing as an MK operative. Mamasela promised them access to AK47s and hand grenades, and offered to train them. But the group did not pursue this offer and, in all likelihood, it saved their lives.[127] In Duduza in the East Rand, members of a similar group blew themselves up after being given hand grenades timed at zero

122   Rueedi, '"Siyayinyova!"'; M. Marks, '"We Are Fighting for the Liberation of Our People": Justifications of Violence by Activist Youth in Diepkloof, Soweto', *Berkeley Journal of Sociology*, 41 (1996–97), pp.137–65.

123   T. Lodge, *Sharpeville: An Apartheid Massacre and its Consequences* (Oxford, Oxford University Press, 2011), p.298. On the PAC and APLA during this period, see K. Kondlo, *In the Twilight of the Revolution: The Pan Africanist Congress of Azania (South Africa), 1959–1994* (Basel, Basler Afrika Bibliographien, 2009); T. ka Plaatjie, 'The PAC's Exile Politics, 1980–1990', in SADET (ed.), *The Road to Democracy, Volume 4* (Pretoria, Unisa Press, 2010), pp.1227–64; and Letlapa Mphahlele's autobiography, *Child of this Soil: My Life as a Freedom Fighter* (Johannesburg, Mwalimu Books, 2010).

124   Themba Goba, interview with author, Vereeniging, 18 June 2010; see Rueedi, '"Siyay-inyova!"'

125   Sarhili 'Toy' Manqa, interview with author, Vereeniging, 26 May 2011; Oupa Masankane, interview with author, Vereeniging, 29 June 2010; Themba Goba, interview with author, Sebokeng, 2 December 2011.

126   Sarhili 'Toy' Manqa, interview with author, Vereeniging, 26 May 2011.

127   One of their members was allegedly warned about Mamasela.

seconds by Mamasela. Orders for what become known as 'Operation Zero Zero' had been given by General Johan van der Merwe to quell the revolts in the townships.[128] Operation Zero Zero not only cost the lives of these young activists, it also undermined MK's ability to recruit others, as Veli Mazibuko, MK commander from Duduza, recalls.[129]

Another group, which was formed in 1986, was Ace Mates under the leadership of Lekgotla 'Ace' Motaung.[130] Like VALIMO's members, most of Ace Mates' activists had cut their teeth in COSAS and later VASCO, and were in their late teens. Ace Mates mostly operated in Zone 7 in Sebokeng and came to be feared by anyone associated with the apartheid regime. The group consisted of a handful of members who had been trained and politically educated by a seasoned activist who was released from Robben Island in 1984, and who also allegedly provided them with weapons such as AK47s and hand grenades.[131] Lekgotla 'Ace' Motaung, codenamed Joseph Ntuli, became the commander of the group and in charge of operations, Moeketsi Benedict 'Tina Turner' Mashoke was the political commissar, and Thabo Memela handled ordnance. Their unit was modelled after an MK unit, with each member having a clear task. Some of Ace Mates' most militant members were young women: Dineo 'Mapikoko' Mokoena, who had joined the group in her late teens, came to play a leading role.[132]

Whether or not the former Robben Islander had received instructions to identify and train youth in the townships remains unclear. It is likely that he used his networks as a former political prisoner and ANC activist to access weapons and to impart political education. In contrast to trained MK cadres, the training and education of Ace Mates' members was brief: rudimentary military training included knowledge on how to shoot, use an AK47 and a hand grenade, how to take cover and conduct basic surveillance. Their armoury included three hand grenades, as well as rifles such as R1s and R4s, which they had obtained

---

128   Johan Velde van der Merwe, interview with author, Pretoria, 18 May 2011; Truth and Reconciliation Commission Amnesty Hearings, 3 August 1999, Willem Frederik Schoon, AM4396, http://www.justice.gov.za/trc/amntrans/1999/99080205_pre_990803pt.htm, retrieved 15 May 2020.

129   Veli Mazibuko, interview with author, Johannesburg, 28 February 2019.

130   See Rueedi, '"Our Bushes Are the Houses"'.

131   Lekgotla 'Ace' Motaung, interviews with author, Sebokeng, 22 November 2011 and 9 July 2016; Lekgotla 'Ace' Motaung and Dineo 'Mapikoko' Mokoena, interview with author, Sebokeng, 28 June 2016; Nthabiseng Christina Mofolo, Dineo 'Mapikoko' Mokoena and Lekgotla 'Ace' Motaung, interview with author, Sebokeng, 22 October 2011.

132   While these groups were often heavily dominated by men, young women were also involved in structures espousing violence. See E. Bridger, 'Soweto's Female Comrades: Gender, Youth and Violence in South Africa's Township Uprisings, 1984–1986', *Journal of Southern African Studies*, 44/4 (2018), pp.559–74.

by disarming police. In contrast to trained MK cadres who were instructed to use DLBs, Ace Mates stored their weapons at home, and their safe houses were selected based on networks of familiarity and trust.[133]

Groups such as Ace Mates were at the forefront of people's war in the townships. Largely beyond the direct control of the ANC's command structures, Ace Mates, like many other similar groups, fought police in the ANC's name and embraced the ANC's call to render the country ungovernable. The weak presence of MK and the political ANC underground, and the lack of a domestic command structure tasked to guide people's war, resulted in considerable freedom for units such as Ace Mates to interpret the ANC's strategic objectives. Their lack of training and education also made them vulnerable: openly displaying their weapons in the townships, Ace Mates aimed to mark their presence and instil hope, yet they also attracted the attention of the police. Ace Mates not only targeted the houses of policemen and informers, they also planned to attack the police station in Vereeniging, where the head office of the security branch was located, as well as a white high school. The latter was not in line with the ANC's policies, which emphasised avoidance of soft targets.

Not long after their formation and before they could carry out their plan to attack General Jan Smuts High School, Ace Motaung and other members of Ace Mates were arrested. They were viciously tortured by the police, who were desperate to uncover where the weapons had come from. While Motaung was eventually sentenced to 24 years on Robben Island, and Mokoena was placed under house arrest, one of the group, Moeketsi Benedict 'Tina Turner' Mashoke, died in detention in March 1987.[134] Police alleged he hanged himself, but his family suspect that he died as a result of his torture.[135] During the same year, Motubatsi, Mogotsi and others were arrested for aiding MK operatives to infiltrate the region and sentenced to various prison terms in what became known as the 'Potchefstroom Seven' trial.

By then, South Africa was changing. Many of the country's uprisings had been quelled and the police had re-established their coercive capacities. Many activists were in detention or had gone into exile. But even though the apartheid regime had seemingly gained the upper hand in curbing the revolts, power relations had shifted. The negative publicity South Africa's white minority regime attracted led to the loss of major domestic and international allies. Pretoria's propaganda war was failing, and for many global audiences apartheid had to be dismantled. Secret talks between the ANC's imprisoned leader Nelson Mandela and the apartheid regime had been ongoing, paving the way for a negotiated settlement. The fall of the Berlin Wall in 1989, heralding the end of the Cold War, deprived Pretoria of one of its key justifications for its war against the liberation movements; the 'threat' of communism was no longer real.

133   Rueedi, '"Our Bushes Are the Houses"'.
134   The circumstances of Mashoke's death remain unclear.
135   Rosalinah Mashoke, interview with author, Sebokeng, 8 October 2016.

The release of Govan Mbeki in 1987, Walter Sisulu in 1989 and Nelson Mandela and others in 1990 gave hope to activists that South Africa would soon be liberated. During the same year, the ANC, the PAC and the South African Communist Party were unbanned and many ANC cadres began preparations to return from exile. Dorcas and Esau Ralitsela returned in early 1991; Mokhele only saw the country of his birth again in 1993, when he entered South Africa to attend the funeral of Chris Hani. Most of the Delmas trialists were acquitted (some over a technicality) or released with pending sentences. Gcina Malindi, Thomas Manthata, Moss Chikane, Terror Lekota and Popo Molefe, who were serving their sentences, were released from Robben Island after the unbanning of the ANC. After years on death row, Sefatsa and the other accused in the Sharpeville Six trial were reprieved and finally released as well. But while the National Party and the ANC embarked on negotiations to prepare for a transfer of power, parts of the country, including the Vaal Triangle and the East Rand, descended into some of the worst violence the country had ever witnessed.

Conclusion:
Dream Deferred

On 2 September 2014, a crowd gathered in Sebokeng. The day was sunny and mild, the mood festive. The air was filled with the sound of drums and a dance show entertained those that were present. The crowd had come to pay tribute and respect to the thousands of people who had assembled in the same place 30 years earlier. Planning to retrace the steps of the original marchers, they were flanked by high-powered local luminaries in expensive cars.[1] Young and old were in the streets, just as they had been in 1984. Many were wearing African National Congress (ANC) T-shirts, others wore clothing that signified their place in the struggle for freedom: 'Robben Island' said the zip-up top of one prominent activist. Some were marching in military uniforms to emphasise their contribution to the armed struggle. Former activists of the Vaal Civic Association (VCA) and the Congress of South African Students (COSAS), who had been at the forefront of protest politics during the 1980s, were among the crowd. Many were happy that this watershed moment was being commemorated and that the Vaal Triangle's role in ending white minority rule was being acknowledged. Born-frees, who never experienced the brutality of apartheid, were quoted as saying that they were proud of their region's history. And politicians voiced their commitment to prosperity and progress. David Makhura, the chairperson of ANC Gauteng, in his speech spoke about the need to 'reindustrialise' the region to create employment and combat poverty. MP Paul Mashatile affirmed, 'Now that we have brought about freedom and democracy, we must build a better life for all our people.'[2] Other speakers used the occasion to remind residents to pay their rent 'to make this new government work'; in the Vaal Triangle, the rent boycott has become so entrenched that 25 years after the dawn of democracy it is still ongoing.

---

1   M. Makhanya, '1984: A Bygone Year?', *City Press*, 9 September 2014.
2   N. Shelembe, 'Sebokeng Residents Encouraged to Do Business', *South African Government News Agency* (4 September 2014), https://www.sanews.gov.za/south-africa/sebokeng-residents-encouraged-do-business, retrieved 5 March 2020.

But despite the festivity and cheer, the dissatisfaction of some was palpable. Reid Mokoena of the Sharpeville Six angrily proclaimed, 'My sacrifice for the country seems to have been for some people to have big cars and big houses.'[3] Others refrained from attending the commemoration. These sentiments are not new and are regularly expressed as the anniversary of the Vaal Uprising approaches. For many, the date is a reminder of their sacrifice, their pain and the hardship they went through during the struggle against oppression and white minority rule. And it is symbolic of the hopes, aspirations and dreams that shaped the struggle for freedom, many of which remain unfulfilled. As Trevor Ngwane, leading member of the now defunct Anti-Privatisation Forum (APF) emphasises, '[P]eople want the transition from apartheid to democracy to lead to a significant improvement in the conditions of their everyday lives. They want a level of material comfort and security that goes beyond the abstract rights that they supposedly enjoy.'[4]

This lack of material comfort is glaringly visible in African townships: 'The township looks exactly like it did before, when we took action against the Apartheid government. The roads are still bad, streetlights still not working,' Thabiso Ratsomo, former Delmas trialist, bemoaned in 2012.[5] Sebokeng's roads continue to be largely untarred, electricity frequently goes off, the faulty stormwater drainage leads to flooding, access to water remains a privilege, violent crime is rife and in 2018, the unemployment rate in the Sedibeng region was a staggering 50 percent.[6] Unemployment rates for Emfuleni municipality, of which Sebokeng forms a part, were even higher. The once booming industrial towns of Vereeniging and Vanderbijlpark are experiencing recession, retrenchments and severe economic decline.[7] The Sedibeng District Municipality, which encompasses the Vaal Triangle region and includes the municipalities of Emfuleni, Lesedi and Midvaal, had the lowest 'human development and GDP per capita' in the entire Gauteng province in 2016.[8]

3   Reid Mokoena, quoted in Makhanya, '1984: A Bygone Year?', *City Press*, 9 September 2014.
4   T. Ngwane, '"Insurgent Democracy": Post-Apartheid South Africa's Freedom Fighters', *Journal of Southern African Studies*, 45/1 (2019), p.230.
5   G. Marinovich, 'Sebokeng: The Lessons of 1984', *Daily Maverick*, 30 November 2012.
6   T. Zwane, 'Young Graduates Fear Falling into a Trap of "Nothingness"', *Mail and Guardian*, 14 August 2015; Gauteng Province, 'Socio-Economic Review and Outlook', 2020.
7   D. McKinley and A. Veriava, '"Forgotten" Voices in the Present: Alternative, Post-1994 Oral Histories from Three Poor Communities in South Africa' (South African History Archive, Alternative Histories Project, 2008), pp.99–160. http://www.saha.org.za/resources/docs/Publications/FVITP.pdf, retrieved 22 April 2020.
8   'Gauteng Province: Socio-Economic Review and Outlook 2018', http://www.treasury.gov.za/documents/provincial%20budget/2018/3.%20Estimates%20of%20Prov%20Rev%20and%20Exp/GT/1.%20Budget%20Overview/GT%20-%20EPRE%20-%20Budget%20Overview.pdf, retrieved 15 May 2020.

The landscape of the Vaal Triangle not only serves as a stark reminder of the ongoing poverty and hardship many black people continue to face, but it also bears the scars of the struggle for freedom. Some of the houses that were burnt down on 3 September 1984 were never rebuilt; others are marked by bullet holes and some continue to show the signs of 'people's war': the painting over of house numbers serves as a memorial of a bygone era. The area around the post office, once the site of fierce street battles between young activists and police, looks the same as it did 30 years ago. Another key site, the Roman Catholic Church in Evaton Small Farms, appears dilapidated; plans to turn the church into a memorial site have yet to materialise. Sites where major confrontations and violence took place during the 1980s and during the horrific conflict of the 1990s evoke traumatic memories for those who witnessed this violence. The commemoration of the Vaal Uprising remains sporadic, reflecting the scant attention the Vaal Triangle has received within the broader history of the struggle for freedom. No memorial site exists that commemorates those who lost their lives during the turbulent 1980s, nor is there a museum that preserves the history and legacy of the uprising, and that provides a platform for public engagement with the past. Soweto, the Vaal Triangle's famous neighbour, continues to loom large in the popular imagination and collective memory.

Democracy and the Legacy of Inequality and Poverty

Twenty-five years after the first democratic government was voted into power, South Africa remains the most unequal society in the world.[9] While South Africa's transition to democracy has been hailed as a successful example of a negotiated settlement that took the country from a racially discriminatory state to a politically inclusive new system, the transition to majority rule has not yet been able to overcome the deep divisions and the pernicious socio-economic legacy of apartheid on society. Informal settlements, where people live in abject poverty, jostle for their existence while the wealthy suburbs and glittering high-rise buildings of Johannesburg continue to promise the dream of a 'better life for all' that underpinned the first democratic elections in 1994. The townships remain barren sites of want and hardship; for many, 'matchbox houses' continue to evoke a complex set of aspirations, hope and rejection. Informal settlements that dot the landscape remind of ongoing poverty, inequality and a lack of housing and services.

---

9   See W.B. Hurlbut (ed.), 'Overcoming Poverty and Inequality in South Africa: An Assessment of Drivers, Constraints and Opportunities' (Washington, The World Bank, March 2018); E. Sekyere, S. Gordon, G. Pienaar and N. Bohler-Muller, 'Is South Africa Winning the War on Poverty and Inequality? What Do the Available Statistics Tell Us?' in E. Durojaye and G. Mirugi-Mukundi (eds), *Exploring the Link Between Poverty and Human Rights in Africa* (Pretoria, Pretoria University Law Press, 2020), p.34.

With the advent of democracy, the new government committed itself to addressing the legacy of apartheid-era spatial planning, poverty and inequality. By 1994, public policy was largely racially non-discriminatory.[10] South Africa's post-apartheid constitution has enshrined a set of socio-economic rights that includes the right to 'housing, social security, healthcare services, food and water, and non-basic education'.[11] Through the constitution, the state therefore deracialised citizenship rights and redefined what constitutes a right. At the centre of the remaking of early post-apartheid policy was the 1994 Reconstruction and Development Programme (RDP), which focused on social development and addressing poverty and inequality.[12] One of the key concerns when the ANC took power was a severe shortage of housing and the inadequate living conditions of millions of black South Africans.[13] During the first three years of democracy, 154 roads were built in rural areas, 1.3 million people gained access to clean piped water and 1.4 million homes were electrified.[14] Salahuddin and colleagues identify three different types of poverty-reduction policies that were implemented: the distribution of social grants such as pensions, child grants and grants for people with disabilities; economic empowerment through the Broad Based Black Economic Empowerment programme, which contributed towards the emergence of a new elite; and an increase in resources for social services.[15] In 2015, as Natasha Vally shows, the South African Social Security Agency (SASSA) paid out 16.9 million grants to 11 million beneficiaries, such as the elderly, children and people with disabilities.[16] The sheer scale of social assistance is extraordinary, and evidence suggests that social grants have played an important role in addressing poverty.[17]

10   J. Seekings and N. Nattrass, *Class, Race, and Inequality in South Africa* (New Haven and London, Yale University Press, 2005), p.36.

11   M. Langford, 'Introduction: Civil Society and Socio-Economic Rights', in M. Langford, B. Cousins, J. Dugard and T. Madlingozi (eds), *Socio-Economic Rights in South Africa: Symbols or Substance?* (Cambridge, Cambridge University Press, 2014), p.5.

12   Ibid., p.6.

13   For an early assessment of the RDP programme, see T. Lodge, *South African Politics since 1994* (Cape Town, David Philip, 1999), pp.28–39.

14   Ibid., p.32.

15   M. Salahuddin, N. Vink, N. Ralph and J. Gow, 'Globalisation, Poverty and Corruption: Retarding Progress in South Africa', *Development Southern Africa*, 37/4 (2020), p.618.

16   N.T. Vally, 'Insecurity in South African Social Security: An Examination of Social Grant Deductions, Cancellations and Waiting', *Journal of Southern African Studies*, 42/5, Special Issue: Labour, Insecurity and Violence in South Africa (2016), pp.965–82. Vally's research demonstrates the complexities of collecting these grants.

17   T. Satumba, A. Bayat and S. Mohamed, 'The Impact of Social Grants on Poverty Reduction in South Africa', *Journal of Economics*, 8/1 (2017), pp.33–49.

To address the severe housing shortage, the construction of RDP housing was subsidised under the National Housing Subsidy Scheme (NHSS), among other subsidy schemes, with the aim to provide low-cost housing for the impoverished majority.[18] By 2001, one million RDP houses had been constructed.[19] But the construction of these new RDP houses could not keep up with the rapidly growing backlog, and houses were built at the periphery of the cities, thus reinforcing spatial divisions.[20] The smallness and poor quality of these houses led some to conclude that they were mere 'dog kennels' and 'chicken coops'.[21] In other words, as Fiona Ross has argued, '[t]he provision of housing to the poor people in urban areas, [...] has not necessarily directly ameliorated people's living conditions beyond the basics of shelter'.[22]

Malcolm Langford identifies three trends that impacted on social development from the mid-1990s. First, in 1996, the Growth, Employment and Redistribution (GEAR) strategy replaced the RDP and brought in neoliberal economic policies.[23] Secondly, government spending on health, education, social welfare, housing and community development increased drastically from 47 percent of total expenditure in 1998 to 60 percent in 2008; this increase is significant but cannot address the pernicious legacy of racial oppression and inequality. Finally, since the reformation of municipalities in 2000, the onus of providing and financing access to water, sanitation, local economic development and housing lies largely with local municipalities. Much of the popular anger over a lack of housing and services is therefore directed at local government. The implementation of GEAR heralded a decline in central government funding to local municipalities, which, in response, increasingly resorted to measures to recover and cut costs.[24] Low economic growth and high levels of unemployment on the

18   J. Dugard, M. Clark, K. Tissington and S. Wilson, 'The Right to Housing in South Africa', in Foundation for Human Rights, *Socio-Economic Rights – Progressive Realisation?* (Foundation for Human Rights, Johannesburg, 2016), p.169. http://www.fhr-mirror.org.za/files/8015/1247/0285/Socio_Economic_Rights.pdf, retrieved 30 March 2020.

19   M. Langford, 'Housing Rights Litigation: Grootboom and Beyond', in Langford, Cousins, Dugard and Madlingozi (eds), *Socio-Economic Rights in South Africa*, p.190.

20   Ibid.

21   R. Pithouse, 'The University of Abahlali baseMjondolo', http://abahlali.org/node/2814/, retrieved 20 April 2020.

22   F. Ross, *Raw Life, New Hope* (Cape Town, UCT Press, 2010), p.205.

23   Langford, 'Introduction', pp.7–8.

24   T. Madlingozi, 'Post-Apartheid Social Movements and Legal Mobilisation', in Langford, Cousins, Dugard and Madlingozi (eds), *Socio-Economic Rights in South Africa*, p.106. For a left critique of the post-apartheid state, see, for example, P. Bond, *Elite Transitions: From Apartheid to Neoliberalism in South Africa* (London, Pluto Press, 2000); A. Desai, *We Are the Poors: Community Struggles in Post-Apartheid South Africa* (New York, Monthly Review Press, 2002); H. Marais, *South Africa: Limits to Change –*

one hand, and misappropriation of state funds, mismanagement of public enterprises and corruption on the other, have further undermined the state's capacity to deliver services and address inequality.[25] Consequently, and even though the South African constitution protects and guarantees a wide range of socio-economic rights, access to housing and services has remained uneven. Access to basic services and housing has increased, but is still 'heavily conditioned on apartheid spatial geography'.[26] Disconnections from water and electricity, and evictions of shack dwellers, remain a daily reality.

Socio-Economic Struggles: Rights and Protests

For many, political rights have therefore not been matched by far-reaching social and economic transformation. Across the country, protests expressing dissatisfaction with poor living conditions, lack of housing, services and a lack of prospects (often referred to in the media as 'service delivery protests') remind of the incomplete nature of the transition to democracy.[27] In Sebokeng, angry residents took to the streets in February 2014, a few months prior to the thirtieth anniversary of the Vaal Uprising, to demand RDP houses.[28] Burning tyres and rocks were pushed into the roads and running battles between police and protestors led to the death of one protestor at the hands of the police. Among the targets of popular anger were local councillors, who were accused of failing to promote progress. As elsewhere in the country, these protests are frequent and aimed at disrupting the status quo.

Three different strategies and tactics are worth mentioning in this context: spectacular community protests, legal approaches aimed at overcoming material deprivation through water and electricity reconnections, and land occupation. The early 2000s saw a proliferation of social movements focusing on socio-economic grievances, and a drastic increase in community protests.[29] Out of a

The Political Economy of Transition (London, Zed Books, 2001). On cost recovery, see D.A. McDonald and J. Pape (eds), *Cost Recovery and the Crisis of Service Delivery in South Africa* (Cape Town, HSRC Press, 2002). As McDonald and Pape show, the implementation of neoliberal measures was far from linear.

25   S. Plagerson, L. Patel, T. Hochfeld et al., 'Social Policy in South Africa: The Route to Social Development', *World Development*, 113 (2019), p.8.

26   Langford, 'Introduction', p.10.

27   The term 'service delivery protest' has been replaced by the more inclusive term 'community protest'. See P. Alexander, C. Runciman, T. Ngwane, B. Moloto, K. Mokgele and N. van Staden, 'Frequency and Turmoil: South Africa's Community Protests 2005–2017', *South African Crime Quarterly*, 63 (2018), pp.27–42. For a critique of the term 'service delivery protest', see R. Pithouse, 'The University of Abahlali baseMjondolo'.

28   RDP houses are subsidised houses built by government and sold to low-income families.

29   The literature on post-apartheid social movements and collective action is expan-

total of 604 community protests between 2007 and 2011, 21 percent of protestors complained about a lack of adequate and affordable housing, 10 percent were motivated by a lack of access to water and 10 percent by a lack of access to electricity.[30] The most common combination of grievances was a lack of quality housing and electricity.[31] Peter Alexander has therefore labelled these protests a 'rebellion of the poor'.[32] He also argues that not all protests during this period were related to socio-economic concerns but also concerned corruption, maladministration and misappropriation of funds. The increase in disruptive community protests, and the increasingly violent nature of these protests, have led scholars to conceptualise the post-apartheid order as a 'violent democracy'[33] and as an 'insurgent democracy'.[34] Julian Brown argues that disruptions caused through public protests or courtrooms are fundamental to the workings of the political order; disruptions reflect the assertion by 'ordinary men and women' that they are 'equal citizens'.[35] They are therefore productive and reflective of the ongoing process of citizenship-making. The policing of collective protests has been criticised, either for failing to prevent violence (during xenophobic attacks for example) or for escalating tensions through insensitive and aggressive conduct.[36] The Marikana massacre, where police shot dozens of miners on 16 August 2012, is the most chilling example.

---

sive. For an overview of the debates, see Langford, 'Introduction'; T. Madlingozi, 'Post-Apartheid Social Movements and the Quest for the Elusive "New" South Africa', *Journal of Law and Society*, 34/11 (2007), pp.77–98. For an analysis of data trends, see Alexander, Runciman, Ngwane, Moloto, Mokgele and van Staden, 'Frequency and Turmoil' and C. Runciman, P. Alexander, M. Rampedi, B. Moloto, B. Maruping, E. Khumalo and S. Sibanda, 'Counting Police-Recorded Protests: Based on South African Police Service Data', South African Research Chair in Social Change Report No.2 (Johannesburg, 2016).

30   It appears that protests regarding housing increase during the winter months, suggesting that the impact of a lack of access to quality housing is particularly acute during the colder months.

31   J. Karamoko and J. Hirsh, 'Community Protests in South Africa: Trends, Analysis and Explanations' (Local Government Working Paper No.1, Cape Town, Community Law Centre, updated 2011).

32   P. Alexander, 'Rebellion of the Poor: South Africa's Service Delivery Protests – A Preliminary Analysis', *Review of African Political Economy*, 37/123 (2010), pp.25–40.

33   K. van Holdt, 'South Africa: The Transition to Violent Democracy', *Review of African Political Economy*, 40/138 (2013), pp.589–604.

34   Ngwane, '"Insurgent Democracy"'.

35   J. Brown, *South Africa's Insurgent Citizens: On Dissent and the Possibility of Politics* (London, Zed Books, 2015), p.6.

36   See, for example, K. van Holdt, M. Langa, S. Molapo et al., *The Smoke that Calls: Insurgent Citizenship, Collective Violence, and the Struggle for a Place in the New South Africa* (Johannesburg, Centre for the Study of Violence and Reconciliation & Society, Work and Development Institute, 2011).

Tshepo Madlingozi distinguishes national movements from movements that are rooted in, and responding to, local grievances.[37] National movements are often rights-based and composed of 'collectives of marginalised actors who develop a collective identity; who put forward change-oriented goals; who possess some degree of organisation; and who engage in sustained, albeit episodic, extra-institutional collective action'.[38] Rights-based strategies, as several scholars have emphasised, undermine the possibility for transformative politics that shift the parameters of what is politically and economically feasible.[39] They 'hold the government to constitutionally enshrined rights within the current liberal order'.[40]

Community movements, on the other hand, are 'counter-hegemonic'.[41] As Madlingozi shows, they often struggle to 'achieve their goals in the context of inaccessible and unresponsive political structures and prevailing strategies that tend toward their exclusion'.[42] For these movements, a rights-based approach cannot help in their struggle for the decommodification of basic services such as water and electricity, and the 'radical redistribution of economic and political power'.[43] Many of them, such as the APF and Abahlali baseMjondolo, foreground the importance of class; a socialist order is seen as the solution to ongoing inequality, while neoliberalism is seen as its leading cause.[44] For some of these movements, and the left more broadly, the ANC's strategy of a two-stage revolution, which foregrounded the attainment of political power and envisaged the implementation of a socialist order only during the second stage, partly explains government's shift towards neoliberalism. Movements such as the APF serve as a reminder of the promises the ANC made during the transition to democracy; they

37   Madlingozi, 'Post-Apartheid Social Movements'.
38   Ibid., p.93.
39   For an overview of this critique, see Langford, 'Introduction', pp.16–17. Langford distinguishes between the critique from the left, which emphasises the foreclosing of alternative political strategies, and the critique from the right, which emphasises that rights are 'too strong', undermining 'cooperative relationships' and creating a sense of entitlement.
40   R. Ballard, A. Habib and I. Valodia, 'Conclusion: Making Sense of Post-Apartheid South Africa's Voices of Protest', in R. Ballard, A. Habib and I. Valodia (eds), *Voices of Protest: Social Movements in Post-Apartheid South Africa* (Pietermaritzburg, University of KwaZulu Natal Press, 2006), p.400.
41   Madlingozi, 'Post-Apartheid Social Movements'.
42   Ibid., p.123.
43   Ibid.
44   Ibid., p.106. For an analysis of the decline of the APF, see C. Runciman, 'The Decline of the Anti-Privatisation Forum in the Midst of South Africa's "Rebellion of the Poor"', *Current Sociology*, 63/7 (2015), pp.961–79.

'are now demanding this "second phase"', as Kelly Rosenthal notes.[45] In the long term, the aim of these movements is therefore to implement a socialist order; in the medium term, they campaign for the state to provide 'free basic water and electricity supply, subsidised housing and social security'.[46]

Some of these movements, such as the now defunct APF, therefore consider themselves to be the true champions of struggles for redistribution as outlined in the Freedom Charter.[47] As Marcelle Dawson shows, the APF's ideological programme 'reprioritises some of the objectives that are spelled out in the Freedom Charter', while also aiming to go 'beyond these goals' to formulate an alternative socialist future.[48] Other movements have 'espoused radical democratic ideas in principle, and highlighted the division of wealth in the society', but did not adopt socialist language and ideology.[49] In that regard, there are important ideological overlaps between the latter and some community formations during the 1980s, as William Beinart observes.[50] But overall, the emergence of these social movements has to be viewed within a context of global struggles against the neoliberal order, and the impact of global capital.[51]

Beyond public protest action, litigation has become a significant tactic in post-apartheid South Africa, and housing has become the most litigated socio-economic right.[52] Housing is a 'deeply emotive issue [...], having secure access to a home is the basis for living as a human being'.[53] Access to basic ser-

---

45   K. Rosenthal, 'New Social Movements as Civic Society: The Case of Past and Present Soweto', in W. Beinart and M. Dawson (eds), *Popular Politics and Resistance Movements in South Africa* (Johannesburg, Wits University Press, 2010), p.264.

46   Madlingozi, 'Post-Apartheid Social Movements', p.106

47   M. Dawson, '"Phansi Privatisation, Phansi!": The Anti-Privatisation Forum and Ideology in Social Movements', in Beinart and Dawson (eds), *Popular Politics and Resistance Movements in South Africa*, pp.266–85. The degree to which the Freedom Charter is a socialist document has been debated by scholars and activists. See, for example, G. Williams, 'Celebrating the Freedom Charter', *Transformation*, 6 (1988).

48   Dawson, '"Phansi Privatisation, Phansi!"', p.285.

49   W. Beinart, 'Popular Politics and Resistance Movements in South Africa, 1970–2008', in Beinart and Dawson (eds), *Popular Politics and Resistance Movements in South Africa*, p.13.

50   Ibid.

51   Anne-Maria Makhulu discusses the global literature on struggles against neoliberalism. See A.-M. Makhulu, *Making Freedom: Apartheid, Squatter Politics, and the Struggle for Home* (Durham, Duke University Press, 2015), pp.21ff. See also Desai, *We Are the Poors*.

52   Dugard, Clark, Tissington and Wilson, 'The Right to Housing in South Africa', p.156.

53   Ibid., p.157.

vices such as water, electricity and sanitation is strongly related to one's ability to access housing. Housing therefore determines quality of life in multiple ways. This became apparent during the case *Government of the Republic of South Africa* v *Grootboom* in 2001, which is widely acknowledged as a landmark in confirming the state's obligations with regard to housing.[54] In 1998, respondent Irene Grootboom and other residents of an informal settlement in the Western Cape occupied land that had been earmarked for the development of low-cost housing. Subsequently, they were evicted and their possessions bulldozed. In 2000, the residents turned to the courts for relief; judgment confirmed that based on the constitution, the residents had a general right to access to housing (section 26), and that children had a right to shelter (section 28).[55] Yet even though this case confirmed that socio-economic rights such as housing are justiciable, their enforcement remains flawed.[56] Furthermore, the Grootboom judgment 'laid the first conceptual foundation stone of SER [Socio-Economic Rights] jurisprudence, namely, evaluation of the reasonableness of the measures taken by the state to fulfil its SER obligations progressively within its available resources'.[57] The right to adequate housing, while enshrined in the constitution, is therefore not absolute but contingent on the state's capacities and the reasonableness of demands. As suggested above, scholars have questioned the usefulness of litigation in addressing poverty and inequality.[58]

A third set of tactics aimed at gaining access to housing, services and land uses illicit means. By reconnecting electricity meters and water, and by occupying land, impoverished people claim what they consider to be theirs, and what remains otherwise inaccessible.[59] These tactics are not only a way of addressing poverty and a lack of access to resources, they also 'enable actors to claim belonging and recognition, or [...] a mode of citizenship'.[60] Furthermore, in many townships across the country the boycott of payments for rent and ser-

54 See http://www.saflii.org/za/cases/ZACC/2000/19.html, retrieved 2 April 2020; Langford, 'Housing Rights Litigation'.

55 Langford, 'Housing Rights Litigation'; Dugard, Clark, Tissington and Wilson, 'The Right to Housing in South Africa'.

56 Langford, 'Housing Rights Litigation'.

57 A. Sachs, 'Introduction', in Foundation for Human Rights, *Socio-Economic Rights*, p.30. In his introduction, Albie Sachs reflects on the debates and processes that led to the judgment.

58 Langford, 'Housing Rights Litigation'. See also Madlingozi, 'Post-Apartheid Social Movements'.

59 See, for example, A. von Schnitzler, 'Citizenship Prepaid: Water, Calculability, and Techno-Politics in South Africa', *Journal of Southern African Studies*, 34/4 (2008), pp.899–917; Dawson, '"Phansi Privatisation, Phansi!"'.

60 Makhulu, *Making Freedom*, p.11.

vices has been ongoing since the 1980s, leading to what some have labelled a 'culture of non-payment'.[61] It becomes clear that access to basic services and housing remains central in people's struggles for improved living conditions and that the inability to access them constitutes a form of 'collective unfreedom'.[62] The slogan 'No freedom without basic services', chanted during a protest in 2006, captures this sentiment.[63]

The Legacy of the 1980s

This takes us back to the struggles against rent increases and the Black Local Authorities during the 1980s. At a first glance, some of the issues at the heart of post-apartheid mobilisation appear strikingly similar to the grievances and demands that triggered the revolts of the 1980s, namely access to housing and services. Yet as most scholars have noted, there are key differences between the civic struggles of the 1980s and new social movements of the post-apartheid period.[64] Post-apartheid social movements respond to the material conditions, political and economic opportunities and constraints of the post-apartheid state.[65] As Gary Kynoch notes, community protests object to 'the performance of government, not the legitimacy of the state'.[66] They are 'driven by the struggle for local advantage and by frustrated expectations'.[67] Significantly, as Kynoch and others argue, some community protests are led by ANC members whose factions have been excluded from patronage networks; they therefore build on popular grievances to gain more leverage. Allegations of corruption, mismanagement and misuse of funds continue to spark popular anger.[68]

61   This label may be misleading, as it obscures the fact that many impoverished South Africans simply do not have the financial resources to pay for rent and services. See von Schnitzler, 'Citizenship Prepaid', footnote 26 on p.906. Von Schnitzler shows how government discourse has linked the payment of services to 'empowerment' and 'active citizenship'.

62   L. Hamilton, 'Collective Unfreedom in South Africa', *Contemporary Politics*, 17/4 (2011), pp.355–72.

63   Quoted in Beinart, 'Popular Politics and Resistance Movements in South Africa', p.22.

64   Ibid.

65   For a comparison of popular struggles pre- and post-1994, see Rosenthal, 'New Social Movements as Civic Society'.

66   G. Kynoch, 'Apartheid's Afterlives: Violence, Policing and the South African State', *Journal of Southern African Studies*, 42/1 (2016), p.68.

67   Ibid.

68   It is beyond the scope of this chapter to examine in detail the debates on corruption, maladministration and nepotism in post-apartheid South Africa. For an insider's account, see C. Olver, *How to Steal a City: The Battle for Nelson Mandela Bay, an Inside Account* (Johannesburg, Jonathan Ball, 2017).

For all the critique that has been levelled at the ANC, the post-apartheid political dispensation is based on democratic principles and thus radically different from its apartheid predecessor. In contrast to apartheid legislation, which used a wide range of tools to criminalise extra-parliamentary dissent, the right to protest is enshrined in the post-apartheid constitution. But the revolutionary rhetoric of the liberation struggle that emphasised the dismantling of racial capitalism and the pursuit of socialism has been replaced by 'tamer words such as rights, citizenship, liberal democracy, nation-building, transformation, black economic empowerment, and so on', as Steven Robbins notes.[69]

There are nevertheless continuities that are worth noting. Some of the neo-liberal measures employed by the post-apartheid government date back to the late 1970s and 1980s. The installation of water meters, as Antina von Schnitzler shows, was a direct consequence of the rent boycotts of the 1980s.[70] The privatisation of township housing (see Chapter 2), has its origins in the restructuring of housing policy during the mid-1970s, and the subsequent opening up of the township housing market for private investors. During the early 1980s, houses became available for purchase during the 'big sale', even though they remained out of reach for the majority. By 2012, most of the 500,000 township houses built during the apartheid era were in private hands.[71]

Repertoires of protest show a striking similarity: the street barricades and collective mobilisation of the 1980s, and the strikes and boycotts that shaped contentious politics during this period, have resurfaced and once more capture the popular imagination. Images of burning tyres and roads blocked by overturned cars and rubble are broadcast into the homes of domestic and global audiences. Yet these tactics have been widely deployed by protest movements across the world and are therefore not unique to South Africa. Other strategies and tactics have gained greater significance in the post-apartheid era. Even though the law was used during the 1980s in the struggle for urban and socio-economic rights, this strategy emerged more fully in the post-apartheid era.[72] Some organisations employed legalistic tactics to fight the implementation of rent increases (see

---

69 S.L. Robbins, *From Revolution to Rights in South Africa* (Woodbridge, James Currey, 2008), p.3.

70 von Schnitzler, 'Citizenship Prepaid', p.911.

71 L. Marais, M. Sefika, J. Ntema, A. Venter and J. Cloete, 'Towards an Understanding of the Outcomes of Housing Privatisation in South Africa', *Urban Forum*, 25 (2014), pp.57–58.

72 For an analysis of the use of law during the apartheid era, see R. Abel, *Politics by Other Means: Law in the Struggle against Apartheid* (New York, Routledge, 1995). Two organisations that were at the forefront of providing (legal) assistance and advice were the Legal Resources Centre (LRC) and Black Sash. See M. Burton, *The Black Sash: Women for Justice and Peace* (Johannesburg, Jacana, 2015).

Chapter 4), and therefore challenged discriminatory practices from 'within'. But by 1985, the more common response was the rejection of the system and the establishment of alternative structures that took over the functions of the state. Street committees played a significant role in combating evictions (by assisting those evicted to move back into their houses) and in providing basic services. Popular conceptions of the state's duties, and the role local government should play in social upliftment and welfare, date back to the apartheid era, as this book has shown.

The two most important outcomes of popular protests during the 1980s were the establishment of popular democratic structures through the introduction of street, block and area committees, and localised understandings of freedom and emancipation that were rooted in everyday demands and grievances of the township population. Together they shaped grassroots articulations of emancipatory citizenship that continue to infuse post-apartheid political discourse. While some of the new social movements espouse a much more open socialist vision, the rhetoric and programme of the civic movements of the 1980s contained socialist, welfarist and redistributive ideas that cohered around equal access to affordable quality housing and services and infrastructure, as well as education and equal pensions. These articulations, instead of openly advocating for a socialist order, reflected ideals more closely aligned to those of a social democratic welfare state. As noted, these ideas need to be situated within their longer history of denied citizenship and rights, and the consequences of apartheid social engineering that produced new political subjectivities.

Denied Citizenship and the History of Emancipatory Politics

In contrast to many analyses that take the implementation of reforms as the starting point for the 1980s revolts, this book traces the development of new political subjectivities that were at the core of the 1980s mass mobilisation back to the mid-twentieth century. As Chapter 1 has shown, the Vaal Triangle witnessed rapid industrialisation and urbanisation during the 1940s; for many rural migrants, the Vaal Triangle's booming industries were an attractive alternative to the gold mines of the Witwatersrand. Sharpeville, established during the 1940s, was regarded as the 'pride of the municipality' and served as a prototype for township planning during the 1950s. Sharpeville offered facilities and infrastructure that surpassed those in other townships; its housing, many said, was superior and attracted the socially aspirant. It also boasted a lively cultural scene and a string of famous boxing and soccer champions that placed the township firmly on the radar of South Africa's sports enthusiasts. Yet Sharpeville's reputation as a 'model township' was short-lived. On 21 March 1960, police shot 69 women, men and children who had gathered outside the Sharpeville police station to protest against the pass laws. The images of protestors shot in the back and lying on the ground, with police nonchalantly standing by, epitomised apartheid's brutal disregard for African life. The Sharpeville massacre, as this event came to be known, heralded a period of apparent 'quiescence' that was marked by a lack of public protest action and the banning of the liberation movements.

But while open political resistance diminished, politics located in the domestic sphere gained in importance. For apartheid's architects, the 'homelands' were the real home of Africans, and their aspirations for citizenship and rights were therefore confined to these entities. With the denial of urban rights, and the constant threat of forced removals, the African population's claim to the city expressed itself through home renovations and the stylisation of interiors. Setting up home therefore not only contained the physical act of moving furniture and other belongings into a house, but was also reflective of the process of claiming permanence in South Africa proper. The 1960s and 1970s, then, gave rise to new subjectivities with aspirations for a settled, dignified life in the urban areas. These ideals were particularly significant in the Vaal Triangle, where a history of forced removals had led to a sense of precarity and unsettlement. The ideals generated during this period, and the failure of the model townships to provide improved living conditions, would significantly shape protest action later on.

While Sharpeville descended into survival mode and local authorities were eager to remove Sharpeville's residents to eradicate the memory of the shooting, another model township was built: Sebokeng would soon come to be the new darling among apartheid's social engineers. Plans to build one large township to concentrate the African workforce in the region had already been made in 1954, when the Mentz Committee recommended a new blueprint for social engineering in the Pretoria–Witwatersrand–Vereeniging region. Sebokeng, like Sharpeville, was considered to be a success story by local authorities and government alike. For many who had been renting shacks in neighbouring Evaton, Sebokeng offered improved living conditions. The houses, known as NE51/6 or matchbox houses, promised a suburban life of stability and progress. But, as we have seen in Chapter 2, these modest aspirations were frustrated early on. The channelling of money into the development of the bantustans, and the dwindling of state subsidies to build houses and to develop African townships, soon led to a severe lack of housing, overcrowding, stilted development and poor living conditions. Race relations were tense in the small towns of Vereeniging and Vanderbijlpark, as numerous people recall.[73] Racist assaults were common and shaped the ways in which African people navigated these towns. Compounded by frequent pass and liquor raids, the daily assault on Africans' dignity was key in shaping the political subjectivities of a new generation of activists, who would be catapulted to the forefront of the freedom struggle during the 1980s.

73   Tsietsi 'Stompi' Mokhele, interview with author, Bophelong, 18 September 2011.

Even though officials of the Vaal Triangle Administration Board (which became the Orange Vaal Administration Board in 1979, and the Orange Vaal Development Board in 1984) praised themselves for the 'stellar work' they were doing in keeping the area pacified, discontent on the ground was brewing. While the socio-economic situation of residents was nowhere near as dire as it would be a few years later, sporadic protests and confrontations served as a reminder that all was not well. Under the control of administration boards, townships were required to be self-financing, yet a serious lack of revenue hampered any prospect of this. By the late 1970s, most administration boards were facing a severe fiscal crisis as their deficits accumulated. Within this context, the development of a set of reforms under the administration of Prime Minister P.W. Botha would have significant consequences. The Durban strikes of 1973 and the student uprisings of 1976 had brought into sharp relief the political and economic crisis the country was facing, and the inability of the administration boards to contain the crisis. From the late 1970s, the Botha government therefore set in motion plans to strengthen the African middle class, which would serve as a buffer zone, and to fulfil their economic and social aspirations. As a result, African permanence was now accepted in the urban areas. Consequently, many townships were in dire need of upgrading and development to accommodate the expectations of this new emerging middle class, and new houses needed to be built. The costs for this were to be covered through rent increases (see Chapter 2). Between 1977 and 1984, rent was increased by more than 400 percent. Owing to a lack of revenue, rent increases (and the raising of tariffs, rates and levies) were seen as the only option to balance the books, yet for residents they undermined their capacity to make ends meet. The intensity of material grievances in this region, as compared to Soweto, for example, is one of a number of reasons why the Vaal Triangle was soon at the forefront of popular protests.[74] By 1984 the Vaal Triangle was the most expensive area for African people to live. Frequent rent increases therefore paved the way for mass mobilisation; townships that saw no increases during this period often remained tranquil for longer.

The housing crisis and the reformation of local government, which aimed to gloss over the exclusion of the African majority in national political affairs, set the pace for growing mass mobilisation. The elections of community councils in 1977 received widespread opposition. While some residents held out hope that councillors would promote their welfare, the reality soon proved otherwise. Rumours of maladministration, corruption and nepotism abounded, and by 1984, councillors were regarded as 'puppets' and 'sell-outs', whose main interest was to enrich themselves; they were held responsible for their constituents' frustrated aspirations for a better life. Notwithstanding this

---

74   J. Seekings, 'Why Was Soweto Different? Urban Development, Township Politics, and the Political Economy of Soweto, 1977–1984' (African Studies seminar paper, University of the Witwatersrand, 1988).

negative perception, some councillors undoubtedly tried to improve the lot of their constituencies, yet fiscal strictures and an authoritarian climate within the council silenced them.

Before long, local discontent and dissatisfaction began to translate into more organised forms of opposition (see Chapter 3). In 1980, a local branch of the Congress of South African Students was formed, followed by the establishment of the VCA in 1983 and the Vaal Organisation of Women in 1984. The formation of these three organisations signified the ascendancy of Charterist politics in the region, and the increasing ideological influence of the ANC. Struggles for housing and services were key in shaping popular protests during this period and informed the way in which ordinary people envisioned their freedom and emancipation. As noted in Chapter 3, the VCA espoused ideals that resembled those of a social democratic welfare state, which would ensure equal access to pensions, housing and other basic services. The meaning of emancipatory citizenship and the rights that would come with it therefore gained centre stage. By then, ANC underground units had been established and even though their capacity to stir mass mobilisation remained modest, they played an important role in framing bread-and-butter issues within a broader vision of freedom. The hesitance of ordinary residents to be elected into leadership positions of the VCA opened up space for these ANC underground activists to shape the discourse and direction of civic politics. Many of the founding members of the VCA were directly or indirectly linked to the ANC in exile. Significantly, the ideals of the Freedom Charter of 1955 tallied with the hopes and aspirations of ordinary people on the ground.

Hence, while the Black Consciousness Movement was in the forefront of emancipatory politics during the 1970s, it was eclipsed by the rise of Charterism in the townships, which found its apogee in the formation of the United Democratic Front (UDF) in August 1983. The UDF was initially formed to oppose the constitutional reforms, and the introduction of the tricameral parliament more specifically. These reforms once more excluded the African majority from representation at a national level. To gloss over this exclusion, the Black Local Authorities Act of 1982 was passed, granting augmented powers to African councillors in the townships. By 1984, the conflict between councillors and residents was escalating. Frequent violent confrontations bore testimony to their lack of legitimacy and their inability to address popular grievances. Hence, in contrast to other townships such as Maokeng, relationships between local residents and African councillors were exceptionally fraught and left little room for peaceful negotiations.[75] This history of violent confrontations is vital for understanding the violence that occurred during the uprising.

---

75   T. Moloi, *Place of Thorns: Black Political Protest in Kroonstad since 1976* (Johannesburg, Wits University Press, 2015).

3 September 1984: A Turning Point?

The final straw was the announcement in early August 1984 by the mayor of the Lekoa Town Council and the mayor of the Evaton Town Council to increase rent by an average of R5.90 (see Chapter 4). Anger was mounting, and during the month of August frequent meetings took place to plan for mass action. Eventually, a decision was taken to call for a stay-away on 3 September. Businesses belonging to councillors would be boycotted, councillors asked to resign and a protest march would be led to the offices of the Orange Vaal Development Board to hand over a memorandum with grievances and demands. But it was not to be. Tensions increased in the days prior to 3 September, when violence began to escalate in the township of Bophelong. By 2 September, the air was redolent with trepidation and skirmishes between police and youth were ongoing. The protest march itself never reached its destination, as it was stopped after a few kilometres by a heavily armed contingent of riot police, who began shooting at the crowd. It was at that moment when 'all hell broke loose'. During the course of the uprising that followed, dozens were shot dead by the riot squad. The brutal shooting of young children inflamed the already volatile situation and demonstrated once more that the police had little regard for African life.

As Chapter 4 has argued, violence was not an inevitable outcome of public protest action, nor did it simply erupt. Violence was partly contingent on and triggered by police and councillors' shooting, and partly adopted as a tactic by more radical (and mostly young) activists who regarded a protest march as insufficient. The manner in which liberation and freedom should be achieved was therefore contested. While some regarded violence as the most effective tactic to overcome white minority rule, others favoured collective action in the form of strikes, boycotts and stay-aways, and yet others located their politics at the intersection between the two. New tactics were invented that shaped contentious politics in the aftermath of the uprising. The meaning of the street and its relation to the home shifted and the boundaries between the domestic and the public became blurred. The relative 'success' of the uprising gave new hope to activists that the balance of power was shifting and that liberation was imminent.

In the immediate aftermath of the uprising, the social and political order was upended (see Chapter 5). The civic and student leadership had to go into hiding, while others, such as Dorcas and Esau Ralitsela, who had spearheaded the formation of civic structures and who had been actively involved in the ANC underground, went into exile. New actors soon gained centre stage to fill the lacuna left by collapsing civic structures. Churches, as Chapter 5 has highlighted, were thrust into the forefront and provided much-needed financial and logistical assistance, leadership and pastoral care.

The impact of 3 September was far-reaching. Other regions in South Africa soon followed suit and by 1985, a large percentage of African townships had become ungovernable. Heavy-handed repression such as the deployment of troops, the use of courts and the escalation of 'dirty tricks' all signified the police's inability to maintain control (see Chapter 6). Conversely, government embarked on a propaganda war to win over domestic and international public opinion. At the local level, authorities developed a multi-pronged approach to break the rent boycott, but to no avail. In many areas the rent boycott would continue into the post-apartheid era.

If the early 1980s witnessed the ascendancy of Charterism, the insurrectionary period of 1984 to 1986 saw a partial translation of these ideals into practice. 'People's power' became one of the key tenets of the struggle for freedom during this period. The rupture of the uprising therefore opened up space for the reconfiguration of possibilities and for new visions of freedom and democracy to emerge. While government held on to a version of diminished and partial rights, the mass movements demanded full emancipation and an alternative order based on popular democracy. Besides the development of these popular democratic forms, the insurrectionary period also saw the formation of clandestine youth units that considered themselves to be part of the armed struggle. They fought a 'people's war' in the townships, aimed at creating favourable conditions for the exiled ANC to establish itself in the country. As Chapter 7 has argued, many of these units were beyond the direct control of the ANC and their lack of training and discipline often exposed them to police surveillance and arrest.

If strategies and tactics were contested, so was the meaning of 'people's power'. People's power as envisioned by the ANC leadership in exile was different from the way it was practised by grassroots organisations. For the ANC, people's power was essentially the outcome of the struggle for liberation and was therefore equivalent to state power; for grassroots organisations it was a popular democratic practice that encouraged people to take control over all aspects of their lives.[76] Many within the ANC were committed to implementing the ideals espoused in the Freedom Charter. Theirs was a world that would be underpinned by 'racial equality, social justice and human emancipation'.[77] In 1996, the new constitution was signed in Sharpeville, affirming the region's significance in scripting an alternative future. Yet for many South Africans, the dream for a better life has been deferred as they continue their quest for full emancipation; the struggle for the home remains deeply political and embedded in emancipatory politics.

76   Seekings, *The UDF*, p.169.

77   J. Soske, A. Lissoni and N. Erlank, 'One Hundred Years of the ANC: Debating Struggle History after Apartheid', in A. Lissoni, J. Soske, N. Erlank et al. (eds), *One Hundred Years of the ANC: Debating Liberation Histories Today* (Johannesburg, Wits University Press, 2012), p.29.

Bibliography

Archival sources

University of the Witwatersrand, Historical and Literary Papers (WHP)

AC623	South African Council of Churches
AE862	The Black Sash
A2084	Helen Suzman Papers
AK2117	*State v Baleka and 21 Others*, Case No.482/85 (records of the Delmas treason trial)
A2243	*State v Sefatsa and 7 Others*, Case No.698/85 (records of the Sharpeville Six trial)
AK2340	Trial sheets
AK2305	*State v Nhlapo and 5 Others*, Case No.344/86
A2561	Oliver Tambo Papers
AG2613	SACBC, Justice and Peace Division
A2675	Karis-Gerhart Collection of Political Materials
AG2918	Kairos, Dutch Anti-Apartheid Organisation
AG3298	Legal Resources Centre Oral History Project

South African History Archive (SAHA)

AL2457	Original SAHA Collection

National Archives Pretoria (NAP)

BAO	Department of Bantu Administration and Development

University of the Western Cape, Mayibuye Archive (UWC MA)

MCH01	African National Congress
MCH02	African National Congress
MCH31	International Defense Aid Fund (IDAF)

Private Collection Matthew Chaskalson (MS)

SMA	Sebokeng Municipal Archive
Notes and unpublished papers	

Vaal Teknorama (VT)

CPN   Collection Patrick Noonan

Police Files in the Possession of the Missing Persons' Task Team, National Prosecuting Authority (MPTT NPA)

Case Dockets, 1984–86

Private Collection of Photographs, Pule Zwane

Photographs, 1984/85

Online resources

http://www.nelsonmandela.org/omalley
http://www.unrisd.org
http://www.saha.org.za
http://www.aluka.org
http://truth.wwl.wits.ac.za
http://www.anc.org.za
http://www.csvr.org.za
http://www.disa.ukzn.ac.za
http://www.saflii.org.za/
http://www.justice.gov.za/trc

Recorded interviews with author, 2006–19

Bizos, George, Oxford, 23 February 2011
Crowe, Sarah, Johannesburg, 11 May 2006
Du Toit, Andries, West Rand, 10 May 2011 (name has been changed)
Erasmus, Gerrit Nicholas, Johannesburg, 22 May 2006
——Johannesburg, 6 May 2011
——Johannesburg, 15 August 2011
Goba, Themba, Vereeniging, 18 June 2010
Harris, Kevin, Johannesburg, 15 May 2006
Hlomoka, Oupa, Vanderbijlpark, 9 July 2010
Johnson, Sipho, Vanderbijlpark, 7 June 2010 (name has been changed)
Ka Plaatjie, Thami, Vanderbijlpark, 14 June 2010
——Johannesburg, 26 May 2011
Khumalo, Leonard, Rust-ter-Vaal, 9 May 2011
Khumalo, Sakhiwe, Vereeniging, 23 June 2010
Kolisang, Samuel, Sharpeville, 6 July 2010
——Sharpeville, 15 July 2010
Lethale, Jeffrey Ramphuki, Evaton, 2 May 2006
Madisa, Dimakatso, Sebokeng, 21 July 2010
Makiti, Ikabot, Sharpeville, 15 July 2010
——Sharpeville, 22 July 2010

Malan, Magnus, Johannesburg, 10 May 2006
Malapela, Phineas, Johannesburg, 29 June 2010
Maleka, Thomas Togo, 21 June 2010
Malindi, Gcina, Johannesburg, 25 March 2010
——Johannesburg, 21 July 2010
Malindi, Khulu, Johannesburg, 22 November 2018
Manthata, Thomas Madikwe, Johannesburg, 23 May 2006
Manqa, Sarhili 'Toy', Vereeniging, 26 May 2011
Marcus, Gilbert, Johannesburg, 18 March 2010
Mareletse, Oupa, Johannesburg, 30 June 2010
Masankane, Oupa, Vereeniging, 29 June 2010
Mashoke, Rosalinah, Sebokeng, 8 October 2016
Matube, Roy, Vereeniging, 20 April 2010
——Vanderbijlpark, 17 June 2010
Mazibuko, Mandla, Vanderbijlpark, 22 June 2010
Mazibuko, Veli, Johannesburg, 28 February 2019
McCamel, Lord, Evaton, 2 May 2006
Mhlobo, Bongani, Vereeniging, 12 July 2010 (name has been changed)
Milani, Mario, Vereeniging, 6 July 2010
Miller, Nick, Alberton, 9 May 2006 (name has been changed)
Modikoane, Oupa Lucas, East Rand, 1 July 2010
Moepadira, Tebogo 'Exec.', Vanderbijlpark, 23 June 2010
Moerane, Gift, Johannesburg, 17 May 2006
——Vereeniging, 29 March 2010
——Vereeniging, 27 November 2018
Mofolo, Nthabiseng Christina, Sebokeng, 22 October 2011
Mogotsi, Kedibone, Vereeniging, 26 July 2010
Moisi, David, Pretoria, 13 July 2010
Mokatsanyane, Tsietsi 'Speech', Pretoria, 13 July 2010
Mokhele, Tsietsi 'Stompi', Bophelong, 18 September 2011
——Bophelong, 21 September 2019
Mokoena, Dineo 'Mapikoko', Sebokeng, 22 October 2011
——Sebokeng, 28 June 2016
Mokoena, Sekwati, Sharpeville, 30 March 2010
Mokoena, Sophie, Johannesburg, 14 July 2010
Mokolo, Richard 'Bricks', Orange Farm, 11 May 2006
——Orange Farm, 17 May 2006
——Orange Farm, 20 March 2010
More, Morris, Sebokeng, 2 December 2011
Motaung, Lekgotla 'Ace', Boipatong, 16 September 2011
——Sebokeng, 22 October 2011
——Sebokeng, 28 June 2016
——Evaton, 9 July 2016
Motaung, 'Ma', Sebokeng, 9 July 2016
Motubatsi, Edward 'Chippa', Vereeniging, 8 April 2010
——Vereeniging, 15 April 2010

——Vereeniging, 22 November 2011
——Vereeniging, 5 December 2011
——Vereeniging, 27 September 2017
——Johannesburg, 6 November 2018
——Bophelong, 21 September 2019
Nhlapo, Peter, Vereeniging, 8 July 2010 (name has been changed)
Niemand, Petrus, West Rand, 10 May 2011
——West Rand, 29 September 2011 (name has been changed)
Noonan, Patrick, Sebokeng, 24 March 2010
Papane, Matime Moshele, Johannesburg, 28 April 2010
——Johannesburg, 6 November 2018
Radebe, Shaka, Vereeniging 23 July 2010
——Vereeniging, 26 July 2010
——Vereeniging, 23 May 2011
Ralitsela, Dorcas, Vereeniging, 1 April 2010
——Vereeniging, 21 July 2010
——Vereeniging, 4 November 2011
Ralitsela, Esau, Vereeniging, 5 April 2010
Ramashamole, Theresa, Vanderbijlpark, 15 June 2010
Sebusi, Tshepo, Vereeniging, 5 July 2010
Sefatsa, Mojalefa Reginald 'Jaja', Vereeniging, 3 July 2010
Tlhopane, Pelamotse Jerry, Sebokeng, 22 November 2011
Tsotetsi, Dikeledi, Vanderbijlpark, 14 June 2010
Van der Merwe, Johan, Pretoria, 18 May 2011

Electronic conversations

Mokhele, Tsietsi 'Stompi', 4 November 2016
Motubatsi, Edward 'Chippa', 25 August 2018
Ralitsela, Dorcas, 28 August 2018
——5 September 2018
Seakhoa, Morakabe 'Raks', 1 September 2018

Unrecorded conversations and interviews

Ka Plaatjie, Thami, Vanderbijlpark and Johannesburg, 21 March 2010 and other conversations
Lennon, Edward, Johannesburg, 10 April 2010
Malindi, Khulu, Sebokeng, 26 March 2010 and other conversations
Mabuye, Peter, Vereeniging, 26 March 2010 and other conversations
Mokoena, Dineo 'Mapikoko', Sebokeng, 22 October 2010 and other conversations
Mokoena, Sekwati, Sharpeville and Sebokeng, 29 March 2010 and other conversations
Motaung, Lekgotla 'Ace', Boipatong and Sebokeng, 16 September 2011
——Sebokeng, 31 May 2016
——Sebokeng and Evaton, 2 July 2016
Motubatsi, Edward 'Chippa', Vereeniging and Sebokeng, 26 March 2010 and other conversations

Ralitsela, Dorcas, Vereeniging, 1 April 2010 and other conversations
Zwane, Pule, Johannesburg and Vereeniging, 5 May 2010 and other conversations

Government publications

Republic of South Africa, *Debates of the House of Assembly* (Hansard)
Republic of South Africa, *Government Gazette*
Republic of South Africa, *Report of the Commission of Inquiry into the Riots at Soweto and Elsewhere from the 16th of June 1976 to the 28th of February 1977* (Cillié Commission), 2 volumes (Pretoria, Government Publisher, 1980)

Newspapers and periodicals

African Communist
Africa Perspective
Bantu
Bula Ditaba tsa Lekoa
Citizen
Ecunews
Guardian
Indicator South Africa
Inter Nos
Mayibuye
Rand Daily Mail
SASPU National
Sechaba
South African Labour Bulletin
Sowetan
Sunday Post
Sunday Times Extra
The Star
Vereeniging en Meyerton Ster
Washington Notes on Africa
Washington Post

Books, book chapters and journal articles

Abel, R., *Politics by Other Means: Law in the Struggle against Apartheid* (New York, Routledge, 1995)
Adi, H., *Pan-Africanism: A History* (London, Bloomsbury Academic, 2018)
Alexander, N., *An Ordinary Country: Issues in the Transition from Apartheid to Democracy in South Africa* (New York, Berghahn, 2003)
Alexander, P., 'Rebellion of the Poor: South Africa's Service Delivery Protests – A Preliminary Analysis', *Review of African Political Economy*, 37/123 (2010), pp.25–40
Alexander, P., C. Runciman, T. Ngwane, B. Moloto, K. Mokgele and N. van Staden, 'Frequency and Turmoil: South Africa's Community Protests 2005–2017', *South African Crime Quarterly*, 63 (2018), pp.27–42

Ally, S. and A. Lissoni, 'Preface: "Let's Talk about Bantustans"', *South African Historical Journal*, 64/1 (2012), pp.1–4

Anderson, D., *Histories of the Hanged: Britain's Dirty War in Kenya and the End of Empire* (London, Phoenix, 2006)

Badat, S., *The Forgotten People: Political Banishment under Apartheid* (Leiden, Brill, 2013)

Baderoon, G., *Regarding Muslims: From Slavery to Post-Apartheid* (Johannesburg, Wits University Press, 2014)

Bank, L., 'The Failure of Ethnic Nationalism: Land, Power and the Politics of Clanship on the South African Highveld 1860–1990', *Africa*, 65/4 (1995), pp.565–91

Bank, L., *Home Spaces, Street Styles: Contesting Power and Identity in a South African City* (Johannesburg, Wits University Press, 2011)

Ballard, R., A. Habib and I. Valodia (eds), *Voices of Protest: Social Movements in Post-Apartheid South Africa* (Pietermaritzburg, University of KwaZulu-Natal Press, 2006)

Barrell, H., 'The Turn to the Masses: The African National Congress Strategic Review of 1978–79', *Journal of Southern African Studies*, 18/1 (1992), pp.64–92

Beinart, W., 'Introduction: Political and Collective Violence in Southern African Historiography', *Journal of Southern African Studies*, 18/3, Special Issue: Political Violence in Southern Africa (1992), pp.455–86

Beinart, W., *Twentieth-Century South Africa* (Oxford, Oxford University Press, 2nd edition, 2001)

Beinart, W. and M. Dawson (eds), *Popular Politics and Resistance Movements in South Africa* (Johannesburg, Wits University Press, 2010)

Beinart, W., P. Delius and S. Trapido (eds), *Putting a Plough to the Ground: Accumulation and Dispossession in Rural South Africa, 1850–1930* (Johannesburg, Ravan Press, 1986)

Bekker, S. and R. Humphries, *From Control to Confusion: The Changing Role of Administration Boards in South Africa, 1971–1983* (Pietermaritzburg, Shuter and Shooter, 1985)

Biehl, J., B. Good and A. Kleinman, 'Introduction: Rethinking Subjectivity', in J. Biehl, B. Good and A. Kleinman (eds), *Subjectivity: Ethnographic Investigations* (Berkeley, University of California Press, 2007)

Bizos, G., *Odyssey to Freedom: A Memoir by the World-Renowned Human Rights Advocate, Friend and Lawyer to Nelson Mandela* (Cape Town, Random House, 2007)

Bond, P., *Elite Transitions: From Apartheid to Neoliberalism in South Africa* (London, Pluto Press, 2000)

Bonner, P., '"Desirable or Undesirable Basotho Women?" Liquor, Prostitution and the Migration of Basotho Women to the Rand, 1920–1945', in C. Walker (ed.), *Women and Gender in Southern Africa to 1945* (Cape Town, David Philip, 1990)

Bonner, P., 'The Russians on the Reef, 1947–1957: Urbanisation, Gang Warfare and Ethnic Mobilisation', in P. Bonner, P. Delius and D. Posel (eds), *Apartheid's Genesis, 1935–1962: Contradiction, Continuity and Popular Struggle* (Johannesburg, Ravan Press, 1993)

Bonner, P., 'African Urbanisation on the Rand between the 1930s and 1960s: Its Social Character and Political Consequences', *Journal of Southern African Studies*, 21/1 (1995), pp.115–29

Bonner, P. and N. Nieftagodien, *Alexandra: A History* (Johannesburg, Wits University Press, 2008)

Bonner, P., P. Delius and D. Posel, 'The Shaping of Apartheid: Contradiction, Continuity and Popular Struggle', in P. Bonner, P. Delius and D. Posel (eds), *Apartheid's Genesis, 1935–1962: Contradiction, Continuity and Popular Struggle* (Johannesburg, Ravan Press, 1993)

Bonner, P., P. Delius and D. Posel (eds), *Apartheid's Genesis 1935–1962: Contradiction, Continuity and Popular Struggle* (Johannesburg, Ravan Press, 1993)

Borer, T.A., *Challenging the State: Churches as Political Actors in South Africa 1980–1994* (Notre Dame, University of Notre Dame Press, 1998)

Bozzoli, B., 'Why Were the 1980s "Millenarian"? Style, Repertoire, Space and Authority in South Africa's Black Cities', *Journal of Historical Sociology*, 13/1 (2000), pp.78–110

Bozzoli, B., *Theatres of Struggle and the End of Apartheid* (Johannesburg, Wits University Press, 2004)

Bozzoli, B. (ed.), *Class, Community, and Conflict: South African Perspectives* (Johannesburg, Ravan Press, 1987)

Brandel-Syrier, M., *Reeftown Elite: Social Mobility in a Black African Community on the Johannesburg Reef* (New York, Africana Publishing Corporation, 1971)

Bridger, E., 'Soweto's Female Comrades: Gender, Youth and Violence in South Africa's Township Uprisings, 1984–1986', *Journal of Southern African Studies*, 44/4 (2018), pp.559–74

Brooks, H., 'Differential Interpretations in the Discourse of "People's Power": Unveiling Intellectual Heritage and Normative Democratic Thought', *African Studies*, 77/3 (2018), pp.451–72

Brooks, H., 'Popular Power and Vanguardism: The Democratic Deficit of 1980s "People's Power"', *Politikon*, 45/3 (2018), pp.313–34

Brown, J., *South Africa's Insurgent Citizens: On Dissent and the Possibility of Politics* (London, Zed Books, 2015)

Brown, J., *The Road to Soweto: Resistance and the Uprising of 16 June 1976* (Oxford, James Currey, 2016)

Buettner, E., *Europe after Empire: Decolonisation, Society, and Culture* (Cambridge, Cambridge University Press, 2016)

Bundy, C., 'Street Sociology and Pavement Politics: Aspects of Youth and Student Resistance in Cape Town, 1985', *Journal of Southern African Studies*, 13/3 (1987), pp.303–30

Bundy, C., 'Survival and Resistance: Township Organisations and Non-Violent Direct Action in Twentieth Century South Africa', in G. Adler and J. Steinberg, *From Comrades to Citizens: The South African Civics Movement and the Transition to Democracy* (London, Macmillan, 2000)

Burton, M., *The Black Sash: Women for Justice and Peace* (Johannesburg, Jacana, 2015)

Carter, C., '"We Are the Progressives": Alexandra Youth Congress Activists and the Freedom Charter, 1983–85', *Journal of Southern African Studies*, 17/2 (1991), pp.197–220

Carter, C., 'Community and Conflict: The Alexandra Rebellion of 1986', *Journal of Southern African Studies*, 18/1 (1992), pp.115–42

Charney, C., 'Vigilantes, Clientelism, and the South African State', *Transformation*, 16 (1991), pp.1–28

Chaskalson, M., 'Apartheid with a Human Face: Punt Janson and the Origins of Reform in Township Administration, 1972–1976', *African Studies*, 42/2 (1989), pp.101–29

Chaskalson, M., M. Jochelson and J. Seekings, 'Rent Boycotts and the Urban Political Economy', in G. Moss and I. Obery (eds), *South African Review 4* (Johannesburg, Ravan Press, 1987)

Cherry, J., 'Hidden Histories of the Eastern Cape Underground', in SADET (ed.), *The Road to Democracy, Volume 4* (Pretoria, Unisa Press, 2010)

Cobbett, W. and R. Cohen (eds), *Popular Struggles in South Africa* (London, James Currey, 1988)

Cobbett, W., D. Glaser, D. Hindson et al., 'A Critical Analysis of the South African State's Reform Strategies in the 1980s', in P. Frankel, N. Pines and M. Swilling (eds), *State, Resistance and Change in South Africa* (London, Croom Helm, 1988)

Cole, J., *Crossroads: The Politics of Reform and Repression* (Johannesburg, Ravan Press, 1987)

Cooper, C., S. Motala, P. Randall et al. (eds), *A Survey of Race Relations: 1982* (Johannesburg, South African Institute of Race Relations, 1983)

Cooper, C., J. Shindler, C. McCaul et al. (eds), *Race Relations Survey: 1984* (Johannesburg, South African Institute of Race Relations, 1985)

Cooper, F., 'Conflict and Connection: Rethinking Colonial African History', *American Historical Review*, 99/5 (1994), pp. 1516–45

Cooper, F., *Africa since 1940: The Past of the Present* (Cambridge, Cambridge University Press, 2002)

Cooper, F., 'Afterword: Social Rights and Human Rights in the Time of Decolonization', *Humanity: An International Journal of Human Rights, Humanitarianism, and Development*, 3/3 (2002), pp.473–92

Cooper, F., *Colonialism in Question: Theory, Knowledge, History* (Berkeley, University of California Press, 2005)

Cooper, F., 'A Parting of the Ways: Colonial Africa and South Africa, 1946–48', *African Studies*, 65/1 (2006), pp.27–44

Cooper, F., 'Possibility and Constraint: African Independence in Historical Perspective', *The Journal of African History*, 49/2 (2008), pp.167–96

Cooper, F., 'Decolonization and Citizenship in Africa between Empire and a World of Nations', in E. Bogaerts and R. Raben (eds), *The Decolonization of African and Asian Societies* (Leiden, Brill, 2012), pp.39–67

Cooper, F., *Africa in the World: Capitalism, Empire, Nation State* (Cambridge, MA, Harvard University Press, 2014)

Crankshaw, O., 'Squatting, Apartheid and Urbanisation on the Southern Witwatersrand', *African Affairs*, 92 (1993), pp.31–51.

Das, V., 'Specificities: Official Narratives, Rumour, and the Social Production of Hate', *Social Identities*, 4/1 (1998), pp.109–30

Das, V., *Life and Words: Violence and the Descent into the Ordinary* (Berkeley, University of California Press, 2007)

Das, V., 'On Singularity and the Event', in J. Laidlaw and B. Bodenhorn (eds), *Recovering the Human Subject: Freedom, Creativity and Decision* (Cambridge, Cambridge University Press, 2018)

Davis, S.R., *The ANC's War against Apartheid: Umkhonto we Sizwe and the Liberation of South Africa* (Bloomington, Indiana University Press, 2018)

Dawson, M., '"Phansi Privatisation, Phansi!": The Anti-Privatisation Forum and Ideology in Social Movements', in W. Beinart and M. Dawson (eds), *Popular Politics and Resistance Movements in South Africa* (Johannesburg, Wits University Press, 2010)

De Kock, E. and J. Gordin, *A Long Night's Damage: Working for the Apartheid State* (Johannesburg, Contra Press, 1998)

Delius, P., *A Lion amongst the Cattle: Reconstruction and Resistance in the Northern Transvaal* (Oxford, James Currey, 1997)

DeMarrais, E. and T. Earle, 'Collective Action Theory and the Dynamics of Complex Societies', *Annual Review of Anthropology*, 46 (2017), pp.183–201

Denis, P., 'Seminary Networks and Black Consciousness in South Africa in the 1970s', *South African Historical Journal*, 62/1 (2010), pp.162–82

Desai, A., *We Are the Poors: Community Struggles in Post-Apartheid South Africa* (New York, Monthly Review Press, 2002)

Diar, P., *The Sharpeville Six: The South African Trial that Shocked the World* (Toronto, McClelland and Stewart, 1990)

Diseko, N.J., 'The Origins and Development of the South African Students' Movement (SASM): 1968–1976', *Journal of Southern African Studies*, 18/1 (1991), pp.40–62

Dlamini, J., *Native Nostalgia* (Johannesburg, Jacana, 2009)

Dlamini, J., *Askari: A Story of Collaboration and Betrayal in the Anti-Apartheid Struggle* (Johannesburg, Jacana, 2014)

Drury, J. and S. Reicher, 'Collective Action and Psychological Change: The Emergence of New Social Identities', *British Journal of Social Psychology*, 39 (2000), pp.579–604

Dubow, S., *Apartheid, 1948–1994* (Oxford, Oxford University Press, 2014)

Dubow, S., 'Closing Remarks: New Approaches to High Apartheid and Anti-Apartheid', *South African Historical Journal*, 69/2, Special Issue: Rethinking 'Apartheid's Golden Age' (2017), pp.304–29

Dubow, S. and A. Jeeves (eds), *South Africa's 1940s: Worlds of Possibilities* (Cape Town, Double Storey Books, 2005)

Ellis, S., *External Mission: The ANC in Exile, 1960–1990* (Oxford, Oxford University Press, 2013)

Evans, I., *Bureaucracy and Race: Native Administration in South Africa* (Berkeley, University of California Press, 1997)

Evans, L., 'South Africa's Bantustans and the Dynamics of "Decolonisation": Reflections on Writing Histories of the Homelands', *South African Historical Journal*, 64/1, Special Issue: Let's Talk about the Bantustans (2012), pp.117–37

Everatt, D., 'Alliance Politics of a Special Type: The Roots of the ANC/SACP Alliance, 1950–1954', *Journal of Southern African Studies*, 18/1 (1991), pp.19–39

Eyoh, D., 'Freedom: Overview', in T. Kepe, M. Levin and B. von Lieres (eds), *Domains of Freedom: Justice, Citizenship and Social Change in South Africa* (Cape Town, UCT Press, 2016)

Fitzpatrick, J. and R.C. Slye, '*Republic of South Africa v. Grootboom*. Case No. CCT 11/00. 2000 (11) BCLR 1169 and *Minister of Health v. Treatment Action Cam-*

paign. Case No. CCT 8/02', *The American Journal of International Law*, 97/3 (2003), pp.669–80

Foster, D.H. and D. Davis, *Detention and Torture in South Africa: Psychological, Legal & Historical Studies* (Cape Town, David Philip, 1987)

Frankel, P., *An Ordinary Atrocity: Sharpeville and its Massacre* (Johannesburg, Wits University Press, 2001)

Frankel, P., N. Pines and M. Swilling, *State, Resistance and Change in South Africa* (London, Croom Helm, 1988)

Freund, B., *The African City: A History* (Cambridge, Cambridge University Press, 2007)

Freund, B., *Twentieth-Century South Africa: A Developmental History* (Cambridge, Cambridge University Press, 2019)

Gerhart, G. and C. Glaser, *From Protest to Challenge: A Documentary History of African Politics in South Africa, 1882–1990. Volume 6: Challenge and Victory, 1980–1990* (Bloomington, Indiana University Press, 2010)

Getachew, A., *Worldmaking after Empire: The Rise and Fall of Self-Determination* (Princeton, Princeton University Press, 2019)

Ginsburg, R., '"Now I Stay in a House": Renovating the Matchbox in Apartheid-Era Soweto', *African Studies*, 55/2 (1996), pp.127–39

Glaser, C., 'Swines, Hazels and the Dirty Dozen: Masculinity, Territory and the Youth Gangs of Soweto, 1960–1976', *Journal of Southern African Studies*, 24/4 (1998), pp.719–36

Glaser, C., '"We Must Infiltrate the Tsotsis": School Politics and Youth Gangs in Soweto, 1968–1976', *Journal of Southern African Studies*, 24/2 (1998), pp.301–23

Glaser, C., *Bo-Tsotsi: The Youth Gangs of Soweto, 1935–1976* (Oxford, James Currey, 2000)

Glaser, C., 'Whistles and Sjamboks: Crime and Policing in Soweto, 1960–1976', *South African Historical Journal*, 52/1 (2005), pp.119–39

Glaser, C., 'Soweto's Islands of Learning: Morris Isaacson and Orlando High Schools under Bantu Education, 1958–1975', *Journal of Southern African Studies*, 41/1 (2015), pp.159–71

Glassman, J., *War of Words, War of Stones: Racial Thought and Violence in Colonial Zanzibar* (Bloomington, Indiana University Press, 2011)

Gould, D.B., *Moving Politics: Emotion and ACT UP's Fight against AIDS* (Chicago, University of Chicago Press, 2009)

Guenther, L., *Solitary Confinement: Social Death and Its Afterlives* (Minneapolis, University of Minnesota Press, 2013)

Guy, J. and M. Thabane, 'The Ma-Rashea', in B. Bozzoli (ed.), *Class, Community, and Conflict: South African Perspectives* (Johannesburg, Ravan Press, 1987)

Hack, K., 'Everyone Lived in Fear: Malaya and the British Way of Counter-Insurgency', *Small Wars and Insurgencies*, 23/4–5 (2012), pp.671–99

Hadfield, L., 'Christian Action and Black Consciousness Community Programmes in South Africa', *Journal for the Study of Religion*, 23/1–2 (2010), pp.105–30

Hamilton, L., 'Collective Unfreedom in South Africa', *Contemporary Politics*, 17/4 (2011), pp.355–72

Harries, P., 'From Public History to Private Enterprise: The Politics of Memory in the New South Africa', in M. Diawara, B. Lategan and J. Rüsen (eds), *Historical*

Memory in Africa: Dealing with the Past, Reaching for the Future in an Intercultural Context (New York, Berghahn, 2010)

Hassim, S., 'Turning Gender Rights into Entitlements: Women and Welfare Provision in Post-Apartheid South Africa', *Social Research*, 72/3 (2005), pp.621–46

Haysom, N., 'Licence to Kill, Part 1: The South African Police and the Use of Deadly Force', *South African Journal of Human Rights*, 3/1 (1987), pp.3–27

Healy-Clancy, M., 'The Family Politics of the Federation of South African Women: A History of Public Motherhood in Women's Antiracist Activism', *Signs: Journal of Women in Culture and Society*, 42/4 (2017), pp.843–66

Heffernan, A., 'Black Consciousness's Lost Leader: Abraham Tiro, the University of the North, and the Seeds of South Africa's Student Movement in the 1970s', *Journal of Southern African Studies*, 41/1 (2015), pp.173–86

Heffernan, A., 'Blurred Lines and Ideological Divisions in South African Youth Politics', *African Affairs*, 115/461 (2016), pp.664–87

Heffernan, A., 'The University of the North and Building the Bantustans, 1959–1977', *South African Historical Journal*, 69/2 (2017), pp.195–214

Heffernan, A., 'Student/Teachers from Turfloop: The Propagation of Black Consciousness in South African Schools, 1972–1976', *Africa*, 81/Supplement 1 (2019), pp.189–209

Heffernan, A., *Limpopo's Legacy: Student Politics and Democracy in South Africa* (Johannesburg, Wits University Press, 2019)

Hendler, P., *Urban Policy and Housing: Case Studies in Negotiations in PWV Townships* (Johannesburg, South African Institute of Race Relations, 1988)

Hendler, P., 'Living in Apartheid's Shadow: Residential Planning for Africans in the PWV Region 1970–1990', *Urban Forum*, 3/2 (1992), pp.37–80

Hindson, D., 'Orderly Urbanisation and Influx Control: From Territorial Apartheid to Regional Spacial Ordering in South Africa', *Cahiers d'Etudes Africaines*, 25/99 (1985), pp.401–32

Hindson, D., *Pass Controls and the Urban African Proletariat* (Johannesburg, Ravan Press, 1987)

Hlongwane, A.K., 'The Mapping of the June 16 1976 Soweto Student Uprisings Routes: Past Recollections, Present Reconstructions', *Journal of African Cultural Studies*, 19/1, Special Issue: Performing (In) Everyday Life (2007), pp.7–36

Holston, J., *Insurgent Citizenship: Disjunctions of Democracy and Modernity in Brazil* (Princeton, Princeton University Press, 2008)

Horrell, M. and D. Horner (eds), *A Survey of Race Relations in South Africa, 1973* (Johannesburg, South African Institute of Race Relations, 1974)

Houston, G., *The National Liberation Struggle in South Africa: A Case Study of the United Democratic Front, 1983–1987* (London and New York, Routledge, 1999)

Houston, G., 'The ANC's Internal Underground Political Work in the 1980s', in SADET (ed.), *The Road to Democracy, Volume 4: 1980–1990* (Pretoria, Unisa Press, 2010)

Houston, G. and B. Magubane, 'The ANC Political Underground in the 1970s', in SADET (ed.), *The Road to Democracy in South Africa, Volume 2: 1970–1980* (Pretoria, Unisa Press, 2006), pp.371–451

Hund, J. and M. Kotu-Rammopo, 'Justice in a South African Township: The Sociology of *Makgotla*', *Comparative and International Law Journal of Southern Africa*, 16/2 (1983), pp.179–208

Hunter, E. (ed.), *Citizenship, Belonging and Political Community in Africa* (Athens, Ohio University Press, 2016)

Hyslop, J., *The Classroom Struggle: Policy and Resistance in South Africa* (Pietermaritzburg, University of Natal Press, 1999)

Jeeves, A. and J. Crush, 'Introduction', in A. Jeeves and J. Crush (eds), *White Farms, Black Labor: The State and Agrarian Change in Southern Africa, 1910–1950* (Oxford, James Currey, 1997)

Jeffery, A., *People's War: New Light on the Struggle for South Africa* (Johannesburg, Jonathan Ball, 2009)

Jeffrey, I., 'Street Rivalry and Patron Managers: Football in Sharpeville, 1943–1985', *African Studies*, 51/1 (1992), pp.69–94

Jochelson, K., 'Reform, Repression and Resistance in South Africa: A Case Study of Alexandra Township, 1979–1989', *Journal of Southern African Studies*, 16/1 (1990), pp.1–32

Kakar, S., 'Rumors and Religious Riots', in G. Fine, V. Campion-Vincent and C. Heath (eds), *Rumor Mills: The Social Impact of Rumor and Legends* (New Brunswick, Aldine Transaction, 2005)

Kalyvas, S., 'The Ontology of "Political Violence": Action and Identity in Civil Wars', *Perspectives on Politics*, 1/3 (2003), pp. 475–94

Kalyvas, S., *The Logic of Violence in Civil War* (Cambridge, Cambridge University Press, 2006)

ka Plaatjie, T., 'The PAC's Exile Politics, 1980–1990', in SADET (ed.), *The Road to Democracy, Volume 4: 1980–1990* (Pretoria, Unisa Press, 2010), pp.1227–64

Keegan, T., 'The Sharecropping Economy, African Class Formation and the 1913 Native's Land Act in the Highveld Maize Belt', in S. Marks and R. Rathbone (eds), *Industrialisation and Social Change in South Africa* (London and New York, Longman, 1982)

Keegan, T., 'The Making of the Rural Economy: From 1850 to the Present', in Z.A. Konczacki, J. Parpart and T.M. Shaw (eds), *Studies in the Economic History of Southern Africa, Volume Two: South Africa, Lesotho and Swaziland* (New York, Routledge, 2013)

Kenny, B., *Retail Worker Politics, Race and Consumption in South Africa: Shelved in the Service Economy* (Cham, Palgrave Macmillan, 2018)

Kepe, T., M. Levin and B. von Lieres (eds), *Domains of Freedom: Justice, Citizenship and Social Change in South Africa* (Cape Town, UCT Press, 2016)

Klein, G.L., 'Publicising the African National Congress: The Anti-Apartheid News', *South African Historical Journal*, 63/3 (2011), pp.394–413

Kleinman, A., 'The Violences of Everyday Life: The Multiple Forms of and Dynamics of Social Violence', in V. Das, A. Kleinman, M. Ramphele and P. Reynolds (eds), *Violence and Subjectivity* (Berkeley, University of California Press, 2000)

Kleinman, A. and E. Fitz-Henry, 'The Experiential Basis of Subjectivity: How Individuals Change in the Context of Societal Transformation', in J. Biehl, B. Good and A. Kleinman (eds), *Subjectivity: Ethnographic Investigations* (Berkeley, University of California Press, 2007)

Kondlo, K., *In the Twilight of the Revolution: The Pan Africanist Congress of Azania (South Africa), 1959–1994* (Basel, Basler Afrika Bibliographien, 2009)

Kotzé, D.A., 'The Witzieshoek Revolt 1940–1950', *African Studies*, 41/1 (1982), pp.127–41

Kynoch, G., 'From the Ninevites to the Hard Livings Gang: Township Gangsters and Urban Violence in Twentieth-Century South Africa', *African Studies*, 58/1 (1999), pp.55–85

Kynoch, G., *We Are Fighting the World: A History of the Marashea Gangs in South Africa, 1947–1999* (Scottsville, UKZN Press, 2005)

Kynoch, G., 'Crime, Conflict and Politics in Transition-Era South Africa', *African Affairs*, 104/416 (2005), pp.493–514

Kynoch, G., *Township Violence and the End of Apartheid: War on the Reef* (Johannesburg and Woodbridge, Wits University Press and James Currey, 2018)

Landau, P.S., *Popular Politics in the History of South Africa, 1400–1948* (Cambridge, Cambridge University Press, 2010)

Landau, P., 'The M-Plan: Mandela's Struggle to Reorient the African National Congress', *Journal of Southern African Studies*, 45/6, Special Issue: Reassessing Mandela (2019), pp.1073–91

La Hausse, P., '"The Cows of Nongoloza": Youth, Crime and Amalaita Gangs in Durban, 1900–1936', *Journal of Southern African Studies*, 16/1 (1990), pp.79–111

Langford, M., 'Housing Rights Litigation: Grootboom and Beyond', in M. Langford, B. Cousins, J. Dugard and T. Madlingozi (eds), *Socio-Economic Rights in South Africa: Symbols or Substance?* (Cambridge, Cambridge University Press, 2014)

Langford, M., B. Cousins, J. Dugard and T. Madlingozi (eds), *Socio-Economic Rights in South Africa: Symbols or Substance?* (Cambridge, Cambridge University Press, 2014)

Lee, R., *African Women and Apartheid: Migration and Settlement in Urban South Africa* (London, Tauris Academic Studies, 2009)

Lefebre, G., *The Great Fear of 1789: Rural Panic in Revolutionary France*, trans. Joan White (New York, Pantheon Books, 1973)

Lekgoathi, S., '"You are Listening to Radio Lebowa of the South African Broadcasting Cooperation"': Vernacular Radio, Bantustan Identity and Listenership, 1960–1994', *Journal of Southern African Studies*, 35/3 (2009), pp.575–94

Lekgoathi, S., 'The African National Congress's Radio Freedom and its Audiences in Apartheid South Africa, 1963–1991', *Journal of African Media Studies*, 2/2 (2010), pp.139–54

Lekgoathi, S., 'The United Democratic Front, Political Resistance and Local Struggles in the Vaal and West Rand Townships in the 1980s', in SADET (ed.), *The Road to Democracy in South Africa, Volume 4: 1980–1990* (Pretoria, Unisa Press, 2010)

Lodge, T., '"We Are Being Punished because We Are Poor": The Bus Boycotts of Evaton and Alexandra, 1955–57', in T. Lodge, *Black Politics in South Africa since 1945* (London and New York, Longman, 1983)

Lodge, T., 'State of Exile: The African National Congress of South Africa, 1976–86', in P. Frankel, N. Pines and M. Swilling (eds), *State, Resistance and Change in South Africa* (London, Croom Helm, 1988), pp.229–58

Lodge, T., *South African Politics since 1994* (Cape Town, David Philip, 1999).

Lodge, T., *Sharpeville: An Apartheid Massacre and its Consequences* (Oxford, Oxford

University Press, 2011)

Lodge, T., B. Nasson, S. Mufson et al., *All, Here, and Now: Black Politics in South Africa in the 1980s* (Cape Town, David Philip, 1991)

Mabin, A., 'Comprehensive Segregation: The Origins of the Group Areas Act and its Planning Apparatuses', *Journal of Southern African Studies*, 18/2 (1992), pp.405–29

Mabin, A., 'Varied Legacies of Modernism in Urban Planning', in G. Bridge and S. Watson (eds), *A Companion to the City* (Oxford, Blackwell, 2000)

Mabin, A. and D. Smit, 'Reconstructing South Africa's Cities? The Making of Urban Planning 1900–2000', *Planning Perspectives*, 12/2 (2000), pp.193–223

Macmillan, H., *The Lusaka Years, 1963–1994: The ANC in Exile in Zambia* (Johannesburg, Jacana, 2013)

Macqueen, I., 'Students, Apartheid and the Ecumenical Movement in South Africa', *Journal of Southern African Studies*, 39/3 (2013), pp.447–63

Macqueen, I., *Black Consciousness and Progressive Movements under Apartheid* (Pietermaritzburg, University of KwaZulu-Natal Press, 2018)

Madlingozi, T., 'Post-Apartheid Social Movements and the Quest for the Elusive "New" South Africa', *Journal of Law and Society*, 34/11 (2007), pp.77–98

Madlingozi, T., 'Post-Apartheid Social Movements and Legal Mobilisation', in M. Langford, B. Cousins, J. Dugard and T. Madlingozi (eds), *Socio-Economic Rights in South Africa: Symbols or Substance?* (Cambridge, Cambridge University Press, 2014)

Magaziner, D., *The Law and the Prophets: Black Consciousness in South Africa, 1968–1977* (Athens, Ohio University Press, 2010)

Makhulu, A.-M., *Making Freedom: Apartheid, Squatter Politics, and the Struggle for Home* (Durham, Duke University Press, 2015)

Mamdani, M., *Citizen and Subject: Contemporary Africa and the Legacy of Late Colonialism* (Princeton, Princeton University Press, 1996)

Manganyi, C., 'Crowds and Their Vicissitudes: Psychology and Law in the South African Court-Room', in C. Manganyi and A. du Toit (eds), *Political Violence and the Struggle in South Africa* (London, Macmillan, 1990)

Mangcu, X., 'African Modernity and the Struggle for People's Power: From Protest and Mobilization to Community Organizing', *The Good Society*, 21/2 (2012), pp.279–99

Marais, H., *South Africa: Limits to Change – The Political Economy of Transition* (London, Zed Books, 2001)

Marais, L., M. Sefika, J. Ntema, A. Venter and J. Cloete, 'Towards an Understanding of the Outcomes of Housing Privatisation in South Africa', *Urban Forum*, 25 (2014), pp.57–68

Marks, M., '"We Are Fighting for the Liberation of Our People": Justifications of Violence by Activist Youth in Diepkloof, Soweto', *Berkeley Journal of Sociology*, 41 (1996–97), pp.137–65

Marks, M., *Young Warriors: Youth Politics, Identity and Violence in South Africa* (Johannesburg, Wits University Press, 2001)

Marks, S. and R. Rathbone (eds), *Industrialisation and Social Change in South Africa* (London and New York, Longman, 1982)

Martin, G., 'Collective Behaviour', in B.S. Turner (ed.), *Wiley Blackwell Encyclopedia of Social Theory* (Oxford, Wiley Blackwell, 2017)

Marx, A., *Lessons of Struggle: South African Internal Opposition, 1960–1990* (New York, Oxford University Press, 1992)

Matzukis, N., 'Nature and Scope of Common Purpose', *South African Journal of Criminal Justice*, 1/2 (1988), pp.226–34

Mayekiso, M., *Township Politics: Civic Struggles for a New South Africa* (New York, Monthly Review Press, 1996)

Mazibuko, N., *Spring Offensive: Youth Underground Structures in South Africa during the 80s* (Johannesburg, Timbila Publishing, 2006)

McDonald, D.A. and J. Pape (eds), *Cost Recovery and the Crisis of Service Delivery in South Africa* (Cape Town, HSRC Press, 2002)

Mendelsohn, R., *Sammy Marks: The Uncrowned King of the Transvaal* (Cape Town and Athens, David Philip and Ohio University Press, 1991)

Mkhabela, S., *Open Earth and Black Roses: Remembering 16 June 1976* (Johannesburg, Skotaville Publishers, 2001)

Moloi, T., *Place of Thorns: Black Political Protest in Kroonstad since 1976* (Johannesburg, Wits University Press, 2015)

Moloi, T., 'The Botswana Connection: The Re-invigoration of Confrontational Politics in Thembisa Township, 1979–1990', in A. Lissoni and A. Pezzano (eds), *The ANC between Home and Exile: Reflections on the Anti-Apartheid Struggle in Italy and Southern Africa* (Napoli, Universita degli studi di Napoli L'Orientale, 2015)

Moloi, T., 'Zamdela Township: The Explosion of Confrontational Politics, Early 1980s to 1990', *Journal of Contemporary History*, 43/1 (2018), pp.111–16

Morris, M. and V. Padayachee, 'State Reform Policy in South Africa', *Transformation*, 7 (1988), pp.1–26

Morris, P., *A History of Black Housing in South Africa* (Johannesburg, South Africa Foundation, 1981)

Mphahlele, E., 'The Evaton Riots', *Africa South*, 1/1 (1957)

Mphahlele, L., *Child of this Soil: My Life as a Freedom Fighter* (Johannesburg, Mwalimu Books, 2010)

Mufson, S., *Fighting Years: Black Resistance and the Struggle for a New South Africa* (Boston, Beacon Press, 1990)

Murray, C., 'Struggle from the Margins: Rural Slums in the Orange Free State', in F. Cooper (ed.), *Struggle for the City* (London, Sage Publications, 1985)

Mzamane, M.V. and B. Maaba, 'The Azanian People's Organisation, 1977–1990', in SADET (ed.), *The Road to Democracy, Volume 4: 1980–1990* (Pretoria, Unisa Press, 2010)

Naidoo, K., 'The Politics of Youth Resistance in the 1980s: The Dilemmas of a Differentiated Durban', *Journal of Southern African Studies*, 18/1 (1991), pp.143–65

Nattrass, N., 'Economic Growth and Transformation in the 1940s', in S. Dubow and A. Jeeves (eds), *South Africa's 1940s: Worlds of Possibilities* (Cape Town, Double Storey Books, 2005)

Ndebele, N., *Rediscovery of the Ordinary: Essay on South African Literature and Culture* (Johannesburg, COSAW, 1991)

Ndlovu, S.M., *The Soweto Uprisings: Counter Memories of June 1976* (Johannesburg, Picador Africa, 2017)

Neocosmos, M., 'Civil Society, Citizenship and the Politics of the (Im)possible: Rethinking Militancy in Africa Today', *Interface: A Journal for and about Social Movements*, 1/2 (2009), pp.263–334

Neocosmos, M., *Thinking Freedom in Africa: Toward a Theory of Emancipatory Politics* (Johannesburg, Wits University Press, 2016)

Nesbitt, F.N., *Race for Sanctions: African Americans against Apartheid, 1946–1994* (Bloomington and Indianapolis, Indiana University Press, 2004)

Ngwane, T., '"Insurgent Democracy": Post-Apartheid South Africa's Freedom Fighters', *Journal of Southern African Studies*, 45/1 (2019), pp.229–45

Nieftagodien, N., 'High Apartheid and the Erosion of "Official" Local Politics in Daveyton in the 1960s', *New Contree*, 67 (2013), pp.35–55

Noonan, P., *They're Burning the Churches: The Final Dramatic Events that Scuttled Apartheid* (Bellevue, Jacana, 2003)

Nqakula, C., *The People's War: Reflections of an ANC Cadre* (Johannesburg, Mutloatse Arts Heritage Trust, 2017)

O'Brien, K., *The South African Intelligence Services: From Apartheid to Democracy, 1948–2005* (London and New York, Routledge, 2011)

Olver, C., *How to Steal a City: The Battle for Nelson Mandela Bay, an Inside Account* (Johannesburg, Jonathan Ball, 2017)

O'Meara, D., *Forty Lost Years: The Apartheid State and the Politics of the National Party, 1948–1994* (Johannesburg, Ravan Press, 1996)

Pandey, G., *Remembering Partition: Violence, Nationalism and History in India* (Cambridge, Cambridge University Press, 2001)

Parker, P. and J. Mokhesi-Parker, *In the Shadow of Sharpeville: Apartheid and Criminal Justice* (Basingstoke and New York, Macmillan and NYU Press, 1998)

Pauw, J., *Into the Heart of Darkness: Confessions of Apartheid's Assassins* (Johannesburg, Jonathan Ball, 1997)

Pavlich, G., 'People's Courts, Postmodern Difference, and Socialist Justice in South Africa', *Social Justice*, 19/3 (1992), pp.29–45

Peterson, B., 'Culture, Resistance and Representation', in SADET (ed.), *The Road to Democracy in South Africa, Volume 2: 1970–1980* (Pretoria, Unisa Press, 2006)

Pile, S. and M. Keith (eds), *Geographies of Resistance* (London, Routledge, 1997)

Pillay, P., 'The Development and Underdevelopment of Education in South Africa', in W. Nassan and J. Samuels (eds), *Education: From Poverty to Liberty* (Cape Town, David Philip, 1990)

Pinto de Almeida, F., 'Framing Interior: Race, Mobility and the Image of Home in South African Modernity', *Social Dynamics*, 41/3 (2015), pp.461–81

Plagerson, S., L. Patel, T. Hochfeld et al., 'Social Policy in South Africa: The Route to Social Development', *World Development*, 113 (2019), pp.1–9

Pohlandt-McCormick, H., '*I Saw a Nightmare…*': *The Soweto Uprising, June 16, 1976* (New York, Columbia University Press, 2005)

Posel, D., 'A "Battlefield of Perceptions": State Discourse on Political Violence, 1985–1988', in J. Cock and L. Nathan (eds), *War and Society: The Militarisation of South Africa* (Cape Town, David Philip, 1989)

Posel, D., 'Curbing African Urbanisation in the 1950s and 1960s', in M. Swilling, R. Humphries and K. Shubane (eds), *Apartheid City in Transition* (Cape Town, Oxford University Press, 1991)

Posel, D., 'Influx Control and the Urban Labour Markets in the 1950s', in P. Bonner, P. Delius and D. Posel (eds), *Apartheid's Genesis 1935–1962: Contradiction, Continuity and Popular Struggle* (Johannesburg, Ravan Press, 1993)

Posel, D., 'Race as a Common Sense: Racial Classification in Twentieth Century South Africa', *African Studies Review*, 44/2 (2001), pp.87–113

Posel, D., 'The Case for a Welfare State: Poverty & the Politics of the African Family in the 1930s & 1940s', in S. Dubow and A. Jeeves (eds), *South Africa's 1940s: Worlds of Possibilities* (Cape Town, Double Storey Books, 2005)

Posel, D., 'Marriage at the Drop of a Hat: Housing and Partnership in South Africa's Urban African Townships, 1920s–1960s', *History Workshop Journal*, 61 (2006), pp.57–76

Posel, D., 'The Apartheid Project, 1948–1970', in R. Ross, A. Mager and B. Nasson (eds), *The Cambridge History of South Africa, Volume 2: 1885–1994* (Cambridge, Cambridge University Press, 2011)

Potgieter, D., *Total Onslaught: Apartheid's Dirty Tricks Exposed* (Cape Town, Zebra Press, 2012)

Rantete, J., *The Third Day of September: An Eye-Witness Account of the Sebokeng Rebellion of 1984* (Johannesburg, Ravan Press, 1984)

Rayner, M., 'Law, Politics, and Treason in South Africa', *Human Rights Quarterly*, 471 (1986), pp.471–86

Reynolds, P., *War in Worcester: Youth and the Apartheid State* (New York, Fordham University Press, 2013)

Robbins, S.L., *From Revolution to Rights in South Africa* (Woodbridge, James Currey, 2008)

Robinson, J., 'Administrative Strategies and Political Power in South Africa's Black Townships, 1930–1960', *Urban Forum*, 2/2 (1991), pp.63–77

Ross, F., *Raw Life, New Hope: Decency, Housing and Everyday Life in a Post-Apartheid Community* (Cape Town, UCT Press, 2010)

Ross, R., 'A Respectable Age', *African Historical Review*, 47/1 (2015), pp.1–15

Rousseau, N., 'The Farm, the River and the Picnic Spot: Topographies of Terror', *African Studies*, 68/3 (2009), pp.351–69

Rousseau, N., 'Counter-Revolutionary Warfare: The Soweto Intelligence Unit and Southern Itineraries', *Journal of Southern African Studies*, 40/6 (2014), pp.1343–61

Rudé, G., *The Crowd in the French Revolution* (Oxford, Clarendon Press, 1959)

Rueedi, F., 'Narratives on Trial: Ideology, Violence and the Struggle over Political Legitimacy in the Case of the Delmas Treason Trial, 1985–89', *South African Historical Journal*, 67/3 (2015), pp.335–55

Rueedi, F., '"Siyayinyova!" Patterns of Violence in the African Townships of the Vaal Triangle, South Africa, 1980–86', *Africa*, 85/3 (2015), pp.395–416

Rueedi, F., 'The Politics of Difference and the Forging of a Political "Community": Discourses and Practices of the Charterist Civic Movement in the Vaal Triangle, 1980–84', *Journal of Southern African Studies*, 41/6 (2015), pp.1181–98

Rueedi, F., '"They Would Remind You of 1960": The Emergence of Radical Student Politics in the Vaal Triangle, 1972–1985', in A. Heffernan and N. Nieftagodien (eds), *Students Must Rise: Youth Struggle in South Africa Before and Beyond Soweto* (Johannesburg, Wits University Press, 2016)

Rueedi, F., '"Our Bushes Are the Houses": People's War and the Underground during the Insurrectionary Period in the Vaal Triangle, South Africa', *Journal of Southern African Studies*, 46/4 (2020), pp.615–33

Rueedi, F., 'The Hostel Wars in Apartheid South Africa: Rumour, Violence and the Discourse of Victimhood', *Social Identities*, 26/6 (2020), pp.756–73

Runciman, C., 'The Decline of the Anti-Privatisation Forum in the Midst of South Africa's "Rebellion of the Poor"', *Current Sociology*, 63/7 (2015), pp.961–79

Sapire, H., 'Politics and Protest in Shack Settlements of the Pretoria–Witwaters-rand–Vereeniging Region, South Africa, 1980–1990', *Journal of Southern African Studies*, 18/3, Special Issue: Political Violence in Southern Africa (1992), pp.670–97

Sapire, H., 'Apartheid's "Testing Ground": Urban "Native Policy" and African Politics in Brakpan, South Africa, 1943–1948', *Journal of African History*, 35/1 (1994), pp. 99–123

Sapire, S., 'Township Histories, Insurrection and Liberation in Late Apartheid South Africa', *South African Historical Journal*, 65/2 (2013), pp.167–98

Satumba, T., A. Bayat and S. Mohamed, 'The Impact of Social Grants on Poverty Reduction in South Africa', *Journal of Economics*, 8/1 (2017), pp.33–49.

Saunders, C., 'Britain, the Commonwealth, and the Question of the Release of Nelson Mandela in the 1980s', *The Round Table: The Commonwealth Journal of International Affairs*, 106/6 (2017), pp.659–69

Schärf, W. and B. Ngcokoto, 'Images of Punishment in the People's Courts of Cape Town, 1985–7: From Prefigurative Justice to Populist Violence', in C. Manganyi and A. du Toit (eds), *Political Violence and the Struggle in South Africa* (London, Macmillan, 1990)

Seekings, J. 'The Origins of Political Mobilisation in PWV Townships, 1980–84', in W. Cobbett and R. Cohen (eds), *Popular Struggles in South Africa* (London, James Currey, 1988)

Seekings, J., 'Political Mobilisation in Tumahole, 1984–85', *Africa Perspective*, 1/7–8 (1989), pp.105–44

Seekings, J., 'People's Court and Popular Politics', in G. Moss and I. Obery (eds), *South African Review 5* (Johannesburg, Ravan Press, 1989)

Seekings, J., 'Gender Ideology and Township Politics in the 1980s', *Agenda*, 10 (1991), pp.77–88

Seekings, J., 'Trailing behind the Masses": The United Democratic Front and Township Politics in the Pretoria–Witwatersrand–Vaal Region, 1983–84', *Journal of Southern African Studies*, 18/1 (1992), pp.93–114

Seekings, J., 'From Quiescence to "People's Power": Township Politics in Kagiso, 1985–1986', *Social Dynamics*, 18/1 (1992), pp.20–41

Seekings, J., *Heroes or Villains: Youth Politics in the 1980s* (Johannesburg, Ravan Press, 1993)

Seekings, J., 'The Decline of South Africa's Civic Organizations, 1990–1996', *Critical Sociology*, 22/3 (1996), pp.135–57

Seekings, J., 'The Origins of Social Citizenship in Pre-Apartheid South Africa', *South African Journal of Philosophy*, 19/4 (2000), pp.386–404

Seekings, J., 'Visions, Hopes and Views about the Future: The Radical Moment of South African Welfare Reform', in S. Dubow and A. Jeeves (eds), *South Africa's 1940s: Worlds of Possibilities* (Cape Town, Double Storey Books, 2005)

Seekings, J., '"Not a Single White Person Should be Allowed to Go Under": *Swaart-gevaar* and the Origins of South Africa's Welfare State, 1924–1929', *Journal of African History*, 48/3 (2007), pp.375–94

Seekings, J., 'Whose Voices? Politics and Methodology in the Study of Political Organisation and Protest in the Final Phase of the "Struggle" in South Africa', *South African Historical Journal*, 62/1 (2010), pp.7–28

Seekings, J., *The UDF: A History of the United Democratic Front* (Cape Town, David Philip, 2nd edition, 2015)

Seekings, J. and N. Nattrass, *Class, Race, and Inequality in South Africa* (New Haven and London, Yale University Press, 2005)

Sekyere, E., S. Gordon, G. Pienaar and N. Bohler-Muller, 'Is South Africa Winning the War on Poverty and Inequality? What Do the Available Statistics Tell Us?', in E. Durojaye and G. Mirugi-Mukundi (eds), *Exploring the Link between Poverty and Human Rights in Africa* (Pretoria, Pretoria University Law Press, 2020)

Shakinovsky, T., S. Court and L. Segal, *The Knock on the Door: The Story of the Detainees' Parents Support Committee* (Johannesburg, Picador Africa, 2018)

Simpson, T., '"Umkhonto we Sizwe, We Are Waiting for You": The ANC and the Township Uprising, September 1984–September 1985', *South African Historical Journal*, 61/1 (2009), pp. 158–77

Simpson, T., *Umkhonto we Sizwe: The ANC's Armed Struggle* (Cape Town, Penguin Books, 2016)

Sitas, A., 'The Making of the "Comrades" Movement in Natal, 1985–91', *Journal of Southern African Studies*, 18/3, Special Issue: Political Violence in Southern Africa (1992), pp.629–41

Soske, J., A. Lissoni and N. Erlank, 'One Hundred Years of the ANC: Debating Struggle History after Apartheid', in A. Lissoni, J. Soske, N. Erland et al. (eds), *One Hundred Years of the ANC: Debating Liberation Histories Today* (Johannesburg, Wits University Press, 2012)

Stolten, H.E. (ed.), *History Making and Present Day Politics: The Meaning of Collective Memory in South Africa* (Uppsala, Nordiska Afrikainstitutet, 2007)

Sutcliffe, M., 'The Crisis in South Africa: Material Conditions and the Reformist Response', *Geoforum*, 17/2 (1986), pp.141–59

Suttner, R., 'The African National Congress (ANC) Underground: From the M-Plan to Rivonia', *South African Historical Journal*, 49 (2003), pp.123–46

Suttner, R., *The ANC Underground in South Africa to 1976: A Social and Historical Study* (Johannesburg, Jacana, 2008)

Suttner, R., 'The Freedom Charter @60: Rethinking its Democratic Qualities', *Historia*, 60/2 (2015), pp.1–23

Swilling, M., 'Urban Social Movements under Apartheid', *Cahiers d'Etudes Africaines*, 99 (1985), pp.363–79

Swilling, M., 'The United Democratic Front and Township Revolt', in W. Cobbett and R. Cohen (eds), *Popular Struggles in South Africa* (London, James Currey, 1988)

Swilling, M., R. Humphries and K. Shubane (eds), *Apartheid City in Transition* (Cape Town, Oxford University Press, 1991)

Thomas, M. and G. Curless, 'Introduction: Decolonisation, Conflict and Counter-Insurgency', in M. Thomas and G. Curless (eds), *Decolonization and Conflict: Colonial Comparisons and Legacies* (London, Bloomsbury Academic, 2017)

Tom, P., *My Life Struggle* (Johannesburg, Ravan, 1985)

Trapido, S., 'Putting a Plough to the Ground: A History of Tenant Production on the Vereeniging Estates, 1896–1920', in W. Beinart, P. Delius and S. Trapido (eds), *Putting a Plough to the Ground: Accumulation and Dispossession in Rural South Africa, 1850–1930* (Johannesburg, Ravan Press, 1986)

Tshwete, S., 'Understanding the Charter Clause by Clause', in R. Suttner and J. Cronin, *30 Years of the Freedom Charter* (Johannesburg, Ravan Press, 1985)

Vail, L. (ed.), *The Creation of Tribalism in Southern Africa* (Berkeley, University of California Press, 1989)

Vally, N.T., 'Insecurity in South African Social Security: An Examination of Social Grant Deductions, Cancellations and Waiting', *Journal of Southern African Studies*, 42/5, Special Issue: Labour, Insecurity and Violence in South Africa (2016), pp.965–82

van Holdt, K., 'South Africa: The Transition to Violent Democracy', *Review of African Political Economy*, 40/138 (2013), pp.589–604

van Holdt, K., M. Langa, S. Molapo et al., *The Smoke that Calls: Insurgent Citizenship, Collective Violence, and the Struggle for a Place in the New South Africa* (Johannesburg, Centre for the Study of Violence and Reconciliation & Society, Work and Development Institute, 2011)

van Kessel, I., '"From Confusion to Lusaka": The Youth Revolt in Sekhukhuneland', *Journal of Southern African Studies*, 19/4 (1993), pp.593–614

van Kessel, I., *Beyond Our Wildest Dreams: The United Democratic Front and the Transformation of South Africa* (Charlottesville, University Press of Virginia, 2000)

van Niekerk, R., 'The African National Congress: Social Democratic Thinking and the Good Society, 1940–1962', in E. Webster and K. Pampallis, *The Unresolved National Question: Left Thought under Apartheid* (Johannesburg, Wits University Press, 2016)

van Onselen, C., *The Seed Is Mine: The Life of Kas Maine, a South African Sharecropper 1894–1995* (Johannesburg and Cape Town, Jonathan Ball, 1996)

von Schnitzler, A., 'Citizenship Prepaid: Water, Calculability, and Techno-Politics in South Africa', *Journal of Southern African Studies*, 34/4 (2008), pp.899–917

Webster, E. and J. Mawbey, 'Revisiting the National Question', in E. Webster and K. Pampallis (eds), *The Unresolved National Question: Left Thought under Apartheid* (Johannesburg, Wits University Press, 2016)

Williams, G., 'Celebrating the Freedom Charter', *Tranformation*, 6 (1988), pp.73–86

Wylie, D., *Art and Revolution: The Life and Death of Thami Mnyele, South African Artist* (Johannesburg, Jacana, 2008)

Unpublished theses, papers and reports

Albertyn, C., 'A Critical Analysis of Political Trials in South Africa 1948–1988' (PhD thesis, University of Cambridge, 1991)

Barrell, H., 'Conscripts to Their Age: African National Congress Operational Strategy, 1976–1986' (DPhil thesis, University of Oxford, 1993)

Bekker, S., 'The Local Government and Community of Sebokeng' (University of Stellenbosch, Occasional Paper No.3, 1978)

Bureau of Market Research, 'Income and Expenditure Patterns of Urban Black Multiple Households in the Vaal Triangle, 1980' (Pretoria, University of South Africa, Research Report No.94.3, 1981)

Bureau of Market Research, 'Income and Expenditure Patterns of Urban Black Multiple Households in the Vaal Triangle, 1985' (Pretoria, University of South Africa, Research Report No.94.3, 1986)

Chaskalson, M., 'The Road to Sharpeville' (African Studies seminar paper, University of the Witwatersrand, 1986)

Dugard, J., M. Clark, K. Tissington and S. Wilson, 'The Right to Housing in South Africa', in Foundation for Human Rights, *Socio-Economic Rights – Progressive Realisation?* (Johannesburg, Foundation for Human Rights, 2016)

Frankel, P., 'Socio-Economic Conditions, Rent Boycotts and the Local Government Crisis: A Vaal Triangle Field Study' (unpublished report, June 1987)

Hurlbut, W.B. (ed.), 'Overcoming Poverty and Inequality in South Africa: An Assessment of Drivers, Constraints and Opportunities' (Washington, The World Bank, March 2018)

Jeffrey, I., 'Cultural Trends and Community Formation in a South African Township: Sharpeville, 1943–1985' (MA thesis, University of the Witwatersrand, 1991)

Karamoko, J. and J. Hirsh, 'Community Protests in South Africa: Trends, Analysis and Explanations' (Local Government Working Paper No.1, Cape Town, Community Law Centre, updated 2011)

Kumalo, V.R., 'The African Struggle for Independent Education: A History of Wilberforce Institute, Evaton 1905 to 1950s' (PhD thesis, University of the Witwatersrand, 2018)

Kunene, P.S., 'From Apartheid to Democracy: A Historical Analysis of Local Struggles in Phomolong Township, Free State, 1985–2005' (MA thesis, University of the Witwatersrand, 2013)

Mabin, A. and S. Parnell, 'The Question of Working Class Home Ownership', Second Carnegie Inquiry into Poverty and Development in Southern Africa, Paper No.159 (Cape Town, 13–19 April 1984)

Martiny, J. and J. Sharp, 'Second Carnegie Inquiry into Poverty and Development in Southern Africa. An Overview of Qwa Qwa: Town and Country in a South African Bantustan', Second Carnegie Inquiry into Poverty and Development in Southern Africa, Paper No.286 (Cape Town, 13–19 April 1984)

Nieftagodien, N., 'The Implementation of Urban Apartheid on the East Rand, 1948–1973' (PhD thesis, University of the Witwatersrand, 2001)

Nieftagodien, N., 'Vaal Squatters in the 1940s: Occupiers, Speculators and Eye of the City' (unpublished paper, 2012)

Niehaus, I., 'Relocation into Tseki and Phuthaditjhaba: A Comparative Ethnography of Planned and Unplanned Removals in Qwa Qwa' (University of the Witwatersrand, African Studies seminar paper No.260, 1989)

Rueedi, F., 'Mobilisation, Violence and Control in the Townships of the Vaal Triangle, South Africa, c.1976–1986' (DPhil thesis, University of Oxford, 2013)

Ruiters, G., 'South African Liberation Politics: A Case Study of Collective Action and Leadership in Katorus, 1980–1989' (MA thesis, University of the Witwatersrand, 1995)

Runciman, C., P. Alexander, M. Rampedi, B. Moloto, B. Maruping, E. Khumalo and S. Sibanda, 'Counting Police-Recorded Protests: Based on South African Police Service Data' (South African Research Chair in Social Change report No.2, Johannesburg, 2016)

Sachs, A., 'Introduction', in Foundation for Human Rights, *Socio-Economic Rights – Progressive Realisation?* (Johannesburg, Foundation for Human Rights, 2016)

Seekings, J., 'Why Was Soweto Different? Urban Development, Township Politics, and the Political Economy of Soweto, 1977–1984' (African Studies seminar paper, University of the Witwatersrand, 1988)

Seekings, J., 'Broken Promises: Discontent, Protest, and the Transition to Confrontation in Duduza, 1978–1985' (African Studies seminar paper, University of the Witwatersrand, 1990)

Seekings, J., 'Quiescence and the Transition to Confrontation: South African Townships, 1978–1984' (DPhil thesis, University of Oxford, 1990)

Seekings, J., 'Powerlessness and Politics: "Quiescence" and Protest in Pretoria–Witwatersrand–Vaal Townships, c.1973–1985' (Southern Africa in the Nineteenth and Twentieth Centuries seminar paper, Institute of Commonwealth Studies, University of London, 1991)

Sparks, S., 'Apartheid Modern: South Africa's Oil from Coal Project and the History of a South African Company Town' (PhD thesis, University of Michigan, 2012)

Vanderbijlpark Town Council, 'Vanderbijlpark – Founded for Progress, Planned for People' (Vanderbijlpark, no date)

Van der Walt, T., 'Report on the Investigation into Education for Blacks in the Vaal Triangle Following Upon the Occurrences in September 1984 and Thereafter' (Pretoria, Government Printer, 1985)

Vally, N.T., 'The "Model Township" of Sharpeville: The Absence of Political Action and Organisation, 1960–84' (MA thesis, University of the Witwatersrand, 2010)

Wilkinson, P., 'The Sale of the Century? A Critical Review of Recent Developments in African Housing Policy in South Africa', Second Carnegie Inquiry into Poverty and Development in Southern Africa, Paper No.160 (Cape Town, 13–19 April 1984)

Documentaries

The Struggle from Within, directed by Kevin Harris (Johannesburg, Kevin Harris Productions, 1984/8)

Index

NOTE: PREPOSITIONS in sub-entries are not used for alphabetical ordering and numbers are ordered by their letters.

www.ingramcontent.com/pod-product-compliance
Lightning Source LLC
Chambersburg PA
CBHW051959270326
41929CB00015B/2713